THE STUDY OF RELIGIONS IN IRELAND

Also available from Bloomsbury

Experience, Identity & Epistemic Injustice within Ireland's Magdalene Laundries
Chloe K. Gott

Religious Diversity in Europe: Mediating the Past to the Young
Edited by Riho Altnurme, Elena Arigita and Patrick Pasture

Young Muslims and Christians in a Secular Europe
Daan Beekers

THE STUDY OF RELIGIONS IN IRELAND

Past, Present and Future

Edited by
Brendan McNamara and Hazel O'Brien

BLOOMSBURY ACADEMIC
LONDON · NEW YORK · OXFORD · NEW DELHI · SYDNEY

BLOOMSBURY ACADEMIC
Bloomsbury Publishing Plc
50 Bedford Square, London, WC1B 3DP, UK
1385 Broadway, New York, NY 10018, USA
29 Earlsfort Terrace, Dublin 2, Ireland

BLOOMSBURY, BLOOMSBURY ACADEMIC and the Diana logo are trademarks of
Bloomsbury Publishing Plc

First published in Great Britain 2022
This paperback edition published 2024

Copyright © Brendan McNamara, Hazel O'Brien and contributors, 2022, 2024

Brendan McNamara and Hazel O'Brien have asserted her right under the Copyright,
Designs and Patents Act, 1988, to be identified as Editors of this work.

For legal purposes the Acknowledgements on p. xv constitute an extension
of this copyright page.

Cover design: Tjasa Krivec
Cover image © Round Tower at St. Kevins monastery, Glendalough, Co. Wicklow.
Photo (using star-trail technique) by Keith Gordon

All rights reserved. No part of this publication may be reproduced or transmitted
in any form or by any means, electronic or mechanical, including photocopying,
recording, or any information storage or retrieval system, without prior permission
in writing from the publishers.

Bloomsbury Publishing Plc does not have any control over, or responsibility for,
any third-party websites referred to or in this book. All internet addresses given in this
book were correct at the time of going to press. The author and publisher regret any
inconvenience caused if addresses have changed or sites have ceased to exist,
but can accept no responsibility for any such changes.

A catalogue record for this book is available from the British Library.

Library of Congress Control Number: 2021952917

ISBN: HB: 978-1-3502-9174-4
PB: 978-1-3502-9178-2
ePDF: 978-1-3502-9175-1
eBook: 978-1-3502-9176-8

Typeset by Newgen KnowledgeWorks Pvt. Ltd., Chennai, India

To find out more about our authors and books visit www.bloomsbury.com
and sign up for our newsletters.

We dedicate this book to all those who have worked on the study of religions in Ireland as researchers, writers, academics, activists and volunteers.

CONTENTS

List of Contributors	ix
Preface	xiii
Acknowledgements	xv

Part I
DISCIPLINARY OVERVIEW OF THE STUDY OF RELIGIONS IN IRELAND

Chapter 1
THE STUDY OF RELIGIONS IN IRELAND: AN ENTANGLED HISTORY 3
   Alexandra Grieser and Brian Bocking

Chapter 2
HISTORICAL PERSPECTIVES: IRISH NATIONALIST WOMEN'S
RELIGIOUS AND POLITICAL REVOLUTIONS 20
   Amy Heath-Carpentier

Chapter 3
REFLECTIONS ON IRISH FOLKLORE AND RELIGION 32
   Síle de Cléir

Chapter 4
THE ACADEMIC DISCIPLINE OF RELIGIOUS EDUCATION AT PRIMARY
LEVEL IN IRELAND 45
   Patricia Kieran

Chapter 5
UNDERSTANDING THE SOCIOLOGY OF RELIGION IN
CONTEMPORARY IRELAND 62
   Gladys Ganiel

Part II
THEMES IN THE CONTEMPORARY STUDY OF RELIGIONS IN IRELAND

Chapter 6
ESOTERICISM, ROMANTIC NATIONALISM AND THE BIRTH OF THE IRISH STATE 77
    Jenny Butler

Chapter 7
AFFIRMATIONS OF IRISHNESS: ASSESSING IRISH PROTESTANT IDENTITY 90
    Deirdre Nuttall and Tony Walsh

Chapter 8
SITUATING NEW RELIGIOUS MOVEMENTS IN CONTEMPORARY IRELAND 106
    Vesna Malešević

Chapter 9
MIGRANT RELIGIONS AND THE IRISH STATE 119
    Abel Ugba

Chapter 10
IRISH CATHOLICISM: WHERE HAS IT BEEN AND WHERE IS IT GOING? 132
    Brian Conway

Chapter 11
THINKING BEYOND THE ISLAND: BUDDHISM, IRELAND AND METHOD IN THE STUDY OF RELIGIONS 144
    Laurence Cox and Brian Bocking

Postface
MAPPING THE RELIGIOUS FIELD IN IRELAND 158
    Tom Inglis

Notes 163
References 175
Index 213

CONTRIBUTORS

Brian Bocking is Emeritus Professor of the Study of Religions at University College Cork, Ireland. From 1999 to 2007 he was Professor of the Study of Religions at SOAS, University of London. He became Professor and Head of the newly established Study of Religions Department at University College Cork in 2008 and retired in 2015. Publications include the first English translation of the fifth-century Chinese text of Nagarjuna's *Middle Treatise*, a study of a Japanese religious scroll (the *sanja takusen* or 'Oracles of the Three Shrines'), a Dictionary of Shinto, and journal articles and edited works including *Religious Education in a Global-Local World*, *Representing Sikhism: Essays in Memory of the Irish Scholar Max Arthur Macauliffe* and a 2017 special issue of the *Journal of the Irish Society for the Academic Study of Religions* (*JISASR*) with Prof. Christopher Shackle of SOAS. He has recently co-researched and authored *The Irish Buddhist: The Forgotten Monk Who Faced Down the British Empire* (2020).

Jenny Butler is a lecturer in the Study of Religions Department at University College Cork, Ireland. Her interests converge in the study of national identity, religious movements and emergent spiritual traditions, and popular culture. She is the founder of the Irish Network for the Study of Esotericism and Paganism (INSEP), a regional research network of the European Society for the Study of Western Esotericism (ESSWE). She has published widely on Irish contemporary Paganism as well as traditional culture and national identity in Ireland.

Brian Conway is Assistant Professor of Sociology at Maynooth University, Ireland. His recent research has been published in the *International Journal of Comparative Sociology*, *Sociology Compass*, *Sociological Perspectives* and *Social Science History*. He received a PhD in sociology from the University of Notre Dame. He also studied at the University of Pittsburgh, USA, where he earned a master's in social work with a specialization in community organization. He is the former editor of the *Irish Journal of Sociology*. Prior to his role at Maynooth University, he was Lecturer in Sociology at Robert Gordon University, Scotland.

Laurence Cox is Associate Professor of Sociology at Maynooth University, Ireland. Recent publications include *Buddhism and Ireland* (2013), *The Irish Buddhist* (with Brian Bocking and Alicia Turner; 2020), 'Japanese Buddhism and Ireland' (*Journal of Religion in Japan*, with John Ó Laoidh), 'Early Western Lay Buddhists in Colonial Asia' (*JISASR*, with Mihirini Sirisena) and 'The First Buddhist Mission to the West' (*DISKUS*, with Brian Bocking and Yoshinaga Shin'ichi). He maintains the Dhammaloka Project website (https://dhammalokaproject.wordpress.com/)

covering research on early western Buddhists in Asia, and on Ireland and Buddhism.

Síle de Cléir is a lecturer in Irish language and literature at the University of Limerick, Ireland. She is the author of *Popular Catholicism in 20th-Century Ireland: Locality, Identity and Culture* (2017). She has also researched and written about Irish cloth and dress traditions, along with transformations from folk to fashionable dress. Her current research is centred on Irish-language heroic narrative in the nineteenth and twentieth centuries.

Gladys Ganiel is Reader in Sociology at Queen's University Belfast, UK. She has authored/co-authored six books, more than forty-five peer-reviewed journal articles and book chapters, a co-edited book and two co-edited journal special issues. Her specialisms include religion on the island of Ireland, religion and conflict in Northern Ireland, evangelicalism and the emerging church. Her book *The Deconstructed Church: Understanding Emerging Christianity* (2014), co-authored with Gerardo Marti, was winner of the 2015 Distinguished Book Award of the Society for the Scientific Study of Religion.

Alexandra Grieser is Assistant Professor for the Theory of Religion at Trinity College Dublin, Ireland. Her research focuses on method and theory in the Academic Study of Religions; European pluralism (from 1800 to the present; interferences between religion, art, science and technology); the history and theory of knowledge; and aesthetics of religion. She has published on religious change (*Transformations of Immortality*, 2008), on knowledge production in museums (2011), on religious and scientific imagery (2014, 2017), on the aesthetics of religion as a bio-cultural approach (*Aesthetics of Religion: A Connective Concept*, 2017) and on the history of the study of religion (*Religion in Culture – Culture in Religion*, 2021).

Amy Heath-Carpentier lectures in gender, sexuality and international affairs in the Global Studies programme at Washington University in St. Louis, USA. She studies the connections between revolutionary/progressive politics and religious transformation among Irish feminists. In addition, she contributes to international dialogue on transdisciplinary research and transnational feminist theories and praxes. She is the editor of the first comprehensive collection of essays in English by the French philosopher/sociologist Edgar Morin.

Tom Inglis is Emeritus Professor of Sociology at University College Dublin, Ireland. He has written extensively about culture, mostly in relation to religion, meaning, the body and the media, particularly in relation to Ireland. He published two editions of *Moral Monopoly: The Rise and Fall of the Catholic Church in Modern Ireland* (1998). His other books include *Global Ireland: Same Difference* (2008) and *Meanings of Life in Contemporary Ireland: Webs of Significance* (2014).

Patricia Kieran teaches religious education at Mary Immaculate College (MIC), University of Limerick, Ireland. She is Director of the Irish Institute for Catholic Studies and a British Foreign and Commonwealth Chevening Scholar. Prior to working in MIC, she lectured in the area of theology and religious education in Newman University, Birmingham, UK. She is a member of the Mid-West Interfaith Network and the Religions and Beliefs in Changing Times Research team. She has co-written and edited seven books, journal articles and book chapters on a range of topics including decolonizing the religious education curriculum, inter-belief dialogue, Catholic religious education, religious education in an intercultural Europe, Catholic theology, children and Catholicism, and trends and challenges in education. She was a team member of the Enquiring Classroom Project which sought to develop strategies to support teachers and students in engaging in difficult ethical conversations about identity, religions and beliefs, democratic values, diversity, belonging and violence. Her most recent edited book *Connecting Lives: Inter-belief Dialogue in Contemporary Ireland* (2019) focuses on dialogue among belief diverse communities.

Vesna Malešević is a lecturer at National University of Ireland, Galway. She is a sociologist whose primary focus rests on the topics of religion, secularization, minorities, sexualities and health. From 2015 to 2016, she led a research project called 'Mental Health and Suicide among Travellers: A Sociological Pilot Study', which was funded by The Exchange House National Traveller Service where intersections between religion, sexualities and mental health were investigated. Currently, she is engaged in the GenderNet Plus Project 'Violence against Women, Migrants and Refugees: Analysing Causes and Effective Policy Response'.

Brendan McNamara is a lecturer in the Study of Religions Department in University College Cork, Ireland. His research interests include East/West connections in the early twentieth century, the discourse around religions in that period, Orientalist constructions of knowledge and Ireland and Empire. He has published journal articles, a book chapter and edited a volume of essays. His recent monograph is titled *The Reception of 'Abdu'l-Bahá in Britain; East Comes West* (2021).

Deirdre Nuttall is an ethnologist, independent researcher and writer. She has a particular interest in religion as a cultural identifier, in symbolic thoughts and behaviours, and in narratives of the supernatural and macabre. She has a master's in social anthropology from the University of Durham, UK, and a PhD in Folklore/Ethnology from University College Dublin, Ireland, and has carried out fieldwork in Ireland, Newfoundland and Guatemala. Deirdre is also a ghostwriter in the fields of memoir, biography and non-fiction generally, and in this capacity she has produced a large number of mass-market and niche books. Recent publications on the topic of Irish Protestantism include 2020's *Different and the Same: A Folk History of the Protestants of Independent Ireland*.

Hazel O'Brien is a lecturer in Sociology at Waterford Institute of Technology, Ireland. Her research is currently focused on the adaptations of tradition inherent within Global Mormonism, and she is working on a monograph related to this topic. Other recent publications include 2020's 'What Does the Rise of Digital Religion during Covid-19 Tell Us about Religion's Capacity to Adapt?' in *Irish Journal of Sociology*. She is a participant in the 'Consultation on Latter-day Saint Women 2019–2021' at the Maxwell Institute, Brigham Young University, USA, which brings together the foremost scholars of Mormonism and Gender from across the globe.

Abel Ugba is a lecturer based in the School of Sociology and Social Policy at the University of Leeds, UK. He is a sociologist of religion and media scholar who is interested in the dynamics of religiosity in immigration contexts and in the multilayered and complex entanglements of religion with the media. For over a decade, Abel has studied the dynamics of transnational Pentecostalism among Europe's new African diasporas, focusing on the implications of religiosity for self-understanding and the delineation of social boundaries and commonalities in precarious and racialized immigration contexts. He is the author of *Shades of Belonging: Pentecostal Africans in Twenty-First Century Ireland* (2009). Abel currently serves as the vice-president of the African Association for the Study of Religion (AASR).

Tony Walsh was, until his recent retirement from Maynooth University, Head of the Department of Adult and Community Education. He continues as Director of the Centre for the Study of Irish Protestantism at Maynooth University and is a Fellow of the Young Centre for Anabaptist and Pietist Studies at Elizabethtown College, Pennsylvania, USA. A licensed systemic constructivist psychotherapist, he is engaged in writing, consultancy and social inquiry engagements in the United States, the UK, Palestine, Liberia and Ireland (including Northern Ireland). Current research emphases include (1) the experience and culture of the Irish Protestant minority, (2) a narrative study of the Old German Baptist Brethren (an Amish-like Plain church), (3) the role of reflexivity in radical adult education and (4) narrative and auto-ethnographic inquiry.

PREFACE

The Study of Religions in Ireland: Past, Present and Future was conceived as a project to celebrate, summarize and synthesize some of the best academic work ongoing within the interdisciplinary field of the study of religions in Ireland and on Ireland. Its publication coincides with the hosting of the European Association for the Study of Religions (EASR) annual conference in University College Cork in 2022, the first time this significant gathering of scholars has convened in Ireland. Both conference and publication synchronize with the centenary of the birth of the Irish Free State, the culmination of a process intimately connected to religions and religion, and a prelude to a profound interplay.

The conference aims to provide a space for theoretical and methodological reflection and for empirical and historical research on freedom in, from and of religion. *The Study of Religions in Ireland: Past, Present and Future* speaks to these debates, reflecting upon Ireland's complex interrelationship between religions and the state. In early planning, the editors envisaged that the treatment would comprehensively encompass an all-island experience, but as the work progressed it became clear that this would necessitate a much larger volume and would be a far bigger project than constraints will allow. Therefore, for the most part (though certainly not entirely), the contributors discuss the study of religions in what is commonly referred to as the 'Republic of Ireland' or 'Ireland',[1] the successor of the Irish Free State.

Whilst research and writing in the academic study of religions (ASR) has been greatly augmented across Ireland's vastly changing social, cultural and economic landscape, no volume has yet brought together key figures in the field to provide an overview of the discipline or to outline new developments. Some of Ireland's pre-eminent scholars of religions have been tasked with showcasing a sample of the ongoing work in progress on the study of religions as Ireland moves into the state's second century. The editors felt it important to provide a collection capable of fulfilling a dual role. On the one hand, we wanted this volume to be a useful resource for religions specialists who are interested in the study of religions in Ireland and how key points of discussion in the field are being addressed in an Irish context. On the other hand, we wanted to provide a 'go-to' text that provides undergraduate and postgraduate students of religions with a comprehensive overview of how the field has developed, what themes have driven its progression and what opportunities and challenges may lie ahead. Not every specialism can be covered however, and the editors are conscious that this volume does not fully capture the wonderful complexity of the religious field in Ireland. The availability of work in progress, and the perpetual heavy workloads for academics, has inevitably affected efforts to create a fully representative volume.

As we reflect, we consider that an expanded volume could have included the work of scholars researching, for example, the sociology of religions, Judaism, Hinduism and aspects related to the study of Islam not possible to include here. There are relevant themes surrounding Ireland, religion and the state which are not addressed here, such as the place of the Irish diaspora, the experience of sectarianism or a more central discussion of the commonalities and divergences in experiences of religion North and South of the border. Future publications will surely redress these omissions.

Nonetheless, we believe this to be a volume that presents a unique combination of cutting-edge theory and research in the study of religions. Part I provides a disciplinary overview of the study of religions in Ireland, opening with a comprehensive introductory chapter that outlines where the study of religions is located within the Irish academy and followed by contributions exemplifying developments within the fields of sociology, religious education, folklore and history. Part II is a discussion of the key themes which have emerged from the study of religions in Ireland, such as religions and the state, methods in the study of religions, majority-minority relationships and secularization. Catholicism, the Church of Ireland, Pentecostalism, Buddhism and New Religious Movements are all examined. The volume will therefore engage specialists and students with contemporary topics whilst illuminating for them how these themes have been experienced from a variety of religious perspectives. The Postface for the volume is contributed by Prof. Emeritus Tom Inglis, who deftly synthesizes the past, present and future of the religious field in Ireland. He emphasizes that to understand the contemporary moment, we must understand what has gone before and its significance for all our futures.

It is our hope that this offering will be a precursor to many more publications covering a wide variety of themes and topics around the study of religions in and on Ireland.

ACKNOWLEDGEMENTS

This volume would not have been possible without the support of many. The committee of the Irish Society for the Academic Study of Religions (ISASR) and its wider membership were enthusiastic about this project from the start.

We particularly appreciate the role played by Dr Alexandra Grieser in her capacity as the president of ISASR and the advice and assistance provided by ISASR members Dr James Kapaló and Dr Jenny Butler. Their encouragement and practical help has been invaluable.

Emeritus Prof. Brian Bocking has played a foundational role in the progress of the study of religions in Ireland and he has been most generous and supportive as this project has progressed.

We thank our editors and reviewers at Bloomsbury for their diligence, patience and expertise. We are also grateful for funding received under Waterford Institute of Technology's 'Research Connexions' programme which has assisted the editors in the completion of this project.

Finally, we wish to express our sincere gratitude to all our contributors. The professional, collegiate and generous spirit which characterized the project from the outset made the work of the editors most enjoyable.

Part I

DISCIPLINARY OVERVIEW OF THE STUDY OF RELIGIONS IN IRELAND

Chapter 1

THE STUDY OF RELIGIONS IN IRELAND: AN ENTANGLED HISTORY

Alexandra Grieser and Brian Bocking

Relating the two themes 'Ireland' and 'religion' to one another probably invokes, for many, memories of a country that has gone through 'the Troubles', with religiously defined opposing parties and a culture hard to understand in its historically evolved constellation. For others, 'Irish religion' might stand for the presence of a living 'paganism', the cradle of a 'Celtic spirituality' that has shaped Irish culture to the present day and has now globalized, as other indigenous traditions have done. This book aims to widen the horizon and offer a deeper understanding of Ireland and Irish religions in the light of the European, and indeed global, history of religions.

The title of this book could mean two things: *The Study of Religions* in Ireland, meaning the academic discipline, or the study of *Religions in Ireland*, meaning the historical and contemporary role of religion in Irish culture. Rather than resolving the ambiguity before moving forward, in this introduction we embrace both meanings and will use them productively. As the disciplinary history of the study of religions has shown, the ways in which the subject has developed against different cultural backgrounds is closely intertwined with the religious history of a country or, better, the history of the religious and the secular and the place of the study of religions within it (Kippenberg 2002; Fujiwara, Thurfjell and Engler 2021). The present volume as a whole, as is evident from the Table of Contents, covers almost exclusively Ireland-related religious topics; yet, by doing so, it also tells the reader much about the background from which the study of religions in Ireland and elsewhere has developed, and will develop further.

Covering both a comprehensive history of religions in Ireland and an overview of how the academic study of religions (ASR) has developed over the last decades worldwide is obviously impossible within the scope of a single volume. Rather, the editors saw an opportunity to provide a map for those scholars who in June 2022 will come to attend the first annual conference to be held by the European Association for the Study of Religions (EASR) in Ireland. The event will be organized by the Study of Religions departmental team at University College Cork (UCC) in cooperation with the Irish Society for the Academic Study of Religions

(ISASR). For many participants, the 2022 EASR conference may well offer a first sustained encounter with Ireland and with the complexities of Irish culture and history, particularly the past and present of Irish religiosity. Conversely, for many Irish readers familiar with Ireland and the ways in which the topic of religion in Ireland has traditionally been addressed, and indeed for a global audience acquainted with Irish studies, the perspectives presented may provide fresh views. It can be hoped that it will serve as a 'Guide for the Perplexed' regarding Ireland and religion and may help to start productive conversations.

Each of the chapters in this volume makes its own significant contribution to the goal of expanding the horizon of understanding. Most, though not all, of the contributors to this volume are themselves Irish.[1] As a result, the discussions within these pages draw not only on the authors' extensive research into their particular areas of scholarly interest but often reflect personal experience of developments in the island of Ireland over decades in which significant changes have taken place. The chapters in this book are not, however, accounts which unreflectively privilege the 'insider', whether of country, epoch or religion. The approach taken throughout the book exemplifies the second meaning of the title: The Study of Religions in Ireland. In other words, the chapters reflect a non-confessional ASR approach of the kind fostered in Ireland by ISASR, in Europe more widely by the EASR and globally by the International Association for the History of Religions (IAHR).[2] In this introduction, we attempt to add a glimpse of both the diverse research interests of scholars of religions working in Ireland and some of the structures that shape their work.

The 'academic study of religions' or ASR is a term not very commonly used (yet) in the wider world of the study of religions,[3] but it has proved tactically useful in Ireland and Europe generally where the topic of 'religion' tends to be limited to the history of Christianity or where it is widely assumed (including by many of today's students schooled by the internet of strong opinions) to demand an approach which 'takes sides'. Often this expectation presupposes a naive 'world religions' perspective and looks for a teacher who is an 'insider', a theologically correct exponent of the supposedly unitary 'religion' he or she is employed to teach about. Basic methodological questions arise from adopting such an approach in higher education, such as who will be resurrected to teach about the past, how 'other' religions fit into this perspective and what kind of 'insider' could be appointed to teach and research transcultural, multireligious topics such as gender, ethnicity, clerical abuse, religion and politics and so forth. The background of these questions and the identity politics linked with it need to be addressed with students at an early stage of their course in the study of religions.

While the IAHR and its subsidiaries have wrestled for some time with the question of whether the academic study of religions ought to be called (in English) 'scientific',[4] such a claim would have little chance of gaining traction in Irish academia, where, as things stand, it would be interpreted as a 'stroke' – a term for any ingenious and disingenuous stratagem – in this case an attempt by a 'Humanities' or 'Social Sciences' subject to join the rather more generously funded Science, Technology, Engineering and Mathematics (STEM) subjects. ASR, then, indicates an approach which – like other humanities and social science subjects – values rigorous theory and evidence-based research of the kind which yields results capable of being checked, verified, debated and no doubt in due course improved upon by any competent and responsible scholar, regardless of that scholar's personal religious orientation, politics, gender, ethnicity and so forth.

If this seems to the reader a modest and uncontroversial ambition in a European country, the chapters in this book will help to explain why in Ireland academic detachment in matters of religion has seldom seemed a viable option. ASR has developed relatively late in comparison with other national cultures in the field, such as the phenomenological tradition in the early twentieth century in the Netherlands (G. van der Leeuw), Sweden (N. Söderblom), Germany (from R. Otto via F. Heiler to G. Mensching), Italy (with figures such as R. Pettazzoni) and the UK (with F. M. Müller); the anthropological tradition coming from J. Frazer and E. B. Tylor; and more recently N. Smart's 'methodological agnosticism'. In this connection, Gladys Ganiel's chapter in Part I of this volume on the sociology of religion in contemporary Ireland and Deirdre Nuttall and Tony Walsh's chapter in Part II on Protestant identity in the Republic together offer a valuable conspectus of key religious developments in a sociopolitical context within the island of Ireland over the last hundred years.

A non-confessional approach to religions is indeed a relatively new phenomenon in Ireland.[5] As in many countries, the development of ASR has not been linear, and a historical approach needs to recognize changing activities within the dominant structures. A good example is the fact that 'religious studies' was long taught to intending schoolteachers within colleges of education. Many such colleges have recently been incorporated into universities. Teaching programmes that were part of the Mater Dei Institute and St Patrick's College, for example, have now been transformed and located in the School of Theology, Philosophy, and Music of Dublin City University (DCU).[6] While there is still a strong theological element in programmes such as 'Theology and Religious Studies', 'World Religions and Theology' or 'Bachelor of Religious Education with History/English/Music', there is an increasing role for ASR not only in terms of engagement with what are still often offensively referred to as 'non-Christian' traditions but also in the way in which Christianity and more traditional subjects such as 'sacred texts' are dealt with.[7]

Another example of a historical development specific to the Republic can be seen in the establishment of the Irish School of Ecumenics (ISE), founded in 1970 by the Jesuit Michael Hurley against the will of church authorities and dedicated to the initiation and development of the peace process. Ecumenics, in the understanding of the ISE, recognizes the role of religion in conflict and peacebuilding and requires, in addition to inter-religious and intercultural dialogue, a multidisciplinary field of academic study. Today, the institute is housed in the School of Religion of Trinity College Dublin (TCD) with a campus also in Belfast, running postgraduate programmes and hosting research projects on the role of religion in the field from different perspectives. The School of Religion in TCD is itself a recent construct that brings together the ISE, the Loyola Institute and the former Department of Religions and Theology.[8] ASR is present here in the distinctive combination of expertise in different religious traditions and their history ('World Religions') and a position in the 'Theory of Religion', a combination that provides methodologies and approaches for studying religion in relation to media cultures and other social systems such as science, economy, politics and art.

These examples show how religion – as a subject of academic analysis – has received increasing attention in Ireland over the last decade. This has led to ASR now being taught, in practice, at different universities at different levels of intensity and under different labels. The contributions of scholars trained in ASR are often interwoven in more general programmes, often without clear institutional visibility. Examples would include BA and MA programmes in arts with religious studies (such as in Waterford Institute of Technology, WIT), in religion programmes including theology, biblical studies and ethics (e.g. in TCD); in psychology (e.g. in WIT), in religious education (RE, e.g. in DCU), in theology with religious studies, in ethics and philosophy, in chaplaincy and healthcare education, and modules added to sociology programmes and electives designed to include ASR elements (e.g. in Maynooth University, MU), responding to the challenge to convey not only empirical knowledge but also the different dimensions of thinking about and researching religion.

Before the early years of the twenty-first century, however, no department for the study of religions as a social and cultural science had been established in any of Ireland's universities. A side effect of this was, crucially, that those who studied religions in Ireland across a variety of disciplines were not part of the European EASR and global IAHR networks. This is why, as recently as 2007, Ireland was characterized by Michael Stausberg, in his overview of the development of the study of religions in Europe, as being (with Portugal) one of the remaining 'blind spots' for the academic study of religion(s) in Western Europe (Stausberg 2007: 296). While academic studies of religious topics had developed to some extent within disciplines including sociology, folklore, political science, Biblical, Jewish and Near Eastern Studies, and history,[9] researchers from those various disciplines were, in the absence of a substantial and officially recognized Irish networking organization such as ISASR, often unaware of each other's shared interests and thus of the extent of Irish research in the study of religions.

Laurence Cox (2010) provided a succinct contemporary account of the situation of Irish studies of religions around that time in his report on the 2009 international conference 'Alternative Spiritualities, the New Age and New Religious Movements in Ireland' organized by a group of colleagues in the social sciences and held at MU in October 2009. To the pleasant surprise of the organizers, that conference, the first of its kind in Ireland, attracted nearly seventy participants from '3 continents, 11 countries and 15 disciplines' (Cox 2010; Cosgrove et al. 2011: 4). An appetite for expansion of the field of the study of religions was evident, certainly to the academic leadership at UCC, and Stausberg noted in a correction to the final instalment of his essay that things had begun to change quite rapidly around this time (Stausberg 2009: 278n). The Study of Religions department at UCC and its 'Religions and Global Diversity' undergraduate programme were inaugurated in academic year 2007–8, academics of international standing in the field of the study of religions were recruited and interest in the study of religions (plural), both within and beyond Ireland, began to spread. ISASR was launched in 2011, with its first president Patrick Claffey (TCD-based) and first secretary Brian Bocking (UCC-based) among a committee drawn from a range of higher education institutions. Soon after, the ISASR journal *JISASR*[10] saw its first volume published, and regular annual ISASR conferences were organized in different universities throughout the island of Ireland, a first joint conference with the British Association for the Study of Religions (BASR) being held at Queen's University Belfast in 2018.[11]

One of the consequences of the rapid increase in research and teaching activity over recent years is that any appraisal of the current state of ASR in Ireland which focuses mainly on *Irish* religious topics misses the bigger picture. Complementing a renewed and reinvigorated interest in Ireland's own – and, as soon became apparent, unexpectedly diverse – religious past and present, much of the new Ireland-based scholarship in the study of religions has been geographically and linguistically outward-looking and global in scope, with skilled and linguistically prepared researchers studying topics in India, the Middle East, Japan, the Americas, Eastern Europe and other areas, initiating debates and developing approaches in a diversity of ways. In some cases, such research has followed the trail of neglected émigré Irish figures such as Dhammaloka or Macauliffe (see below). Hence, in what follows, we very purposively start by drawing attention to some of the significant research projects and publications by ASR scholars in Ireland whose research is directed wholly or mainly outside Ireland and for that reason is not much represented elsewhere in this book. For the most part, the scholars and their research projects and publications are already internationally recognized. However, it is not always appreciated that the work for which they are best known originates in Irish universities.

It should be understood that the following account of research activities across the broad canvas of ASR specialisms in Ireland is indicative rather than exhaustive. We have restricted publications, where cited, to just one or two for individual researchers mentioned, as well as highlighting mainly members of ISASR and those who identify as ASR or Study of Religions scholars. Where known, website addresses of research projects are provided in the endnotes. Naturally, the works cited and others too numerous to mention here provide a much fuller picture of a scholar's research activities and interdisciplinary connections than we can offer in a brief introduction, and we apologize for possibly having overlooked important work.[12]

Among Ireland-based and internationally focused research projects in ASR, probably the best known at time of writing is the collaborative EU-funded project 'Creative Agency and Religious Minorities: Hidden Galleries in the Secret Police Archives in Central and Eastern Europe' directed by James Kapaló (UCC), a specialist in Eastern European Christianity (Kapaló 2019; Kapaló and Povedák 2021).[13] In 2013, Kapaló co-founded with Lidia Guzy (UCC) the Marginalised and Endangered Worldviews Study Centre (MEWSC) (Guzy and Kapaló 2017) which hosts regular international conferences and workshops.[14] Guzy's anthropological research, primarily in South Asia, is founded on ethnography, museum research and the documentation of hitherto unknown and endangered traditions of sacred music of rural India and indigenous world views (Guzy 2013). Alexandra Grieser (TCD) focuses on European pluralism (religious and secular), the history of, and theory building in, the Study of Religions, and the networked and newly developing approach of an Aesthetics of Religion that studies the relationship between religious systems and the human senses on an individual and societal level (Grieser and Johnston 2017; Grieser 2021).

Amanullah De Sondy (UCC) approaches Islamic studies through the lens of gender, sexuality, race, ethnicity and pluralism (De Sondy 2013), while his role as a public intellectual in the wider field of Islam as one of the 'Abrahamic' faiths is reflected in a co-authored work on Jewish, Christian and Islamic monotheism (De Sondy, Gonzales and Green 2020). Rachel Woodlock (UCC) studies Islamophobia and the social inclusion of Muslim minorities in Western societies, focusing particularly on self-identified religious Muslims in Australia (Woodlock 2012, 2016). James Carr (University of Limerick, UL) has also published extensively on Muslims, Islamophobia and integration in Ireland, including *Experiences of Islamophobia: Living with Racism in the Neoliberal Era* (2016) and on Muslim dilemmas (Carr and Fanning 2019).

In her work on the intertextuality between the Qur'an and the Hebrew Bible, Zohar Hadromi-Allouche (TCD) develops comparative perspectives; specializing in the portrayal of figures of women in classical and modern scholarship on Islam adds not only the reflective prism of gender approaches but also the reflexive question of how the production of knowledge about religion changes throughout history (Hadromi-Allouche 2018a, 2018b). Daniele Pevarello (TCD) combines his expertise in Greek and Roman Mediterranean history of religion with a focus on its reception in the religious discourse of early Christianity and how classical *paideia* (educational cultures), above all Graeco-Roman literature and Hellenistic philosophy, were received and used in the formation of Christianity, with a special interest in ascetic practices (Pevarello 2017, 2018).

Gwilym Beckerlegge (Open University, UK), who as professor at UCC during 2006–7 designed and secured academic approval for UCC's pioneering 'Religions and Global Diversity' programme, has recently documented the remarkable translocal life of the social and educational activist Sister Nivedita (the Irish-born Margaret Noble), revising conventional 'emic' accounts which view her primarily as a disciple of Swami Vivekananda (Beckerlegge 2021). In similar biographical vein, Tadhg Foley (National University of Ireland Galway, NUIG) has pioneered the study of two Irish-born scholars of religion, each of whom made his name far from Ireland. William Edward Hearn (1826–1888) in Australia authored works on jurisprudence, political economy and religion; he was a cousin of the somewhat better-known Lafcadio (Foley 2016). The renowned (except in Ireland) and linguistically gifted Max Arthur Macauliffe spent most of his chequered life in the Punjab, first as a judge and then in lengthy retirement as a devoted scholar of Sikhism (Foley 2017). A special issue of *JISASR* contains papers by scholars from Ireland, the United States and the UK delivered at a 2013 UCC conference mounted with the active support of members of the Irish Sikh community to mark the centennial of Macauliffe's death (Shackle and Bocking 2017). Another international UCC conference, 'RE21: Religious Education in a Global-Local World', engendered a volume of essays on RE in contexts as diverse as Mali, Russia, Sweden and Indonesia as well as Ireland (Berglund, Shanneik and Bocking 2016).

Abel Ugba (now at Leeds and Bayreuth) has carried out extensive research on African Pentecostals in Ireland (Ugba 2009, 2011, this volume). His current projects address divine healing practices among Pentecostal Africans in Germany[15] and health and healing practices among diaspora African Pentecostals in London, Cape Town, Kampala and Nairobi.[16] Tatsuma Padoan (UCC) has researched ritual apprenticeship in Japanese mountain asceticism (Katsuragi Shugen) and leads a British Academy research project on pilgrimage as a social and semiotic practice in Japan, Italy, Ireland and Spain entitled 'A Semiotics of Sacred Geography: Understanding Pilgrimage and Holy Sites in a Comparative Perspective' (Padoan 2019, 2021). Research by Brendan McNamara (UCC) on the vibrant religious milieu in Britain prior to the First World War (McNamara 2019) and in particular engagement with religious ideas and figures from 'the East' by home-grown religious reformers and innovators of the time has been published as *The Reception of 'Abdu'l-Bahá in Britain; East Comes West* (McNamara 2021). Bocking (UCC) collaborated with Cox (MU) and Yoshinaga Shin'ichi (Ryukoku University, Kyoto) to research the career, spent largely in Japan, of a forgotten nineteenth-century pioneer Irish Buddhist missionary and Japanophile, Charles Pfoundes (Bocking, Cox and Yoshinaga 2014). Together with Alicia Turner (York University, Toronto) and Cox, Bocking helped to recover the extraordinary Asian monastic career of the working-class 'Irish Buddhist', U Dhammaloka (Turner, Cox and Bocking 2020).[17]

A number of ASR scholars in Ireland combine expertise in Irish religion with international research interests, while others focus almost exclusively on Irish religions. The first large-scale government-funded research project conducted by members of the newly established UCC Study of Religions department from 2008 to 2011 was led by Oliver Scharbrodt; it addressed for the first time the multifaceted history of Islam in Ireland. Published outcomes included *Muslims in Ireland* (Scharbrodt et al. 2015) and individual works on aspects of Islam in Ireland by researchers already experienced in the international study of Islam (Ibrahim 2011; Khan 2013; Sakaranaho and Martikainen 2015; Shanneik 2015). Jenny Butler (UCC), who conducted the first major ethnographic research project on contemporary Paganism in Ireland (Butler 2020a, 2020b) went on to lead the Ireland/Canada/UK-funded ethnographic project 'Fairy Lore and Landscapes', covering Ireland, Iceland and Newfoundland.[18] Cox (MU) completed his comprehensive *Buddhism and Ireland* (Cox 2013; Cox and Bocking, this volume) while co-researching the forgotten 'Irish Buddhist' U Dhammaloka across the United States, Burma, Sri Lanka and other parts of Asia, drawing on his long-standing international research into radical social movements.

Ganiel's (QUB) extensive work on religion, conflict and reconciliation in Northern Ireland has moved understanding of evangelicalism beyond the stereotyped combative evangelicalism of the Revd Ian Paisley to demonstrate evangelical contributions to peacebuilding and identity change. She has also highlighted the unsung role of ecumenical peacemaker Catholic Fr Gerry Reynolds and through research with the Presbyterian church has revealed the diversity of Christian approaches to and roles in conflict and reconciliation (Ganiel and Yohanis 2019). Addressing recent religious changes in Ireland, Ganiel's concept of 'extra-institutional religion' (Ganiel 2016) helps to explain how pockets of religious vitality persist on a secularizing, 'post-Catholic' island. Brian Conway's (MU) research into different aspects of changing Catholicism has examined features such as workforce trends, sexual scandals and episcopal discourses in Ireland (Conway, this volume) and across numerous countries within the global research field surveyed in his 'The Sociology of Catholicism' (Conway 2021). Other established scholars in the field with a particular interest in Northern Ireland include the UCC sociologist Joseph Ruane (Ruane 2021; Ruane and Todd 2010) and politics and international relations specialist Jennifer Todd of University College Dublin (UCD) (Todd 2018; Todd and Ruane 2016).[19]

Dianne Kirby (TCD) has made extensive use of oral history in two areas: 'Religious Women and the Troubles' ('the Troubles' in this case referring to the decades of ethnonationalist conflict centred in Northern Ireland from the 1960s to the late 1990s) and 'Religion and the Cold War' which covers a wider international canvas. These topics are documented in the Oral History Online Witness seminar series 'Religious Voices on Conflict Resolution, War and Peace'[20] and in related publications (Kirby 2017, 2021). Gerard Madden (NUIG) has also published on the Cold War, here focusing on Irish religion and anti-communism in the middle decades of the twentieth century (Madden 2014, 2018). Crawford Gribben (QUB) has worked extensively on early modern religion, with a particular interest in Calvinist literary cultures. He directed the 'Radical Religion in the Trans-Atlantic World, 1500–1800' project[21] and has published widely, including *God's Irishmen: Theological Debates in Cromwellian Ireland* and *The Rise and Fall of Christian Ireland* (Gribben 2007, 2021).

Patrick Claffey (TCD) has published on Christianity in both Africa (Dahomey-Benin) and in Ireland (Claffey 2007; Claffey, Bereska and Szustek 2016) while Brad Anderson's research (DCU) over the past several years has focused on the use and impact of sacred texts, particularly the Bible, in Ireland and beyond, addressing Jewish, Islamic and Christian perspectives, some of this research jointly with Jonathan Kearney (DCU) (Anderson 2020; Anderson and Kearney 2018). Patricia Kieran (Mary Immaculate College, MIC) has written extensively on religion, education, and religious education in Ireland (Kieran 2021; Kieran and McDonagh 2021; Kieran, this volume).

Hazel O'Brien (WIT) has written on Irishness, community and belonging in relation to Irish Mormons, and on digital religion in Ireland and beyond (O'Brien 2019, 2020), while Adrian Stringer's (MU) work has examined issues within the Anglican church in both Northern Ireland and the United States (Stringer 2016, 2019). Walsh's writing on Protestantism in the Irish Republic (Nuttall and Walsh, this volume) is complemented by a specialist interest in American 'Plain' churches

(Walsh 2021). Nuttall is an ethnologist, researcher and writer with particular interests in religion as a cultural identifier, in symbolic thoughts and behaviours, and in narratives of the supernatural and macabre. Her research has embraced Ireland, Newfoundland and Guatemala (Nuttall 2019, 2020). Síle de Cléir (UL) researches popular Catholicism in twentieth-century Ireland, its connections to Irish folk tradition and local identities, and the heroic narrative tradition in Irish folklore (de Cléir 2014, 2017, this volume). Amy Heath-Carpentier (Washington University, St Louis) works on the transformation of political engagement by religion in the lives of Irish women (Heath-Carpentier 2021, this volume) while Vivianne Crowley (Nottingham Trent University, UK) specializes in contemporary Paganism and Jung (Crowley 2019) and has made a special study of the Irish High Priestess of Isis, Olivia Durdin-Robertson (1917–2013) (Crowley 2017).

The Island of Ireland: An introduction through the study of religions

Some prefatory remarks may be necessary when turning to the chapters of this book and the topic of Ireland as a special focus for research in the area of religions. This is because the essays in this volume courteously assume that the reader is familiar with at least the basics of modern Irish history, including what is called the 'revolutionary period' (1912–23) and its enduring aftermath.[22] Recent and much-publicized disputes over Brexit and the Irish border have revived the international public's memories of the 'Good Friday Agreement' of 1998 which seemed to offer a peaceful resolution of the long conflict between pro-UK unionists and all-Ireland nationalists in Northern Ireland, and a new relationship between two jurisdictions (the independent Republic and the UK), both, by then, part of the European Union (EU).

However, transformative events in Ireland which took place almost a century earlier are less well understood. These events still resonate strongly across the whole island of Ireland, for the revolutionary period of often violent resistance to British rule ended in 1922–3 with the establishment of the Irish 'Free State' (now the Republic of Ireland) and the Civil War. But the British would not, in 1922, yield the whole of the island. A partition, to some extent comparable with the creation of a national border between India and Pakistan in 1947, was the result. The Protestant-dominated 'six counties' in the North (part of the ancient region called Ulster) remained, and remain, under UK rule as part of 'The United Kingdom of Great Britain and *Northern* Ireland'. As in many periods of postcolonial transition elsewhere, the open conflicts and violence mirrored the structural violence of preceding centuries that, for Ireland, goes back to the sixteenth century and presents a very special constellation of the pan-European turmoil labelled as 'religious wars'. It shaped a society in which, through the 'Penal Laws', access to political participation, property, marriage, language and education were restricted – on the basis of religion – for Catholics. Neither the conflicts surfacing during the twentieth and twenty-first centuries nor the role of Catholicism, Protestantism and the rising forms of secularism in Irish society can be understood without appreciating that religion was both a dominant force in a restrictive society and the warrantor of identity in the multilayered situation of a colonized country.

Teaching the topics of religion and colonialism or taking a pluralist approach to the history of religions therefore differs, in Ireland, from teaching them elsewhere. Everyone on the island, whether from the North or the Republic, along with many in the vast Irish diaspora,[23] knows of and has feelings about these epochal events, not least because their significance for today's Ireland is likely to be interpreted very differently according to one's ethnic-religious ('Irish', 'British', 'Catholic', 'Protestant', etc.) perspective. By contrast, people in Great Britain, including those who go into politics, are for the most part ignorant of – and/or indifferent to – Irish history, as has become painfully evident in negotiations over Brexit and in particular the UK's only land border with Europe, the border created in 1922. Because the partition of Ireland was literally divisive, narratives have tended to stereotype the protagonists of Irish history in respect of religion as, for example, uniformly 'Catholic' or 'Protestant' in their attitudes and beliefs, drowning out dissonant themes relating, for example, to gender and class, religious ideas and practices beyond the Catholic–Protestant binary, the Irish diaspora and alternative visions of Ireland's future.

This context becomes particularly relevant when looking at recent decades since the 1990s. Massive changes have taken place in both parts of the island, stimulated by the fall of the land border between them, with the active promotion of joint tourism and cultural, trade, health, infrastructure and other projects sponsored by the EU. Especially in the Republic, the economic extremes of the 'Celtic Tiger' period followed by recession around 2008 hit the higher education sector hard, among many other sectors and people. Alongside these developments, the pace at which societal norms have changed can be measured by the referendums held during the last decade, the public debates they stimulated and the landslide majorities by which Irish society decided to change practices closely intertwined with its religious history: same-sex marriage (2015), the repeal of the Eighth Amendment that contained strict regulations on abortion (2018), blasphemy (2018) and divorce (2019). The debate about holding a referendum on euthanasia is currently under way. For more on these and other changes in religion, migration and education, see, for example, Gray (2016), Faas, Foster and Smith (2020), Neary, Gray and O'Sullivan (2018) and Kieran (this volume).

Teaching ASR during this dynamic time encounters the simultaneity of the non-simultaneous when engaging with a generation of students who seem to be untouched by concerns about a religious or political divide between countries, friends and families, and yet discussions can become tense when classes consist of students from both jurisdictions on the island. Oftentimes German scholar Grieser, co-author of this introduction, has had chats with students about the process of *Vergangenheitsbewaeltigung* ('coming to terms with the past') and what she thinks about this with regard to Ireland's recent – and not so recent – history.[24] Students' dissertation topics demonstrate how religious agents are involved in campaigns for and against the changes that are seen as steps towards a modern Ireland; how the religious and the secular is being renegotiated; how religion, while used as a rhetorical weapon, also plays a role in the self-understanding of Irish people, their sexualities, attitudes and emotional and embodied practices.

The chapters in this volume show through close analysis of religious factors how complex, interesting, frequently tragic but often inspirational, the reality of life in Ireland was – and is.

Survey of chapters

In 'Historical Perspectives: Irish Nationalist Women's Religious and Political Revolutions', Heath-Carpenter takes a historical, biographical and feminist approach to the study of a number of notable women from Ireland's revolutionary period, adopting the heuristic concept of 'kyriarchy', 'a system of overlapping webs of domination, oppression and submission within which intersectional experiences of oppression and privilege unfold'. 'Intersectional' means that a multiplicity of systems is involved – the Irish women studied here sought not only as Irishwomen to be free of domination by the British but also as women to be free of submission to men. The innovative figures principally considered in relation to these struggles are Ella Young (1867–1956), Maud Gonne (1866–1953), Hanna Sheehy Skeffington (1877–1946), Dr Maud Joynt (1868–1940) and the sisters Constance Markievicz (1868–1927) and Eva Gore-Booth (1870–1926). To Kate Rigby's themes of 'rejection, replacement and reconstruction', Heath Carpenter offers a new theme, 'renegotiation', to account for how these women, both Catholic and Anglican, added or substituted elements from outside the canon of their native religion, such as spiritualism, theosophy, reincarnation and other aspects of Western esoteric traditions, to enable them to negotiate their position in relation to both politics and religion.

De Cléir in 'Reflections on Irish Folklore and Religion' addresses the terminology used to discuss 'folk religion' ('folk religion' being only one of such terms). Descriptors such as 'unofficial', 'popular' or 'vernacular' religion have helped scholars to pursue research into aspects of religion which might otherwise fall under the academic radar, but wherever there is a distinction there is an inequality, and any 'two-tier' approach – contrasting, for example, 'official' and 'unofficial' religious ideas and activities – generally marks the 'unofficial' as somehow inferior wherever the distinction is employed. By contrast, in Ireland, as de Cléir points out, interest in folklore was driven by a cultural nationalism which accords great respect to 'vernacular' traditions preserved in the Irish language. More recently, developments in other disciplines such as history (and indeed ASR) indicate a helpful convergence of perspectives recognizing the centrality of idiosyncratic 'lived experience'. As de Cléir puts it, 'Recognition of the complexity not just of religious culture, but of individuals and of their lived experience is now a cornerstone of research into religious tradition.' This understanding is carried into a fascinating exploration of examples of religious themes, beliefs and actions from the ancient Irish past to the present, positioned, as de Cléir suggests, on two axes: one axis with 'Christian themes and beliefs' at one extreme and 'otherworld themes and beliefs' at the other, and another axis of 'discourse' morphing into 'action'. A history of such 'lived' experiences can in principle be recovered, but much remains unexplored.

Kieran in 'The Academic Discipline of Religious Education at Primary Level in the Republic of Ireland' addresses the issues facing those who wish to advance Irish RE. Some broader background for the newcomer to this topic might be helpful. In the Republic, the government (i.e. the taxpayer) provides all the funding for primary schools but has negligible influence on their activities. Almost 90 per cent of schools are for historical reasons owned and run by the Catholic church, and they devote significant curriculum time to preparing pupils for Catholic sacraments, a situation increasingly anomalous in today's ever more multireligious (or anti-religious) Ireland.[25] Most local primary schools inevitably foster a 'Catholic versus other' mentality among Irish children at an early age (Shanneik 2016). RE under whatever name in Ireland (nomenclature around the subject is itself a major problem, as Kieran adroitly explains) has a long and emotionally and politically charged history, while the levers of change are limited, as government attempts to diversify the system have repeatedly demonstrated. Plans to have four hundred schools multi-denominational by 2030 through 'divestment' from church control (requiring an average of fifty per year) have succeeded in only eight cases since 2016 (O'Toole 2019; Loughlin 2020). Kieran's engaging and comprehensive analysis of the current situation demonstrates just how complex and entangled are the issues involved. A notable strength of the chapter is that the diverse voices in the debate about the future of Irish RE are treated with equal respect despite the inequalities of power. While fully aware of the difficulties in achieving consensus and action on a form of RE which will benefit children growing up in a global age, Kieran is guardedly optimistic. Amongst other things, an expansion in the study of RE as an academic discipline to PhD level in Irish universities is enhancing the range and quality of publications and debate on the subject.

Sociologists of religion in Ireland, though few in number, have made very significant contributions to the study of religions in recent decades. Ganiel in 'Understanding the Sociology of Religion in Contemporary Ireland'[26] takes the reader through the major issues arising in the two geographical areas that constitute the island of Ireland: first, processes of Catholic secularization and religious persistence in the Republic of Ireland; second, religion, conflict and peacebuilding in Northern Ireland. In respect of the Republic, Ganiel points to Tom Inglis's *Moral Monopoly: The Catholic Church in Modern Irish Society* (1987) as 'the foundational sociological text for explaining the Catholic church's all-encompassing role during much of the twentieth century'. Taking a line through Inglis's work, he writes in 1987 of a totalizing Catholic *habitus* moulding people's values, attitudes and behaviour, while the second edition in 1998 now documented the 'fall' of this all-encompassing *habitus*, as social, constitutional and economic changes transformed the relationship between clergy and many laity (Inglis 1998). A decade later, Inglis's 'individualist' type of Catholic (the least 'orthodox') became the 'disenchanted' Catholic, opposed to the church. Nevertheless, church attendance and census returns have kept Ireland high in the religiosity rankings in Western Europe, so that the relative persistence of Catholicism in the face of 'secularizing' forces also needs explaining (see Inglis, this volume), perhaps by the convergence of post-conflict ethnic and religious identity found in other postcolonial Catholic societies (Conway 2013). Northern Ireland, meanwhile, remains less secularized than the Republic, with Protestantism a more important marker of ethno-national identity than for Northern Ireland Catholics. Both Protestantism and Catholicism provide an important source of value and meaning within communities – an aspect that tends to be neglected in comparison with the high level of international interest in the relationships between religion, conflict and peacebuilding in Northern Ireland.

Part II of the volume begins with 'Esotericism, Romantic Nationalism and the Birth of the Irish State' in which Butler takes us to the revolutionary period and the foundation of what became the Republic of Ireland. Studies of Western esotericism have of course advanced in leaps and bounds in recent years, and it provides a helpful lens through which to view ideas and practices which contributed to the Irish campaign for self-rule. Although the Republic after 1922 took the form of Inglis's totalizing Catholic *habitus* and for most of the twentieth century offered little space to alternative forms of religiosity, the revolutionary period itself had involved competing visions of the future of a free Ireland, by no means all Catholic or indeed particularly Christian. Butler examines the contribution of a wide range of artists, writers and activists of both Catholic and Protestant backgrounds who contributed to ideas and ideals of what 'Irishness' might mean if only Ireland could be free of the British yoke. The Celtic Revival, occultism, magical groups such as the Hermetic Order of the Golden Dawn, and the Theosophical Society were influential in these circles, and, as Butler notes, the optimism and sense of connection with a distant past helped to some extent to overcome prevailing sectarian and partisan attitudes. While Protestants were emphatically sidelined within the Catholic self-image of the Free State, 'their occult involvement and romantic leanings were an instrumental force in shaping a cultural nationalism that still pervades today'.

In 'Affirmations of Irishness: Assessing Irish Protestant Identity', Nuttall and Walsh examine the experience of Protestants in the Republic of Ireland over the last century, explaining, 'For a range of historic, political and cultural reasons the experience of this tiny minority in the Republic is completely different to that of the majority Protestant community in Northern Ireland, which remains part of the United Kingdom.' The chapter opens with a striking vignette of a nonconformist minister's accidental presence at the Catholic celebration of Corpus Christi in his home town where his 'small farm' family had lived for three hundred years. He felt, 'I was an alien in my own country, a stranger in my own home.' An account of the undoubtedly problematic circumstances in which the Protestantism of the British took root in Ireland explains, in part, why popular resentment of the Protestant 'ascendancy' (landed gentry) during the revolutionary period extended to many ordinary Protestants, who were targeted as 'traitors'; many were intimidated and emigrated after 1921. While the new Irish government made efforts to accommodate Protestants, a good number of whom had supported the revival of Gaelic culture and had valuable professional skills in areas such as law, medicine and finance, the atmosphere changed as the new state asserted its distinctive (non-British) identity through a blend of nationalism and a divisive brand of strict Catholicism (see Ganiel, this volume). Seventy years later, in the 1990s as the economy boomed and the hold of the Catholic church weakened, with immigrants and disillusioned ex-Catholics being added to the Protestant ranks, Protestants found themselves once again significant, if still 'other', to mainstream Catholic identity. Drawing on Foucault, the authors invoke concepts of 'power', 'discourse', 'resistance', 'community' and 'silence' to articulate the precarious situation and strategies of resistance of Irish Protestants faced with an often terrifying ethno-religious environment – personified in the triumphalist and divisive figure of Archbishop John Charles McQuaid (1895–1973).

Malešević sets out to situate new religious movements (NRMs) in the Irish context with a survey of the largely sociological literature on NRMs, including secularization, as it has been measured and identified in a number of different societies, and a trend towards 'desecularization' in which the capacity and indeed persistent tendency for human beings to refresh, reinvent and reformulate religious ideas and practices wherever they can becomes most apparent. As Malešević puts it, 'Regardless of what concept we use to explain the terms religious change, post-secularism, post-Christianity, secularization, de-secularization or pluralization, there is one common denominator between them, namely the idea of religious vitality.' Other flexible terms including 'new religious movements' or 'alternative spiritualities' come in useful when tracking this religious vitality across a multitude of diverse and sometimes seemingly quite unrelated phenomena which may include, for example, Billy Graham's four missions to Ireland between 1946 and 1972, revivals of folk religion, a Catholic priest who was a member of the Magic Circle, atheism, yoga, Islam and migrant African Pentecostalists. What this chapter vigorously demonstrates is that religious orthodoxy or stability is not the norm. Religions are never timeless; 'new' or 'alternative' religious movements are currents which help to make up the mainstream. As Malešević puts it, 'A subjunctivized religiosity was as prevalent in eighteenth century Ireland as it is today.'

Ugba in 'Migrant Religions and the Irish State' observes that when African transnational Pentecostalism was first growing in the Republic of Ireland it was, like Islam, something that 'the Irish state and much of the public could not understand or engage with'. There is an irony here not lost on anyone aware of Ireland's record levels of mass *emigration* over the centuries and the well-known issues of racism and religious suspicion faced by Irish emigrants on arrival. Evidently this experience did not prepare the Irish remaining in Ireland for the migration of significant numbers of non-Irish people *into* the country during the 'Celtic Tiger' era of the 1990s, where Ugba's discussion of migrant religions and the Irish state begins. Since then, the rapid growth in Ireland of African forms of religion, particularly Christianity and Islam, has brought issues of multiculturalism, integration, secularism and the position of cultural and religious minorities in Western democracies to the fore. Ugba's very comprehensive study of

African Pentecostal Christianity in Ireland (Islam has received significantly more research attention) points to numerous factors that have encouraged Africans to look to Ireland for their home, with historic Irish missionary activity, amongst other things, raising African expectations – largely unmet – of a notably 'Christian' country, while, on the Irish side, inherited colonial attitudes of superiority as well as anti-immigration rhetoric, hostile citizenship legislation and an ambivalent relationship of Pentecostals with the dominant Catholic church have hindered an equal meeting of minds and reduced the potential benefits to Ireland of the African presence. In the twenty-first century, the movement towards an ever more liberal, secular, agnostic and anticlerical Ireland has proved particularly challenging for African Pentecostals, for whom the transformative power of the Holy Spirit is a central concern.

Conway in 'Irish Catholicism: Where Has It Been, and Where Is It Going?' applies Stolz's theory of religious-secular competition to Irish Catholicism. As an alternative to secularization theory, this approach looks at specific cases where secular alternatives have competed with, modified or supplanted religious ideas and practices. This approach has the potential to avoid the pitfalls of overgeneralization and neglect of historical factors in relation to secularization by focusing on specific cases at individual, organizational and societal levels. At the individual level, religious-secular competition is evident in, for example, increased preference for secular rather than priestly counselling, lowering of church attendance and an ageing profile among those who do attend due to competition from work, sport and other secular activities, though some churches have successfully adapted their provision. The consequences for future church attendance of the shift to online services during the Covid-19 pandemic are as yet unknown. At the organizational level, traditional sodalities and confraternities have declined, due to both secular and alternative religious openings for community involvement. Since the 1960s, vocations for nuns have fallen by more than half and numbers of those training for the (all-male) priesthood have plummeted. At a societal level, the media has taken on a 'prophetic' role in its critical approach to the church, accentuated by clerical abuse scandals, while, on the other hand, the church has gained respect for its local and international charitable and developmental work. Close attention to areas of competition at each level may indicate the likely trajectory of the church in future few decades.

Cox and Bocking in 'Thinking Beyond the Island: Buddhism, Ireland and Method in the Study of Religions' draw on recent work in the study of Buddhism in Ireland, including research into early Irish Buddhists in colonial Asia, to highlight broader issues in the study of religions, including the role of religion in colonial enterprises, whether collusive or resistant; the long history of Buddhist contacts with Ireland; the nature of religious dissent; and the growth of Irish Buddhism in recent decades. Because Buddhism is a global religion which received negligible attention in Irish academia during the twentieth century, approaching Buddhism from an Irish and ASR perspective has thrown up many neglected and rewarding avenues of investigation, something true of very many other Irish religious topics which fell outside the traditional Catholic–Protestant binary. Tracking the movements of a range of translocal Buddhist individuals, organizations and activities across Europe, Asia, America and elsewhere has encouraged research collaboration involving scholars with specialist linguistic and archival knowledge, as well as increasing use of new methodologies, particularly in the digital humanities. The chapter briefly outlines Irish-Buddhist connections from the Roman era onwards, offers some fresh discoveries relating to 'the Irish Buddhist' U Dhammaloka and outlines the current state of both Buddhism and Buddhist studies in Ireland and their future prospects.

What to expect, what to wish for and what to work on further: Prospects for ASR in Ireland

Predicting the future of any of the humanities subject areas in a time of economic scenarios shaped by Covid-19 and climate change is particularly difficult. There are reasons, however, to regard ASR as well prepared to play a bigger role in Irish universities and in the wider society. It has been recognized in Ireland, as elsewhere, that religion plays a central role in understanding cultures, at home and globally. In a region still adapting to now being a place of immigration, an increasingly visible level of ethnic and cultural diversity raises the level of curiosity and willingness to learn about the variety of 'ways of world-making' (the title of Goodman 1978) across the island. Ireland has become an attractive place for university students and staff, and the long experience of the Irish in having to emigrate for a variety of reasons but frequently staying in contact with 'home' and often coming back with new perspectives garnered abroad makes Ireland a highly connected place, open to cultural mobility. ASR, no longer confined to philology or the 'world religions' paradigm, has developed strong and systematic connections with other academic fields, helping to deepen understanding of the interconnectedness between world views, economies, localities, technologies and politics. Sub-disciplinary fields have developed, such as economics of religion, the cognitive science of religion, aesthetics of religion/material religion, religion and media studies and others.[27] Such specializations offer an ideal way of connecting with recent interdisciplinary structures, for example, in digital humanities or the 'neuro-humanities'. While it would be desirable for ASR to be more visible than it often is in the academic structures – and to be in a better position to offer well-equipped programmes capable of organizing this richness of approaches and topics with sufficient people power – ASR can find advantage in being integrated, as is often the case, in other and more general programmes. Situating ASR in this way within a multidisciplinary context proves the usefulness of the systematic and analytical questions it asks, enables sharing of the critical comparative competence it has developed and enhances the reflexivity that reaches beyond traditional religions and includes ideology-critical analysis of secular knowledge cultures, including the sciences as a form of cultural practice.

In this way – learning from and contributing to a wider and deeper cultural analysis which draws on European and global perspectives – ASR can also take an important position in what is sometimes termed the 'post-secular university'. Being deeply aware that knowledge is positioned and cannot reach a 'point zero' of objectivity, yet refusing to take this as licence to prejudge what has yet to be properly studied, scholars of ASR have often served as moderators, providing a platform for discussing contested issues but also making clear that in academic work the best and most robust approach is secured by skilled theorization and by identifying a suitable and transparent methodology. For some of the issues Ireland will have to come to terms with over the next decades, a position that neither defends nor condemns religious positions and structures yet persists in asking searching questions will undoubtedly find a place as a provider of knowledge and a unique platform for Irish self-reflection, societal development and constructive public debate.

As the contributions in this volume show, there is a cultural vitality across the whole island of Ireland that signals a special relationship between change and inertia. This vitality extends to both secularism in its many forms and a continuing religious productivity that makes this country a laboratory for debates around a global history of religion and contested concepts of modernity, secularity and relationships between the global and the local. ASR can add historical depth and critical comparative knowledge to these developments. In recent years, ASR in Ireland has emerged as a vibrant field of enquiry. We are confident that this book will awaken even more interest in 'the study of religions in Ireland: past and present'.

Chapter 2

HISTORICAL PERSPECTIVES: IRISH NATIONALIST
WOMEN'S RELIGIOUS AND POLITICAL REVOLUTIONS

Amy Heath-Carpentier

To-day life *is* 'politics'. Finance, economics, education, even the ever-popular (in England) subject of divorce is all mixed up with politics to-day. I can't invest my money, without politics; buy clothes without politics. Art is all political, music is battle tunes or hymns of hate or self-glorification.
  Constance Markievicz to her sister, Eva Gore-Booth, c.1918[1]

In this excerpt from a letter sent to her sister Eva Gore-Booth (1870–1926) while she was imprisoned in Holloway jail, Constance Markievicz (née Gore-Booth) (1868–1927) prefigures the 1960s feminist slogan 'the personal is political'. What is unsaid in this passage sends as powerful a message as what is. Markievicz does not mention gender or religion in her litany – both are assumed. Many Irish advanced nationalist women[2] bridged what Markievicz described in 1913 as the 'three great movements going on in Ireland at the time – the National movement, the Women's Movement, and the Industrial movement [*sic*]' ('Irish Suffrage Activities' 1913: 154). Historians of Irish women's history demonstrate that women were at the heart of Irish nationalism, including the Easter Rising (1916), the Irish War of Independence (1919–21) and the Irish Civil War (1922–3). Through organizations such as Inghinidhe na hÉireann, they interacted with women from other socio-economic classes, sexualities and religions, and these encounters sometimes unmoored religious and political identities.

Much has been said about the Irish revolution being Catholic. Reductionist historiographies reify boundaries between nationalism and Catholicism, and unionism and Protestantism. Further, due to the Catholic church's religio-political role in the Irish Free State and Republic and the legacy of 'the Troubles', explorations of the diverse ways that gender, religion and nationalism intersected in the revolutionary period have been limited to sanctioned narratives. Political scientists frequently freeze religion into a variable and generalize combatants' beliefs based on religious affiliation with little regard for individualization, gender differentiation or patterns of dissent.

This chapter seeks to shift these narratives. As sociologist of religion Wade Clark Roof (1993: 303) highlights in an address,

> We do ourselves and religious study generally a disservice when we assume stereotypical unities that do not exist, and at the same time overlook phenomenological unities that do. Narratives are windows into the real worlds in which people live, allowing us to get a bit closer to the operative religious meanings by which they live.

Too often, analysis of religion and conflict are reductionist, based on dominant, androcentric interpretations of sacred texts and traditions. Thus, scholars doubly marginalize women when studying religion and Irish nationalism. Percentage-wise, lifelong Catholics may have dominated the ranks of Cumann na mBan ('The Women's Council') and Irish Citizen Army,[3] but their religious journeys may not have been linear, and few had time to write about them in the midst of a revolution. Some did, though, and this initial examination reveals phenomenological unities that unhinge stereotypes about gender, religion and conflict in the revolution. In this chapter, I explore how a cohort of advanced nationalist women negotiated religion and politics. This study derives from reading and analysis of the lives of advanced nationalist women using primary sources such as letters, writing, diaries, memoirs and Bureau of Military History witness statements. I also rely on the biographies of several women released by Irish women's historians.

Kate Rigby (2001: 23–44) identifies phenomenological unities of *rejection*, *replacement* and *reconstruction* in how twentieth-century feminists did the same. The first two are self-evident. The third, reconstruction, occurs when a woman sees 'not only an oppressive legacy but also emancipatory possibility' in her religion and remodels it (Rigby 2001: 25). I find that advanced nationalist women often demonstrate multiple themes across a lifespan. Therefore, I propose an addition to Rigby's rubric, *renegotiation*, which incorporates what Gladys Ganiel terms extra-institutional religion. Extra-institutional religion includes 'various methods and strategies people use to keep their faith alive *outside* or *in addition to the institutional* Catholic Church' (2016: 5). Among the women I discuss in this chapter, several were baptized Protestant, so my usage is inclusive. 'Kyriarchy', which was coined by feminist theologian Elisabeth Schüssler Fiorenza, designates a system overlapping webs of domination, oppression and submission within which intersectional[4] experiences of oppression and privilege unfold. This term is quite useful in the revolutionary context of Markiewicz's three great movements. In stating 'the first step on the road to freedom is to realize ourselves as Irishwomen – not only or merely as women, but as Irish women doubly enslaved, and with a double battle to fight', Markievicz provides an intersectional analysis of Irish women's position in the kyriarchy (1909: 14).

For this cohort, Western esotericism was a significant resource that informed their religious replacements and reconstructions. Wouter Hanegraaff (2006) and Antoine Faivre and Christine Rhone (2010) define Western esotericism as a contested term for interrelated subcurrents within Western religion that 'have, at one time or another, come to be perceived as problematic (misguided, heretical, irrational, dangerous, evil, or simply ridiculous) from the perspectives of established religion, philosophy, science, and academic research' (Hanegraaff 2006: xi–xiii). I adopt Faivre's (1994) rubric for the boundaries of Western esotericism, concentrating on living nature or animated landscape, which resonates with cultural nationalism.[5] The Theosophical Society and the Golden Dawn espoused heterodox views on gender, and Joan Dixon (2001) and Siv Ellen Kraft (2013) thoroughly explore why progressive, particularly Protestant, women joined.[6] The Theosophical Society had a self-identified Irish woman, Annie Besant, at the helm from 1893 to 1933.[7] Outside of Besant, histories of Irish esotericism centre on William Butler Yeats (1836–1939) and George William Russell (1867–1935), known as Æ.[8] If one shifts the focus to Irish women with Western esoteric ties, such as Charlotte Despard (1844–1939),[9] Margaret Cousins (1878–1954) or Eva Gore-Booth, a different social network emerges that fuses revolutionary politics with Western esotericism. Due to limited space, I concentrate on the innovations of Ella Young (1867–1956), Maud Gonne (1866–1953), Hanna Sheehy Skeffington (1877–1946), Dr Maud Joynt (1868–1940) and sisters Constance Markievicz and Eva Gore-Booth. When possible, I indicate other women whose religious biographies intersect with these women.

Rejecting religion

> I began to take religion seriously.
>
> Young (1945: 5)

In her memoir, *Flowering Dusk*, Young introduces her deconversion from Presbyterianism with this poignant sentence. Taking religion seriously meant recognizing its role in structuring and enforcing kyriarchy. For example, the ideology of separate spheres ascribed men to the public sphere of economics, politics, law and industry, while women functioned within the private, domestic sphere managing the education of children, household staff and the household and religious life. This gendered hierarchy underpinned all relationships in Victorian Ireland. Protestant-born Constance Markievicz and Dr Maud Joynt and Catholic-born Hanna Sheehy Skeffington address the ideology of separate spheres and religion.

Contrast Markievicz's quote that opens this chapter with this description she gives of her life among her Protestant Ascendancy family and friends: 'No-one was interested in politics or economics … Everyone accepted the *status quo*, almost as if it had been the will of God' (1923: 2–3). Markievicz's divinely willed status quo included patriarchy, British imperialism and a largely Protestant upper class who historically exploited urban and rural workers, that is, a kyriarchy. Androcentric religion[10] too often buttressed gendered ideologies that afforded middle- and upper-class women, like Markievicz, the luxury of ignorance about the systems of gendered structural oppression that obfuscated politics in their lives. In a 1912 article in the *Irish Citizen*, Joynt described the repercussions of those obfuscations:

> Her interests and her sympathies, she was taught, were not to go beyond the threshold of her own dwelling and the members of her own family. She was to be a pattern within her own four walls, of course; but her virtues were to be strictly for home-consumption. What went on outside, in the country, in the world at large, was not her concern. So long as her larders were well stocked with pies, it was not her business if other women's children had not enough to eat. … Her destiny was 'to fatten the household sinners': and often while practicing the virtue of self-abnegation, she developed a prodigious selfishness on the part of the men of her family. (27)

Catholic and Protestant religions alike taught 'that women's highest mission was to make man comfortable' (Joynt 1912: 27). Joynt pinpoints how the virtues religion taught women, such as self-denial, reinforced male selfishness, which in turn perpetuated social inequality in 'the world at large'. Hanna Sheehy Skeffington, arguably one of the most progressive feminists of her day, professed 'to read or think oneself outside of the Church is a hazard of becoming a feminist' (Sheehy Skeffington, H., cited in MacCurtain 1987: 143). While attending university, Hanna demonstrated how her feminist consciousness challenged her Catholicism. In 1901, she authored a short story, 'Life's Choosing', featuring two teenage girls considering their futures after their priest lectures on the ideology of separate spheres (Levenson and Natterstad 1986: 12). One girl follows the religious and societal expectations to her ruin while the other embraces independence as a journalist and has a fulfilling career. Hanna found her way through that false dichotomy when she married Francis Skeffington. Catholicism played no role in her or their future life. In 1909, the Sheehy Skeffingtons defended their choice not to baptize their son Owen, from the criticism of family members (Sheehy Skeffington, M. 2017). By 1911, they refused to provide their religion to the census enumerator (National Archives Ireland 1911a). Nearing her death, Hanna told her son, 'I want you to remember, Owen, that I am an unrepentant pagan. If I die, as I must someday, it is *you* who will have all the trouble from the Christians: not only the Catholics but the Prods, when you carry out my instructions' (Sheehy Skeffington, A. 1991: Loc. 2722). Hanna negotiated her religion and politics by rejecting religion, as did others, such as Dorothy Macardle (1889–1958) and Muriel MacSwiney (née Murphy) (1892–1982).

Replacing religion

> Not for thee, O' Maeve, is the song of the
> Wandering Harper sung,
> For men have put lies on thy lips, and treason
> and shrieking fear;
> Because thou wert brave, they say thou wert
> bitter and false of tongue:

> They mock at thy weakness now, who once fled
> From thy flaming spear.
>
> Gore-Booth (1904: 49)

Rigby's theme of replacement is associated with the late-twentieth-century ecofeminist and feminist spirituality movements. Replacement is the attempt to shift the symbolic system that maintains kyriarchy by replacing it with egalitarian, female symbolism and divinity. In 1973, radical lesbian feminist Mary Daly (1973: 13) wrote, 'If God in "his" heaven is a father ruling "his" people, then it is in the nature of things and according to divine plan and the order of the universe that society be male dominated.' Just as the Christian God could choose maleficence or benevolence towards humanity, so too could men choose how to relate to women, children and men with less social capital. Christian theologies incorporated Aristotelian concepts of women as deformed or less evolved versions of men, less capable of rational thought and in need of guidance. Masculinity/male defined the standard; femininity/female became anomalous, a hazard to mitigate and control. As Markievicz ([1915] 1995: 46) observed, 'Today we are in danger of being civilised by men out of existence.'

Rigby highlights feminist theologian Carol Christ's 1978 keynote 'Why Women Need the Goddess' as representative of the replacement theme.[11] Applying Clifford Geertz's ([1973] 2000) theory of religion as a cultural system, Christ (1982; 2012: 246) examines the psychological, social and political impacts of a male godhead and concludes,

> In cultures where God is symbolized exclusively or primarily as male, maleness is consciously and unconsciously understood to be divine ... it feels true, right, and just for females to be subordinated to male power. In such cultures, no one questions the right of fathers and husbands to demand obedience from wives and daughters, nor do people find it remarkable that religious and political leaders are male or that men make laws that women must obey.

Christ (2012: 277) adds that 'the simplest and most basic meaning of the symbol of the Goddess is the acknowledgement of the legitimacy of female power as a beneficent and independent power'. Christ is not alone in her assessment, but she is the first classically trained theologian to insist that female images of the divine are central to addressing the damage androcentric religion has inflicted.[12] Christ and others in the amorphous feminist spirituality movement invented and reinterpreted theologies, rituals, symbols, leadership structures and practices. They found malleable source material in Western esotericism, folklore, mythology and neo-paganism (Eller 1993). In a similar political project of symbolic replacement, beginning in the 1880s, Irish intellectuals like Douglas Hyde (1860–1949) commenced decolonizing Ireland by fighting the denigration and repression of Irish language and culture. Irish cultural nationalism promoted Irish language, folklore, mythology, sports and arts. They interrupted the characterization of 'all things Irish' as uncivilized, base, illogical and unrefined.[13] Anglo-Irish women, such as Gonne and Young, perceived popular religion in rural Ireland as a syncretic blend of Catholicism, folklore and place-based religious practice.[14]

Most Irish nationalist organizations, particularly militant ones, prohibited women from joining. Inghinidhe na hÉireann, founded in 1900 by Gonne, bridged militant nationalism, cultural nationalism and feminism. Inghinidhe became a training ground for everything from Irish language and mythology to community organizing and civil disobedience.[15] Membership spanned women baptized Catholic[16] and Protestant.[17] Just as Christ recommends, Inghinidhe replaced the symbol of Victorian womanhood with figurations they crafted from Irish mythic, folkloric and historic women. Brigid, goddess and saint, was Inghinidhe's patron, and members researched, wrote and presented essays on mythic and historical women at their meetings. Máire O'Brolchain (née Ní Cillín) recounts presentations on 'Goddess Bride, Saint Brigid, Rose, wife of Fiach, M. N. O' Byrne, Margaret of Offaly, Maeve, Cliona, Macha' (1949: 9). Inghinidhe members authored literature featuring these figures, and some interpreted them through the lens of Theosophy's New Woman.[18] For example, having grown up in the shadow of Maeve's cairn on Knocknarea, County Sligo, Gore-Booth wrote poems and a play, *The Three Resurrections and Triumph of Maeve* (1905), featuring the Queen of Connacht. After the Easter Rising, Gore-Booth released the play *The Death of Fionavar from the Triumph of Maeve* (1916) and Markievicz illustrated it while she was serving her prison sentence. Young wrote about Fionavar, Maeve, Niamh and Brigid over the course of her career, including *Poems* (1906), *Celtic Wonder-Tales* (1910), *The Weird of Fionavar* (1922) and *Marzilian and other Poems* (1938). Gonne illustrated *Celtic Wonder-Tales*. By replacing symbols of Victorian womanhood, Inghinidhe created a repository of empowering symbols that legitimized women's political agency and valued women's communities. Historian Margaret Ward (1995b: 86) assesses, 'Had Inghinidhe not existed, a whole generation of women would never have developed the self-confidence which eventually enabled them to hold their own in organizations composed of both sexes.'

Some Inghinidhe members believed Maeve, Brigid and so forth were more than symbols. Born into a Northern Irish Reformed Presbyterian family, Young explored Western esotericism and cultural nationalism in Dublin in the 1890s, travelling with Helen Laird (1874–1957)[19] to meet Besant in Limerick.[20] During a Celtic Literary Society meeting in 1901, she followed E. E. Fournier's lecture on 'the chief characteristics of the Druidical religion' with 'a survey of Celtic mythology, accounting for its superiority over the systems of Greece and Rome' ('National Literary Society' 1901: 7). By the time she met Æ, Yeats and Gonne, she was replacing her religion of birth with neo-paganism. By 1916, Young was addressed, by some,[21] as Druidess.

As Adrian J. Ivakhiv (2001: 8) notes, 'Proponents of contemporary earth spirituality ... speak of the Earth itself as being an embodiment, if not *the* embodiment of divinity.' Routinely, neo-paganism genders the earth as female, overlapping with conceptions of Ireland as woman, such as Roisin Dubh, Kathleen Ni Houlihan and Shan Van Vocht. Figurations of the land as divine are rarely innocuous. European history is marked with movements that weaponized 'the motherland' to rouse hate.[22] However, Young's neo-paganism was bioregional and thus not exclusive to Ireland.

In *Flowering Dusk*, Young recounts how Æ wrote a rhyme describing how each member of the Hermetic Society[23] conceived of divinity. Then, he posted these rhymes in the building and pretended Helen Laird wrote them. Æ composed for Young:

> My sister, Ella, takes of you (God)
> A territorial sort of view:
> I think an Island is her notion
> Somewhere in the Atlantic Ocean. (Young 1945: 35)

Æ's 'territorial view' of the divine refers to Young's bioregional, neo-pagan religion. A decade later, when the census enumerator visited Young, she was living with poet and Irish language teacher Móirín Nic Shionnaigh.[24] Both women listed their religion as Pagan (National Archives Ireland 1911b). Their official response of Pagan as their religion is remarkable for the period and indicates the continuity of Young's neo-paganism.

Young established at least two religious organizations. In a 1966 interview, Young's friend Gavin Arthur recounts that Young founded the Fellowship of the Four Jewels in the wake of the Judge Crisis within the Theosophical Society in 1891.[25] Aidan Kelly (2012) contradicts Arthur, stating that the Fellowship was founded in the wake of the Easter Rising, Beltaine 1916, as a collaboration between Young, Yeats, Gonne, Æ and others. This is quite a discrepancy. However, the second organization, the Fine, established in 1900, bridged Western esotericism, neo-paganism and Irish nationalism according to Gonne (1995: 335), who states, 'The object of the Fine was to draw together for the freeing of Ireland the wills of the living and of the dead in association with the earth and the elements which to her seemed living entities.'

If Gonne's memory is correct, Young established the Fine prior to meeting Gonne in 1901 because she thought that the Eastern mysticism prevalent in Æ's group of mystics 'was not suitable for Ireland's needs' (1995: 335). The fate of the Fine is unknown, as is the relationship between the Fine and the Fellowship of the Four Jewels. Young suggested visualizations to other women in the early 1900s, and the Fine received small bundles of heather from Slieve Gullion (Annat 2016: 194). Young recollects gifting heather from Gullion to Gonne when they were introduced (1945: 58).[26] Gonne and Young's concentration on Irish sources to construct their neo-paganism is unique among their Western esoteric compatriots who focused on Theosophy, Buddhism and Hinduism.

Young hosted friends on pilgrimages to significant sites in Ireland's mythic landscape, where she would attempt to communicate with mountains and streams. During the Fine's Beltaine trips to Ireland's Eye, Gonne (1995: 335) recounts that the ritual fire would also function to heat the kettle and burn incense made of herbs gathered across Ireland 'to unite all'. Arthur, Markievicz and Young made a pilgrimage to River Boyne laden with votive offerings for the river, which is sacred to the Goddess Aunya (Young 1945: 193). Young offered small rituals to honour the earth spirits and poured libations of wine or whiskey, according to Arthur (1966). Elsa Gidlow (1898–1986)[27] recalls, 'If we went on a picnic she would never touch food until she had poured a libation of wine to "Earth, Air, Fire, Water, and – in Gaelic – The Great Goddess"' (1986: 313). Talk would turn to invoking a god or goddess, hearing *ceol sídhe* (faery music) or contemplating the return of the Lia Fail.

When Young moved to the United States in 1925, she transitioned her connection to the land from Ireland to California where she accepted the chair of Celtic Studies at the University of California, Berkeley. The Fellowship of the Four Jewels morphed into the Fellowship of Mount Shasta (Kelly 2016: 52). Of New Mexico, Young (1945: 257) reflects, 'This is a country that possesses, like Ireland, the ancient magic.' Young localized her neo-pagan practice and was never shy about discussing her beliefs and practices. Near the end of her life, beat poet Alan Watts (1915–1973) interviewed Young. These recordings offer a rare audio glimpse into Young's religion. Watts asks about the spirit of a mountain, Young (1950: 4.10) replies,

> Well, you see, to begin with the mountain is alive. And to go back further than that, the Earth is alive. The Earth is a great living being, and the Earth is greater than we are. The Earth has many things that we haven't, but we haven't got anything that the earth hasn't got.

Throughout these interviews, Young always refers to nature and the earth as female and as the core divinity. She teaches listeners how one might communicate with a mountain or another part of nature – greet it regularly and attempt to build a relationship with it (1950: 7.15). While her neo-paganism was welcomed in Theosophical circles, it was distinct from it. Thus, an Irish innovation birthed in the revolutionary period was transported to the United States in 1925 and began to develop fourteen years prior to the formation of the Church of Aphrodite and thirty-eight years prior to Ray and Rosemary Buckland's arrival.[28]

Unapologetically neo-pagan and a nationalist throughout her life, Young influenced many women through Inghinidhe and otherwise, including Dorothy Macardle and Cesca Trench (1891–1918).[29] In anticipation of fighting in the Easter Rising, Helena Molony prioritized hand-delivering a letter to Young on Holy Saturday, angering James Connolly (Molony 1934). Markievicz entrusted her keys to her keeping,[30] and the two discussed omens, astrology and recovering the Lia Fáil.[31] In her diary, Cesca Trench (2005: 158) records visiting Young and Móirín Ní Shionnaigh in 1914, whom she describes as 'very Celtic Twilighty'. In the aftermath of Roger Casement's (1864–1916) execution, Trench (2005: 250) sat with the Druidess by the Carrigaholt bay and heard 'singing, men's voices, out in the sea where it meets the sky … my soul went out to meet it and the great beings there'. Dorothy Macardle (1956) reports walking with Young on the Hill of Howth where Young encouraged her to separate herself from politics to concentrate on writing. Macardle followed Young's example rather than her advice, as Young was involved in hiding guns. Macardle's stories written while she was imprisoned in Mountjoy and Kilmainham Gaols during the Civil War demonstrate Young's influence, particularly 'The Return of Niav' (Macardle 2020). In 1939, the two unexpectedly reunited in Berkeley when Macardle travelled there for a lecture. When Young died in 1956, Macardle (1956) authored her obituary for RTÉ, testifying that Young was still writing about Niamh and Fionavar and keeping the Irish pagan holidays while in America.

Reconstructing religion

Rigby's theme of reconstruction involves women contributing publicly to theological or religious discourse. In the case of Ireland during the revolutionary period, some women laboured to chart a path forward within their Christian religions. Against this backdrop emerged Eva Gore-Booth, one of Ireland's and the world's first feminist Christian theologians. Yet, when she is recognized beyond her relationship with her militant sister Constance Markievicz, it is for her labour activism and poetry rather than her revolutionary theology. Gore-Booth was a prolific theologian and ethicist, publishing numerous articles and several books. These include an autobiographical sketch, 'The Inner Life of a Child' (1929), and theological works: her magnum opus *A Psychological and Poetic Approach to the Study of Christ in the Fourth Gospel* (1923),[32] *The Inner Kingdom* (1926) and *The World's Pilgrim* (1927). She reconstructed Christian theology and ethics in light of contemporary ethical challenges, such as war and peace, the death penalty, gender relations and human rights. Her Christian belief in God as love was socially engaged just as her sister Markievicz's belief was. She organized and lobbied on behalf of women's labour and suffrage organizations in Manchester, England, where she joined her life partner, Esther Roper, in 1897 (Tiernan 2012).

Gore-Booth was an avid reader of religious texts and engaged in interreligious dialogue and reflection. An early example of her attempts to reconstruct religion was a diary she kept in 1894 as she travelled in North America with her father. Gore-Booth employs poetry rather than prose to consider the consequences of replacing the norms of Victorian womanhood with those of the *fin-de-siècle* new woman, as she was described by fellow Irishwoman Sarah Grand (1854–1943) (Grand 1894). In this draft poem, Gore-Booth depicts Mary Magdalene as an advocate for the 'modern woman' who faces St Peter at Heaven's gate after she dies. 'She heard S. Peter's / Sentence Said / & would not bow her rebel head' (Gore-Booth 1894: MIC 590 Reel 5). Just in time, Jesus arrives, flanked by his mother Mary and Mary Magdalene. The poem ends:

> Then Mary Magdalene walked forward
> My friend, my beloved
> She said seizing the
> New woman by both hands
> Then for the like of Mary Magdalene
> They opened the gate and let her in. (Gore-Booth 1894: MIC 590 Reel 5)

Gore-Booth positions Magdalene as sympathetic to the struggles of the 'New Woman' under the rule of the Church of St Peter. In Mt. 16.18, Jesus makes Peter 'the Rock of the Church' – the first Pope. For many feminists, St Peter represents patriarchy in Christianity. Magdalene, however, is the first person to encounter Jesus after the resurrection, and while Catholic theology rarely ascribes the position to her, she is the first person to bear the gospel of Christ's resurrection to his disciples. Gore-Booth's poem signifies a shift in her religion. Magdalene addresses the new woman as friend and beloved, and Magdalene's authority overrides Peter's. Janet Liebmann Jacobs (1989: 132) notes, 'At the deepest levels of commitment and love, rejection of the spiritual father symbolizes the failure of a morality that is grounded in the theology of dominance and control.' Magdalene's egalitarian and relational theology overrides Peter's.

Gore-Booth's decision to write her first attempts at theology in poetic form instead of prose is significant. Poetry allowed her to take steps in exploring her own theological ideas. Women's feminist theological musings, as with most theologically subversive ideas, often take artistic form. A poem does not directly challenge the patriarchal control of the theologians on their own turf (pulpit, divinity schools, etc.). Approaching theology through the arts allows subaltern thinkers to contribute their voices when they are barred from sanctioned paths. Despite having a primarily male canon, poetry is an art that breaks boundaries. While both poetry and theology have emancipatory potential, historically the discipline of theology reinforced male lineage and hierarchical gender norms by initiating participants into the androcentric discourse of the field. Feminist theologians, such as Judith Plaskow (1947–present) and Carol Christ (1945–2021) (2016), attest to the struggle of being among the first female graduate students in theology. Gore-Booth's untitled draft poem is an early example of her forays into authoring feminist theology as she seeks to renegotiate Christianity in light of her commitments to feminism and pacifism. Nearly thirty years later, Gore-Booth returned to poetry as a hermeneutical framework in her *A Psychological and Poetic Approach to the Study of Christ in the Fourth Gospel* (1923).

Conclusion: Renegotiating religion

> Women are everywhere today in a position of inferiority. And the Churches, both Catholic and Protestant, are to blame for this, for both foster the tradition of segregation of the sexes … be prepared to go your own way depending for safety on your own courage, your own truth and your own common sense. (Markievicz [1915] 1995: 47)

Rigby's (2001) themes of rejection, replacement and reconstruction provide a generative framework for evaluating how advanced nationalist women struggled to bridge their religions with their politics in the face of multiple revolutions against kyriarchy. As readers familiar with the historiography or biographies of advanced nationalist women may have realized already, these women's journeys do not fit neatly into just one of these themes. Advanced nationalist women rejected their religions of birth, read the Vedas, attended meetings of the Theosophical Society, went on pilgrimages to the Hill of Tara and dabbled in spiritualism. Therefore, I propose adding a theme of *renegotiation* to account for how women add or substitute elements from outside their religion's canon, what Ganiel (2016) identifies as extra-institutional religion. This differs subtly from Rigby's theme of *reconstruction*. Reconstruction occurs when a woman contributes to her religion's theological or ethical discourse in a public forum (i.e. publications and lectures). Key to Ganiel's formulation of extra-institutional religion and mine is that community and dialogue are central to renegotiation. Renegotiation unfolds, not individually as Ulrich Beck (2014) proposes, but in dialogue with an established tradition and within intimate communities of friends.

Some examples of renegotiation include Trench, Sheehy Skeffington and Gonne. Artist and nationalist Trench's father came from a line of prominent Church of Ireland leaders, and her mother, a unionist, was nonetheless a proud Irishwoman who taught her daughters respect for their Irish heritage. Born and educated in England, Trench studied the Irish language, joined the Gaelic League and later joined Cumann na mBan after returning to Dublin from studying art in Paris. Trench's diary (2005) reveals her belief in and experiences of reincarnation, her support for Irish language integration in the Church of Ireland through Cumann Gaelach na hEaglaise and her experiences hearing ceol sídhe, as mentioned above. Hanna rejected Catholicism but experimented with spiritualism and consulted friend and Theosophist Margaret Cousins after Francis was murdered during the Easter Rising (Ward 2019). She believed that Francis's spirit continued beyond death and that they would be reunited one day (Ward 2019). Baptized Anglican, Gonne converted to Catholicism in 1903 but continued her interest in Western esotericism. Writing to Yeats from Paris in 1914, she described what she learned from a spirit, Teig O'Driscoll, with whom she, along with Molony, one of the Gifford sisters, and her daughter Iseult, communicated using a planchette (Gonne and Yeats 1993: 328). In 1928 Gonne defined her vision of reincarnation, naming the creator 'Great Mother': 'I fight until the long rest comes – out of that rest I believe the Great Mother will refashion beauty & life again' (Gonne and Yeats 1993: 445). Trench, Hanna and Gonne were not attempting to reform religion on a larger scale; rather, they were renegotiating their own and influencing one another.

The renegotiation theme is key to comprehending a wider range of women's responses to clashes between their politics and religions. Renegotiation has inherent political implications as well. As I discussed in the introduction, many historiographies of the revolutionary period are reductionist, collapsing nationalism and Catholicism. Further, diversity in Catholic belief and practice is sacrificed for a unified, androcentric definition of Catholic. This obfuscates the experiences of non-religious nationalists, nationalists of other religions and Catholic nationalists who engaged in extra-institutional religion, such as Gonne. Reconstruction is not enough to account for this diversity. Men dominated post-secondary theological education and scholarship, and though Ireland's St Patrick's College, Maynooth University,[33] appointed theologian Jessie Rogers as its first female and first lay Dean of Faculty in 2021, they still do in many religions. However, historically, most women could not access education, set aside the time for reflection and writing or wield the prestige necessary to reconstruct religion in a public forum. Through smaller, individual acts of renegotiation, they shifted their individual religions and influenced others in their immediate communities. Renegotiation makes visible micro and meso religious shifts, which are significant in the study of gender, politics and religion.

One final observation. For some, Irish nationalism functioned as extra-institutional religion, regardless of whether they were Catholic, Protestant, Buddhist, Theosophist or neo-pagan. If we utilize Geertz's ([1973] 2000: 90) definition of religion as 'a system of symbols which act to produce powerful, pervasive, and long-lasting moods and motivations', this is not surprising. Advanced nationalist women frequently described their political experiences in religious language, such as Marie Flanagan (née Perolz; 1949: 4) reflecting, 'Those were great times and I would crawl on my knees to do it all again,' as if the revolutionary period were a pilgrimage site. The overlaid Catholic–Nationalist identity created conditions by which extra-institutional, nationalist religious practices were less challenging to Catholic orthodoxy. However, once the Free State was established, these egalitarian and inclusive nationalisms *and* religions were sidelined. Markievicz's 1915 address to the Irish Women's Franchise League, which opens this conclusion, is a haunting reminder of how quickly multiple revolutions against kyriarchy can be consolidated once one is in sight. As an interdisciplinary set of scholars struggle to unpack the divergence in the Free State and Republic from the progressive idealism of the Easter Rising, Rigby's themes and my addition of renegotiation may be helpful in understanding women's experiences of and methods for coping with androcentric religion.

Chapter 3

REFLECTIONS ON IRISH FOLKLORE AND RELIGION

Síle de Cléir

Introduction: Terms and concepts

Folklore is generally thought of as a discipline which is focused on the oral traditions of a particular community, and in Ireland's case this aspect has loomed very large in the history of the subject at both academic and popular levels. The richness and variety of Irish storytelling, along with the combination of circumstances which led to its extensive collection from the late nineteenth century through to the 1970s, has led to the assembly of a unique cultural resource in the National Folklore Collection, now housed in University College Dublin and recently inscribed into the UNESCO Memory of the World register (National Folklore Collection 2017). The study of popular culture has also been promoted by museums and museum curators, while the fusion of folklore studies with oral history methodologies has also been significant (National Museum of Ireland n.d.; UCC Anthropology n.d.). The hybridity of the Irish-language literary tradition, incorporating as it does significant bodies of material which also existed in oral culture, has ensured that the study of folklore is an important aspect of research and teaching in Irish-language departments as well as in departments of folklore and ethnology at third-level educational institutions such as universities.[1]

In his wide-ranging discussion of the culture of Irish traditional communities, Diarmuid Ó Giolláin (2005: 76–81) has drawn on international studies and comparative material to demonstrate the role of both belief and religious practice in the everyday life of pre-modern societies. The centrality of religion in the world view of these communities has made this an important area of research in the discipline of Irish folklore. Even the most cursory glance at any bibliography of Irish ethnological research will yield many types of studies about religion and religious tradition throughout the twentieth century, from early classics such as Douglas Hyde's (1906) *Religious Songs of Connacht* through Kevin Danaher's (1972) *The Year in Ireland* to Lawrence J. Taylor's (1995) *Occasions of Faith: An Anthropology of Irish Catholics*. In such a multifaceted area of research and analysis, it is not surprising to find that the terms used to define the field of study have been the subject of some discussion. While the term 'religion' would seem to apply comfortably to discursive and behavioural elements relating to the supernatural phenomena of the Christian faith or to those of other global religions, it has also been used to characterize practices and beliefs which are separate from these traditions.

Meanwhile, the word 'belief', while having the potential to depict phenomena outside of organized religion, could be said to express a state of mind and a metaphysical position rather than encompassing both this and the behaviours associated with it. The same points could be made about the equivalent Irish terms *reiligiún* (religion) and *creideamh* (belief) – though the latter has traditionally been used in the Irish language to express religious denominations, through the addition of qualifying adjectives such as *Caitliceach* (Catholic) and *Protastúnach* (Protestant). It seems that qualifying adjectives have often been necessary in any case, in the description of the religious phenomena which comprise such a significant part of the traditional cultures of many countries, including Ireland. Mid-twentieth-century scholars such as John Messenger (1972) were comfortable with the term 'folk religion', seeing it as a natural adaptation of the word 'folklore' to a more ethnographically based field of analysis, though it is important to note the questioning of the concept of 'folk' as the century progressed (Dundes 1980: 1–19).

The later twentieth-century interest in popular culture, pioneered by historians such as Peter Burke (1978) and Keith Thomas (1971) led to the use of the term 'popular religion' as an alternative to 'folk religion'. The word 'popular' has the advantage of not being primarily associated with rural communities, but folklorists of the 1970s were, in any case, calling for wider recognition of urban communities – and of other types of communities – in the study of folklore (Dundes 1980: 5–8). Leonard Primiano, however, has argued more recently that terms such as 'folk', 'popular' and 'unofficial' characterize religious beliefs and practices as residual and marginal, not just setting them in opposition to more official versions of religion, but also implying their inherent inferiority to these. This leads to a 'two-tiered model' for the study of religion, which dichotomizes 'official' and 'unofficial' religiosity. Primiano argues strongly for the use of the term 'vernacular' instead. With its potential to indicate cultural elements emanating from a group or a locality, along with more personal or private contexts, the word 'vernacular' does seem to embody the relevant concepts without the same sense of divisiveness inherent in terms such as 'unofficial' and 'popular' (1995: 37–40). However, while there is no doubt of the validity of Primiano's perspective for ethnological research in general, it is important to filter his comments through the experience of folklore scholarship in Ireland and to acknowledge the specificity of different cultures in their approaches to traditions and their analysis. In Ireland, the ideology of cultural nationalism – the main driving force of folklore collection from the late nineteenth century – and, more specifically, the importance of the Irish language in this project meant that many aspects of traditional life and culture, including vernacular religious discourse as encountered by scholars and collectors in the Irish-speaking Gaeltacht areas, were frequently regarded with a deep respect for their linguistic richness and for their longevity and centrality in the tradition. It is true to say that this was sometimes mixed with a desire to explain the existence of certain features of their content, as Seán Ó Súilleabháin's preface to the 1952 *Scéalta Cráibhtheacha* (translated into English and published as *Miraculous Plenty* in 2012) shows. But this is far from their being categorized as an inferior form of religion.

Looking at Ó Súilleabháin's work on customs (1967), it is probably true to say that an explanatory and somewhat reductionist instinct was more in evidence when he was dealing with non-Christian areas of belief, most especially in the area of traditional medicine. Even then, he is careful to acknowledge the realization on behalf of medical science that many traditional cures were efficacious, and his respect for these is palpable (1967: 59–60). It must also be pointed out that other types of ideological underpinnings in the collection and study of folklore in Ireland could lead to different hierarchies of value being applied to ritual behaviours and religious practices – the higher value placed by collectors on older, rural customs, for instance, even if these were dying out, than on equivalent urban customs, which were perceived to be more modern, more disruptive and less 'safe'.[2]

It is perhaps the search for the origins of a particular cultural or religious phenomenon that may lead scholars to categorize them as emanating from different sources, thus labelling them 'official' and 'unofficial' in the process. In fieldwork, this was and is part of the process of asking whether people are doing something because of being told to by the clergy, or because their grandparents did it. As for the value judgement supposedly inherent in this, that the traditional practice is somehow inferior to the church-led one, my own experience is that most fieldworkers and collectors would regard the latter answer – attributing the practice to family custom – as having much more research potential than the former. Therefore, the supposed prejudice is much more likely to be in favour of the unofficial practice than the official. But it is true to say that oppositional perspectives can lead to oversimplification of the cultural processes underpinning traditional religious discourse and practice, and this is true for both historical and contemporary ethnographic research.

Recognition of the complexity not just of religious culture but also of individuals and of their lived experience is now a cornerstone of research into religious tradition, as Sabina Magliocco (2014: 146) points out: 'It is based on taking the experiences and perceptions of individual believers seriously while balancing them with an empathic scholarly perspective that situates them within their cultural and performative context.' It is interesting to note that the approach outlined by Magliocco for folklore scholarship is very much like that of Alana Harris (2013: 15) in her recent history of English Catholicism, which she describes as an exploration of 'lived religious experience'. The increasing similarity of research methodologies in folklore and history, along with shared concerns around interpretation, show how scholars with different disciplinary backgrounds are increasingly examining the phenomenon that is 'religion' – without the need for qualifying adjectives. Questions around origins and influences are still important, but increased awareness of the complexity of people's lives, in both historical and contemporary contexts, necessitates a broader view of cultural process than the crude labelling of material as official or unofficial, elite or popular. Gearóid Ó Crualaoich has said that 'images such as that of a sea or ocean of knowledge can give some sense of the ceaseless surging back and forth of cultural creativity, together with its transmission and transformation of meaning'. Ó Crualaoich characterizes individuals and groups as forming 'dynamic islands of identity, cultural creativity and meaningfulness', stating that this is an ongoing and ever-changing process (2003: 6). This approach allows for the complexity of culture, while acknowledging the patterns created by groups and individuals – and, crucially, allows for change around and within these cultural patterns.

Understanding religion in Irish folk tradition

While keeping the centrality of lived experience and cultural complexity as outlined above in mind, it is also the case that the nature of religious culture itself will sometimes shape its study and interpretation. This is the case for the wide repertoire of Irish-language oral religious tradition in the form of songs, laments, stories and prayers collected by individual scholars from the late nineteenth century and also by the Irish Folklore Commission and its predecessors from the early part of the twentieth century to the 1970s. In an essay discussing religious singing, Ríonach Uí Ógáin (2012: 36) has noted how *Scéalta cráibhtheacha*, a volume of some two hundred stories collected by the Commission between 1935 and 1950, demonstrates both the popularity of this material in the community and the centrality of religious lore in people's lives during that period. Uí Ógáin (2012: 38) mentions how religious references can be found in many different types of song, something which shows the way in which everyday discourse was permeated by religion and religious practice. Douglas Hyde's (1906: vii) reflection on his research in Connacht at the beginning of the twentieth century gives some sense of the sheer size and reach of the material in the experience of one of its early collectors:

> While collecting the poetry of the province of Connacht ... I found that those Poems which touched upon piety or religion were very numerous. I found, moreover, that prayers put in a setting of poetry, melodious 'paidirs', and short petitions composed in metre were very numerous also ... I found at the same time charms or 'orthas' or 'amhras', I found pieces concerning the Church, I found pieces praising or dispraising people for their religion, I found stories about the Church, or about the persecution of the Church, or about some saint or other, I found blessings, I found curses, and I put all these things down here with the rest.

We know that religious items – whether this is material relating to Christianity, as outlined by Hyde above, or material relating to other kinds of belief – formed an important part of the lore of major Irish storytellers, as demonstrated in the volumes of individual repertoire published by the Folklore of Ireland Council and others. In all these books there are substantial sections devoted to prayers, stories of the saints and pious legends, legends of the dead and the fairies, and stories of people with supernatural powers or other magical beings and events.[3] The beliefs embodied in these stories and anecdotes also served to underpin a wide range of religious behaviours, as evidenced in both ethnographic studies of Irish communities and in other classic textbooks of Irish folklore and folklife.[4]

It is helpful to group these materials according to characteristics and influences in order to further explore their functioning in both practical and cultural contexts. A study of the characteristics will show whether the religious phenomenon is embodied in language – a part of the oral tradition of the community – or whether it is an action, a behaviour based on belief, carried out by people on certain occasions or on a regular basis. Looking at influences will help to decide whether the item of discourse or the action is using Christianity as a term of reference or whether it is more related to an otherworld sensibility. The term 'otherworld' is used deliberately, as many other terms used to characterize the type of belief embodied in fairy legends or avoidance strategies such as *piseoga* are problematic. To many people, 'pagan' is still a pejorative term, especially when used in a historical context; 'pre-Christian' implies that everything exists in relation to Christianity, and 'Celtic' can involve both an implied oversimplification of Celtic religious culture and frequently a confusion between Celtic religion and what was actually early Irish Christianity. The fact that the latter was heavily influenced by Celtic sensibilities is not in doubt, and it is important to point out that people's creative development of their own spirituality in the contemporary world may of course involve drawing on Celtic and early Irish Christian ideas and concepts (O'Connor 2012: 363–74). However, this does not mean that all the non-Christian religious phenomena of a much later period can be labelled with the catch-all term 'Celtic'. At the same time, it is necessary to understand that there is, of course, a strong Celtic influence in parts of the tradition, with the emphasis in calendar custom on the four head-festivals the most obvious, but by no means the only, example of this.

In distinguishing these groups of beliefs, behaviours and narratives from each other in terms of characteristics and influences, it is important not to see them as opposing or separate categories. Many religious elements, such as prayers, for instance, involve both words *and* actions. Influential qualities can also be mixed in one element, as illustrated by the strong *Samhain*-influenced protection rituals around the feast of St Martin (MagFhloinn 2016: 282–301). For this reason, it is perhaps more helpful to think of each idea as a continuum, with different elements located along various points on an axis. One axis would have otherworld themes and beliefs at one end, and Christian themes and beliefs at the other, with these shading into each other in the centre. The other axis would have discourse at one end and action at the other – again with a combination of the two in the centre. Thus, fairy legends and other stories of the supernatural would lie in the discourse-otherworld part of the quadrant, but a local legend about suffering souls would be nearer the middle, as it shades into Christian belief. Actions such as burying eggs or raw meat in a neighbour's farm in order to steal the fertility of the land, or making sure not to build a house in a place considered to be inhabited by the fairies, would belong firmly in the otherworld-action category while pilgrimage and holy well visits would be on the Christian-action side (Ó Súilleabháin 1967: 22; Ó hEochaidh and Ó Catháin 1977: 94–7). Prayers, involving both ritual and language, would be in the Christian category but lie somewhere between action and discourse, while the kind of stories found in *Scéalta Cráibhtheacha*, along with the religious songs discussed by Hyde, would be located in the Christian-discourse quarter of the scheme; laments, richly linguistic, but also with ritualized aspects, would be placed a little further towards the action quadrant.

Meaning and interpretation

While the above scheme is useful in disentangling the influential and practical contexts underpinning religious discourse and action, it is also important to explore to some extent the meaning of this cultural world for the people who inhabited it. As with much historical material, it is not possible today to carry out a deeply contextualized study of the role this repertoire played in people's lives, nor is it possible to say what the reply would have been had the people who contributed material like this to collectors been asked what it 'meant' to them. As Bengt Holbek (1982: 24; original emphasis) has pointed out in relation to another major genre of folklore, 'if the meaning of a fairytale could have been exhaustively and satisfactorily explained in ordinary prose, there would hardly have been any point in expressing that meaning in the form of a tale. In a profound sense, *meaning and artistic expression are one*.' Applying Holbek's idea to religious material, it could be said that the songs, the legends, the prayers, the blessings, the curses, the anecdotes and the actions themselves provide plenty of scope for exploration of the religious sensibility and the metaphysical imagination expressed in them. This essay provides the opportunity to look more closely at some aspects of religion in terms of meaning and expression.

There are many different areas that could be examined in a longer discussion. Religious sense-experience, most notably achieved through singing, is one; the combination of narrative and behaviour used to explain the unknown and deal with pain, perhaps most apparent in life-cycle and calendar custom, is another. The question of the relationship between religion and identity is also of interest. This often-localized aspect of religion can be found in many different contexts: some of these will be discussed below. In exploring the connections between religion and senses of locality and identity, oral narrative is a good place to start. Religious folklore constitutes an important part of the international folk narrative repertoire, as is attested to by the some one hundred stories in this category in the ATU international tale-type index (Uther 2004a: 397–477). It is necessary to point out that these one hundred stories are those which explicitly refer to the beliefs and supernatural phenomena of organized religion. If stories concerning other supernatural concepts are included, the amount is much larger, but this is a more difficult number to estimate as some of these may be wonder tales, where magic is functioning as part of a fantasy rather than illustrating supernatural belief and its functions in the real world. In some wonder tales, elements of organized religion – as opposed to magic – are mixed with fantasy, however.[5] It is interesting to see that religious jokes and anecdotes are also part of the international tale-type index, with some 125 titles included (Uther 2004b: 397–457). Out of all these types of oral narratives, it is perhaps the explicitly religious story that tells us most about the creative intersection between folklore and religion in the life of the traditional community, amply illustrated in Ireland by Ó Súilleabháin's *Miraculous Plenty* mentioned above. Anne O'Connor (2012: 373) describes it as follows:

> Many of the narratives contained in Ó Súilleabháin's *Scéalta Cráibhtheacha* concern the fate of the soul in the Afterlife, the Return of the Dead, the Virgin Mary, saints and sinners, Satan and the Fallen Angels, the return of the spirits of the dead for various benevolent and malevolent purposes, the true nature of the priesthood and issues of significance in terms of Roman Catholic doctrine and liturgy. Many of these religious tales are apocryphal, others are didactic and are examples of medieval *exempla* and *mirabilia*, medieval religious themes predominate throughout, all indicative of the inherited and vibrant folk religion of the Irish people.

Pádraig Ó Héalaí's (2012) more recent index of stories about New Testament characters and its accompanying discussion together constitute a significant addition to the study of Bible-related folklore in Ireland. Local legends with a religious theme are perhaps the best way to examine the connections between religion and the life of a community in a particular area, and saintlore is one of the most expressive types of narratives in this context. Although the following discussion concerns two specific saints, it is important to realize that there were many more than these, both male and female, in the repertoire of traditional communities. Some of these, such as St Brigid and St Patrick, were well known throughout the country, whereas others had a more local profile. In looking at examples of these, Peig Sayers's (1873–1958) oral narrative repertoire is very useful, not just because of the large amount of material involved and the variety of types of oral narrative recorded from her,[6] but also because she had a lively interest in religion and a strongly held faith (MacCurtain 1989). It helps too that unlike other storytellers in the tradition, and especially women storytellers, considerable information about her life and her experiences in Kerry in the nineteenth and twentieth centuries is available to scholars, because of her autobiographical and other published work.[7] '*Naomh Cuán agus an Phiast*' (St Cuán and the Serpent) is a short story collected from Peig by Kenneth Jackson between 1932 and 1937. The collector summarizes it as follows: 'St. Cuán stops the ravages of a water-serpent living in Loch Chill Chuáin, by putting a cauldron on its head and telling it to stay so till Monday. The serpent is tricked because the Monday of Doomsday is meant' (1939: 91).[8]

This legend is an interesting example of how the conflict between different kinds of supernatural forces was narrated. The point of the story is, of course, that

St Cuán wins out over the serpent and, in doing so, saves the people of the area from further damage inflicted by her. At its most obvious level, the legend serves to illustrate the dangers of negative supernatural forces associated with the natural world and the importance of Christianity in the fight against these. The serpent's gender is emphatically female and not just brought about by the fact that 'piast/ péist' is a feminine noun in Irish. Peig uses many female pronouns, prepositional pronouns and female possessive adjectives throughout: 'She was doing a lot of damage but nobody could put a stop to her ... The serpent lifted her head ... she opened her big mouth to swallow him' (Jackson 1939: 62-3).[9] Ó Crualaoich has discussed the significance of the feminine in the Irish mythological tradition, and there are echoes of that here (Ó Crualaoich 2003: 25-37). The fact that it was the serpent's custom to appear every May Day morning connects her more strongly to Celtic culture, and the story of St Cuán, taking on the serpent while surrounded by a large crowd, is also set on '*maidean Lae Bhealltaine*' (the morning of May Day). St Cuán's importance is highlighted not just by the plot of the story but also by many other narrative techniques used by the storyteller. The opening lines situate the story in the local area: 'A little story that happened in Paróiste Múrach a long time ago. The lake is still there, and will always be: it is called Loch Chíl Chuáin' (Jackson 1939: 62). At the end of the story, the geographical location is referred to again, and the story is given a contemporary angle:

> 'You will never eat anything again,' said Cuán, 'no-one need have any fear of your doing so.' He was right, because nothing of that sort was ever experienced in Loch Chíl Chuáin since. St Cuán himself is buried in that townland, and there is a graveyard there and Catholics often go on pilgrimage around it. (Jackson 1939: 63)

Cill Chuáin is still in use as a graveyard, and the local community still gathers in that location to pray for those who are buried there.[10] Peig may have been speaking almost one hundred years ago, but her closing comment – despite the difference between pilgrimage and prayers for the dead – is still relevant, something which illustrates the remarkable continuity of religious tradition in the area. Having situated the story geographically by telling the listener about the existence of the lake, the storyteller then situates it historically by saying that there was a magic serpent there '*sa tseanaimmsir*' (in the old days) and then goes on:

> But on the coming of St Patrick, a lot of miracles started happening from that time on. One of the saints in Ireland after his death happened to be going around, the name of this saint was St Cuán. He was situated around Mount Brandon, where St Brendan spent a period of his life a good few years after this story happened. (Jackson 1939: 62)

St Cuán, though important in the Corca Dhuibhne area of West Kerry, was not a nationally known saint. Nóra Ní Shéaghdha, the writer and schoolteacher who taught on the Great Blasket Island and also in Scoil Naomh Eirc, near Cill

Chuáin (anglicized as Kilquane), recalled the sarcastic and dismissive attitude of a Department of Education inspector when a child in the class told the story of 'Naomh Cuán' on one of his visits: he said that he had never heard of that saint. The fact that a local teacher was using the story in the class shows the importance of religious folklore in the culture of the area, and Nóra Ní Shéaghdha, though she did not argue with the inspector on the day, continued to teach local stories to the children (Tyers 1982: 143). Peig's narrative technique helps to bolster this confidence in local lore and to validate St Cuán by bringing him into the historical arena already populated by St Patrick and St Brendan. Thus, the story is framed in both time and space: Peig situates the story in the local area but also manages to connect it to the larger narrative of the history of Christianity in Ireland.

The larger narrative of Irish Christianity is also present in local contexts, however. It is interesting to compare the story of St Cuán with a legend concerning St Brendan, recorded from the same storyteller by W. R. Rodgers of the BBC in 1947.[11] In this short narrative, St Brendan is to say Mass at the summit of Mount Brandon on Easter Sunday; he forgets his Mass book and mentions this to the cleric who is standing beside him. The cleric turns to the person beside him and the story goes from person to person until it reaches the bottom of the mountain. The last person to hear it makes the short journey to the chapel to retrieve the book and brings it to the person who told him; this person hands it to the next person and so the book makes its way up the mountain from hand to hand until finally it is given to St Brendan. He then says Mass and blesses the people. On this occasion, Peig begins by locating the story in time and space in her opening lines, mentioning that this is a story she heard from her father:

> About St Brendan when he was a saint here with us in Kerry. At that time his place of dwelling was Cnoc Bréanainn … Brandon Hill in English, and he was respected and honoured by all the people around there. He used to say Mass every morning up on top of the mountain, and every Sunday and holy day he used to say a special Mass, but on Easter Sunday especially, he used to give a big long sermon instructing the people and the congregation that followed him. (Almqvist and Ó Héalaí 2009: 203)

Once again, Peig concludes the story by making it relevant to the contemporary scene; she states that Easter Sunday is a special day for all Catholics since then, in that they celebrate the memory of St Brendan on that day at the summit of Mount Brandon. In that way, St Brendan 'has left his work and the mark of his labour behind him, thanks be to God'. In the final few sentences, she uses both historical and contemporary imagery in order to reinforce the sense of continuity even more:

> In those days there were steps going down from the top of the hill, down the side of the hill, where the saint and his huge congregation would ascend every day of the week to the top of the mountain. The little chapel is still there and the rounds are still made, and there is a holy well there and people are making the rounds

there every Easter Sunday, unless the weather is very poor entirely. That is still done to honour St Brendan. (Almqvist and Ó Héalaí 2009: 204)

St Brendan (d. *c.*575) was a famous figure in the early Christian church, both in Ireland and abroad. A native of Kerry, he was very well-travelled, not just in Ireland but also in Scotland, Wales and Brittany. The story of Brendan's travels and adventures, the *Navigatio Sancti Brendani* – thought to date from the ninth century – was based on biographical accounts of the saint written in both Irish and Latin in the preceding hundred or so years (Ó hÓgáin 1990: 52–4). Peig's narrative, however, does not concern itself with St Brendan's national or international activities. Instead, it emphasizes St Brendan's connection to the locality and describes his work and that of his clergy in the area. Unlike the St Cuán legend, this story does not include any otherworld supernatural features. It is firmly located in the Christian scene, with a strong message throughout about the importance of the Easter celebration. It is not hard to imagine the quiet crowd assembled on the mountain for Mass on a beautiful Easter Sunday with St Brendan waiting peacefully for his book to make its way to him. The stillness and serenity of the scene is conveyed by the narrator's emphasis on the fact that nobody turned or moved in the slightest from where they were. The centrality of the written word in the Christian liturgy is clear, and yet it is beautifully subverted here: the message that the saint has forgotten his book is orally transmitted '*ó bhéal go béal*' (from mouth to mouth), the book is transported '*ó láimh go láimh*' (from hand to hand) and the problem is solved not by saints or clerics but by the community talking to each other and cooperating quietly and discreetly. Dáithí Ó hÓgáin has noted that this story, or a story like it, was told about a number of other Irish saints as well (Ó hÓgáin 1990: 382).

Both of the above legends concern Christianity, but while the St Brendan one is at the Christian end of the continuum, the one about St Cuán shades into otherworld belief. These are not to be seen as mutually exclusive. Both were told by the same narrator, and her repertoire also included a story about how, as a young man, her father was shown a vision of his future wife by a wise woman, one Sunday morning while everyone else was at Mass. This story illustrates the widespread belief in the special powers of 'Ollthaigh' or 'Ulsterwomen' in certain areas in south Munster.[12] Thus, we see a variety of religious understandings and areas of belief being employed in the process Ó Crualaoich has called 'transmission and transformation of meaning' to create and continuously reinforce the 'island of identity' inhabited by the storyteller and by other people at that time and in that place. Peig's use of concepts of time and place give the narratives power and relevance for the community, but they also elevate the stories to the level of belief and action based on that belief, by their statements about the long-standing practices of the community and the insistence on their continuation.

The expressive use of religious concepts and ideas is very apparent in the material discussed above. But it must be remembered that this kind of creativity around religion and identity was also to be found in other communities and contexts. For instance, religion in the city of Limerick in the first half of the twentieth century was very organized and regimented. The Redemptorists' Archconfraternity of the Holy Family (also known as the 'Fathers' Confraternity' and 'The Confraternity'), which at its height had ten thousand members, was the most striking example of this high level of organization. However, research has shown that devotion in this context also served to reinforce local identity, though in a different way to the legends above (de Cléir 2010). The oral nature of organized religious activities at the time, along with jokes, anecdotes and humorous adaptations of texts such as the catechism (O'Flynn 1998: 182–3), led to a religious experience that was deeply connected to place and people, with both behavioural and narrative aspects present (de Cléir 2017: 170–83). Examples such as this, along with others from different times and places, show that the expressive use of religious tradition, and the creativity associated with this, is not confined to rural areas or to communities with extensive oral narrative repertoires (Wildman 2011). The use of singing and street decorations – the latter a crucial part of urban religious activity – can also be seen as powerful assertions of identity as well as major contributors to the sense-experiences associated with religion (Sciorra 1999; de Cléir 2017: 154–9).

Conclusion: Oppositions, continuities, revolutions and revivals

It is important to note that the 'islands of identity' created by local communities, wherever and whenever these occur, are not unconnected to larger worlds of religion and belief, and the concluding section of this essay will try to assess the intersection of traditional discourse and practice with the increasingly public nature of religion in Ireland in the nineteenth and twentieth centuries. Peig's frequent use of the term 'Catholic' shows her awareness of the politics of religion in Ireland over the preceding few hundred years, and another item in her repertoire bears this out (Almqvist and Ó Héalaí 2009: 205). In terms of identity, Peig, like many other people, had a strong sense of her own locality but would also have seen herself as an Irish woman and a Catholic. The steadily increasing profile of the Catholic church in the post-Famine period is a factor that cannot be excluded from any discussion of Ireland's religious tradition. Emmet Larkin's (1976: 57–85) characterization of the changes occurring in the Catholic religion from around 1850 as a 'devotional revolution' indicates that organized, church-centred devotion took the place of practices carried out at older locations such as holy wells and other long-standing places of pilgrimage; moreover, the accelerated language change from Irish to English during the same period would have led to the decline of traditional prayers. This is how the history of religious tradition in Ireland is generally understood, and while this picture is largely correct, it is necessary to make some additional points about it.

The first point is that while it is definitely true to say that the Catholic religion in Ireland experienced significant growth at this time and that this was characterized by a more international outlook as far as devotion was concerned, it is also important to realize that there were some continuities between older traditions and the practices of this late-nineteenth-century growth and development. Thomas

McGrath (1991) has argued that many of the devotions identified by Larkin as new are actually rooted in the Counter-Reformation period and are Tridentine in nature rather than originating in the second half of the nineteenth century. Úna Nic Einrí (2001: 72–3; 53), while she has noted the emphasis on the English language in the Catholic church during the eighteenth century, has also shown how Counter-Reformation devotional movements – most notably the cult of the Sacred Heart – found their way into Irish-language poetry during the same period. But the phenomenon which most illustrates the complexity of religious tradition is perhaps the rosary prayer. This was introduced by the Dominican Order in the early thirteenth century, and it went on to become a widespread and long-standing ritual throughout Ireland. Patricia Lysaght (1995) has demonstrated its importance in the Donegal oral tradition, including its creative adaptation to the culture of the area. By the time of its promotion in the post-Famine era, the rosary had already been the subject of at least one revival (Lysaght 1995: 19) and would go on to be the centre of another prayer crusade in the 1950s (Fuller 2002: 25). It could be said that one of the reasons that the modernization of popular Catholic practice was so widespread and so successful was because it was, at least in some respects, built on such long-standing and embedded religious tradition. This can be clearly seen in the case of the rosary, despite its ongoing transformation and, some of the time, translation. It had a strong recognition factor and could be easily understood and adapted to a new religious narrative and a modern devotional context.

The second point about the relationship between traditional religion and modern Catholicism is that while church-centred forms of devotion were heavily promoted, mostly through English, from the last quarter of the nineteenth century, the scholarly interest in the Irish language on the part of some members of the clergy along with a growing sense of cultural nationalism meant that an interest in holy well traditions, older pilgrimage practices and Irish-language religious material began to be apparent by the beginning of the twentieth century.[13] The promotion of the Croagh Patrick pilgrimage in 1903 by the combined efforts of the Archbishop of Tuam, Dr Healy, and the parish administrator in Westport, Fr McDonald, is an example of this (Hughes 1991: 24). The pilgrimage – shown by Máire MacNeill to be a long-standing tradition connected with the Celtic festival of *Lughnasa* – had not died out, in any case, although an attempt had been made in 1883 to transfer the penitential exercises carried out from the summit to the base of the mountain (1962: 79). From 1903, the pilgrimage was expanded and adapted to a more modern setting, with trains and buses coming from different parts of the country, some of them leaving in the early hours of the morning so that the participants could be in time for Mass on the summit at noon (de Cléir 2017: 67).

This illustrates my third point, that religious tradition was vibrant and creative in many different ways and contexts. There were some areas, many of them in the Gaeltacht, where older traditions, prayers and beliefs had not yet died out and were still in use in the early twentieth century. Added to this is the fact that even in urban areas, such as the city of Limerick, for instance, it was still possible to collect local sayings and anecdotes about St Patrick as late as the 1970s (Harrold 1994: 67–70). This is not to suggest that all these items were survivals from the early Christian period or even from the era before the modernization of Irish Catholicism in the late nineteenth century – they may have been read in books or mentioned in school – but their meaningful presence in the culture is what is significant. The study of religion is not about the search for origins, nor is it about labelling elements according to their source and derivation, however interesting an exercise this may be. It is really about looking at the meaning of religion in people's lives. The examples discussed above and the variety of places, times and practices mentioned give some idea of the complexity, the dynamism and the ongoing creativity in the expression of religion and religious culture. It is an area rich in concepts, ideas and meanings, and much of it is yet to be explored.

Chapter 4

THE ACADEMIC DISCIPLINE OF RELIGIOUS EDUCATION AT PRIMARY LEVEL IN IRELAND

Patricia Kieran

Introduction

Religious education (RE) is a complex, contested academic discipline whose diverse and distinctive styles have developed largely in response to the unique history of religion and education on the island of Ireland (Titley 1983; O'Donoghue 1999; Akenson 2012). This chapter outlines the evolving nature of this relationship as RE navigates rapid change, new challenges and exciting opportunities. It provides an overview and analysis of diverse types of RE emergent in distinct contexts, as well as their underlying aims, methodologies and rationale. While exploring terminological, historical, legal and educational factors impacting on RE, the chapter simultaneously reflects on the methodological and conceptual complexity of the discipline as well as opportunities for further development. Ireland is distinctive from many of its European counterparts since it has developed a predominately publicly funded system of private faith schools at primary level rather than a nation-wide system of state schools (Coolahan, Hussey and Kilfeather 2012). For most of the twentieth century, RE was conceptualized almost exclusively within a denominational and Christian context. Since the founding of the Free State in 1922, practically all of the national schools were managed by boards whose membership was determined partly by church decision while being chaired *ex officio* by clergymen (O'Buachalla, 1988). Furthermore, the legal trustees of the school property often came from the ranks of senior diocesan clergymen and church parochial officers.

In contemporary Ireland, 94.4 per cent of all primary schools are managed by churches, with 88.9 per cent under the patronage of the Catholic church, 5.5 per cent under the patronage of the Church of Ireland (C of I), 4.8 per cent under multi-denominational patronage and 0.8 per cent under the category of 'other' (Department of Education 2019). The multi-denominational sector is complex and there are several patron bodies (e.g. Education and Training Boards Ireland (ETBI), Educate Together (ET), An Foras Pátrúnachta) offering various models of education. At post-primary level, Catholic pupils account for 47.6 per cent of the entire school population (O'Brien 2019) with 3 per cent of schools being C of I, 48.7 per cent being multi-denominational and 0.7 per cent Other (Department of Education 2019). Protestant ethos schools include Presbyterian, Methodist and Society of Friends schools (Wilkinson 2021). In the current educational configuration, not all denominational patrons are Christian, and, significantly, there are two Muslim and one Jewish primary schools in Ireland's faith school sector. In the past decade, change is evident as over one hundred Catholic primary schools have closed as other school types, most notably multi-denominational schools, increase in popularity.

In the absence of a nation-wide state system of primary schooling or a state curriculum for RE at primary level, there is a lack of cohesion and unity within RE, and the discipline inhabits what Arniika Kuusisto and Liam Gearon (2017) refer to as a pedagogically and politically contested space. Since RE is one vital aspect of the school's ethos in the patronage system, diverse forms of RE have been incubated within different patron's programmes and curricula. Indeed, over the past century, the vast majority of RE has taken place within formal schooling in an ecclesial context. In general, RE has tended to focus on specific patron's programmes and there has been insufficient exploration of the discipline's foundational principles, philosophical rationale, sociocultural context, inter-belief contribution and connection with global movements in education and religion (Kennedy 2021). While there have been interesting empirical studies (Byrne and Francis 2019; McGrady, Francis and McKenna 2019), new research groups (Whittle 2021), multiple conferences and links to European and international research (Ziebertz and Riegel 2009; Byrne and Kieran 2013; Smyth, Lyons and Darmody 2013; Tuohy 2013), overall, in Ireland, debate on RE has tended to be more inward-looking and pragmatic. Indeed, in Ireland, RE has not always been positioned or seen as a force for democracy, conflict resolution, active citizenship, intercultural engagement, social cohesion and anti-racist education (Keast 2007; OECD 2007). It is often situated as a subsection of a larger public debate on the involvement of religious bodies in education (Lodge and Lynch 2005; Darmody and Smyth 2013) as well as school patronage, governance, equality legislation, admissions policies, inclusion and parental choice (Mawhinney 2012; Nugent and Donnelly 2013; Parker-Jenkins and Masterson 2013; Selim 2014; Heinz, Davison and Keane 2018). Despite experiencing what has been called a recent renaissance of multidisciplinary interest in religion and education (Whittle 2021), RE in Ireland also has a history of occupying a highly charged, somewhat territorial and divisive space (Van Nieuwenhove 2012; Nugent and Donnelly 2013; Park 2019).

Proliferation of terms

In twenty-first-century Ireland there has been a renegotiation of the central place and potency (Lane 2007; Smyth, Lyons and Darmody 2013; Conway 2015; Faas, Smith and Darmody 2018; O'Connell 2018) of RE in the primary school curriculum, as well as a fundamental change in perception of its nature, identity

(Shanahan 2017; Henry 2021) and purpose (Tuohy 2013; Renehan 2014; Hession 2015). RE at primary level inhabits a fractured, complex and changing space in the educational landscape that is increasingly devoid of a common language and shared rationale. This is evident in the confusing and competing nomenclature applied to the area (Coolahan, Hussey and Kilfeather 2012). At primary level, the term 'religious instruction' (RI) gained widespread currency in policy documents after the founding of the Free State (1922), in the Constitution (Government of Ireland 1937), in the Rules for National Schools (Department of Education 1965) and in the 1971 curriculum (Department of Education 1971).

However, the term 'religious education' was used in 1831 in the Stanley Letter at the founding of the national system of education (Coolahan 1981), as well as in the 1998 Education Act. Despite the fact that RE was identified as one of seven curricular areas in the 1999 Curriculum (Department of Education and Skills 1999: 58), in twenty-first-century Ireland, there is a lack of common purpose evident in the discipline as increasingly confusing and competing titles are applied to it. Finola Cunnane speaks of RE's 'babel of language' (2004: 2) while Mary Shanahan outlines some of the discipline's many terms including denominational, multi-denominational, interdenominational, education about religion and beliefs (ERB), religious studies, religious instruction, catechetics/catechesis, religious and moral education and religious formation (Shanahan 2017).

More recently at primary level, policy makers and academics have added further distinction and nuance as new terms such as multi-belief education, inter-belief dialogue (Irwin 2013; NCCA 2018; Kieran 2019) and equality-based education (Educate Together 2004; Conboy 2016) emerge. Donna Doherty's research on lifelong learning in religious book publishing in Ireland suggests that this variety of terms might be due, in part, to the fact that in the contemporary context words connected with religion and 'religious' can be encumbered (Doherty 2020). Nearly one-quarter of Doherty's research participants interpreted the word 'religion' or 'religious' as narrowly doctrinal, lacking in critical thinking, leading to pious labelling and inhibiting dialogue with those from secular traditions (Doherty 2020). Precisely because the language surrounding religion is so loaded, ET and Community National Schools (CNS) do not use the term 'religious education' and apply the term 'Ethical Education and Goodness Me Goodness You!' to their respective multi-belief and values curricula in schools. Indeed, there are tensions (Irwin 2013) as language is stretched to accommodate new evolving contexts.

As a consequence of the lack of a unitary, consistent vision and vocabulary for RE in Ireland, diverse terms are used in different contexts with multiple meanings. Understandably, given this absence of a common language, it is challenging to facilitate cross-sectoral academic dialogue and research on the nature, purpose and future of RE in Ireland. This lack of linguistic clarity inhibits the kind of philosophical and conceptual coherence necessary for the academic discipline to flourish (Biesta et al. 2019; Kennedy 2021). While there are positive curricular developments, multiple initiatives and new energies around different types of RE, there is also confusion and uncertainty. Áine Hyland and Brian Bocking (2015: 252) suggest that 'RE in Ireland is in a process of erratic and unpredictable transition' as 'private, mainly Catholic church control of the overwhelming majority of schools, is seemingly clashing head-on with the demands of an increasingly multi- and non-religious civil society'.

Recently, the *Draft Primary Curriculum Framework* (2020) for Ireland dropped sole use of the term 'religious education' (Department of Education and Skills 1999) in favour of an awkward new constellation of terms, 'Religious/Ethical/Multi-Belief Education – Patron's Programme' (NCCA 2020). While this cumbersome compound term may have been inspired by a well-meaning desire to be inclusive, it reveals in stark manner the general lack of coherence and connection in the discipline of RE. Conversely, as there is renewed scholarly energy around RE in Ireland, this proliferation of terms could be interpreted as a call to dialogue and engagement among and between practitioners, policy makers and academics at a time when there are also great signs of innovative research and scholarship. This is especially evident in the exciting proliferation of curricula and programmes for different types of RE in schools and the increased research output in the discipline.

The historical backdrop to the academic study of RE

In order to understand why the discipline of RE at primary level is so fragmented, one must explore the past to trace the causal factors leading to this fractured contemporary configuration of religion and education. Under colonial rule, the penal laws from 1695 to 1829 had a devastating impact on the right to education and freedom of religion in Ireland. While the penal laws were not always universally enforced (Scally 2021), all those who were not members of the established Anglican church, especially Catholics and Protestant dissenters including Baptists, Methodists, Palatines, Presbyterians and Quakers, could not legally promote or teach their faith (Rogan 1987). When the laws were finally abolished in 1829, religious authorities, and in particular the Catholic church, ventured on a period of rapid educational and religious expansion. Charitable schools (King 1970) were founded and newly established religious orders founded denominational primary and second-level schools to provide education and RI for the poor (Darmody and Smyth 2013). RI through Bible reading in Protestant schools or catechism in Catholic schools became a key aspect of the schools' educational mission.

In 1831, the chief secretary of Ireland, Edward G. Stanley (1799–1869), wrote a letter founding an experimental, free, religiously mixed or interdenominational national system of education (Durcan 1972; Coolahan and O'Donovan 2009). Within this interdenominational system, RE was conceptualized as a form of denominationally specific, clergy-led Christian education in religion. As a scholastic discipline, RE was originally partitioned from 'secular' subjects, to be delivered by Protestant or Catholic clergy, and positioned outside of the school day (Kieran and Hession 2005). However, with a backdrop of oppressive Penal Laws (Mitchel 1913: 10), Catholic authorities tended to view interdenominational schools as attempts at subversion and proselytism and engaged in decolonial (Kieran and McDonagh 2021) acts of resistance. While there was a sizable number of religiously mixed schools (Fitzgerald 2010), there was also considerable opposition to them. Protestant religious authorities resisted joint schooling and in 1839 the C of I created the Church Education Society to run its schools. In 1850, Catholic bishops condemned denominationally mixed education and warned that 'the separate education of Catholic youth is, in every way, to be preferred to it' (Coolahan 1981: 18).

As Catholic bishops lobbied for full civil rights (O'Donoghue and Harford 2012: 338), the proliferation of denominationally specific schools in the nineteenth century laid the foundations for the system of education that is largely operative in contemporary Ireland. At the time of the 'devotional revolution' (Larkin 1972) in the mid-nineteenth century, Catholic bishops banned all Catholic children and teachers from attending interdenominational schools and training colleges (Coolahan 1981). As the national system of education was established by a letter and not an act of parliament, Ireland's education system became, *de facto*, and not *de jure*, a denominational system by the end of the nineteenth century (Kieran and Hession 2005: 77).

When the Irish Free State came into being in 1922, it did not initiate any wholescale restructuring of the pre-existing educational arrangements. The future shape of RE in Ireland was sealed as the State ceded management of the vast majority of primary schools to religious bodies with denominationally specific RE. This meant that at primary level, there was no state system of schooling and Ireland developed a 'parochially organized, denominationally segregated and clerically managed' system (Walsh 2016: 11–12). The Catholic bishops had a policy of resisting state involvement in education (Department of Education 1926: 18) and especially in the area of RI where religious authorities designed programmes for their own schools. Anne Lodge (2021) notes that following independence, the Protestant minority learned to keep a low profile. In 1934, Zion National School was founded to provide children with a national school education within a Jewish ethos (Stratford NS 2019). The Dalkey School Project in 1978 marked the beginning of Ireland's multi-denominational primary school sector (Hyland 1989). In 1990, the first Muslim national school opened, followed in 2000 by the Weekend Islamic School and in 2001 by a second Muslim national school providing Islamic RE including Arabic, Qur'an and religious studies. In 1993, An Foras Pátrúnachta was established to provide Irish-medium schools and it is currently patron to Catholic, multi-denominational and interdenominational schools. In 2008, the first CNS opened providing a new form of multi-denominational education (Conboy 2017).

The legal context

Dympna Glendinning notes that education in Ireland is largely a church–state cooperative, enshrined in the Constitution, enacted in legislation and upheld by the Supreme Court (Glendinning 2012). Article 42.4 of the Constitution affirms that the State shall provide 'for free primary education' (Government of Ireland 1937). The crucially important word 'for' places the state at one remove from educational provision as the state does not provide free primary education. With the exception of a handful of Model schools and an increasing number of CNS, the state does not provide education. This is vitally important for RE as it has given rise to multiple school patrons with distinctive school ethoi, each generating their own form of RE or alternative education. The 1998 Education Act stresses the rights of the different church authorities to design and supervise the teaching of curricula in RE at primary level. Therefore, patron bodies and not the Department of Education are responsible for RE in primary schools and there is no prescribed curricular content for RE. The Department of Education recommends a time allocation of thirty minutes per day for RE (Department of Education and Skills 1999: 70), while Rule 69 of the Rules for National Schools reinforces the parental right to withdraw children from RI of which they do not approve (Department of Education 1965). The 1999 curriculum acknowledges the school's duty to be flexible in making alternative organizational arrangements for those who do not wish to avail of its particular RE (Department of Education and Skills 1999: 58).

Main types of RE in Ireland

In Ireland, there is a growing realization that RE's educational rootedness means that the discipline is focused not only on religion and beliefs but also on its 'underlying pedagogy, its understanding of teaching and learning, its aims, methodologies and contents' (Cullen 2013: 127). As an educational discipline, RE aims to facilitate higher-order thinking and religious literacy (Biesta et al. 2019) as it invites critical thinking when religion meets education (Hession 2015: 88). John Sullivan (2017: 7) notes that

> RE offers a space like no other: for encounter, explanation, and empathy; for expression, interpretation, and imagination; for interrogation, questioning, and reflection … It gives an opportunity for students to experience and to bring into dialogue with one another both insider and outsider perspectives with regard to religious issues. It prompts pupils to think about similarities and differences between people and, in so doing, to reflect upon their own uniqueness and forms of belonging.

There are multiple forms of RE that address the diversity 'evident in the rich kaleidoscope of ages, competencies, cultures, ethnicities, family structures and backgrounds, home languages, religions, sexual identities, and worldviews characteristic of classrooms in twenty-first century Ireland' (NCCA 2020: 3). The 1999 Curriculum hints at both confessional and multi-belief forms of RE when it states that RE 'enables the child to develop spiritual and moral values and to come to a knowledge of God' while also recognizing 'the importance of tolerance towards the practice, culture and life-style of a range of religious convictions and expressions, and aspires to develop in children a tolerance and understanding towards the beliefs of others' (Department of Education and Skills 1999: 58). Sandra Cullen (2013) draws attention to the contextual aspect of the discipline where different forms of RE are shaped by distinct types of schools. In Ireland these include Catholic, C of I, CNS, ET, interdenominational, Jewish, Methodist, multi-denominational, Muslim, Presbyterian, Quaker and other school types, each with their own approach to RE or ethical and multi-belief education.

In 2012 the Forum and Patronage and Pluralism Report marked a new departure in the field. At primary level, it recommended establishing a mandatory multi-belief, state-designed and assessed education about religion and beliefs and ethics (ERBE) curriculum/programme for primary schools to ensure basic standards of religious and belief literacy in all schools. The Forum recommended that schools should teach ERBE including the celebration of festivals from different beliefs (Coolahan, Hussey and Kilfeather 2012: 10). It wished to promote greater inclusiveness in schools and recommended that schools have a beliefs' display wall to celebrate the range of religions and world views (Coolahan, Hussey and Kilfeather 2012: 6). For the first time in the history of the state, it was proposed that the National Council for Curriculum and Assessment (NCCA) would design and monitor an ERBE curriculum for primary schools. It affirmed that all children should be educated to respect adherents of a range of religions and beliefs (Irwin 2013) and 'have an informed awareness of the main theist and non-theist beliefs and of key aspects of their cultural manifestations' (Coolahan, Husse and Kilfeather 2012: v). This had implications for the discipline of RE at third level when pre-service teacher programmes developed modules in ERBE in primary initial teacher education programmes in Ireland.

Overall, at primary level, RE in Ireland can be situated within the three main approaches of *learning into, learning about and learning from* religion and beliefs. With differing emphases, these three approaches to RE act to form (*learning into*), inform (*learning about*) and transform (*learning from*) individuals and communities (Lane 2021: 19–29) in a formal educational context. Historically, many Catholic schools tended to provide exclusively catechetical RE programmes with a focus on evangelizing and faith transmission. These approaches aimed to foster encounter with the divine and lead students to increased commitment in one faith tradition (Grimmitt 1973: 18; Hull 1984) with an emphasis on forming and transforming individuals and communities (Hession 2015: 102–3). Dermot Lane terms this a 'learning into' religion approach.

In contemporary Ireland, Catholic RE is conceptualized as developing religious ways of thinking, feeling and doing, which give expression to the spiritual, moral and transcendent dimensions of life with the possibility of personal and social transformation (Irish Episcopal Conference 2010: 38). As an invitational approach, RE focuses on the possibility of personal faith commitment (Irish Episcopal Conference 2010: 32–42; Lane 2013: 27–8) within one religious tradition while simultaneously educating learners about other faith communities. As an educational activity, this approach fosters religious literacy and critical thinking, not just within one faith tradition but also across a spectrum of religions and beliefs. Other confessional approaches, with various degrees of nuance, are also found in contemporary interdenominational, Jewish, Muslim and Protestant schools.

In many contemporary faith schools, a blend of approaches to RE may be simultaneously applied. For instance, the Jewish primary school provides learning into RE for Jewish children including general Jewish knowledge, study of the five books of Moses, prayers, Hebrew writing, reading and grammar. This school welcomes children from a diverse range of religious and cultural backgrounds while creating an inclusive learning environment, and in the past it has facilitated learning into RE for Catholic children through sacramental preparation and Catholic RE (Stratford NS 2019). Likewise, in Protestant schools, while children are introduced to worship and prayer in accordance with the Reformed Christian tradition, they are also invited to explore their own unique identities and to make informed independent choices about their own beliefs in a diverse and inclusive context.

Phenomenological and experiential approaches (Smart 1968) have impacted on RE in Ireland as RE curricula focus on different approaches to learning about a range of religious and secular world views and, for some, a 'bracketing' of the learner's own faith or belief perspectives in a desire to appreciate the perspective of others. Michael Grimmitt's 'learning about' RE approach focuses on learners' understanding the teachings and practices of the world's religions and beliefs, through learning information, facts, stories and rites about religions (Lane 2013: 27–8). Derek Bastide (2006) succinctly summarized this as the 'giving them the facts' approach. This differs in emphasis to Grimmitt's 'learning from' approach which foregrounds what pupils learn about themselves when they explore religion and beliefs in an educational setting as 'it focuses more on their own experience' (Grimmitt 1987: 225). 'Learning from' concentrates on learners' personal engagement with, reflection on and response to the religion or belief being studied (Lane 2013: 25). Multidenominational and equality-based RE in Ireland fall into both Grimmitt's learning about and learning from categories.

In Ireland's multi-denominational schools, children are educated in an informed empathetic and experiential manner about a range of ethical perspectives, religions and beliefs through learning about and learning from religion approaches. They provide pluralist, wide-ranging learning experiences on a variety of human rights, environmental, ethical, religious, spiritual and belief traditions including humanist, atheist and non-religious perspectives. It would be simplistic and binary to present the three learning about, learning from and learning into religion approaches as disconnected and isolated. Lane notes that 'there is a logical and educational progression in learning about, to learning from, to learning into a particular faith tradition. This progression can go in either direction – what is important is the critical coherence and integration of the three-way movement' (Lane 2013: 29). Grimmitt's 'learning about' and 'learning from' (Groome 2011: 263) approaches are also found in C of I, Presbyterian, Methodist and Catholic schools where they are combined, in nuanced and diverse ways, with learning into religion approaches. In many faith schools, the human search for meaning (Lane 2013: 37) and inter-religious learning forms a key part of curricular content and methodologies (Wilkinson 2001-10; Irish Episcopal Conference 2015). While Catholic RE prioritizes children's engagement with the Catholic tradition, it simultaneously foregrounds human rights and inclusion, and facilitates learning about other religious and belief traditions, thus enabling them to enrich their own lives and the lives of others (Hession 2015: 102-3).

RE in Catholic schools

From the Stanley Letter up until Vatican II (1962-5), a confessional and doctrinal approach based on the Catechism (embodying both methodological approach and curricular content) became so identified with RI in Catholic schools that the two almost became identical. Indeed, Thomas O'Donoghue comments on 'the equation of religious education with the teaching of the catechism' up until the 1960s which served to stultify any consideration of social change (O'Donoghue 1999: 138).

J. D. King described Vatican II's documents on revelation, church, education and inter-religious engagement as giving rise to a 'revolution' in RE in Ireland in the 1960s and 1970s (King 1970). In the 1970s, kerygmatic approaches placed scripture, Christ and biblical stories at the heart of RI in Ireland. Catholic RI in the *On Our Way* series (McConville 1965) moved away from the doctrinally laden approach of the catechism and focused more on Christ and the scriptures. A more radical anthropological approach presented RE as a transforming force for social justice with a greater emphasis on the child's experiences while making religious reality accessible to the child's consciousness (King 1970: 159). The first National Catechetical Programme gave rise to two distinctive Catholic RE series in the form of the *Children of God* series (1973-2005), succeeded by the *Alive O* (1996-2004) programme. The *Children of God* series embodied a form of 'learning into' religion as it aimed to communicate 'Christian Revelation to children in their concrete situation with a view to fostering faith' (Irish Episcopal Conference 1977: 7). Catholic RE was influenced by the disciplines of anthropology and sociology through the work of writers such as Gabriel Moran who argued that catechesis had to address the learners' needs. The eclectic *Alive O* programme, titled from St Irenaeus' phrase 'the glory of God is people fully alive', was a biblically based, anthropological and bilingual programme, tailored to children's ability, age and stage of faith development and life experience. Both of these Catholic programmes were designed to enable students to acquire the knowledge, beliefs, skills, values, attitudes and sensibilities that being Christian involves (Kieran and Hession 2005).

In 2011 the National Directory for Catechesis in Ireland, *Share the Good News*, set down a framework for the presentation of and engagement with the Good News of Jesus Christ in Catholic RE (Byrne and Kieran 2013). *Share the Good News* presents Catholic RE as informed by a pluralism which 'at its best upholds positive respect for and interest in the quest for truth engaged in by individuals, by faith communities and other groups in society' (Irish Episcopal Conference 2010: 21).

Contemporary Catholic RE is rooted in the Catholic tradition and emphasizes the voluntary, inclusive, invitational and educational nature of its RE programmes.

'In embracing young people from beyond the Catholic community, the Catholic school treats them with the greatest honour. It respects the faith and beliefs of all young people under its care. The right of parents to withdraw their children from denominational religious education and formation has always been respected. Clearly, young people should not in any way be subjected to proselytizing or indoctrination' (Irish Episcopal Conference 2010: 101). While 'utterly respectful of everyone's belief system' (Irish Episcopal Conference 2010: 148), in an increasingly secular and belief-diverse Ireland, Catholic RE emphasizes the dignity and rights of the learner, freedom of choice, critical thinking and higher-order skills. It condemns absolutely all forms of coercive imposition on the conscience of pupils (Byrne and Kieran 2013: 9). In 2015 the Irish Episcopal Conference (IEC) published an inaugural RE curriculum framework for primary schools in Ireland North and South, with an aim 'to help children mature in relation to their spiritual, moral and religious lives, through their encounter with, exploration and celebration of the Catholic faith' (Irish Episcopal Conference 2015: 31). Across five levels (from preschool and primary school) and in its special educational needs (SEN) guidelines, this curriculum outlines the knowledge, understanding, skills and processes of its four interconnected strands: Christian Faith, Word of God, Liturgy and Prayer, and Christian Morality (Irish Episcopal Conference 2015). This child-centred, spiral curriculum provides clarity about curricular content, learning outcomes and possibilities for flexible differentiation.

The curriculum outlined the complex pedagogical and theological underpinning of its approach rooted in Christ, scripture and the Catholic tradition (Irish Episcopal Conference 2015: 25–9) as it aimed to develop five key interrelated skills of children's religious literacy (understanding, communicating, participating, developing spiritual literacy and developing inter-religious literacy) across the curriculum (Irish Episcopal Conference 2015: 34). While identifying key truths, doctrines and practices of the Catholic religious tradition, it stresses the importance of intercultural, inter-religious, moral, ecological, information and computer technology, and SEN perspectives. Catholic schools may include children who adhere to other religions or other stances for living. While mindful of their duty to educate in the distinctive beliefs, values and practices of the Catholic community, teachers will bear witness to an attitude of respect for and appreciation of all (Irish Episcopal Conference 2015: 15).

This 2015 curriculum resulted in the authorized *Grow in Love* (2015–20) programme for Catholic primary schools (Irish Episcopal Conference 2015). As an invitational and conversational child-centred sacramental and confessional approach (Catholic School Partnership 2015; Mahon and O'Connell 2015), it finds its theoretical basis in Tom Groome's (2011) shared Christian praxis. Groome's kerygmatic and experiential (Groome 2011: 267) approach was inspired by Jesus' story-based pedagogy in the gospels, especially the Emmaus story (Lk. 24.13-24). In *Grow in Love*, the Christian story and vision is correlated to the students' prior learning, world views and lives. Shared Christian praxis aims to make connections between the learner's experience and the Christian theme. Its pedagogy invites learners to bring their 'lives to their faith and their faith to their lives' (Groome 2011: 262). A 'Life to Faith to Life' movement combines an inductive approach that invites learners to reflect on their own lives, with a deductive process focused on instruction in the Christian faith (Groome 2011: 268).

The *Grow in Love* programme is steeped in the Catholic tradition and it scaffolds children's skills of inter-religious literacy, higher-order thinking and the development of empathy for and sensitivity towards people of other religions and cultures, while fostering awareness of shared values such as justice, peace, solidarity, tolerance and freedom (Irish Episcopal Conference 2015: 37). Notwithstanding, it is important to recognize that in some Catholic schools there can be mission and ethos dissonance (Sullivan 2017; Dineen 2021). Researchers have emphasized the need for teacher in-service and support to contribute to the successful delivery of Catholic RE programmes (Meehan and O'Connell 2021) and to support inter-belief dialogue in schools (Kieran 2021). In a crowded curriculum, another major challenge facing Catholic RE is the fact that the discipline is not always taught in schools. In 2001, INTO research suggested that 10 per cent of teachers did not want to teach, or did not teach, RE in primary classrooms (INTO 2003). More recent research suggests that many teachers in Catholic primary schools do not teach the Catholic RE programme on a regular basis (Dineen and Lundie 2017) and that pre-service teachers may not intentionally teach RE according to curricular guidelines (O'Connell, Ryan and Harmon 2018: 85). Other challenges facing Catholic schools include the tensions inherent in achieving full inclusion of LGBTQI families, staff and pupils whilst adhering to the Catholic ethos (Neary 2013; Neary, Gray and O'Sullivan 2018) as well as the tension of delivering sacramental and faith-based RE in an increasingly secular and multi-belief context (Hession 2015). While Seán Henry (2021) challenges the heteronormativity of RE, Catherine Stapleton speaks of the kaleidoscope of identities in Catholic schools (2021). There is much talk of inclusion, yet there is a total absence of inter-religious learning in Level One of the Catholic primary curriculum and insufficient engagement with many of the great religious traditions of the world including Buddhism, Hinduism, Sikhism and others. Finally, the short time allocated for inter-religious literacy (e.g. 1.5 hours per year in Level Two and 2.5 hours in Level Three and 5 hours in Level Four) is inadequate.

RE in C of I, Methodist, Presbyterian and Society of Friends schools

The C of I is a Christian church with 126,400 members and 175 primary schools (Wilkinson 2021). In 1871 after the Disestablishment of the Church of Ireland, the General Synod Board of Education became responsible for RE in C of I Schools. As the second-largest patron body for 5 per cent of schools in the Republic of Ireland, the C of I is patron to co-educational primary schools that are 'diverse in population and inclusive in enrolment' (Wilkinson 2021: 81). In 2001, a child-centred, biblically based RE programme was published after a period of consultation and piloting. This *Follow Me* (FM) (Wilkinson 2001–10) programme caters for a diverse intake of children from a variety of belief traditions (Lodge, Tuohy and Fennelly 2011) and is used in primary schools under C of I, Methodist, Presbyterian and Society of Friends patronage. In C of I schools, FM builds upon and supports each school's uniquely manifest ethos or climate (Lodge and Jackson 2014). As an RE programme, it aims to enable children to 'develop a knowledge and understanding of beliefs, worship and witness of the Christian faith, and in particular of the Church of Ireland and other principal reformed traditions' (Wilkinson 2001–10: viii).

This child-centred, biblically based RE programme sets out to develop learners' 'own religious beliefs, values and practices through a process of personal search and discovery' while developing 'an awareness of and a sensitivity towards those of other faiths and none' (Wilkinson 2001–10: viii). The programme's seven strands focus on key themes:

1. Celebrations, festivals, ceremonies and customs
2. Sacred writings, stories and key figures
3. Beliefs
4. Sacred places, worship and symbols
5. Moral values and attitudes
6. Personal search: the natural world, relationships and moral values, ultimate questions
7. Awareness of those of other faiths and none (Wilkinson 2001–10: ix).

FM is an RE programme for denominational schools, yet it differs from Catholic approaches in its emphasis on reformed theology and worship. It has a distinctive strand content rooted in the Reformed tradition that allocates a central place for worship in school assemblies. This confessional, thematic, biblically based, child-centred programme provides regular opportunities for sung, spoken or silent prayer and worship through school assembly or church services such as carol services. Interestingly, FM does not present teachers as agents for transmitting or forming children's faith through worship and witness. Instead, precisely because faith is seen as a deeply personal matter, in FM the child is invited to engage in their own unique journey of discovery to develop their own personal beliefs and practices through open-ended, higher-order thinking and discussion activities that foster independent thought. FM invites children to 'learn about' and 'learn from' C of I and other Reformed traditions' beliefs and practices as they explore religious faith and ultimate questions. The FM programme also educates about a diversity of perspectives incorporating people of diverse faiths and none.

Equality-based and multi-denominational RE in Ireland

At primary level, there are three main types of multi-denominational schools in Ireland: ET schools, An Foras Pátrúnachta's Irish-medium multi-denominational schools and CNS, each with their own approach. In 1978, ET schools were established to respond to parental demand (Hyland 1989; Faas, Smith and Darmody 2018) to provide greater educational choice through an alternative model of schooling (Darmody and Smyth 2013) and to counteract the exclusion and marginalization of minority-belief children in Ireland's denominational educational system (Hyland 2018). ET schools were founded so that 'children of all faiths and none would have equal right of access and would be equally respected' (Hyland 2018: 5). In Ireland, multi-denominational and equality-based schools provide inclusive multi-belief learning experiences in a human rights framework for children of all faiths and none (Faas, Smith and Darmody 2018: 4). In the very early stages of this ET movement (Mullally 2018: 21), it was suggested that during the school day, this model might provide all children with forms of RE aligned to their parents/guardians' convictions. However, given ET's co-educational, child-centred, democratic and equality-based principles, it became evident that the segregation of children along religious or belief lines was unworkable and inconsistent with the charter for ET schools (Fischer 2016: 99).

In 1990, the ET Charter had been established to address the religious rights of all families in ET schools without favour or discrimination. In this model, no one belief tradition is promoted or prioritized. In 2004, ET produced its patron's curriculum called the *Learn Together Ethical Education Curriculum* (Educate Together 2004). This curriculum was collaboratively written by principals, parents and educators to reflect its ethos based on equality and respect, embodied in the motto that 'No child is an outsider'. The four strands of the *Learn Together* programme include Moral and Spiritual Development, Equality and Justice; Belief Systems and Ethics and the Environment. Importantly, *Learn Together* is not described as a form of RE, as *Learn Together* is conceptualized as a distinct patron's curriculum with a focus on ethical education where belief systems form one strand of a broader framework.

In 2015, ET stopped using the term 'multi-denominational' when describing its schools and adopted what it viewed as the more inclusive term 'equality-based' education. Daniel Faas, Aimee Smith and Merike Darmody (2018: 5) contend that *Learn Together* is an 'ethics curriculum, which comprises ethics and values with a comparative view of world religions where pupils learn about religion instead of being instructed in religion'. As a spiral curriculum it aims to 'provide children with a range of dispositions and skills to enable them to participate in and contribute to the democratic process and become responsible, fair minded and socially responsible citizens' (Educate Together 2004: 10). It celebrates diversity, respect for difference and self-esteem, while placing an emphasis on multiculturalism and pluralism. Through this integrated curriculum learners are invited to explore the ethical, moral and spiritual dimensions of life as well as belief systems. A number of resources such as *Signposts: Lessons for Living* (Dermody, Kelly and Ward 2010) and *Lessons on Humanism* (Educate Together and Humanist Association of Ireland 2017), have been developed to support the delivery of the curriculum. At first glance it appears that ET's approach is one of learning about religions and beliefs. The Belief Systems strand explains and explores the major belief systems in the world in an educational manner, teaching children about these faiths and beliefs without endorsing any particular one as religious truth. The educational aim of this work is to model positive information about world faiths in a respectful atmosphere which highlights rights and responsibilities. (Educate Together 2018)

Yet ET's exploratory approach also embodies a form of 'learning from' diverse beliefs, ethics and world views as learners 'are encouraged to gain personal understandings in a creative and supportive learning environment. They are encouraged to evaluate information, form judgements and articulate these judgements in a supportive, respectful and safe environment' (Educate Together 2018). ET is currently in the process of engaging in wide consultation as part of revising and re-presenting its ethical education curriculum.

Community National Schools

In 2007, a new state CNS model of multi-denominational schools was established. It originated from an educational crisis when eighty children from diverse linguistic and cultural backgrounds were left without school places in West Dublin. The then minister for education, Mary Hanafin T. D., promised,

> The new schools will be open to children of all religions and none. They will be inter-denominational in character, aiming to provide for religious education and faith formation during the school day for each of the main faith groups represented. A general ethics programme will also be available for children whose parents opt for that and the schools will operate through an ethos of inclusiveness and respect for all beliefs, both religious and non-religious. (Teach Don't Preach 2007)

In 2008, the first CNS was opened and, since then, the model has been evolving (Conboy 2016). As state, multi-denominational, co-educational schools underpinned by the core values of excellence in education, care, equality, community and respect, these schools have reconfigured the relationship between religion and education in Ireland in an innovative way.

In the early years, through an initial *Goodness Me Goodness You!* (GMGY) experimental programme, CNS ambitiously sought to combine learning 'into' religion approaches with learning 'about' and learning 'from' approaches. This hybrid approach attempted simultaneously to combine the type of confessional faith formation and sacramental preparation found in Catholic schools with Islamic and other forms of faith formation, alongside phenomenological learning about and learning from approaches. From 2008 to 2015, in the one classroom, teachers were engaged in the delivery of confessional and multi-belief approaches as the GMGY programme sought to nurture the beliefs of all children within the school day (Mullally 2018: 21). Seamus Conboy describes this combined approach as 'generic religious education and religious instruction for all within the school day' (Conboy 2019: 25).

Although children were taught the GMGY programme together for most of the year, they were provided with belief-specific teaching (BST) and separated for four weeks each year into generic groups (e.g. Muslim or Catholic) to learn more about their own beliefs. It was during this time that Catholic children were given sacramental preparation (Conboy 2019). This approach was controversial and research recommended the suspension of BST (Faas, Smith and Darmody 2018). Indeed, the original GMGY programme ran into difficulties as it simultaneously sought to cross-fertilize 'learning into' the distinctive and diverse religious traditions of each child in the school with a phenomenological learning about and learning from religion and belief approaches. Children from religious homes were invited to pray during GMGY while non-religious children were invited to recite a meaningful reflection. Some perceived BST as inequitable. Others expressed reservations about teachers having the capability to teach multiple religious traditions as truth when they were from non-religious backgrounds. As the model evolved, BST and faith-formational approaches were dropped as teachers spoke of the challenges around nurturing the faith of each child in a multi-belief context.

Further, a movement away from the 'learning into' approach had occurred in 2014 when the term 'faith formation' was replaced with the more inclusive term 'belief nurturing' to include children from secular, atheist and non-religious backgrounds (Mullally 2018: 12). A further dismantling of the original hybrid confessional and phenomenological approaches came in 2016 when the ETB sector announced that sacramental preparation for Catholics would be moved outside the school day. In 2015, through a process of consultation, the NCCA supported ETB's development of a new GMGY curriculum. This current multi-belief and values education curriculum draws on a multidisciplinary framework to enable

> children to encounter identity education, values education, philosophy and multi-denominational religious education. GMGY contributes to the holistic development of the child and as such aims to enable every child to realise their potential as a unique individual. (NCCA 2018: 4)

GMGY is a process curriculum that evolves with schools. While there is no cross-sectoral agreed definition of the term 'multi-denominational' in Irish education, in CNS it is interpreted as culturally responsive education (NCCA 2018: 28) that respects the equality of beliefs of school and community members.

The GMGY curriculum was generated through drawing collaboratively on the voices of children, parents and teachers in CNS as well as inputs from ETBI, NCCA and Department of Education staff. As part of its pluralist approach (NCCA 2018: 8), it contains four strands: My Stories, We Are a Community National School, Thinking Time, and Beliefs and Religions. These strands enable children 'to share their beliefs and values and to encounter the beliefs and values of others in a learning environment of enquiry and respect' (NCCA 2018: 7). GMGY affirms that it does not promote any one perspective or tradition (NCCA 2018: 14) and is influenced by the *Toledo Guiding Principles* through sponsoring study about religions and beliefs without imposing 'any particular view' (Organisation for Security and Co-operation in Europe 2007: 21). Further, CNS do not present GMGY as an RE programme. RE is used only in relation to the belief strand which is described as multi-denominational RE. Faas, Smith and Darmody (2018: 8) note that since beliefs and religions 'is only one of four, the GMGY senior curriculum can be more accurately described as a values and ethics curriculum rather than purely religious'.

From 2015 onwards, the GMGY curriculum moved entirely away from previous approaches of learning into religion so that it now embodies a learning 'about' and 'from' religions and beliefs approach (NCCA 2018: 14). Of particular note is GMGY's use of inter-belief conversation/dialogue as a methodology for 'cooperative, constructive and positive interactions between children of different belief backgrounds, both religious and non-religious' (NCCA 2018: 38). The curriculum 'combines the formative pedagogy of values education with the constructivist approach of philosophy with and for children and the exploratory and dialogical pedagogy of multi-denominational religious education' (NCCA 2018: 8). Indeed, GMGY is heavily influenced by Philomena Donnelly's work on philosophy with children (Donnelly 2001, 2004) and Julia Ipgrave's dialogical approach where children engage actively with religious questions and negotiate their way through different viewpoints and understandings (McKenna, Ipgrave and Jackson 2008). Robert Jackson's interpretive approach has also been influential in shaping the curriculum's commitment to engaging with the real-life experiences and the interests of children as well as local representations of diverse religious and belief communities in family projects (McKenna, Ipgrave and Jackson 2008: 16).

Conclusion

In contemporary Ireland, primary RE is undergoing rapid transition and its complex nature, integrity and existence is subject to ongoing debate. Indeed, the predominance of Catholic RE in denominational schools has led to critique and resistance to faith schools in the form of Atheist Ireland's 'Teach Don't Preach' campaign (Nugent and Donnelly 2013; Park 2019). In a more secular Irish society (Lodge 2021), the educational basis of RE has sometimes been underappreciated and viewed as potentially indoctrinatory and discriminatory (Meehan and O'Connell 2021: 199). With an increasing focus on 'Wellbeing' in the curriculum (NCCA 2020), there is debate about the future status of RE and fear that it will be eclipsed by Wellbeing and ERBE. Some see ERBE as a wake-up call for the Catholic church (Conway 2012) and the state's attempt to secularize faith schools and replace confessional RE (Van Nieuwenhove 2012).

Overall, a lack of terminological and conceptual clarity in the area has resulted in the absence of agreed foundational principles or a common understanding of the discipline's location within the educational and academic landscape. While language around RE can be viewed as encumbered and a proliferation of confusing terms are found in the NCCA's Draft Primary Curriculum Framework (2020), there is a simultaneous realization that the multiple forms of learning in, from and about RE operative in Ireland have contributed to a growing curiosity about diverse approaches, as well as a creative and nuanced desire to expand the discipline and engage in the work of clarifying and refining its foundational principles and terminology. Current research and debate is moving beyond simplistic binaries through an appreciation that confessional RE is not inherently indoctrinatory and that ERBE and multi-denominational RE do not represent a neutral and objective, value-free engagement with religious data.

Further, it is also appreciated that multiple forms of RE can be operative in the one school or classroom where one learner's affective, experience-based and personal engagement with a faith tradition is not necessarily replicated by the learner sitting next to them who may have a more impersonal and factual response to identical material. While research in RE has tended to foreground pragmatic issues around patronage, schooling, ethos and rights to access or withdraw from specific types of educational programmes in Ireland, there are also exciting new developments exploring the queering of RE (Henry 2021), belief fluidity (Harmon 2018), multi-denominational RE (Hyland 1989; Irwin 2013; Conboy 2017; Mullally 2018), the foundational principles of RE (Shanahan 2017) and RE's hermeneutical task in Ireland (Kennedy 2021).

Overall, while there is confusion and uncertainty, there are many positive scholarly and curricular developments, multiple initiatives and new energies around primary RE in Ireland. There are clear signs of revitalization through RE's expansion as an academic discipline with the establishment of doctoral programmes in many universities. In recent decades, there has been a marked increase in high-quality interdisciplinary scholarship and publication output. The twenty-first century has witnessed much greater cross-sectoral, educationally informed academic collaboration situating RE in Ireland within a wider international and academic context. There has also been a greater spirit of partnership, collegiality and ecumenical and inter-religious dialogue through collaboration between the Catholic and C of I programmes and through ERBE programmes. In 2021, the Islamic Cultural Centre of Ireland generated new online RE programmes to educate teachers and students in all school sectors about Islam and Quranic Studies. With increasing research and a cross-fertilization of ideas as well as innovative dialogical inter-belief approaches, which acknowledge, respect and support difference, there is great hope for the future of the discipline.

Chapter 5

UNDERSTANDING THE SOCIOLOGY OF RELIGION IN CONTEMPORARY IRELAND

Gladys Ganiel

Introduction

This chapter explores sociology's contributions to understanding religion in contemporary Ireland. While most studies analyse either the Republic of Ireland or Northern Ireland, it takes an all-island approach.[1] There are good reasons why sociologists have limited their analysis to one part of the island: even though churches remained organized on an all-island basis after partition in 1921, the different relationships between churches and the state in each jurisdiction helped create very different religious contexts.[2] This chapter ultimately argues that scholarship would be enhanced by more all-island studies and hopes to inspire such a trend. Having said that, the chapter is organized in an admittedly 'partitionist' manner, in that it first considers sociology of religion in the Republic before turning its attention to Northern Ireland. This simply reflects the scholarship in the field: the main debates in the Republic have coalesced around secularization, especially the dramatic decline of the Catholic church, while the violence of 'the Troubles' (*c.*1968–98) has meant that scholars working on Northern Ireland concentrated on relationships between religion, conflict and peacebuilding. These sections analyse sociological contributions to these debates, before a third and final section identifies ongoing and new areas for research in an all-island context. Of course, the sociology of religion has been enriched by its interaction with other disciplines.

The chapter's primary concern is Christianity, recognizing that many of the best studies of other religions have been carried out by scholars in other disciplines. But in order to analyse sociology's unique contributions, this chapter limits its engagement with studies from other disciplines, though some are mentioned briefly to provide broader context. Accordingly, the chapter focuses on works that have engaged with existing sociological concepts and theories or created new concepts or ideal types to help explain religion on the island.

Secularization and religious persistence in the Republic of Ireland

For a generation of sociologists, secularization has been a dominant paradigm for analysing religion in Western societies. Until the late 1990s, Ireland was often presented as a highly religious outlier to secularizing trends (Nic Ghiolla Phádraig 1995, 2009). In more recent years, the Republic has secularized at breakneck speed, catching up with or surpassing other Western societies with its indicators of religious decline (Turpin 2019). Understandably, the sociology of religion in Ireland has been concerned with explaining religion's sudden decline. In line with patterns in other secularizing societies, religion's decline can be measured in three main ways (Casanova 2006): (1) the separation of religion from politics; (2) religion's decline in public influence and the privatization of religious belief; and (3) declines in religious practice, belief and identification. The studies discussed below shed light on declines in these three areas.

First, some brief historical context provides a sense of the importance of religion before its recent decline. Partition reflected and solidified religious differences between Catholics and Protestants, which overlapped with opposing ethno-national identities. The Irish Free State, later Republic, was overwhelmingly Catholic.[3] The Catholic church was entrusted with education and healthcare, and influenced social policies in areas like divorce, contraception and abortion. The state's early economic policies were agrarian and protectionist, in line with Catholic social teaching that urged caution about industrialization and capitalism, stunting economic development. Censorship was widespread and generally supported by a conservative population. Catholicism was a key component of national identity, which was conceived as not British and not Protestant. By 1972, weekly church attendance in the Republic was still over 90 per cent (Ganiel 2016a: 34). Of course, churches had once played important political and social roles in other Western nations, so the Republic was not unusual in this regard. What was unusual is that quite strong religious influence persisted throughout the 1960s and beyond, when it was declining elsewhere.

Tom Inglis's *Moral Monopoly: The Catholic Church in Modern Irish Society* is the foundational sociological text for explaining the Catholic church's all-encompassing role during much of the twentieth century. First published in 1987, it describes a totalizing Catholic *habitus* that moulded people's values, attitudes and behaviours. The Catholic church was a key shaper of *habitus*, achieving symbolic domination of Irish life. The church was highly clerical, with the deference and devotion of laity expected and by and large received. At the same time, *habitus* was maintained by people's everyday social interactions and their perceptions of what it meant to be a good person, which were grounded in Catholic teachings around sexuality, fertility, humility and so on. The second edition of the book was published in 1998, with a telling new subtitle: *The Rise and Fall of the Catholic Church in Modern Ireland*. Like the first edition, it analysed the factors that had been contributing to declines in religiosity since the 1960s, such as the end of protectionism and tentative economic growth, and the role of a more assertive media.

Inglis also devoted substantial analysis to the changing role of women, describing how a partnership of priests and mothers that had worked so effectively to socialize generations began to break down as more women began working outside the home and making decisions for themselves about sexuality and reproduction. The experiences of women were further explored in Betty Hilliard's (2003) study of Catholic women between 1975 and 2000. Hilliard documented how women's relationships with the Catholic church moved from ones of domination, to resistance, to altered consciousness and changed practices. Inglis (1998) also took into account the acceleration of secularization related to the economic growth of the Celtic Tiger (late 1990s to c.2008) and mentioned the impact of clerical sexual scandals, although many more revelations about the extent and management of abuse were still to come.[4]

The decisive role of the media in unravelling the Catholic church's moral monopoly was also taken up by Susie Donnelly (2016; see also Inglis 2000). She argued that journalists' coverage of the Second Vatican Council was a watershed for more critical coverage of the church, which paved the way for the reporting of clerical scandals from the 1990s onwards. This new journalistic approach was accompanied by greater accessibility to television. *The Late, Late* chat show promoted liberalizing debate, while sitcoms depicted desirable, materialistic lifestyles at odds with a humble, traditional Catholic *habitus* (Donnelly and Inglis 2010). For Donnelly and Inglis (2010: 1), the media's role in dismantling Catholic power has been so decisive that it has 'replaced the Catholic Church as the social conscience and moral guardian of Irish society'. Media coverage of a series of reports on inquiries into abuse between 2009 and 2021 provided occasions for the Catholic church to be depicted as evil – and for the media itself to assume the moral high ground through its exposure of abusers (see also Weatherred 2014).

The results of a series of referenda illustrate the weakening of the relationship between church and state, and the public's abandonment of conservative Catholic mores. In 1973, the public voted by referendum to remove the 'special position' of the Catholic church from the constitution. Contraception was legalized in 1980. Other referenda legalized divorce (1995), same-sex marriage (2015) and repealed the Eighth Amendment of the Constitution, which had prohibited abortion in all but the most restrictive of cases (2018). There were also drops in religious practice, belief and identification. In the Republic, Mass attendance had fallen from 66 per cent in 1997 to 35 per cent in 2016, with figures much lower in some urban parishes.[5] Between 1981 and 2008, there were small but steady declines in the importance people placed on religion in their lives; declines in belief in a personal god, life after death, heaven, hell and sin; and declines in confidence in the Catholic church (Breen and Reynolds 2011; Ó Féich and O'Connell 2015).[6] Identification as Catholic on the Census fell, from 94 per cent in 1971, to 88 per cent in 2002, to 78 per cent in 2016. There was an increase in those identifying as 'no religion', from 2 per cent in the 1991 Census to around 10 per cent in 2016. After Catholic, 'no religion' was the second-most popular option on the 2016 Census, ahead of the Church of Ireland (about 3 per cent). Pew's 2017 survey found 15 per cent identified as 'religiously unaffiliated', and the 2018 European Social Survey put this figure at 32 per cent (Pew Research Center 2018; O'Connell et al. 2019).

But even with this much decline, Pew's survey found that 24 per cent of people in the Republic were 'highly religious', ranking fifteenth in Europe and third in Western Europe, behind only Portugal and Italy.[7] As such, sociologists of religion also have been concerned with explaining religious persistence in the midst of decline. Inglis (2007) was among the first to explore religious persistence, describing it as 'de-institutionalisation'. He observed that Catholics were increasingly detaching themselves from the 'institutional' church, identifying with a Catholic religious heritage while picking and choosing beliefs and practices. Drawing on a major qualitative study (2003–5), as well as European Values Survey data, he developed a fourfold typology of Irish Catholics: (1) orthodox: 'loyal members of the institutional Church' who practice regularly and conform to the teachings of the institutional church (Inglis 2007: 214); (2) creative: Catholics who 'both believe and belong' but select their beliefs and practice from a range of options within Catholicism and other religions (Inglis 2007: 215); (3) cultural: Catholics who are detached from the institutional church yet still avail of its sacraments on occasion (especially baptisms, first communions, weddings, funerals) (Inglis 2007: 215–16); and (4) individualist: those who identify as Catholic but reject the institution and have 'developed a nebulous New Age orientation to religion that revolves around a search for personal authenticity' (Inglis 2007: 216). Inglis noted that the orthodox variant was small and declining, while arguing that being Catholic was not part of most Irish people's 'everyday image of themselves'. Yet he concluded,

> Irish Catholics still like the Catholic way of being spiritual and moral; they like being recognised and accepted as part of a community and the feeling of belonging and bonding. Being Catholic is part of their cultural heritage. It will not disappear quickly. (2007: 218)

Karen Andersen's (2010: 37) analysis of Irish data in the 'Church and Religion in an Enlarged Europe' survey confirmed Catholics' increasing distance from the institutional church. She argued that there was 'a new Catholic habitus … where being Catholic entails exercising individual choice and being critical and selective'. Michael Breen and Caillin Reynolds (2011: 9) drew a similar conclusion in their analysis of European Values Surveys, while at the same time observing that Ireland remained 'outstandingly religious' compared with the rest of Europe. Pádraig Ó Féich and Michael O'Connell (2015: 240–3) also used European Values Survey data to identify a strand of 'liberal' Catholics, who disagreed with church teachings on homosexuality, euthanasia, divorce, taking 'soft drugs', abortion and prostitution. They calculated that liberal Catholics had increased from 14 per cent in 1981 to 45 per cent in 2008. Similarly, Vesna Malešević explored how religion persisted despite declines in loyalty to the 'institutional' Catholic church. Using a 'neo-secularization' approach that emphasized the decline of religious authority rather than a straightforward decline of religion per se, she argued that the social significance of Ireland's churches would decline further unless they adjusted to their loss of control, with targeted efforts 'to meet the needs' of a changing society (Malešević 2010: 36).

Research carried out around 2009 and thereafter revealed further declines and even more critical attitudes towards the Catholic church. This date coincides with the publication of reports on two state inquiries: The Commission to Inquire into Child Abuse in reformatory and industrial schools (Ryan Report 2009) and the Archdiocese of Dublin (Murphy Report 2009). Both reports were covered extensively in the media and brought the scale and severity of abuse into public consciousness, further damaging the Catholic church's reputation. While it would be too much to claim that these reports accelerated secularization, they may have contributed to people's willingness to express dissatisfaction with the Catholic church.[8] Further, Breen and Amy Erbe Healy's (2014) analysis of European Social Survey data found steeper drops in attendance, prayer and self-rated religiosity after 2008. A substantial interview-based study by Inglis, conducted between 2008 and 2009, signalled a profound change, hinting towards a more rapid 'disappearance' than he anticipated earlier. Inglis revised his fourfold typology: 'individualist' Catholics disappeared entirely in favour of the 'disenchanted' – those who opposed the institutional church. He noted that even orthodox Catholics compartmentalized their practice, a far cry from the all-encompassing *habitus* of previous generations. While the persistence of cultural Catholicism meant religion retained some societal resonance, Inglis concluded that other sources of meaning like sport, family, success, politics and love were of greater concern to most people than god or religion. As he summed it up, 'There were few indications that God was in their minds and hearts and on their lips' (Inglis 2014: 188).

I also found Catholic 'disenchantment' in a major interview-based study conducted between 2009 and 2010 (Ganiel 2016a). It was initially concerned with analysing increasing religious diversity and changing ecumenical relations. But what I discovered was that Irish people – of all religions – could not stop talking about Catholicism. Accordingly, the study morphed into an examination of 'post-Catholic' Ireland, with a major focus on how devout individuals attempted to distance themselves from the 'institutional' church. I developed the concept of 'extra-institutional religion' to capture how people described their own faith practices as 'outside or in addition to' the institutional church (see also Ganiel 2019). Some retained links with the institution while seeking or creating additional religious spaces outside it; others severed links with the institution altogether in favour of new religious spaces. At the same time, I conceived of the Irish religious field as a 'post-Catholic' religious market (Ganiel 2016a). Post-Catholic was an empirical description of how the religious field had changed, not a simplistic claim that Ireland was once Catholic, and now it is not. Rather, the Republic was post-Catholic in the sense that there had been a shift in consciousness in the way people conceived of Catholicism: the institutional church was not esteemed but was distrusted or mocked.

More recently, anthropologist Hugh Turpin (2019) explored new ground with his attention to ex-Catholics, whose perspectives have been neglected in Irish sociology. Turpin found that the two main reasons ex-Catholics chose disaffiliation were dissatisfaction with moral conservatism and clerical abuse. He described a non-religious orientation that was deeply moral in its opposition not only to the church but also to cultural Catholics whose apathy was condemned for propping up a pernicious institution. Further comparative research is necessary, but Turpin (2019: 194) postulated that Irish ex-Catholicism is 'notable' for its energetic opposition to cultural Catholicism. Indeed, a comparative analysis of 2008 European Values Survey data from fourteen countries found the Republic had simultaneously the widest support for religion and the strongest anti-religious sentiment (Ribberink, Acherberg and Houtman 2013). Turpin's documentation of cultural Catholicism was much in line with Inglis's earlier observations, although Turpin emphasized that for many cultural Catholics their religious practice was 'marked by experiences of boredom, irrelevance, and transparent social conformism', with religiosity reduced to a cynical use of the sacraments (baptism to get children into a good Catholic school; a church wedding to please granny) (Turpin 2019: 192).

While the studies discussed above have been almost exclusively focused on the Republic, Breen (2017) and Brian Conway (2014a, 2014b) have consistently situated the Irish case in the comparative, international sociology of religion.[9] Breen's (2017) edited volume contextualized Irish data on secularization and religiosity from European Social Surveys in a wider European context. In a 2018 article, Conway and Bram Spruyt explained variations in Catholic religiosity across fifty-two countries, exploring the impact of major explanatory frameworks in the sociology of religion such as modernization, the dynamics of internal religious markets, existential security (a perspective based on Pippa Norris and Ronald Inglehart's (2011) theory that countries with greater human and material security will be less religious) and historical legacies like the role of the church in constructing national identity, communism, scandal and colonialism. They found the strongest support for the existential security approach; in other words, insecure, precarious societies exhibit higher levels of religiosity. They also found some support for the historical legacies perspective. For example, countries with a history of colonialism and which became independent in the twentieth century have higher levels of Mass attendance. Those factors go some way towards explaining the Republic's higher levels of religiosity when compared to other European nations. This finding was in line with an earlier analysis of European Values Survey data on Catholic church attendance in Ireland, Belgium and Slovenia. Here, Conway (2013) found that the convergence between ethnic and religious identity in Ireland, related to historic conflict, contributed to higher church attendance rates. At the same time, Healy and Breen's (2014) analysis of European Social Survey data after the 2008 economic crisis in Ireland, Spain and Portugal – traditionally Catholic countries that endured stringent austerity measures – did not support the hypothesis that economic insecurity increases religiosity at a societal level. However, there was some evidence supporting the hypothesis at a personal level, especially among recent immigrants.

In a result Conway and Spruyt (2018: 296) describe as 'surprising', there was no statistical support for the legacy of abuse scandals as a factor in eroding religiosity, although they admitted that 'it may be that the impact of relatively recent scandal on religious commitment is a gradual process and thus may best be observed over time in each country, rather than between countries'. The Irish data was from 2008, just before the qualitative research discussed above, began picking up so much 'disenchantment'. Healy and Breen's (2014: 23) work on the more recent European Social Survey data also suggests an accelerated decline in religiosity after 2008, with the abuse crisis identified as a possible contributor.

In sum, Irish sociology of religion's focus on explaining the decline of Catholic church influence and Catholic religiosity has yielded valuable insights and explanatory concepts and frameworks. Irish secularization also has been considered in comparative perspective. At the same time, there has been a relative neglect of other important areas of concern, such as everyday religion, the role of women, young people's religiosity, religion and immigration and non-Christian religions.

The sociology of religion, conflict and peacebuilding in Northern Ireland

The sociology of religion in Northern Ireland has been dominated by 'the Troubles' (*c.*1968–98) and the division between the so-called 'two communities': Catholic-nationalist-republican and Protestant-unionist-loyalist, a division that extends over centuries and is linked with British colonialism. Between partition and 'the Troubles', a Protestant unionist majority dominated political and economic life. Protestant religion had a privileged relationship with unionist political power, and a Calvinist-informed evangelical movement shaped wider Protestant culture. For Northern Ireland's substantial Catholic minority, which did not trust the state, the Catholic church became the most important institution for organizing and shaping communal life. Religious identification and practice were in part a way to identify with one's community, artificially inflating religiosity (Mitchell 2004). In the late 1960s weekly attendance was around 95 per cent among Catholics and 66 per cent among Protestants (Ganiel 2016a: 34–5; see also Hayes and Dowds 2010).[10]

Like the Republic, Northern Ireland has experienced secularization since the 1960s. The churches' relationships with political power weakened substantially during 'the Troubles', especially after the Northern Ireland parliament was prorogued in 1972 (Mitchel 2003). The 1998 Good Friday Agreement established a power-sharing assembly, and although evangelical Protestants retained some influence through links with the Democratic Unionist Party (DUP), this was much reduced (Ganiel 2006; Ganiel and Dixon 2008). Religion became less important in informing social mores and values, including attitudes to homosexuality and abortion, except among those with high levels of religious practice (Hayes and Dowds 2015). Among Catholics, attendance dropped to 81 per cent (monthly) in 1998 to 46 per cent in 2019, while for Protestants monthly attendance was 52 per cent in 1998 and 46 per cent in 2019 (Ganiel 2016a: 34–6; see also Hayes and Dowds 2010).[11] The more dramatic declines in attendance since 1998 – the year of the peace agreement – seem to lend some credence to the idea that religious practice was in part a response to 'the Troubles', especially among Catholics, where the decline was steeper. At the same time, Northern Ireland remains less secularized than the Republic: church attendance figures are higher among both Catholics and Protestants and qualitative studies have found that people are more likely to consider religious aspects of their identity important than in the Republic (Todd 2014, 2018; Ganiel 2016b).

Steve Bruce's work was vital for establishing the social significance of religion in wider interdisciplinary debates about the conflict, especially given a tendency for some scholars to downplay its importance (see McGarry and O'Leary 1995). Bruce's 1986 *God Save Ulster* was a landmark study that grappled with the career of Revd Ian Paisley, founder of both the Free Presbyterian Church (1951) and the DUP (1971). Paisley got his start as an anti-ecumenical and anti-Catholic preacher who warned against the perils of compromise with 'Rome' (Cooke 1996). Though the DUP was at that time the second party of unionism and the Free Presbyterian Church has remained small, Bruce argued that Paisley's prominence revealed the importance of evangelicalism for a wider (even secularizing) Protestant unionist community. For Bruce, evangelicalism provided the basis for the 'core' of Protestant identity, making religion a more important aspect of ethno-national identity for Protestants than it was for Catholics.[12]

Another major contribution was John Brewer's 1998 *The Mote and the Beam: Anti-Catholicism in Northern Ireland*, which developed a distinct 'sociology of anti-Catholicism' at the level of ideas, individual behaviours and social structures. Brewer (1998: 210) characterized anti-Catholicism as a mobilizing resource in group conflict, used 'to defend the socio-economic and political position of Protestants against opposition.' He also identified three 'modes' of active anti-Catholicism: a covenantal mode that conceived of Ulster Protestants as a chosen people, framing Catholicism as a political and existential threat; a secular mode focused on defence of the union, framing Catholicism as a threat to political and civil liberties; and a Pharisaic mode that conceived of Catholics as Christians in error, and sought to evangelize them (Brewer 1998: 133). These modes contributed to greater understanding of the subtle and diverse impact of anti-Catholicism on Protestant conceptions of Catholics and their relationships with them.

Claire Mitchell (2005) moved debate significantly beyond the claim that religion was simply an 'ethnic marker', demonstrating that it structured social life and helped give meaning to the content of ethno-national identities. Most of her fieldwork was conducted in the years immediately following the peace agreement, providing a snapshot of how religion shaped approaches to politics and individual identity formation. She emphasized the importance of evangelicalism and Calvinistic theology for Protestant identity, in politics and in people's everyday lives. At the same time, she challenged the scholarly neglect of the role of religion in the Catholic community, arguing that social and institutional forms of Catholicism were crucial for shaping community life and identity.

Like Mitchell, my fieldwork on evangelicalism was conducted in the decade after the agreement, an unsettled period which brought an end to most violence and a new power-sharing assembly that signalled a decisive end to unionist privilege (Ganiel 2008). Pushing beyond the fundamentalist evangelicalism associated with Paisley, I identified four 'empirical types' of evangelicals: a 'traditional' type similar to Brewer's covenantal mode; a 'mediating' type that sought to reform evangelical ideas and identities in a reconciliatory direction; a 'pietist' type that withdrew from society and politics, focusing on their inner lives; and a 'post-evangelical' type that had become disillusioned with the relationship between evangelicalism and politics and sought more radical religious and political alternatives (see also Ganiel and Marti 2014). A key factor for evangelicals who moved from traditional to mediating identities was learning to critique their own evangelical tradition, including the theological ideas that had justified division and violence. The activism of an organization called Evangelical Contribution on Northern Ireland (ECONI) was crucial in stimulating this process, because it provided biblically based resources like training courses, a magazine and other publications to justify a new, reconciliatory orientation. Because of evangelicalism's historic importance to wider Protestant unionist identity, I argued that ECONI had been the most important faith-based peacebuilding organization during a key period in the 1990s, stimulating grassroots identity change.

Northern Ireland has also featured in the international, comparative study of religion in peace processes. Brewer's work has been pioneering, both in its advocacy for the inclusion of religion in a wider sociology of peace processes (2010) and in its development of a theoretical framework for understanding the role of religion in peace processes (2011). His theoretical framework was informed by his comparative research but developed most fully in *Religion, Civil Society and Peace in Northern Ireland*, where it was applied to the Northern Ireland case. Brewer argued that religion can occupy four civil society 'spaces' in peace processes: (1) intellectual, in which alternative ideas are envisioned; (2) institutional, in which faith-based groups model peacebuilding practices; (3) market, in which faith-based groups devote substantial material and human resources to peace and communicate with policy makers; and (4) political, in which faith-based actors engage with politicians behind the scenes or in formal peace negotiations. Drawing on Brewer, Vladimir Kmec and I argued that religious actors' contributions are maximized when they work at the grassroots, especially in communities where they enjoy high levels of legitimacy; but they risk being compromised by political power if they are too involved in formal peace negotiations (Kmec and Ganiel 2019).

Brewer also noted that religious actors risk being co-opted by ethnic elites, so they may not go far enough in taking risks for peace. Added to that, institutional religions often have unwieldy governance structures and memberships with diverse perspectives on how to approach issues like peacebuilding, resulting in slow, tentative action – or no action at all. In contrast, those from minority religious groups or on the margins of majority religions have more flexibility to critique their own communities and offer creative approaches to peacebuilding, unconstrained by the structures and concerns of larger religious organizations. On the other hand, minority and marginal actors are constrained by a lack of resources when compared to institutional religions and their relatively well-financed structures and activities. Brewer conceptualized these 'marginal' actors as 'mavericks', arguing that in Northern Ireland, they made more significant contributions to peacebuilding than the 'institutional' churches. This argument is readily supported by a substantial interdisciplinary literature on religion and peacebuilding in Northern Ireland, which has emphasized the courageous grassroots efforts of individual clerics and other faith leaders (Wells 2010; Scull 2019), and organizations like ECONI and the ecumenical Corrymeela community (Mitchel 2003; Ganiel 2008; Robinson 2014). Conversely, the role of church leaders in calling for calm and producing statements condemning violence is noted but criticized for not going far enough (Brewer 2011).[13]

The peace ministry of one of those mavericks, Fr Gerry Reynolds, provided the basis for my preliminary theoretical framework for understanding the role of prayer in faith-based peacebuilding, an area that has been neglected in the wider study of religion and peacebuilding (Ganiel 2021a). Combining examples from Reynolds's life with the literature on the sociology of prayer, the framework encompasses two individual effects of prayer: prompting religious identity change and sustaining hope and activism during adversity, with an additional sociopolitical effect of prayer: creating and sustaining real-world initiatives. I argued that prayer should be included as a variable in future research on faith-based peacebuilding, including cross-national studies.

In sum, sociological studies of religion in Northern Ireland have yielded insights on religion, conflict and peacebuilding which contribute to the international literature. The sociology of everyday religion has been neglected, although Mitchell and I (2011) attempted to begin filling this gap in our study of evangelicalism. We described the sociocultural as well as the overtly political aspects of this religious subculture, while emphasizing evangelicalism's internal diversity and capacity for change. Even so, one reviewer remarked that 'the most intriguing aspect of the study is the unusually strong reciprocal relationship of politics and changes in religious identity', highlighting how even studies of everyday religion in Northern Ireland tend to drift back to politics, conflict and peace (Green 2012: 1235–6). In addition, Sandra Baillie's (2002) research on evangelical women shed some light on women's everyday religious attitudes and practices while adopting an 'evangelical feminist' perspective. Adrian Stringer's (2013) studies of Bahá'í, Catholic, Anglican and independent congregations provided further perspectives on everyday religion, emphasizing the importance of familial relationships and wider social networks for maintaining congregational life, while anthropologist Liam Murphy's (2010) study of charismatic Christians explored innovations in religio-cultural identity as well as everyday religious practices. But as in the Republic, the role of women, young people's religiosity, religion and immigration, and non-Christian religions remain under-researched.

Conclusion: Future directions

Among the areas for future research identified above, the study of religion and immigration has gained some momentum in the Republic, where immigration has been more substantial than in Northern Ireland. Antje Röder's (2017) analysis of 2016 Census data in the Republic provides a good starting point, documenting small but significant growth within long-standing Irish Protestant denominations, other Christian traditions and non-Christian religions. Qualitative and ethnographic research has fleshed out the statistical data, including studies of African Pentecostals (Ugba 2009),[14] migrant chaplains (Gray and O'Sullivan Lago 2011), Irish Mormonism (O'Brien 2019, 2020a), Muslims (Scharbrodt et al. 2015) and a German-speaking Lutheran congregation in Dublin (Ritter and Kmec 2017). *Transforming Post-Catholic Ireland* included case studies of three further congregations: the Jesus Centre in Dublin City, a Redeemed Christian Church of God parish;[15] Abundant Life, a multi-ethnic, charismatic congregation in Limerick City; and St Patrick's in Waterford City, a Methodist congregation which had doubled in size due to the attendance of immigrants (Ganiel 2016a). In some ways these studies aligned with international research on immigration and/or multi-ethnic congregations, which emphasize the importance of faith communities for easing immigrants' transitions in their new countries, and the intentional measures required for promoting congregational integration among different ethnic groups. Other findings are more uniquely Irish, such as the conviction of some immigrants that their mission includes 're-evangelizing' the Irish, who they perceive as secular, or the fresh perspectives that those from 'new' Christian communities have brought to ecumenical dialogues previously shaped by historic Catholic–Protestant divisions.

Other new directions were showcased in a 2016 e-forum of the *Irish Journal of Sociology*, which collated articles on religion published between 2009 and 2016. This included research already cited in this chapter, a report on interdisciplinary research on new religious movements (Cox 2012)[16] and articles on parents and the ethos of religious schools (Kitching 2013), Catholic female religious and the transnationalization of care (Yeates 2011), and the industrial schools and child welfare (Pembroke 2013).

In addition, religion's capacity to adapt to social change has been tested by the Covid-19 pandemic (O'Brien 2020b), which prompted most of the island's parishes and congregations to move services online during lockdown in March 2020. Across denominations, the provision of online services increased from 56 to 87 per cent, and there were increases in prayer and lay volunteerism, as well as surprisingly high numbers of people accessing online services (Ganiel 2020, 2021b). Irish clergy – North and South – framed the pandemic as an opportunity to carve out new societal roles in the midst of secularizing societies – despite evidence that some people do not intend to return to in-person services when lockdowns are over (Ganiel 2021c). This research is ongoing and is exploring the impact of the pandemic on the practices of everyday religion across denominations and on ecumenical relationships, North and South.

Future studies in the sociology of religion could fruitfully compare processes of secularization across the island, analysing changing relationships between religion and the state as well as processes of identity change. The impact of the abuse scandals also has been under-researched. Here, North–South comparisons could be especially interesting due to the different roles played and the amount of power previously held by the Catholic church in each jurisdiction. Increases in those identifying as 'no religion' could be compared on an all-island basis, including any links between disaffiliation and disillusionment with the abuse scandals. All-island studies also are necessary for understanding the impact of Brexit on ethno-national and religious identities. Finally, there is plenty of scope for all-island, comparative studies on non-Christian religions, religion and immigration, the role of women, young people's religiosity and how religion adapted during the pandemic.

The sociology of religion has not enjoyed a particularly high profile in universities on the island – despite the best efforts of those (and others) whose work has been considered in this chapter, including scholars who have made considerable contributions to debates beyond Irish contexts.[17] Some generalist sociologists include religion in their analysis, but there are few religion specialists in sociology departments. I have perhaps over-cited my own research here, but that is because I am one of that small band of sociologists of religion. In that light, perhaps the most urgent task for an all-island sociology of religion is to make its case for its importance to social scientific research, reaching beyond the boundaries of the subfield to inform wider sociological and interdisciplinary debates.

Part II

THEMES IN THE CONTEMPORARY STUDY
OF RELIGIONS IN IRELAND

Chapter 6

ESOTERICISM, ROMANTIC NATIONALISM AND THE BIRTH OF THE IRISH STATE

Jenny Butler

While much has been written about the connection between Catholic religiosity and Irish nationalism, and the consequent merging of the two in the state's foundation, much less attention has been paid to the role of esotericism and Romantic nationalism in the birth of the Irish nation. While the prevailing Irish nationalist perspective of the late nineteenth century and early decades of the twentieth century was infused with Roman Catholic values and ideals, it must be acknowledged that intertwined esoteric and Romantic nationalist influences were important in propelling forward the cause of Irish independence. During the establishment of the Irish Free State and since, a cluster of meanings coalesced to form the foremost image projected onto and about the country and its people, that of 'Holy Catholic Ireland'. This image and concept overshadowed the much more intricate cultural and ideological tapestry of the time. Examining the influence of a combination of Romantic nationalist and esoteric ideas on the world views and activities of key figures during the revolutionary period and foundation of the Irish state brings the significance of these cultural forces to light.

Generally, in studies of Irish life, history and the foundation of the state, emphasis is placed on Catholic identity as oppositional to Protestant Englishness. It would seem strange, however, to overlook the occult interests and Protestant background of an entire group given that the Literary Revival was a nexus for political activism and cultural nationalism. The esoteric milieu was important for many of the key players in the fight for Irish independence and must be acknowledged as, at the very least, an adhesive force in bringing particular people together as well as a significant aspect that informed their world view. Prominent figures of the Literary Revival who were involved in esotericism were also engaged directly in revolutionary activities, were outspoken nationalists or were friends and allies of key nationalist and revolutionary figures who were outside of the esoteric and literary scene.

The role of Irish Protestants and those of Anglo-Irish heritage in the independence movement was pushed out of the dominant narrative of the new state. There grew a conceptual basis of an 'Irish Ireland' and 'true Irishness' which excluded Protestants and anyone with a lineage connecting them to the ascendancy class. 'The version of nationalism that developed in the late nineteenth century,' as Deirdre Nuttall (2020: 89) observes, 'became integral to the emerging nation, denying the "true" Irishness of Protestants.' Taking a closer look at the era, prior to the Easter Rising, during the revolution and during the foundation of the Free State, we find that many of the Irish nationalists involved in art and literary scenes were influenced by their interests in Western esotericism or were indeed practising occultists. Mythological tropes alongside spiritual themes of folk culture were utilized by writers, artists and activists of this era in a collective imagining of Irishness.

Protestant lineage, nationalist leanings

The key figures of the Irish Literary Revival, including Maud Gonne, Ella Young, Alice Milligan, William Butler Yeats, George William Russell, John Millington Synge and James Henry Cousins, were instigators of Ireland's Celtic Revival, practicing occultists, folklore collectors or enthusiasts and supporters of Irish nationalism and the fight for independence from Britain. Part of what bonded this group together was esotericism – they shared interests in magical practices and some joined esoteric organizations. These and many others of similar background were significant players in the struggle for an independent Ireland and yet such Protestant identities and experiences were sidelined in the new state's official representation and dominant narratives and images of Catholic Irishness. 'Ascendancy authors Yeats and Gregory,' remarks Karen Steele (2019: 73), 'empowered their cultural nationalism by lionising Protestant republicanism.' While the utilization of Protestant nationalist vigour is true, it worked in tandem with other forces, influences and ideals including Romanticism and esotericism. Others in this circle, such as Synge, rejected Protestant religion and his own class background outright.

Yeats was born in Sandymount, a suburb on the south side of Dublin, to an Anglo-Irish family. As one of Ireland's best-known literary figures, and one of the foremost figures of twentieth-century literature in general, he gave the name 'Celtic Twilight' to the literary renaissance and cultural movement to revive ancient Irish traditions itself, named for the title of his 1893 book. Yeats was instrumental in the cultural nationalist movement and in 1922 was appointed a senator of the Irish Free State and served through two terms up until 1928. Favouring cultural nationalism, which focuses on the inclusiveness of national identity, he expressed his views through writing. Although of an Anglo-Irish background and moving in elite and upper-middle-class social circles, Yeats did much to increase understanding of aspects of Irish culture both in Ireland and Britain and highlighted the existence of a distinct Irish identity. His Romantic leanings meant that his views were presented in a less provocative manner than other forms of nationalism which were based in politics and cultural exclusion and aimed for the segregation or elimination of what was understood as British culture and identities from Ireland.

His earlier volumes of poetry contained 'romantic images of Irish nationalism' (Bradley 2000: 289). It's clear that Yeats saw a connection between creative work and nationalism, and Stephen Regan (2006: 88) records that 'throughout the 1890s Yeats liked to proclaim that "there is no great literature without nationality, no great nationality without literature"' and adds that 'there is no doubt that he saw literature as having a crucial role in revitalising Irish national pride and in creating a unified culture'.

As has been noted, 'Yeats's career – from his first collection of poems, *The Wanderings of Oisin, and Other Poems* (1889), to the 1939 collection *Last Poems and Two Plays* – clearly dominates any account of Revival poetry' (Kelleher 2019: 86), yet the poet's nationalist writings and occult interests and influences have each been largely examined in a stand-alone manner by scholars. Indeed, some historians have viewed the esoteric involvements of this group in quite a pejorative manner. Referring to Irish historian Robert Fitzroy Foster's article 'Protestant Magic: W.B. Yeats and the Spell of Irish History', Selina Guinness (2003: 14) notes that 'Yeats's interest in occultism is here characterized as a sort of occult fiddling while the gentry burns' and rebuffs the view of Foster and others that the occult involvement of this group of Protestant lineage was an escape from Irish history, rather than an engagement with it. Various scholars have remarked on Yeats's position as a member of the ascendancy class who supported Irish nationalism. Anthony Bradley (2000: 290) remarks on Yeats's work, 'imbued as it is with the problematic issues of nationality and identity that arise from Ireland's colonial predicament and Yeats's own membership in the literary and artistic fraction of what had been the colonising class in Ireland'.

Writing on Yeats's work, *A Vision*, Claire Nally (2010: 19, 20) maintains that 'it is critically naïve to detach the arcane from the political impulses in which it was produced' and continues that 'for Yeats, the invention of a tradition was negotiated through an occult belief system, aligned to the Anglo-Irish loss of ascendancy in the early twentieth century'. Engagement with native Gaelic Irish tradition was also mediated through an occult world view. Esotericism provided another door to the other world, accessed by way of their class contacts in Ireland and England, who were partaking in spiritualism, automatic writing, seances, theosophy and other influential ideas and practices. Esoteric interests and activities were something Yeats shared with his social peers, close friends and wider social class.

Both esoteric and folkloric topics and themes fascinated Yeats throughout his life, including spiritualism, reincarnation, spiritual dimensions, communication with the dead, magical practices, theosophy and Eastern philosophies. Yeats connected Celtic culture to Irishness and was influential in uniting together ideas and images from popular religion, magical practices, mythology, landscapes, ancient cultures, values and nationality. With his lifelong interest in folklore, particularly that related to the other-worldly, he collected and published some of the most recognizable and celebrated material in the Irish canon. Alongside Lady Augusta Gregory, Douglas Hyde, Ella Young and John Millington Synge, he gathered folklore material and drew on Irish folk culture for inspiration in his creative work, utilizing folkloric and mythological themes in his poetry and prose.

Esoteric symbols, themes and inspiration from his personal research into the occult, and his own magical practices, feature prominently in his work. Both Yeats and Russell became proponents of the ideas in the theosophist Alfred Percy Sinnett's book *Esoteric Buddhism* (1883), which contained correspondence with an Indian mystic and comprised the tenets of theosophy. In 1885, Yeats became a founding member of the Dublin Lodge of the Hermetic Society with Russell. The Dublin Hermetic Society was an organization founded on 16 June 1885, and in April 1886, it became the Dublin Theosophical Society. Mary Bryson (1977: 32) observes, 'Thus began the Theosophical Movement in Dublin, a force so profound and far-reaching that we are still exploring its influences in Irish studies. It played its role in effecting the Easter Rising – that mystical Armageddon led by poets; and the impact on Irish writers has been demonstrated in figures so seemingly unlikely as James Joyce.' Apparently, the limitation of the organization when it became a branch of the Theosophical Society disappointed Yeats. When his family moved back to London in 1887, Yeats visited Madame Helena Blavatsky, founder of the Theosophical Society, and wrote of his brief interaction with her. He resigned from the 'Esoteric Section' of the Theosophical Society in 1891 for unknown reasons. Despite the membership status and interpersonal issues to do with the Society, Yeats's world view was influenced by theosophy.

In London in March 1890, Yeats was initiated into the Hermetic Order of the Golden Dawn. This was a magical order, offshoots of which still exist today, founded in 1888 by a London coroner, William Wynn Westcott, and Samuel Liddell MacGregor Mathers. Its graded system of initiatory ceremonies and its general operation was based on that of a masonic Rosicrucian organization, the *Societas Rosicruciana in Anglia* (Rosicrucian Society of England), which had been established in 1867 and of which Westcott was secretary general. Yeats remained an active member of the Golden Dawn for over thirty years, becoming involved in the Order's power struggles. After the Hermetic Order of the Golden Dawn splintered into its various offshoots, Yeats remained with the *Stella Matutina* (Morning Star) until 1921, which continued as an initiatory magical order dedicated to the dissemination of the traditional teachings of the earlier Hermetic Order of the Golden Dawn.

It has been noted that almost all the women who were muses for Yeats's poems were themselves involved in the occult, some of them having been introduced to occultism, or at least the magical orders, by way of Yeats. This introduction or further engagement with the occult via Yeats included his love interest Gonne, whom he proposed to and was rejected three times before he married Georgina or 'Georgie' Hyde-Lees. As a child, it was claimed, Hyde-Lees was believed by her family to have the 'second sight', which in Gaelic tradition is an ability to see into or perceive the spiritual realm. Hyde-Lees professed an interest in occultism and was introduced by Yeats to the Hermetic Order of the Golden Dawn in 1914, and she joined in 1915. Yeats and his wife participated in spiritualist practices such as automatic writing which in the early half of the twentieth century had 'emerged as a distinct spiritual and cultural mode of communication' (Nally 2010: 1). Also called psychography, this was a kind of writing produced by someone in trance and is understood as spiritual beings communicating through the person by way of written text. It is similar to the communication through a spiritualist medium by way of speech, sometimes understood as a possession by the spirit of the physical form of the medium. William and Georgie paid close attention to the messages they believed they were incarnating from different spirits and to astrological signs; in tandem with the latter, they partook in the occult practice of sex-magic. As noted by Susan Johnston Graf (2005: 108), 'when the Yeatses decided to have their second child, they were much more careful that the conception would take place exactly when the spirits astrologically planned it' since they apparently believed an avatar for a new age would incarnate through them. Russell communicated his visions of the coming avatar to Yeats and 'both Yeats and Æ felt', Johnston Graf (2005: 106) also notes, 'that the avatar of the coming age would be Irish'.[1] Yeats practiced divination, read tarot cards, was an active astrologer and studied numerology (Mills Harper and Paul 2008: xxix). Numerology was also influential on his work, for example, in the poem 'Easter 1916', written in the months following the Easter Rising. Considering this poem, Margaret Kelleher (2019: 86) remarks on how 'the interweaving of contemporary detail extends to the poem's numerology, the four stanzas of 16, 24, 16 and 24 lines encoding the date of the Rising (24 April 1916)'.

As mentioned above, Synge was like Yeats, a folklore collector, and the material inspired his work. He also had an interest in esotericism, including telepathy, astral travel and theosophy. In a 1924 account by his love interest Cherrie Houghton (née Matheson) published in the *Irish Statesman*, she recollected that Synge, on the day of a surgical operation in December 1897, had asked her if she received the telepathic message he had tried to send her before he was anaesthetized; shortly after, Synge wrote the essay 'Under Ether: Personal Experiences During an Operation', where the narrator, who is an 'initiated mystic', has an other-worldly and revelatory experience during an operation. Alongside folklore, Synge's engagement with esotericism influenced his literary work and, like Yeats, he interpreted some Irish traditions connected to the other world by way of esoteric knowledge systems. As Seán Hewitt (2015: 59) notes, the 'occult had a profound impact on his writing, and was internalized into his approach as a way of reconciling his own contradictory reactions of the ongoing modernisation of the West of Ireland, which he saw not only in terms of cultural and economic changes, but also as a conflict between spirituality and scientific rationalism'.

Synge also drew from esoteric philosophies the idea that spiritual values were to be found among the ordinary people of Ireland, particularly in marginal geographical locations such as the Aran Islands, and that such spirituality was tied to place. Synge, born in Rathfarnham in County Dublin, rejected the Protestantism he was raised with as he associated it with his Anglo-Irish background and connection with Unionism, and favoured instead Irish nationalism and socialist politics. 'Though he rejected his family's Protestantism years before he first encountered the modern theosophical and occultist movements,' Hewitt (2015: 61) notes, 'Synge rewrites his own history in order to plot a trajectory toward this moment of mystic discovery, positing himself as a man instinctively receptive to supernatural experience.' The emphasis in Synge's autobiographical writings on mystical experiences and esoteric matters tells us that this was something perhaps more important to him than commentators on his life and work have generally noticed.

Much more focus has been given to esoteric themes in the work of the painter and writer George William Russell, who has been referred to as 'the Revival's leading mystic' (Kelleher 2019: 87). Russell used the nom de plume Æ representing 'aeon', which in certain spiritual traditions is understood as the first sound in the universe. He was born in Lurgan, County Armagh, and when his father got a job in Dublin, the family relocated there. Russell was educated at Rathmines School and later the Metropolitan School of Art in Dublin, where he met Yeats and with whom he established a lifelong friendship. His first book of poems, *Homeward: Songs by the Way*, was published in 1894 and his collected poems was published in 1913, with a second edition in 1926. *The Candle of Vision: Inner Worlds of the Imagination*, which he wrote in 1918, is popularly described as a 'mystical text'.

Theosophy, its name derived from the Greek *theos* (God) and *sophia* (wisdom) is in a general sense a broad spectrum of esoteric philosophies, often pantheistic in nature and characterized by an emphasis on the hidden tradition passed down in a succession from the ancients. 'The theosophists adopted three basic aims: to promote the brotherhood of man, to investigate the hidden powers of life and matter, and to encourage the study of comparative religion' (Bevir 2003: 100). Theosophy was an important influence on Russell and during the 1880s he lived at the Society's Irish headquarters at the Theosophical Society Lodge at 3 Upper Ely Place in Dublin. Leeann Lane (2003: 165) highlights that 'as a theosophist AE would have been immersed in a belief system which looked to the past in the shape of occult tradition and allied itself with future-orientated programmes for the betterment of human life in the form of feminism and socialism'. Russell's work in the agricultural cooperative movement and his editorship of the Irish Agricultural Organisation Society's newspaper, the *Irish Homestead*, from 1905 to 1923, was also influenced by both theosophy and cultural nationalism.

Russell was said to be clairvoyant and able to see various kinds of spiritual beings, and he had a passionate interest in mythology and folklore. He illustrated his visions in paintings and drawings. His engagement with Celtic mythological themes can be seen particularly in paintings such as 'The Prince of Tir-na-nÓg'. The *sidhe*, other-worldly people of Irish mythology, translated into English as 'fairies', inspired many paintings, including 'A Warrior of the Sídhe', 'The Spirit of the Pool' and 'The Stolen Child'. As with Yeats, Russell's view of the spiritual world and its inhabitants was influenced by esoteric systems he encountered, particularly theosophy. As Lorna Reynolds (1982: 394–5) remarks, 'AE's interest in the occult was as intense as Yeats', his visions of the other world much clearer than any Yeats enjoyed, and of common occurrence in his life; as a painter he had the advantage that he could yield visible evidence of the "plumed yet skinny *sidhe*" that appeared to him.' Mark Williams (2016: 310) examines the use of mythology to create the imagery found in the work of Russell and Yeats and 'specifically the ways in which both men came to crystallize an iconography for the indigenous gods. To do this they built on the work of Standish O'Grady in particular, who had sought with indifferent success to persuade a Protestant landed class to acknowledge a direct connection between Gaelic antiquity and contemporary Ireland'. O'Grady, whose father was the Church of Ireland minister of Castletown Berehaven in County Cork, had a formative role in the development of the Celtic Revival, published mythological tales and made connections between Gaelic heritage and Celtic heroic culture, particularly the Fenian Cycle.

The Literary Revival group had many prominent and prestigious connections in the literary world, and Russell met the young James Joyce in 1902 who introduced him to other Irish literary figures. Russell appears as a character in the 'Scylla and Charybdis' episode of Joyce's *Ulysses*, where he dismisses Stephen's theories on Shakespeare. Russell's house at 17 Rathgar Avenue in Dublin became a meeting place for artists at the time; indeed, his Sunday evenings 'at home' were a notable feature of Dublin literary life. Russell's select group of protégés, including Young, became known as the 'singing birds'. Outside of their literary and artistic contacts, Russell and his friends mixed with significant people in Ireland's freedom fight, an example being the Irish revolutionary leader and politician Michael Collins who became acquainted with Russell in the last months of his life.

A friend of Russell's, James Cousins was an Irish writer, playwright and poet and fellow theosophist. Born in Belfast, Cousins moved to Dublin in 1897 where he became part of the literary circle. He used several pseudonyms, including Mac Oisín and the Hindu name Jayaram, and is believed to have served as a model for the Little Chandler character in Joyce's short story collection *Dubliners*. Cousins had a lifelong interest in the paranormal and reported on several experiments carried out by William Fletcher Barrett, then a professor of physics at Dublin University and one of the founders of the Society for Psychical Research, founded in 1882 in London. Cousins was significantly influenced by Madame Blavatsky's teachings and himself wrote widely on theosophical subjects. He was also impressed and inspired by Russell's ability to reconcile esotericism with a pragmatic approach to social reforms. Colin Duggan (2018: 3) examines the influence of theosophical discourse on the national politics of prominent Irish theosophists including Russell and Cousins, who combined a love of Irish landscape and cultural materials with their theosophical world view and 'both of whom developed their fascination with Irish mythology into ideas and ideals for the future Irish nation despite the universalism and globalism of the society to which they belonged'.

Intellectuals of the era who were members of the Theosophical Society had published their philosophies and social commentary. In the Indian context, theosophists including Annie Besant became involved in Indian nationalist activism, and theosophists evidently had an important role in mobilizing the Indian Home Rule movement. Theosophical writers emphasized the greatness of the Hindu Vedas, shared heritage that derived from a past golden age, and other cultural aspects. They helped to create a national pride in many Indians and 'both Western-educated Indians and Western occultists sometimes used their vision of ancient India, and the organisations through which they promoted it, to advance the political cause of Indian nationalism' (Bevir 2003: 99); theosophy provided the 'framework of action' (Bevir 2003: 106) for key figures involved in political agitation.

Even though theosophy as a philosophy was embedded in Indian culture, some comparison can be made with the situation that developed in Ireland whereby occultists used their vision of ancient Ireland to advance the political cause of Irish nationalism. They motivated people in their social circles as well as much further afield to support the cause by way of their writings and, in some cases, their public speeches. An analogous connexion of elements of textual material in the form of Early Irish Literature, contemporary cultural life, folklore and national pride was cultivated by theosophists in Ireland. Esoteric ideas from theosophy and other systems of thought meshed easily with cultural and Romantic nationalism. Drawing on the idea of bringing ancient wisdom to modern people, different esoteric traditions impacted on concepts circulating about the spiritual values of the 'folk' or 'peasantry' and the creative way this was envisioned as being connected to the ancient Celts. It is noteworthy that it was generally middle-class and upper-class Protestants who most demonstrably utilized a Romantic vision of the Celtic world alongside esoteric and mythological tropes and symbols. It can be argued that those of Protestant backgrounds of this era were enabled to engage with esotericism in ways that Catholics could not, whether in regard to accessibility of materials and social networks or in relation to acceptability of such interests or activities within Catholic communities. 'Pagan' symbols, ancient religious ideas and magical rituals likely had different associations for Catholics in the main.

Romanticism, revivalism and revolution

The Romantic sentiment pulsing around Europe at this time fused a mélange of philosophical ideas, artistic expressions and spiritual yearnings, and projected these onto local landscapes, histories and cultures. Landscapes became idealized: the more rugged and geographically peripheral, the better. This perception of rurality was part of Romantic nationalism around Europe, and Ireland was no different with the agrarian culture and countryside being sentimentalized and connected to spiritual values. Different groups and concerns connected with Romantic nationalism in their own way; for instance, 'Dublin-based members of the Gaelic League considered rural Ireland to be the location of their romantic nationalist ideal, and the Catholic Church saw the romantic conservative ideals of a Catholic Ireland in the countryside' (Githens-Mazer 2006: 6). Birgit Bramsbäck (1971: 59) remarks that ' "folk" to Yeats meant above all the largely illiterate people of the Irish countryside – peasants, farmers, fishermen'. For many participants in the Literary Revival, Ireland's countryside and the so-called 'peasantry' that inhabited it, were the nexus of spiritual values and a link right back to the Celtic world. Living close to the land, farming and fishing and sense of place were together emotionalized in a picture presented of the Irish nation. Bramsbäck (1971: 56) notes that 'popular lore – particularly Irish – was a vital source of inspiration to Yeats and other writers of the Celtic Revival'. Jonathan Githens-Mazer (2006: 86) has pointed out how 'in the Irish case, cultural nationalism was particularly important in crystallising and disseminating national myths, memories and symbols, such as those of origin, golden ages, degeneration and redemption'. Of course, cultural nationalism was utilized in different ways by different groups, with emblems being variously interpreted and symbols holding different resonances. Indeed, there were different golden ages and takes on what part of the distant past was most significant: it could be a golden age of Catholicism prior to the introduction of the Penal Laws, or it could be a peaceful and idyllic golden age of Gaelic culture envisioned as it might have existed before colonization; for the Anglo-Irish group of literary enthusiasts, the golden age was the imagined Celtic world. Romanticism came into play in the ways in which this group of Anglo-Irish engaged with Celtic material. An idealized view of the distant past, and the connecting up of the contemporary people of Ireland to this ancient Celtic world, helped this demographic to transcend more recent problematics of colonization and division.

The tapestry of Ireland's political and cultural life of the time was knotty with different perspectives, ethnic identifications and allegiances; one chosen nationalism or ideological creation of 'Irishness' might be rejected by other nationalist networks or groups. 'The Anglo-Irish were not Gaelic-Irish,' as Nally (2010: 7) explains, 'and therefore were regarded by cultural nationalists as "inauthentic" members of the Irish nation.' Despite their own highly significant contributions as cultural nationalists, their efforts at learning Irish and the production of cultural materials like poems and plays with themes based in Irish mythology, history and society, their class background and British lineage still excluded them, in the minds of some, from being 'fully Irish' in an 'Irish Ireland'. The Ascendancy or 'gentry' were drawn, therefore, to those aspects of Irish culture that pre-dated and transcended the ethnic, social and political divisions since the Anglo-Norman invasion of Ireland in the twelfth century; a useable resource was thus the Celtic world on which much could be projected and from which images and symbols could be drawn and shaped in the absence of recorded detail of the precise world views, practices or lifeways of the Celts themselves.

The pulse of Romantic nationalism was felt around Europe in the nineteenth century. 'Romantics,' writes Giovanni Costigan (1973: 141), 'drew a distinction between nationality and nationalism, between the nation as the vehicle of moral and spiritual values and the nation as a political power tending to aggression and imperialism.' Thus, spiritual values and cultural expressions became increasingly important in forming national identities. Romantic nationalists wished to recapture elements of ancient cosmology and truths. Costigan (1973: 143) remarks on Romantic nationalism and the yearning for 'the sense of depth in history, involving a passionate quest for the origin of national roots in a remote past and an idealisation of folk culture'. This idealization involved much attention to the spiritual aspects of people and also the connection between the other-worldly, landscapes and sites associated with magical practices, ancient religion or more recent legends. Again, popular culture was linked to the ancient Celts. 'In a world growing increasingly industrialized,' as noted by Robert Welch (2000: 197), 'the Celts and other so-called primitive peoples were thought to possess an instinctive understanding and knowledge, qualities reflected in Yeats's *The Celtic Twilight* (1893, 2nd edn. 1902), which grew out of his recollections of Sligo and Howth and showed his respect for the intuitions of Irish country people.' The quixotic 'Celtic spirit' or character was believed to endure in the ordinary people of the Celtic regions and was contrasted by intellectuals and artists of the time with the Saxon character, conceived of as ordered and rational.

Celtic mythology played a significant role as an inspirational resource during the Literary Revival. Young, for example, drew on Celtic mythological themes in her books, *Coming of Lugh* (1909) and *Celtic Wonder Tales* (1910), which were illustrated by her friend Gonne. When she emigrated from Ireland to the United States in 1925, she gave speaking tours on Celtic mythology at universities and held a Chair in Irish Myth and Lore at the University of California, Berkeley, for seven years. At Berkeley, she was remembered for her eccentric persona, giving lectures while wearing her 'druidic' purple robes. She was influential in her academic role and in her creative work in the Californian art scene. Young had a particular interest in spiritual beings such as fairies and elves and, like Yeats and Russell, was influenced by conceptualizations of such beings in theosophy and by ideas of the other world that emerged from spiritualism. Esoteric knowledge systems influenced her understanding of the fairy legends and other folklore material she collected, and, indeed, Young has been described as a 'mystic poet' (Steele 2004: 187).

Young was likewise influenced by a combination of folklore, myth and nationalistic impulses, and, as Rose Murphy (2008: 1–2) describes, the tales she gathered were 'typical of the western Ireland narratives treasured by this Irish writer, storyteller, teacher, poet, mystic, rebel, immigrant and westward adventurer'; Murphy adds that 'her own life story, which included guarding weapons under floorboards for Irish rebels in the 1920s and bringing her Celtic tales to California audiences, has never emerged from the shadows of more famous luminaries'. Born in Fenagh, County Antrim, to a Protestant Anglo-Irish family, Young's family moved to Dublin, to Grosvenor Square in Rathmines, and it just so happened that Russell was her near neighbour living at 67 Grosvenor Square. Young shared an interest in theosophy, which led her to join the Hermetic Society at an early stage. Through the Society, she met the Welsh writer and well-known theosophist, Kenneth Vennor Morris, who often used the Welsh form of his name, Cenydd Morus, and who was also a friend of Russell and who had moved to Dublin in 1896. Young was a staunch nationalist and became friends with Pádraig Pearse, one of the leaders of the Easter Rising. She had a supporting role in the Rising itself and managed to smuggle rifles and other supplies in support of Republican forces and also joined Cumann na mBan ('The Women's Council').

Eva Gore-Booth was similarly a theosophist, political activist and social worker. She and her older sister Constance Gore-Booth, later known as Countess Markievicz, mentioned previously, were born at Lissadell House in County Sligo to an upper-class Irish family. She followed in her sister's footsteps in becoming a nationalist, suffragette and revolutionary. Eva Gore-Booth was a poet, and akin to her friend Yeats, her work was strongly influenced by folklore and mythology.

These themes can be found in the nine poetry collections, seven plays and several collections of spiritual essays she authored.

Mythic Ireland, magic and the Irish freedom fight

Growing up from this underpinning of esotericism came a shared idealism among this group of writers that related to tradition, landscape, built heritage and a nostalgia for a Celtic golden age. This shared vision fed into the attitudes about Irishness and the hope and prospect of a particular kind of Ireland. This optimism for the future and sense of connection with a distant past helped, on an ideological level at least, to bring a unified vision and to rise above the partisan attitudes and sectarianism so prevalent during this period. Gonne is a key figure at the intersection of Irish Romantic nationalism and the esoteric, and Elisabeth Kehoe (2016: 140) remarks how 'Gonne attracted, during her lifetime and after her death, a range of polemic opinions about her role in the shaping of Ireland'. Regardless of these differing viewpoints, she stands out as a devoted nationalist and revolutionary who was called by her French companions *La Grande Patriote* due to her passionate championing of Irish freedom. During the time spent in Dublin, London and Paris, and the groups she mixed with, Gonne was drawn to the occult scene and spiritualism. We are told that much of this interest stemmed from her friendship with Yeats and socializing with his friends, though all accounts of her seem to credit her as a strongly independent-minded person; we can thus assume her occult interests were genuine. In 1891 she briefly joined the Hermetic Order of the Golden Dawn.

In both Ireland and France, Gonne mixed socially with other nationalists who were fervently anti-British and anti-empire. The father of her son Georges was the French politician, Lucien Millevoye, who took an anti-British stance and encouraged Gonne's efforts to continue fighting for Irish freedom. Since Millevoye was a married man, and in the repressive social milieu of the time, the child's birth and life was kept a secret. In 1891, when Georges died at age two of meningitis, 'she hid her deep grief by pretending publicly to be mourning the tragic death of the Irish nationalist leader Charles Stewart Parnell' (Kehoe 2016: 141). Gonne talked about the death of a child she said she had adopted to both Yeats and Russell, and the latter 'shared his belief that a soul could be reborn if another was conceived near his body' (Kehoe 2016: 141). Following this conversation, Gonne persuaded Millevoye to visit the memorial chapel she had built in France for Georges, and this is where her daughter Iseult, born in 1895, was apparently conceived and who Gonne also told others was an adopted child.

Tireless in her freedom-fighting efforts, Gonne funded and wrote much content for the publication *L'Irlande Libre* between 1896 and 1897, and fundraised and lectured in Europe and the United States. Gonne was also an actress and, poignantly, had played the role of the embodiment of Ireland in her 1902 performance as Cathleen Ni Houlihan in the one-act play of the same name, written by Yeats and Lady Gregory. The creation of the symbol of Cathleen Ni Houlihan drew on mythic themes and is an emblem of Irish nationalism, representing Ireland personified in female form. Her nationalism permeated her life and her activities, from writing to acting, as Steele (2004: 188) remarks: 'Gonne's political activism could best be described as street theatre: from her mock funeral for the British Empire in protest of Victoria's Diamond Jubilee in June of 1897 to marshalling all of O'Connell Street in the 1930s on behalf of Republican prisoners.'

The organization Inghinidhe na hÉireann ('Daughters of Ireland') founded by Gonne established a nationalist and feminist journal, *Bean na hÉireann* (The Irishwoman), edited by the prominent Irish Republican Helena Molony with Gonne and Countess Markievicz on staff.[2] Markievicz also contributed to the newspaper, sometimes using the pen names 'Macha', a sovereignty goddess of ancient Ireland, or 'Armid', a variant spelling of Airmid, a member of the mythical people, the Tuatha De Danann, with the ability to resurrect the dead. Similar publications that brought together feminism and nationalism, such as the suffrage newspaper, the *Irish Citizen* (1912–20), 'frequently drew upon romantic and idealized images of the Gaelic civilisation of yore' (Ryan 2020: 25). Ancient Ireland and Celtic myth were used in different agendas to politicize Irish people and images utilized to suit the revolutionary enthusiasm and feelings of the time. These powerful images appealed to both men and women, and especially the 'many Irish suffragists', as Louise Ryan (2020: 24–5) points out, who 'were influenced by the cultural revival movement, which provided an iconography of Gaelic warrior queens as symbols of female empowerment'. Many of the women utilizing such images and references in their writing or campaigning later became involved in the Irish republican women's paramilitary organization Cumann na mBan and participated directly in the Rising.

A playwright key to Ireland's Celtic Revival was Alice Milligan, pen name Iris Olkyrn or I.O., who 'has been marginalized within revivalist doctrine, despite her remarkable achievements as a nationalist propagandist and a creative practitioner' (Morris 2003: 79). Born in Omagh, County Tyrone, and of Methodist background, she became involved with nationalist organizations such as the Gaelic League and the Ulster Anti-Partition Council. Her political work encouraged Ulster people's contribution to the Revival movement. The newspaper Milligan co-edited with Anna Johnston from 1896 to 1899, *Shan Van Vocht*, was titled as a phonetic rendering of the Irish phrase *An tSean bhean Bhocht* ('The Poor Old Woman') and the title of a song dating to the 1798 Rebellion.[3] The newspaper provided an important forum for Northern Irish nationalists to communicate and engage politically. As with her literary circle, she was influenced by Celtic culture and mythology. Remarkably, her sister Charlotte Milligan Fox was a collector of folklore, concentrating on folk songs, and in 1904 founded the Irish Folk Song Society. Sharing a family love of Irish landscape and culture, Alice collaborated with her father to produce the tourist guide *Glimpses of Erin*, published in 1888. Her work brought Ulster more firmly into the Revival movement. In that same year, she moved to Dublin to study Irish language and literature. While there, she attended political gatherings and in June 1891 went to a meeting where she saw Parnell. She was resentful at the Catholic church for rejecting Parnell and articulated her feelings in the poems 'Bonnie Charlie' and 'At Maynooth'. Esotericism also influenced Milligan's work and she experimented with automatic writing (Morris 2012), and these aspects merged into her other interests and activities.

Esotericism, folklore and conceptualizations of the native Irish other world and a Celtic golden age, and a particular brand of Irish national identity, all converged within the life and work of these figures of the Irish Literary Revival. A unique matrix of meaning was created in the late nineteenth and early twentieth centuries which came to the fore in the fight for Irish freedom and the birth of the nation; it is a meaningful framework that underpins forms of Irish nationalism and Irish identities today. While it can be argued that the privileged position of members of the Protestant ascendancy allowed them the freedom to explore esotericism whereas their Catholic countrymen could not, it can't be denied that their occult involvement and Romantic leanings were an instrumental force in shaping a Romantic nationalism that still pervades this country.

Chapter 7

AFFIRMATIONS OF IRISHNESS: ASSESSING IRISH PROTESTANT IDENTITY

Deirdre Nuttall and Tony Walsh

This chapter explores the complexity of culture and experience which typifies the experience of the Protestant minority in the independent Ireland.[1] It concentrates throughout on the life and experience of Protestants in the *political* entity of the Republic of Ireland, rather than the *geographical* entity of the whole island. For a range of historic, political and cultural reasons, the experience of this tiny minority in the Republic is completely different to that of the majority Protestant community in Northern Ireland, which remains part of the UK.[2] Bearing the marked legacy of British colonialism, with political independence in 1922, Irish Protestantism's identity was forged by, and in resistance to, the striations of a state governed by the rigours of an overwhelmingly fundamentalist Catholicism. We open with a vignette of life in the later 1960s, an era when the power and influence of this assumptive world was at its zenith. This narrative[3] conveys the texture of one man's – a nonconformist minister – experience of religious minority status:

> I was walking down the main street of the town where I lived one afternoon on my way home from visiting a member of my congregation. We'd stayed chatting, forgetting it was Corpus Christi.[4] Big Catholic Church holidays could be very strange days for Protestants: we tended to keep our heads well down, to be more invisible than usual. As I headed home, the street was thronged with people. Papal and Irish national flags adorned every lamppost and matching intertwined bunting criss-crossed the street. The whole centre of the town had been totally taken over and there were Gardaí[5] everywhere. The Army were out in force to form guards of honour at various points for the procession. 'Ave Maria' and 'Panis Angelicus' were resounding from loudspeakers attached to every telegraph pole. The singing was interspersed with decades of the Rosary over the loudspeakers, to which the crowd responded on their beads.
>
> I was getting all these looks as I tried to thread my way unobtrusively home before the actual procession arrived. In a small community, everyone knew I was 'one of them', and a preacher to boot. But suddenly the procession was upon us. There was the bishop holding the monstrance containing the Sacred Host

aloft, with a white and gold canopy held above. He was surrounded by hordes of priests in vestments. There were hundreds of acolytes, first communicants, school choirs, church choirs, members of the Legion of Mary, the Vincent de Paul, and so on in the entourage. A contingent of the army band led the way, and the mayor and town council were just behind. As the procession approached, every person in the thronged street fell to their knees in worship of the Eucharistic host.

At first, never having been involved in such an event before, I was fascinated. Then suddenly, with horror, I realized that I was the only one left standing. I didn't want to be discourteous, and yet I couldn't follow the crowd's example; it would have been a betrayal of everything we stood for as evangelical believers to have knelt in adoration. For a moment I was paralysed ... I couldn't even think. Standing there, in my own town, I have never felt so alone, so alien, in my entire life. After a couple of moments the paralysis left, and I darted into an alcove and stood looking into the window of a draper's shop till the procession passed. I couldn't think of anything else to do.

The outstanding memory I have of the experience is of complete isolation and non-belonging. I was an alien in my own country, a stranger in my own home. Who was I to be here at all?

The involvement of the police and army in a sacred procession is noteworthy, as is the powerfully symbolic mixing of national and papal flags, but the narrator's utter sense of alienation is remarkable.

He was born into a 'small farmer' family, who had been in Ireland for well over three hundred years. He had worked all his life in small towns and rural areas. He had contributed greatly to his own community and was noted for his contribution to the wider community too. He was not, and had never been, a member of the aristocracy, the Anglo-Irish Ascendancy 'gentry',[6] which was so resented. He was an Irishman. How can we understand this narrator's sense of alienation? What does it mean – for him, for his community and for Irish society generally? We will return to Robert's tale later, using it as an anchor, as we explore Irish Protestant identity in independent Ireland in the light of Michel Foucault's concepts of power and resistance, noting, too, the dramatic social changes which were, and continue to be, influential in shaping the contours of the religio-cultural minority. We turn first, however, to a brief historical summary of the unique circumstances that led to the events and the emotions described above.

A colonial history

The history of Irish Protestants and Protestantism is intimately related to Ireland's colonial history; an uncomfortable truth (Akenson 1975: 109) that, even now, can be difficult to live with. The diverse Protestant faiths present on the island of Ireland, of which the Church of Ireland is the biggest grouping, descend from events that occurred centuries ago. Unlike other countries, there was no indigenous Reformation in Ireland, and Protestantism was imported 'ready-made', closely associated with Britain and often utilized as a tool in the British conquest of the indigenous Irish. In the seventeenth century, the systematic dispossession of native Irish Catholics and the 'planting' on their land of British Protestants loyal to the crown was a central plank in the colonization of the country. Part of Britain's motivation was to protect itself from the danger of invasion via Ireland by European Catholic powers (Lennon 2005). By the end of the seventeenth century, these processes had resulted in the creation of two broad ethnic categories in Ireland, loosely categorized as 'Catholic' and 'Protestant' (Ó Giolláin 2000: 15). Referring pejoratively to members of the Reformed faiths as 'English', 'planters' or 'West Brits' was once common, and it still lingers.

For centuries in Ireland, the ruling classes were almost uniformly Protestant, and privileged Protestants held positions in government and business that were inaccessible to almost all Catholics (Guinnane 1997: 75) . This association between Protestantism and privilege has often been interpreted as implying that all Protestants were privileged to similar degrees and that all or many aligned themselves with British interests. In reality, Irish Protestants have always been an economically, socially, denominationally and politically diverse group, united more by cultural factors than by a common faith or a commonly held position of privilege (O'Leary 2000: 474). During the War of Independence,[7] the religious minority experienced, to varying degrees, murders, violence and the burnings of Protestant-owned farms,[8] businesses and homes (Crawford 2010; Bury 2017: 85). In some cases, these events were explained in terms of attacks on 'loyalists' or 'traitors'; in other cases they were nakedly sectarian. Notably in County Cork, but also elsewhere, a systematic approach to targeting Protestants seemed intended to dramatically reduce their numbers through intimidation. The ensuing terror contributed to high levels of emigration and to a sense of alienation that lingered for generations (Hart 1996; Megahey 2000; Tanner 2003).

In the early years of independent Ireland, a theoretical tolerance was extended to Protestants, and some gestures were made towards encouraging their integration into the political life of the new state. When the first senate was appointed, Protestants were very well represented, including sixteen members who had previously held unionist views (Akenson 1975). The new government reassured Protestants that they would be regarded 'not as alien enemies, not as planters', but 'part and parcel of the nation'. Twenty out of sixty seats in the senate were reserved for Protestants, a number vastly disproportionate to their numbers overall (Caird 1984: 60) and certainly one that was intended to convey a positive message to the Protestant minority. This apparent acceptance of Protestants as 'part and parcel' was partly in recognition of the reality that many had been deeply committed to, and intimately involved in, the revival of traditional sports, music, language and literature, all the heritage of a Gaelic culture. More pragmatically, wealthy Protestants in industry, business and certain professions were generally treated rather well. At the beginning of Ireland's existence as an independent nation, 40 per cent of the lawyers, 20 per cent of the doctors and well over 50 per cent of the bankers were Protestants, numbers vastly disproportionate to their numbers overall (d'Alton 2009). The new state did not wish to lose either their capital or their professional expertise. Less affluent Protestants, particularly the urban and rural poor, often felt that they were overlooked by both the state and wealthier Protestants and that they experienced significant discrimination (Nuttall 2020).

After centuries of colonization and anti-Catholic discrimination, the process of defining a fresh, concrete identity became an urgent imperative for the emergent state. A rigid brand of nationalism, interwoven with a particularly rigorous expression of Catholicism, supplied the new state with the sense of power, authority and coherence it needed to enforce the distinctiveness of the new nation. 'Valid' Irish identity came to be equated solely with an unquestioning subservience to this model. In later years, this softened into less explicit forms of 'othering', but the social marginalization of Protestants, the sole minority of substantial size in a sea of Catholicism, continued into the latter decades of the twentieth century.[9] As the process of nation-building continued, the new state increasingly adopted a fundamentalist Catholic ethos that came to dominate the social, cultural and political life of the country (Crawford 2010). This would be exemplified in the person of Archbishop John Charles McQuaid, Catholic Primate of Ireland, who was, with conservative episcopal colleagues, to have an extraordinary level of influence on Irish life, culture and politics. Every bill and policy document had to be vetted and approved by him before it could be even presented to the Dáil (parliament). Nakedly triumphalist, McQuaid enforced a particularly divisive brand of Catholicism and is remembered with fear and loathing to this day. Many Protestants still remember him as a barrier to their integration with the wider community, even encouraging some to feel a certain affinity with Britain, due to the ferocity of his anti-Protestant views (Nuttall 2020).

For Catholics, association with Protestants was actively discouraged by priests and bishops; attending Protestant services, even the weddings and funerals of close friends, was forbidden, under pain of excommunication or other forms of social and religious stigma by the hierarchy. The Papal *Ne Temere* decree[10] (whereby the children of religiously 'mixed marriages' had to be brought up Catholic) was enforced with draconian vigilance by the Catholic church, supported by the state[11] and policed by the community. Emigration, which was high in general, was particularly high among Protestants of all social classes, many of whom went to Northern Ireland (Bielenberg 2013) or overseas (Tanner 2003). In a challenging economic era, with lower levels of marriage, and partly because they accepted contraception, their birth rate was 'considerably lower than that of Catholics' (Macourt 2008: 67), well below replacement level. Despite the positive changes heralded by the Second Vatican Council (established in 1962), the growth of interest in ecumenism and growing liberalism, the social 'othering' of Protestants continued into the 1970s and 1980s (Crawford 2010). By 1991, the Protestant population was a third of what it had been in 1911 (Macourt 2008) and the fear of ultimate extinction was becoming a powerful reality.

During the 1990s and into the new millennium, Ireland experienced dramatic change. An increasing awareness of globalization, rising secularism and a period of unprecedented economic affluence, accompanied by unprecedented levels of immigration and growing multiculturalism impacted significantly on what had been a highly traditional society. As Ireland became increasingly liberal and open, the sexual and other scandals that rocked the Catholic church also contributed to the erosion of conservative Catholicism. New narratives emerged to replace traditional and exclusionary interpretations of reality. Quite suddenly, Irish Protestantism found itself a courted 'other', an acceptable alternative rather than an oppositional threat with an unacceptable history. For the first time, many congregations saw their numbers grow, with the arrival of 'new Irish' immigrants and a stream of disaffected Catholics. Census numbers recorded, for example, a significant decline in people identifying as Roman Catholics (although the group is still by far the largest of all those identifying as religious) alongside a significant increase in numbers among certain Protestant denominations, notably Pentecostal and particularly Apostolic churches. This increase takes place in tandem with the ongoing decline, and aging, of the Church of Ireland population in many parts of the country, which nonetheless remains the largest Protestant group in Ireland, with growing numbers of children in primary and in secondary school, and which is one whose history is inextricable from the history of Ireland generally (CSO 2016).

Having explored the historical inheritance and the complexity of the wider Irish context, we will now proceed to examine their legacy on Protestant identity. Ultimately, we will examine four particular expressions of that identity forged in relation to these influences.

Matters of identity

The collective identity of any minority group is always forged, at least in part, in relation to what is happening in the wider society, including the operations of power within that society. Because wider social systems are dynamic, so are the contours of minority identity evolving in relation to the shifts and changes in the wider environment, but also in response to resistance and to the currents of internal alteration, which can be harder to perceive or comprehend. Foucault's particular understanding of the concepts of power and resistance constitute a useful lens through which to examine both societal dynamics and lived experience. Together with his notions of discourse, and its function in making the operations of power visible, these provide a useful theoretical framework to explore the assumptive world of a society and its effects upon the minorities within its boundaries. We will use Foucault's conceptualizations as a framework through which to examine a number of facets of Irish Protestant identity, and we will juxtapose them with commentary and analysis provided by Robert, whose narrative opens our essay.

Power

Foucault (1998) argues that power is everywhere. We are surrounded, formed and, often unwittingly, indwelt by it. He contends that the power of certain interests and positions in society is manifested in social structures, dispersed and made effective in language, societal rituals and everyday social encounters and relationships. The underlying assumptions which uphold and express this power become invisible, remain uncritiqued and come to be accepted as normative reality. They attain the mythical status of well-known facts. The effect is to establish and retain unquestioned a particular dominant way of being, while simultaneously rendering powerless and invalid that of any group whose assumptive world does not fit with such discourses: as Sheila Trahar argues, the complex processes wherby power is institutionalized invariably favour the socially dominant (Trahar 2010). For years, society in independent Ireland was utterly dominated by the hegemony of a fundamentalist Catholic nationalism. This was manifested not only in the structures, legislation and policies of society but also in the minutiae of day-to-day relationships and communication.

The functions of discourse

Foucault's concept of discourse is theorized as the mechanism through which power is made operative (and a tool through which its influences can be made visible) in a society. Discourses are 'socially organized frameworks of meaning that define categories and specify domains of what can be said and done' (Burman 1994: 2). More specifically, Anne Ryan (2005: 23) argues,

> Discourses are regimes of knowledge constructed over time. They include the commonplace assumptions and taken-for-granted ideas, belief systems and myths that groups of people share ... [they] articulate and convey formal and informal knowledge and ideologies.

In the first instance, discourses have a number of basic functions: through them, majorities order, see and make sense of the world and their experiences of it. Discourses define the nature and parameters of what is accepted as 'true' and demarcate ways of being that are seen as valid or acceptable. In Ireland, true Irishness was defined as Catholic, Gaelic and nationalist. Anyone outside this formula was, by definition, non-Irish and other. The Catholic church alone was defined as holding a totality of religious validity and truth; those outside it were an aberration, heretics and, perhaps most significantly, viewed as a threat to national unity. The strategic combination of political and ecclesiastical power which had evolved to convey a unique identity to the emergent state lent great potency to a particular set of discourses. Robert, whose narrative opens our essay, commented,

> You really can't understand Irish Protestant identity without reference to two things. Firstly, there's the legacy of British colonialism here and the extraordinarily oppressive strategies that were part and parcel of that process. These left a terrible legacy of hatred for anything seen as British, or anything or anyone seen as having – particularly English – connections. Secondly – and it was a response to all that – there was the power of a very fundamentalist

Catholicism in the new Irish State – it infiltrated thinking, values, politics, community, social relationships – everything.

Second, through being taken up in the discourses which are regnant in a particular society or culture, members of a dominant grouping enter into a shared grid of common understanding with their peers. This reinforces shared systems of meaning, facilitates communication and excludes and marginalizes those whose meanings, behaviours and assumptive worlds do not accord with it.

Third, discourses maintain the power of a particular society's elites through privileging certain knowledges, assumptions, behaviours and ways of being which then come to be seen as normative, rational and acceptable (Ryan 2001). The Corpus Christi procession described above had the effect of very publicly ritualizing the unquestioned, intertwined power of church and government, and implicitly of a particular version of history and culture. It engaged the town's mayor and public figures, and the police and the state's army, as active participants. This vigorous display of unity had the effect of marginalizing the largest group of 'others' in the community: the Protestant minority. As Robert comments, 'the unrelenting Catholicization of the country resulted in Protestants feeling under siege.' The siege mentality referenced by Robert was most frequently expressed with reference to marriage and the aforementioned *Ne Temere* decree. As he states,

> The enforcement of the Ne Temere decree was tyrannical; Protestants were terrified by it. I've recently heard an Irish – Catholic, actually – academic referring to it as 'the Irish version of ethnic cleansing'. That's certainly how it was experienced by the minority. And it worked; even in my lifetime I've seen whole areas of the country cleared of Protestants. Young people either emigrated because there was no-one of their own to marry here, or they married an RC [Roman Catholic] and, of course, the children, and consequently the subsequent generations, were signed over to Catholicism. Or they didn't marry at all and there were no children. Whichever way it went, it spelled the death of whole small communities.

Making power visible

For Foucault, teasing out the discourses that dominate in a society was a way of shedding light on how that particular society functions (Foucault and Faubion 1994). The concept of discourse creates a lens through which the distribution and operation of power can be rendered visible. In conceptualizing discourse, he was very clear that such meaning repertoires exist *outside* the sense-making processes of individuals or groupings; instead, they are pre-existing, external (and largely unconscious) channels that organize the thinking and assumptive worlds of a society and its members. Individuals and groups in a particular society are unconsciously recruited into these ways of seeing and being.

In Ireland, a unitary and exclusive construction of Irishness was privileged, and those who did not reflect its values and ways of being were rendered outsiders. A particular range of historical narratives were recruited in this process; Catholic nationalism was triumphalist and perceived as the true, and only, inheritor of all things Gaelic and Irish. Protestantism, with its colonial past, and now seen as the defeated usurper, was both marginalized and demonized. In Robert's words,

> I was stationed as a non-conformist minister in a rural town in the mid-to-late-1960s. It was a dreadful time in rural Ireland for everyone; there was huge poverty and the emigration rates were cataclysmic. The Protestant population was particularly badly affected by emigration; communities were often completely numerically unsustainable, and growing more so by the day. While there were often good relations at a personal level between members of the different religious groupings, many Protestants felt that there was little they could relate to in the new state and that they were often barely tolerated. The *Ne Temere* decree was applied with a ferocity unparalleled in other countries. Memories of burnings and boycotts were very close. A pall of depression enveloped everything. It was actually almost endemic in many minority communities; the future appeared immeasurably bleak. We felt completely powerless.

Per Foucault (2019), history is colonized in the service of creating versions of reality implicated in supporting the dominant discourses (and power groupings) of a particular era and in attributing identity. When Ireland became independent, Irish Protestants constituted by far the largest minority whose identity was inconsistent with the new, developing construction of Irishness. Yet many had forebears who had been in the country for over three hundred years, had a deep connection to the country and had never viewed themselves as anything but Irish. In the new environment, they shifted quite suddenly from the position of a minority with influence (because of their historic connections with Britain and a long history of anti-Catholic discrimination) to one of extreme 'outsider' status. Their complete abandonment by co-religionists in Northern Ireland, who were numerically significant and politically well connected, is still a source of ill-feeling (Abbott 2002). The fear of intimidation, violence, threats and burnings terrified members of this minority in the War of Independence and for a long time afterwards; as horrifying as the violence had been, the long shadow that it cast was even worse.[12] In isolated rural areas, a late night knock on a cottage door could induce terror and flight. In the face of hostility, some emigrated, others remained because they felt that they had nowhere to go and many stalwartly refused to leave. They saw their sense of Irishness as valid, even if the dominant discourse did not. For many who remained, the sense of being 'under siege' was a vital facet of their reality.

Resistance

In his groundbreaking commentary on domination, Foucault (1988: 123) disputes traditional definitions that conceptualize power as a unidirectional force which imposes or maintains a simple domination. Instead, he insists that power begets resistance. He assigns such resistance a constitutive site within the designation of power; for him, power and resistance entail a mutual, complex and reciprocal interplay. Of power, he argues, 'We can always modify its grip in determinate conditions and according to a precise strategy.'

Responding to their sense of difference, which was so clearly projected by the state and dominant discourses in society, Irish Protestantism resisted this power. In doing so, they utilized a range of reactions focused on self-protection and the maintenance of boundaries that would enable the survival of an alternative ethos, an assumptive world and, they hoped, numerical sustainability. We will use Foucault's conceptualizations as a framework through which to examine four particular facets of Irish Protestant identity which became central pillars: community, silencing, complexity and liminality.

Community

The formation of a system of close and connected communities has been a hallmark of Irish Protestantism. These served to create a strong social network which linked members, simultaneously nurturing, protecting and reinforcing an ethos and assumptive world distinctive to that of the majority. The prevalence of the *Ne Temere* decree and the existential threat it posed to the survival of the minority was a significant factor in maintaining these communities as tightly bounded systems. The conservation of such bounded communities achieved a degree of success in maintaining a particularly tribal ethos. However, at times Irish Protestantism turned inwards and some members engaged in behaviours that actively facilitated their marginalization within the wider society (Todd et al. 2009). When young people mixed with the wider Catholic community, the spectre of 'mixed' marriages was immediately raised. This instantly brought with it the enforcement of the *Ne Temere* decree and the expectation that future generations, and indeed land or businesses, would be ceded to Catholicism. All implied the extinction of both community and a way of being. Over time, the existence of ruined churches and abandoned schoolhouses provided a powerful, if mute, testimony to vanished communities and the reality of such fears.

Protestant society was characterized by significant internal variety, marked by differing political affiliations, by diverse denominations and by social, class, economic and educational diversity. In these communities, scouts, guides, girls' and boys' brigades, badminton, table tennis, tennis, football clubs, choirs, musical societies and local theatre, and charitable and missionary organizations thrived where there were sufficient numbers. All nurtured the development of cultural capital. The original intricacy of local structures was reinforced by an overarching national framework of voluntary, church, youth or charitable organizations covering the country, all reinforcing a strong sense of belonging, connection and common values.

The community was also served by a distinctly Protestant educational system and by a number of hospitals. Both medical and educational systems operated parallel to, within and yet apart from the wider state provision. The hospital and medical sector was particularly significant in that both operated outside the rigid ethos of Catholicism, particularly around sexual and reproductive health. These became a significant facet of Irish society, quietly and effectively offering their services to members of the majority despite the fulminations of the Catholic hierarchy. Legal firms, banks and businesses also served the minority. Protestants with entrepreneurial spirit and an agentic use of their kinship and community networks were particularly effective at developing small businesses; these periodically grew into significant national and sometimes even international concerns.[13] In provincial towns and major cities, many shops and businesses were Protestant-owned, creating a much-needed boost to employment and contributing to the economic viability of the new state. In this context, the minority achieved a reputation for hard work and honest dealing, but they also attracted resentment, as many Protestant businesses hired Protestants as a matter of preference or reserved managerial positions for Protestants (both traits echoed by Catholic employers) (Nuttall 2020).

Despite lingering memories of the tumultuous years of the 1920s and the difficult decades of the mid-twentieth century, local relationships between members of the minority and majority communities were often good, if 'careful'. A number of community organizations with which Protestants were involved created a distinctive cultural legacy in many areas. Anecdotal evidence suggests that Protestants tended to be disproportionately represented in the leadership of cross-community organizations such as the Irish Countrywomen's Association and Macra na Feirme (an organization for young farmers). With their emphasis on participative church music, choirs, accompanists and soloists were part of the stock-in-trade of the minority; these found expression in the support of national musical performance and competitions (e.g. An Feiseanna Ceoil) which nurtured the musical capital of the nation. Protestants were also particularly active in some areas of sport and in artistic and creative circles. Their more democratic and participative emphases on the nature and running of church created a familiarity with community and a consequent ease with community leadership and dynamics. The structuring of local community activities has long been a core part of Irish Protestant identity. The experience of living in settings which were quite educationally, politically, economically and spiritually diverse, while also essentially cohesive and united, has also provided a significant factor in the community's overall sense of itself.

Silence

Remarkably few Irish Protestant voices have ever spoken out against the 'othering' emanating from the dominant discourses of traditional Irish society, be this active or passive. There was little, if any, public statement, let alone protest, by Protestant community leaders concerning early episodes of murder, boycott, emigration or discrimination. The absence of divorce, the ban on artificial forms of contraception and the effects of the *Ne Temere* decree were rarely the subject of Protestant public comment. In the face of an often hostile environment, where their views were neither sought nor welcome, Irish Protestants resorted to silence; a defence strategically employed to safeguard a minority that experienced itself as vulnerable and exposed. This silence was seen by many as the price for being allowed to remain in Ireland and live in peace. In popular discussion, members of the community were often described as 'nice' or 'quiet'. When some did speak out, they invariably attracted the swift censure of their own community.

For example, during the infamous Fethard Boycott, when a small rural Protestant community was boycotted because a local woman in a 'mixed' marriage had decided to send her children to a Church of Ireland school, efforts to support the beleaguered community were criticized by the Church of Ireland hierarchy as 'senseless provocation' (Butler 1985: 141). Dean Victor Griffin, the uncharacteristically outspoken dean of St Patrick's Church of Ireland Cathedral in Dublin, refers to his mother's horror at some of his statements in the 1970s: 'You'll have us burned out,' she wailed (McGarry 2013). Even within the community, it was rare to openly acknowledge and discuss problematic issues. Perhaps it is easier, or at least more comfortable, to live in denial rather than in continuous engagement with an unwelcome reality. It is interesting to note that, until very recently, almost all the revisionist commentators on Irish history, who have begun to comment on the negative experience of Irish Protestants, are either from a 'cultural' rather than a 'religiously practising' Catholic background, are Irish Protestants now domiciled abroad or are not Irish at all.[14]

The silence that became such a core part of Irish Protestantism was an effective strategy in the early and middle years of the twentieth century in particular. It allowed the community to pass beneath the dominant radar of public scrutiny, allowing quiet difference to survive. However, it did come at a cost. Irish Protestantism appears to have internalized silence as part of its core identity. This has resulted in a systemic reluctance to name or engage with difficult issues and emotions even within the community. The result has been a curtailment of the community's willingness and ultimately its ability for critical reflection, discussion and commentary. This has had implications for issues of power and power abuse within its own community as well as in the broader world. One noted example has been the reluctance of the Protestant churches to explore issues of abuse and intimidation in Protestant-run Mother and Baby Homes (Coulter 2002). Inappropriate actions or behaviours on the part of their own leaders are rarely questioned and certainly not publicly. Where silence becomes a way of being, discussion and critique are curtailed and a dearth in the skills of reflexivity, and reflexive engagement, emerges.

Moreover, because of their preoccupation with silence, public debate on issues of justice, human rights and freedom until recent decades was conducted in Ireland largely without input from the Protestant community. This has both limited and skewed the voice of protest in particular ways. It has also meant that the support and experience and the cultural survival capital of a significant minority grouping has been largely unavailable to other minorities seeking change and inclusivity in the country. The movement for gay rights, groups seeking inclusion and justice for immigrants or other minorities, could have drawn on the experience of Ireland's significant cultural-religious minority, but because of its silence, it could not. Lastly, the strategies and the successful forms of resilience which enabled the survival of a significant minority, whose way of being was so largely oppositional to the dominant discourses, were allowed to go unremarked and largely unrecognized.

Complexity

Despite internal differences, the most noticeable characteristic of Irish Protestantism was an overall cohesiveness, expressed in a robust, if generally ill-defined, notion of common values, beliefs and shared cultural identity. 'An awareness of the enduringly oppositional nature of their tradition remained crucial to the minority's self-conception. ... It is the Catholic majority that keeps most of us defiantly Protestant' (Tobin 2012: 1). The Protestant minority tended to lapse into a sense of vague 'identity in opposition', defining what it was not rather than what it was – particularly as the latter involved a complex blend of values, culture, history and an assumptive world which was alternative, and often oppositional, to the majority's. The community defined itself, in Patrick Semple's (2008: 23) words, as generally 'in being good and in not being Roman Catholic'. This became a convenient, if highly simplistic, catch-all descriptor. The deeper and more intense sense of identity was strongly felt but often difficult to define, particularly to outsiders.

Of course, the experience of Irish Protestants was diverse. There were communities in which there were sufficient numbers and where enough resources existed to maintain sustainable communities, creating an alternative, secure way of being. Adherents were woven into the tight social network of social, educational, sporting, cultural and religious activities; there were differences but they were part of a known landscape and a common, if vaguely defined, assumptive world. In these communities, people could buy what they needed in Protestant shops, attend Protestant doctors and hospitals and be buried by Protestant undertakers. Their children could be employed in a variety of jobs or professions in organizations run by co-religionists. Here, there was little need to engage with the wider community if they did not wish to. In the leafy suburbs of South Dublin, in parts of Counties Cork, Cavan or Monaghan where sufficient numbers existed to maintain the trappings of an alternative community, there was often a sense of complacency, and sometimes of superiority, when relating to the wider community and to less fortunately positioned Protestants.

Where numbers were small, however, particularly in rural, or often in urban working-class, areas, the situation was very different. Here, there was a sense of threat, of living on the margins and of the need to negotiate their positioning with care amidst the dominant discourses of society. Here, it became important to know and understand the assumptive world of the majority in order to fit with it. Anxiety, social positioning and tactical silence served the cause of survival but had other implications too. Paolo Freire (1977) and Boaventura de Souza Santos (2018) argue that such careful manoeuvring is a core response to the dynamics of societal oppression. It is easy for marginalized groups to become domesticated and tamed, losing their critical edge in the service of not threatening the power groupings of society. Freire (1977) maintains that marginalized groups often internalize the position which they have been accorded by the powerful discourses of the majority. Those defined as alien or outsiders come to see themselves as such, deep within, often subconsciously. We see this in the account provided above. The narrator Robert states, 'I was an alien in my own country, a stranger in my own home. Who was I to be here at all?'

Subjected forms of feeling?

Silence and the maintenance of boundaried community networks have constituted significant, agentic sites of resistance to dominant discourse. In this section we approach a different, more contentious area, which recognizes other and more complex layers significant to the formation of identity. For generations, the majority community has interpreted Protestant silence as an incontrovertible demonstration that the minority have lived happy, fulfilled lives in a state where they were accorded equality and privilege. The occasional voice raised drawing any attention to an oppressed status – for instance, to the tyranny of the *Ne Temere* decree – was traditionally castigated as 'whingeing'. A similar reaction has, of course, been the lot of many minorities who comment negatively on the dominant social status quo.

Alongside the explicit effects of hegemonic power and the resistances which these have evoked within the Irish Protestant community, Robert points to another actuality – the potent effect of those discourses on his own subjectivity. On that Corpus Christi evening, he actually experienced the power of official displacement in and upon his own sense of self. Foucault, himself a member of an oppressed gay minority, recognizes the oppressive operations of hegemony in the subjection of personhood. Highlighting the phenomenon became a central focus of his life's work: 'The goal of my work ... has not been to analyse the phenomenon of power, nor to elaborate the foundation of such analysis. My objective, instead, has been to create a history of the different modes by which in our culture, human beings are made subjects' (Foucault 1982: 777).

In Foucault's work, he uses the term 'subject' in two ways: first, to encapsulate the notion of personhood and, second, to recognize the power of dominant discourse in an active process of subjectification and oppression in the context of that very sense of the self. Certain ways of being, certain manifestations of subjectivity are 'licensed' at a particular historical time and in a particular place; they constitute acceptable forms of expression. Others do not. Of that Corpus Christi evening, Robert noted that his identity and his particular expression of subjectivity were other, unacceptable. He felt completely disenfranchised. Alone and alien, his religion, his experience of Irishness, his very way of being, did not accord with the dominant discursive mould. He knew this cognitively from his observations of the crowd's reaction and from his wider life experience. More importantly, he *felt* the marginality of his subjectivity quite profoundly – so much so that he didn't know what to do.

Dominant discourses are active in *creating* reality; they are also profoundly implicated in the construction of subjectivities (Davies and Gannon 2006) and are active in creating feelings (Ryan 2001). Outsiders know and feel themselves to be so. Those who do not subscribe, or who live at variance, to the striations of dominant discourses *know* themselves to be outsiders. Many minority groups have all known similar *felt* realities; such subjectification is the lot of marginal minorities' ways of being. Retreating into cloistered communities, denying ones 'tribe of origin', and sometimes strident struggle, have all been constituted differing ways coping. Tony Walsh (2013) and de Souza Santos (1999) have identified a similar effect on the personhood of the marginalized or oppressed. Bronwyn Davies and Susanne Gannon (2006) maintain that such groups often internalize the position which they have been accorded by the powerful discourses of the majority. Those defined as alien or outsiders come to see themselves as such, subconsciously and deep within. Robert, whose family had farmed the same meagre acres for countless generations, states, 'The outstanding memory I have of the experience is of complete isolation and non-belonging.' According to Friere's conceptual framework, those defined as other or on the margins become domesticated, silenced and cloistered, colluding in their definition and encompassing their positioning as part of their core identity. They became unable even to recognize the dynamics of their oppression or the procedures involved. In this process, marginalized groupings become 'tamed', losing their critical edge, unwitting co-respondents in the service of the power groupings of society and their reality.

Many members of the Irish Protestant community were also continuously exposed to the implications of an existential unsustainability. For years, they saw their numbers fall as young people emigrated or 'married outside', and as communities shrank and evaporated. The narrative that they were doomed to extinction seemed to be visually confirmed by the ruins of closed churches and abandoned schoolhouses, which a generation before had been the centre of small but thriving communities. Of course, all this impacted on the psyche of the Protestant minority. Often, a generalized miasma of depression enshrouded small communities. While experiences of agency, maintenance of boundary and other forms of resistance were characteristics of Irish Protestantism, they existed in a complex weave with other intra-psychic realities that also contributed to identity formation.

Change and liminality

Irish society has changed dramatically in recent decades. The relationships which emerge between prominent versions of the past, the appearance of narratives that define the present and the emergence and texture of those discourses delineating the future are always intricate. Where there is significant change or discontinuity, what Victor Turner (1990: 33) describes as a 'liminal' or 'threshold' space often emerges. Such spaces constitute 'a no-man's land betwixt-and-between ... [with] the mood of maybe, might be, as if, hypothesis, fantasy, conjecture, desire'. Here, time-honoured narratives, functional in providing meaning, predictability and purpose until the recent past no longer apply. Ireland's new openness, increasing secularism, significant immigration and multicultural richness, alongside modern crises in Catholicism, have led to a dramatic turning point for Irish Protestantism. For the first time in the history of the state, and largely thanks to immigration, Protestant numbers are growing and schools and churches recently scheduled for closure are thriving. Exploring more closely, it is clear that, while numbers continue to fall in the aging Church of Ireland population (with considerable regional variance), in the last two decades they have grown dramatically among evangelical and Pentecostal congregations, largely because of immigration from other countries and from the Catholic community.

In other words, an indigenous minority group, belonging to a faith that, pre-independence, benefitted to varying degrees from the social and political capital associated with it, which was marginalized in various ways post-independence, is being organically renewed by congregations and congregants with very different ethnic, cultural and historical influences. On the one hand, this influx of Protestants from diverse non-Irish backgrounds is a source of joy to those who delight in seeing Protestant churches and schools flourish. However, it also invites a degree of ambivalence; the incoming members may share a common faith, but their cultural experience has been different.

Having lived for years with a complex weave of experiences which include vulnerability, endemic depression, rich social networks, agency and a degree of tribalism, those who are descended from that cultural group whose most visible unifier is being Protestant do not always know how to capitalize on the freshness, variety and energy introduced by immigration. Immigrant communities are often, unsurprisingly, unaware of the complex history of the Irish Protestants and more likely to experience marginalization for issues relating to race or immigrant status than for their religious faith. Further complicating the picture, historically a significant factor in Irish Protestantism was its positioning of 'identity in opposition' to fundamentalist Catholicism. Recently, Irish Catholicism, reflecting profound shifts in Irish society, has changed dramatically. Many who still identify as Catholic have jettisoned much that was central to traditional belief and practice. At the same time, many people from all sorts of religious backgrounds now live in secular worlds, rejecting to varying degrees any engagement with religion at all. The rigidly exclusionary notion of Irishness which long dominated has become dilute, permeable and inclusive. In this context, one asks what it now means to be an 'Irish Protestant'.[15]

Foucault's conceptualization of power recognizes the possibility of resistance and a consequent possibility of agentic repositioning. Irish Protestantism has been agentic in responding to dramatic shifts in the wider environment and has survived by adapting to a range of exigencies imposed by many external changes and alterations. It has resisted, but in the process sometimes created, a stifling parochialism and limitation of vision that could reinforce notions of privilege and difference. Today, Irish Protestantism in independent Ireland appears to be entering a new era, characterized by fresh possibilities and open horizons, but also by the ongoing decline of a sense of discrete cultural identity, and by the ongoing decline in numbers among many of those communities traditionally identified as 'Protestant' in the Irish context, even as immigrant and newer communities, often evangelical and Pentecostal, and the revival of many Baptist and Presbyterian communities, inject new life, the promise of a future and abundant research possibilities (Walsh 2006). Anecdotal evidence also suggests active engagement, prevalently in urban areas, with the Church of Ireland on the part of a growing number of self-identified Catholics.

Against a backdrop of a culture that is now overwhelmingly secular in many respects, these processes will demand new forms of agency and the authoring of new narratives of identity and purpose for either traditional or emergent minority groups, as well as for society as a whole. In attending to these new challenges, Irish society can call on the lessons learned from the past, from the resilience of Protestantism in Ireland, both in cultural and in confessional terms, and from its ability to cope with change and from the limitations which such strategies may imply. Clearly, there is still much to explore in this rich and changing cultural and theological landscape, and further research will add to our knowledge not just of the Protestant minority in Ireland but also to an increased conceptual understanding of the dynamics of minority experience in general.

Chapter 8

SITUATING NEW RELIGIOUS MOVEMENTS IN CONTEMPORARY IRELAND

Vesna Malešević

Introduction

Catholicism has been a defining feature of Irish identity since at least the nineteenth century. The Catholic church became a powerful social institution through its political alliances with the nationalist cause since the latter half of the nineteenth century and became a guardian of moral monopoly on truth in post-independence Ireland. While subjugation of Catholicism in the eighteenth century enabled folk religious practices to flourish harmoniously with the Catholic rites and beliefs, once the Catholic church gained prominence in the mid-nineteenth century, it worked steadfastly on eliminating its pagan connections. However, many other religious groups and practices were becoming known such as Buddhists, Mormons, theosophists and spiritualists (Cosgrove et al. 2011; Cox 2014; O'Brien 2018). The increasing invisibility of alternative religious practices in the first decade of the twentieth century was closely related to the formation of a bastion of power personified in the church–state hegemony in political and social matters. Not quite theocracy but not democracy either, as J. H. White explained so studiously in 1971.

Nonetheless, Ireland was not immune to wider social changes affecting Western countries in the 1960s and 1970s. The major social themes became social class, nuclear family and the modern welfare state (Kaelble 2003). In Ireland, political elites became concerned with economic modernization and increasingly less guided by the bishop's approval. A proliferation of (imported) new religious movements (NRMs) such as the Family or the Moonies was accompanied by a revival of folk-Catholicism and New Age spiritualities. The following decades witnessed many social changes including increasing access of women to the paid workforce, economic and social modernization, visual and print media proliferation, access to inclusive education, uptake in foreign travel and material, consumerism and materialism, and inward migration (Corish 1996; O'Connor 2001; Inglis 2002; Seward et al. 2005; Penet 2008). Another crucial factor to influence the change of attitude was the proliferation of knowledge about the Catholic church's historic abuses of women and children.

A secularization thesis that rests on the idea of modernization and urbanization may be criticized for its limited use (Clark 2012). However, it still holds analytical value in an analysis of structural differentiation and individual piety. Regardless of what concept we use to explain the terms 'religious change', 'post-secularism', 'post-Christianity', 'secularization', 'desecularization' or 'pluralization', there is one common denominator between them, namely the idea of religious vitality. In order to understand the multifaceted religious vitality in Ireland, this chapter starts from wider debates on secularization and modernization to situate the emergence of NRMs and alternative spiritualities in a wider context of religious change. Positing personal conviction in religious choices at the centre of the debate on modernization and its effects affords us a closer look at the individual level of religiosity.

Followers of any religion are not sheep; they find in religion the emotional and social bonds that fulfil ontological needs. Something new and different, perhaps holistic, in its relationship with the world and nature may come to a person at just the right time. This 'religious' experience may reinforce one's sense of belonging or help a person's efforts towards self-realization. Various religious groups and spiritual movements have been on the rise in Ireland since the 1970s, and migrant religions of the last thirty years, especially, have proved that coexistence of multiple beliefs enriches us socially and culturally. While there is no one religious truth, there is 'A Religious Truth' depending on your religious leanings. And for most of the population in Ireland, some form of religion or spirituality still holds value.

Secularization and religious change

Since the Age of Enlightenment, secularization and modernization ensued as church–state alliances began to crumble in the face of a changing sociopolitical landscape (Martin 2005). From the moment the steam engine and the printing press were invented, technological and industrial progress kept transforming cultures and societies. Economic and technological modernization increased life expectancy, access to education and national income in Western societies. The process of secularization prompted the questioning of religion's role in society, its effect on social and cultural norms, its input into social cohesiveness and its contribution to the sense of meaning and purpose. If traditional religion is grounded in communal rituals that provide group solidarity and affirm communal values (Durkheim 2012), how does a decline in commitment to traditional religions affect individuals' experience of religion more broadly?

Disillusionment with established religions and modern secular society has given rise to NRMs which offer a sanctuary within which people, especially youth, seem to find solace, community and meaning. In Western societies, whether measured by the participation in services, beliefs or importance of god in everyday life, organized religion is suffering from declining interest in its traditional forms of institutional belonging with younger cohorts reporting no religious affiliation (Beaman 2013). It appears that secularization and modernization create higher levels of prosperity and physical and material security which evoke a sense of agency and autonomy (Mouzelis 2012). Globalization and geographic mobility expand our understanding of different cultures and beliefs and relativize the uniqueness of single truths (Possamai 2015). Increased access to education, and especially higher education, coupled with exposure to scientific world views lessens traditional religions' monopoly over truth about the unexplainable, or the unseen, as trust is increasingly placed on science (Casanova 1994).

An example of the tensions inherent in the complex relationship between science and religion is prominent in the Covid-19 global pandemic management. What has transpired in 2020 and 2021 are interfaith dialogues, prayers and events that bring together religious leaders from various backgrounds. For example, an event organized by the Heavenly Culture, World Peace and the Restoration of Light (HWPL), representatives from the Church of Scientology, Hindus, Muslims, Christian denominations and Buddhists engaged in a three-hour online programme (Scientology Blog 2021). Speakers joined in prayers and responded to questions from the audience. Furthermore, there is evidence that the global Covid-19 pandemic has contributed to the strengthening of faith in some countries.

The Pew Research Center (2021) conducted surveys in 2020 researching religious faith in fourteen countries. They found that nearly one-third of Americans have reported a stronger faith in the summer of 2020 while in other countries the number is one in ten at best and 0.2 per cent at the nadir. White Evangelical Protestant Americans were also found to be most likely to report that the pandemic boosted their faith and the faith in the country overall. On the other hand, if we look at the median for all the countries, 85 per cent of participants did not find that their faith had changed. Interestingly, in the Netherlands and Sweden, more people reported that faith strengthened in the countries than the level of increase of faith at a personal level. For instance, 17 per cent of Dutch people say that religious faith increased in the country while only 7 per cent claim the same for themselves. In Sweden, the percentages are similar (15 and 3, respectively). The median for all the countries in relation to the level of faith in society is at 66 per cent, meaning that over two-thirds of respondents thought that the level of faith stayed the same. What these findings attest to are spiritual needs that come to the fore in times of crisis. When large-scale social system rests on impersonal relations and alienation, religion promises personal relationships and transcends values; it offers a recourse to spiritual awakening, mystical experience or ultimate reality (Wilson 2003). Since March 2020, the Berkley Center for Religion, Peace and World Affairs has started to address the issues of religion, bioethics and Covid-19 vaccination emphasizing the importance that faith communities and their leaders play in matters of ethics and the Covid-19 vaccine rollout among other issues. The building blocks for addressing the pandemic globally is through communal efforts as the message that 'we are all in it together' can only be believed if we shy away from the neoliberal mantra of supremacy of an individual.

The increasing individualism strongly correlated with secularization and economic modernization has been linked to the continued growth of NRMs (Wallis 1984; Chryssides 2011). Secularist tendencies of separation between the church and state, privatization of religion and liberalization of world views have all detrimentally affected established religions and favoured NRMs. While the challenge presents itself at the institutional level, the emotional and social aspect of belonging speak to the vitality of religion preserved through alternative ways of being religious and spiritual. The concept of subjectivization of religion (Heelas et al. 2005) explains well why in Ireland people are substituting Catholicism with alternative religions. It is the 'subjective turn of modern culture' (Taylor 1991: 26) towards inner spirituality that finds outlet in seemingly more fulfilling religious contexts.

What are NRMs?

Different types of religious groups have existed historically, and we often find in NRMs expressions of the world's religions such as Hinduism, Buddhism, Islam, Judaism and Christianity (Saliba 2003). However, 'since the middle of the 1960s a large number of New Religious and Para-Religious movements either have been established, or if already established, have greatly expanded their number of adherents' (Bird and Reimer 1982: 1). 'New religious movements' was a term coined for the new religious groups emerging and growing in popularity from the 1960s (Barker 2015). Proliferation of NRMs in the 1960s and 1970s was linked to the social and cultural revolution (Jameson 1984) prompted by military invasions, the Gay Liberation movement, civil rights movement, migration and youth protests. Murray Rubinstein (2019) contends that NRMs exhibit several common characteristics such as having roots in pre-established ancient religions or traditions, being perceived as countercultural, often drawing on a range of belief systems and commonly relying on a charismatic leader with authoritarian tendencies.

J. Gordon Melton (2000: 87) describes NRMs as being 'primarily religious groups/movements that operate apart from the dominant culture in which they are located and in addition, seek adherents from their now host culture'. Their discourse is imbued by promises of 'an exuberant religious, spiritual and philosophical experience' (Kızılgeçit and Ören 2019: 449). More fundamentalist NRMs emerged in reaction to modernization and secularism (Barker 2015). Incompatibility between modernity and religion is due to historical animosities. From early modern to late global modern society, tradition and collective effervescence have been replaced by either other collective entities (e.g. nation) or individual reflexive biographies (Giddens 1991). The increasingly globalized developments in financial markets and services, electronic communication and the 'compression of time and space' have led to 'detraditionalisation' where tradition and collective certainties disappear (Mouzelis 2012: 209). Thomas Robbins and David Bromley (1999) describe modern dislocation in terms of alienation, anomie or deprivation that create yearning for new structures of meaning and community. What was previously seen as essential has now become a matter of personal choice, and the experience of life in a 'homeless mind' (Kızılgeçit and Ören 2019: 453) is addressed by NRMs through their resistance to secularism, anomie and the lack of moral guidance.

If NRMs are protests against modernity, exactly what are they protesting against? James Beckford (1986) believes that NRMs are a response to the wider social changes. However, young people being affected more directly by the changing social, political and economic contexts are also more drawn to NRMs that create new interpretations and solutions. Robert Bellah (1976) emphasized that emergence of NRMs in the United States coincides with the erosion of the legitimacy of many American institutions including business organizations, local and federal governments, the education system, churches and, very importantly, the family. Mario Diani (1993) affirms the point that NRMs appear as a reaction to the swap of traditional kinship for modernity. Beckford (1986: ix) states that 'in a study of widely differing religious movements occurring within diverse religious and cultural traditions, it would be unwise to impose an excessively restrictive definition on the concept'. John Paul Healy (2011) proposes that NRMs are part of counterculture within the state in which they are located, something that Rodney Stark and William Bainbridge (1985) have identified as one of the three models of cult emergence. The other two models focus on the psychopathology or business acumen of the cult leader. NRMs could take a shape of a sect or a cult depending on their origins in either traditional religions or novel syncretic world views (Kızılgeçit and Ören 2019). What seems to unify different NRMs are 'distinctive ways of interpreting life' and their 'abnormally specialised or narrow … teachings or practices' (Beckford 1986: ix) with the 'desire to carry the ancient truth to modern times and move it into action on a contemporary and secular basis' (Kızılgeçit and Ören 2019: 3). Some NRMs choose seclusion and minimal, if any, contact with the dominant culture; others happily engage with the world, but they all negotiate their existence with modernity by either resisting it or embracing it.

The word 'cult' in particular is commonly laden with negative connotations and a view of cults as extreme, toxic and dangerous 'dehumanizes' the people involved and often paint them as brainwashed and crazy (Olson 2006). However, the media tends to focus on the extreme behaviour of certain cults, often those who have committed atrocities such as the Manson Family murders and the Jonestown massacre. This public perception of cult members as foolish, possibly dangerous and victims of mind control can create a hostile social environment which in turn 'confirms' the guru's rhetoric and reinforces the members' initial decision to join instead of reconsidering the criticism and judgement from the outside world (Olson 2006: 97–106). While use of the term 'cult' has been discredited by academics and the preferred term has become 'new religious movement' (Gallagher 2007), some authors utilize the term 'cult' in their research to denote the perception of such religious groups by either their ex-members (Castaño, Bélanger and Moyano 2021) or the wider public (Olson 2006). In this chapter, both terms are used when addressing the work of particular authors to challenge the reader in their own differentiation between terminology and the understanding of the actual groups.

The joining of NRMs and cults especially is something understood as the rejection of religious and familial values (Richardson 2007: 160). This 'culture-rejecting' explanation is difficult to accept, and a more appealing alternative is the brainwashing theory, that is, assuming that those who join NRMs have not done so voluntarily but have been manipulated through the use of phytotechnology to control members' behaviours through mind control (Richardson 2007). The main issues with the brainwashing theory are that it does not account for the variety of individuals' experiences of involvement (Healy 2011), it is used to justify interventions such as deprogramming and exit counselling (Eggleton 1999), and it is availed of by families of (former) cult members for conservatorship purposes (Bromley 1983).

Charles Glock and Rodney Stark suggest that motivation to join an NRM comes from various types of deprivation produced by social change such as economic, social, orgasmic, ethical and psychic (Flynn and Kunkel 1987). Deprivation refers to 'any and all of the ways in which an individual or group may be, or feel, disadvantaged in comparison to other individuals or groups or to an internalized set of standards' (Glock and Stark 1965, cited in Christopher et al. 1971: 385). Along these lines, the term 'cult' has been used in the United States since at least the late 1950s to account for 'new and unfamiliar in the United States' (Richardson 2017: 39). Further, the American Psychiatric Association uses the term 'cult' and has identified that 'the white middle class, idealistic young people who form the majority in most contemporary cults are often lonely, depressed and fearful of the uncertain future' (Kızılgeçit and Ören 2019: 450). They seek external sources for a feeling of self-worth, a sense of belonging and a reason for living (Kızılgeçit and Ören 2019), which NRMs meet, especially for those who are disappointed with the dominant religious culture. In part, this may be due to the fact that a 'church' which accepts the values of a larger society may create deprivation in some of its members who feel that their church has not evolved in its teachings and is preaching outdated social values (Christopher et al. 1971). Stark and Bainbridge assert that religious belief and commitment provide positive rewards rather than only meeting needs caused by deprivation (cited in Flynn and Kunkel 1987). The compensation theory of religious commitment suggests that an individual's participation in an NRM can provide a supernatural compensation for various kinds of rewards which are unobtainable by secular means (Flynn and Kunkel 1987).

There are various typologies of NRMs that use criteria of membership, religious message, world orientation and leadership to explain hundreds of religious groups that surface, thrive or disappear. The earliest sociological conceptualization of the churches and sects stem from the work of Ernst Troeltsch (1931) and Max Weber (1958, 1963) whose typologies share common characteristics. For instance, churches tend to compromise with the established societal institutions and membership is voluntary while sects are more exclusionary and stand in opposition to the social order. H. Richard Niebuhr (1957) identified denomination as a particular type of religious organization that exists in a plural context having to accommodate and coexist with other denominational groups. Howard Becker introduced the concept of cult into the church–sect typology and Stark and Bainbridge (1985) expanded it further to account for religious groups that are distinctive culturally and socially with loose organizational structure or codified doctrine.

The church–sect–cult typologies continued to be studied and refined to account for groups that were not included before, the proliferation of subtypes or mixed-type groups, new religious groups with permanent or fleeting membership and the historical, social and cultural ethnocentrism. As a result, Bryan Wilson (1970) developed a typology of sects based on the premise of their attitude to salvation. Benton Johnson (1957, 1963, 1971) explored further church–sect typology in relation to the group's relationship with society and thought that the higher the propensity of the group to exhibit sectarian tendencies, the higher the chance that that group is experiencing increasing tension with the outside world. The tension model was adopted and adapted by Roy Wallis (1984, 2017), who identifies three main (ideal) types of NRMs: world rejecting, world affirming and world accommodating. World-rejecting movements (e.g. the Unification Church, the Children of God and ISKCON) tend to attract younger cohorts from middle-class backgrounds. They consider the wider society to be impure, immoral and corrupt, and opt for reclusion within the movement with minimal contact with the outside world. These movements tend to appeal to the rebellious stage of life of a young adult frustrated by the impersonality and individualism of modern life but looking for guidance that the movement provides through cult leaders or gurus who demand an absolute devotion.

World-affirming movements (e.g. Transcendental Meditation, Soka Gakkai and Scientology) accept modern society but teach techniques that promise self-fulfilment, introspection and success in earthly life. Members tend to be educated, privileged and slightly older than members of world-rejecting movements but of a similar middle-class background. Unlike world-rejecting movements, world-affirming movements are more individualistic, secular and universalistic, do not rely on a devotion to a guru and emphasize personal responsibility. Wallis (1984: 99) contends that world-rejecting movements face the problem of 'precariousness of charisma' that needs to be constantly reinforced and legitimized, while the 'precariousness of the marketplace' (Wallis 1984: 85) of world-affirming movements makes them susceptible to failure in meeting the changing personal needs of their members. World-accommodating movements (e.g. Neo-Pentecostalism and Evangelicals) emphasize individual religious experience, collective ritual, return to 'spiritual purity' and original interpretation of scripture that has been compromised by adaptations to the modern life. Wallis's ideal types of NRMs offer a continuum from strictly religious groups to (loosely) spirituality-based groups and, as such, allows for an examination of groups that reject the label of religion, such as Wicca, or find their inspiration in fiction-based material (e.g. the Theosophical Society, Dudeism and Jediism).

David G. Bromley and J. Gordon Melton (2012) further the argument of the group's tension with established social order. They propose that the dominant tradition groups represent the social and cultural traditions shared by many and therefore are in closer alignment with the majority values. The groups that come from and display norms and values different from the established patterns are on the continuum of low to high alignment with the dominant social and cultural norms. Both Wallis's and Bromley and Melton's typologies are meant to account for variations across cultures and between time periods (Bromley 2016).

NRMs and alternative spiritualities in Ireland

While Ireland appears to be deeply embedded in Catholic culture, there are varieties of belief perhaps easily dismissed in light of historical emphasis on Catholicism. While migrant religion explains the continuing growth of new religions in the last few decades such as Islam and different forms of Hinduism, Buddhist and Muslim adherents were already in Ireland prior to 1900 (Cosgrove et al. 2011). Pagan beliefs and folk religion existed from pre-Christian times (de Cléir 2017) and still have practitioners to this day. A belief in the supernatural world in the form of spirits and fairies has a long-standing tradition especially in rural Ireland. From the 1960s, NRMs, sociologically understood as sects and cults, reached Ireland just as they did in the United States and Western Europe. The coexistence of institutionalized religions and alternative spiritualities has a long history fraught with accommodation, tension and subjugation at times.

Folk religion, sometimes referred to as 'folk piety' or 'folk theology', takes inspiration from organized religion and coexists with, but stands outside, the formal structures of religion with adherents making their own interpretation of 'religious mental schema to their everyday of experiences' (Draper and Baker 2011: 625). In Ireland, official Catholicism and popular or folk Catholicism have coexisted since at least the eighteenth century. A series of penal laws were introduced in the first decades of the eighteenth century to encompass mandatory registration of priests with civil authorities. This meant that open-air Mass at a Mass rock was the only way to congregate for official religious rites. Participation in patterns (honouring of patron saints) was approved by Catholic authorities, rosary prayer was already in place since the thirteenth century, pilgrimages to holy wells such as the Well of the Holy Women or sacred places such as Croagh Patrick were expected, and belief in the healing power of water and miraculous cures was common. All communal aspects of religious belonging took place outdoors, and with the lack of priests to mediate, there was a more direct connection between believers and their god.

The nineteenth century saw an increase in the social position of the Catholic church with institutionalization of its practices and doctrines. The devotional revolution (Larkin 1972) ensued due to internal and external factors. The Catholic revival in Europe reached Irish shores with new religious orders being established such as the Christian Brothers, the Sisters of Charity, the Sisters of Mercy and the Sisters of Loretto. All Hallows Seminary was founded in Dublin in 1842 with the aim of training priests for missionary work. The national school system in 1831 meant expansion of literacy across society. The publishing sector printed more prayer books, catechisms and devotional guides to distribute at church Masses every week with the priest at the pulpit. Religious practice became connected with the institution of the church with emphasis on (sacred) texts, in church-held rites and the infallibility of the local priest.

While the nineteenth century was characterized by a Catholic and national revival, other forms of religious expression were present too. The Jewish community and different Protestant groups existed along with Buddhists and Muslims. Global religious movements such as Mormons, spiritualists, theosophists and astrologers found audience. A European anti-clerical movement reached Ireland with few secular societies managing to attract attention (Royle 1974). By the end of the nineteenth century, Irish nationalists developed links with the Asian anti-imperial group. The ethno-religious identification forged from the late nineteenth century and its institutionalization in the 1930s pushed aside alternative religious affiliations, with Catholicism being enshrined in the Constitution of 1937 to a 'special position'.

In the first half of the twentieth century, political, social and cultural dominance of the Catholic church did not deter groups such as the Elim Pentecostalist Church or Jehovah's Witnesses (Butler 2015) to find adherents. By the late 1950s, there was a revival of folk practices such as religious healing practised by both Catholics and Protestants, astrology became more formalized (Roberts 2009) and an Irish Society of Diviners was established in 1954. As NRMs took hold in the United States and Europe in the 1960s and 1970s, Ireland also became a destination for proselytization of new forms of religion. RTE, the national broadcaster, aired a 1971 documentary series called *Irish Religious Beliefs* with Dr Owen Dudley Edwards saying about the religious Irish,

> Their Protestantism is anti-permissive and uncompromising ... Their Catholicism is austere, puritanical, Tridentine, tinged with Jansenism ... Their Judaism is orthodox with paganism still evident in festivals such as Puck Fair and Samhain. (*We the Irish: The Pastor* 1971)

Various manifestations of new religions entering the geography of an island of Ireland became apparent. The American evangelist Billy Graham spoke in Belfast in 1972 for the fourth time, previously visiting in 1946, 1947 and 1961. Transcendental Meditation opened centres in Dublin and in Cork. A Catholic lay charismatic renewal movement was holding two hundred weekly meetings in 1977 (*Praising in Tongues* 1977). The Pentecostal movement held an open-air rally on the Hill of Slane, County Meath, in 1973. Catholic priest Richard Horan was a magician and a member of the Magic Circle in 1971. The legend of the healing powers of the lucky seventh son of a seventh son meant that Finbar Nolan was believed to have healing powers from an early age and would perform healing rituals for health benefits. The Children of God (the Family), the Unification Church (the Moonies), the Divine Light Mission and Wiccans found their way to the people in Ireland among many others (Mulholland 2011).

By the time visionary cults (Allen 2000) appeared with the Marian apparitions, the New Age movement was already flourishing to the extent that the mind–body–spirit umbrella group could develop in the mid-1980s to encompass varieties of New Age practices and spiritualities such as reiki healing, angel card reading, yoga, meditation, complimentary healing and alternative therapies. The proliferation of alternative religions was a target of public criticism too. For instance, the Cult Awareness Centre was set up in Dublin in 1990 to provide information about the workings of cults, and among its supporters were former members of the Moonies, Mormons, Jehovah Witnesses and the Unification Church. The anti-cult sentiment was strong in the United States in the 1970s and 1980s, spreading moral panics and calling for preservation of tradition propagated by organizations such as the Cult Awareness Network (Young 2012).

Many religions are represented in the official Census data in Ireland (Central Statistics Office 2016). Migrant religion (Kmec 2014) has been identified as a source of influx of historically less-represented belief systems, such as African Pentecostal churches with 13,400 members. Many established religions have grown in numbers since the early 1990s; for example, the Muslim community comprised nearly 64,000 members in 2016, in comparison to 3,875 Muslims in 1991. It established the Irish Council of Imams in 2006 from thirty Islamic organizations. Hinduism is represented by over 14,000 adherents with the number more than doubling in a decade. There are nearly 10,000 Buddhists, 24,000 Presbyterians and over 62,000 Orthodox Christians (Greek, Russian or Coptic Orthodoxy). The largest religious group after Catholics (who comprise 78 per cent of the population) is the Church of Ireland with over 125,000 members. When the categories of 'no religion', 'atheist' and 'agnostic' are considered together, there are over 480,000 people in Ireland who do not report an association with religion (Central Statistics Office 2016).

In the Central Statistics Office data collection methodology (2016), any belief system represented by more than thirty people has a designation of religion, which means that there are fifty different religions in Ireland. Some of them fall into a category of NRM such as Jehovah's Witnesses with 6,400 members, Hare Krishna (ISKCON) numbering 87 practitioners and the Church of Scientology having 87 adherents. Apart from these, there are other belief systems, perhaps less well known. There are 78 Satanists, 2,050 Jediists, 92 Pastafarians (the Church of the Flying Spaghetti Monster), 2,922 spiritualists, 2,645 paganists and 114 Rastafarians. While these groups belong to the category of 'other', collectively they now represent over 270,000 people in comparison to 138,000 in 2006 and 38,700 in 1991.

Examining secularization and religious change in Ireland

Religious revival in Western Europe in the 1960s and 1970s has often been associated with the late-modern process of desecularization (Karpov 2010). Purported changes at the level of individual religiosity and the spread of non-traditional and non-institutionalized religious movements have cultivated new spaces within and outside established churches. The proliferation of NRMs and alternative spiritualities in Ireland attest to the search for meaning outside of Catholicism. As pressures grew to harmonize Irish laws and policies more in tune with European expectations, Ireland found itself in a situation where, on the one hand, the state started distancing itself from the Catholic church, while, on the other hand, religion was revitalized in more non-orthodox ways (Ganiel 2016). While secularization does not necessarily have to be accompanied by modernization and modernization does not always imply secularization of society (Spickard 2006), a broader socio-structural reorganization of society would have implications for the role of religion in public and private life.

Where important distinctions are to be made is in the operationalization of society on societal and individual levels in order to assess degrees of religiosity (Mouzelis 2012). At a structural level of objective secularization, we understand how governments and other sectors make rational decisions divorced from religious morality (Hjelm 2018); if religion is losing its 'monopoly on truth', then religious orthodoxy weakens and pluralism finds its way to flourish. When plausibility structures become compromised, individual religiosity becomes increasingly subjectivized (Berger 1967) as increasing pluralization undercuts their assumed ontological foundations. This process may not necessarily lead to a decrease in religiosity (Davie 2013) but to religiosity based on personal conviction. With the revival of folk religious practices, development of New Age spiritualities and (re-)emergence of NRMs since the 1960s, some people in Ireland seem to have concluded that Catholicism is only one of many options to satisfy ontological and spiritual needs or provide a sense of belonging.

From the point of view of secularization theory, social differentiation is the process by which social institutions develop their own logic and values (Mouzelis 2012) independent from religion. For example, Seán Lemass created a government committee in 1966 to review the prohibition of divorce and the constitutionally guaranteed 'special position' of the Roman Catholic Church in Ireland (Fuller 2004, cited in Malešević 2019). To an outside observer, such action may not be controversial. However, such infraction from the established protocol of consultation between the state figures and the Catholic church representatives speaks to the liberalization among political elites and the slow but steady distancing between the two (Malešević 2019). Differentiation in the spheres of competence between the state and church in Ireland meant that in the 1970s and 1980s the marriage bar was lifted, Ireland joined the European Economic Community, print and visual media were less subjected to church censorship and economic development took precedence. Increasing rationalization means that the capacity of religious institutions to coordinate the macro-societal imposition of doctrine diminishes, the role of religion in a person's life changes (Possamai 2015) and expanding global connectedness lends itself to a heterogeneous religious landscape. A range of beliefs in Irish society currently encompasses post-Catholic folk religion, New Age spiritualities and therapies, fiction-based religions and varieties of stricter and more loosely defined NRMs.

On the one hand, diversity diffuses dominance of one religious creed, and secular world views may contribute to a general decrease of religious belief (Molteni and Biolcati 2018). In Ireland, 468,421 people stated that they had no religion in 2016 in comparison to 186,318 in 2006 and 66,270 in 1991 (Central Statistics Office 2016). A growth of numbers in the categories of 'atheist' and 'agnostic' underlines the point about the increase in the more sceptical views on religion (Mouzelis 2012). In the Irish context, the number of atheists grew from 929 in 2006 to 7,769 in 2016 while agnostics amounted to 5,198 cases in 2016 growing from 1,515 cases only a decade earlier (Central Statistics Office 2016). On the other hand, the plurality of religious plausibility structures may lead to an increase in individual religiosity. Adrian Pabst (2012) argues that a decline in traditional and orthodox faiths does not preclude an increase in newer, modernizing creeds. When we look at Ireland, Central Statistics Office data show that membership in the Catholic church declined to 78 per cent in 2016 from 84 per cent just five years earlier. However, so-called migrant religions such as Islam and Orthodox as well as respondents in the category 'Other stated religions' have all recorded significant growth, measuring an increase between 30 and 40 per cent in a space of five years (Central Statistics Office 2011, 2016).

Another important aspect of understanding religious change is the process of individualization that underpins modern desecularization. Anthony Giddens (1991) talks about the 'empty spaces' that emerge when traditional and collectivist social codes disintegrate. In the context of pluralized and globalized societies, individual freedom of choice spreads downwards or, as Nicos Mouzelis (2012) says, it filters down to the non-elite level at the base of society. The de-rationalized religious field is revived through individual conviction and a choice to engage in new religious ideas. Sometimes a surrogate type of religiosity develops. Consumerism and materialism fostered in the Celtic Tiger era in Ireland prove that the gods of capitalism or 'The Money Cult' (Lehmann 2016) transcend individual piety into economic self-realization.

Countries with a strong Catholic culture are said to experience low secularization (Greeley 2003). While Ireland has changed from a society deeply embedded into Catholicism to one where the religious authority of the Catholic church is on a steady decline (Malešević 2010), over a hundred years of Catholic culture has its benefits. The strong presence of Catholic culture breeds a sense of communal belonging that is experienced through generations. With the pluralization of society and the liberalization of views, the expanding religious landscape offers the possibility of recreating a sense of belonging through experimentation with other religious or spiritual creeds. Engaging with alternative religious groups from the 1990s can be partially explained to coincide with the revelations of the Catholic church's institutional abuse of children and by the economic crisis of the late 2000s. Undoubtedly, the public questioning of the Catholic church's historical practices in industrial schools and Magdalene laundries contributed to an increasing lack of trust towards the institution (Donnelly and Inglis 2010). At the same time, economic development, urbanization and expansion of third-level education have led to more urban, educated and critical citizens. But this newly found freedom also meant more individual responsibility; cultural and social capital had to be accrued in new, less familiar ways. Disappointment and disillusionment with organized religion coupled with increasing individualization of a neoliberal kind, and pressures of consumerism have created a sense of invincibility for some who joined NRMs of a world-affirming kind like Scientology or a retreat from materialism for those who preferred more world-rejecting movements like Hare Krishna. The New Age type of spirituality seems to have attracted followers most open to living in harmony with nature and self, though New Age has increasingly become commodified in the recent past due to capitalist demands of regulation and accreditation (Kuhling 2014).

Conclusion

Secularization is often portrayed as a uniquely modern phenomenon confined to Europe and, to a lesser degree, the Anglo-Saxon world, depicting changes to people's degree of Christian religiosity. The regional, national, continental and global differences in degrees of secularity are well documented (Bruce 2002; Malešević 2010; Pabst 2012; Davie 2013). As the concept of desecularization is gaining traction in academic circles (Martin 2005), it becomes more obvious that it is a concept mostly applicable to Western modernity with de-rationalization of the religious sphere translating into 'dechristianisation' (Mouzelis 2012: 215). Modern desecularization is nothing new; the reinvigoration of religion across pre-modern social classes through gentrification and syncretization of popular religions (Possamai 2015) attests to the complexity of religious expression. Expressive individualism and 'turning inwards' against the orthodoxy of organized religion (Mouzelis 2012: 216) requires a quest for personal spiritual fulfilment. A subjectivized religiosity was as prevalent in eighteenth-century Ireland as it is today. The overlap between New Age spiritualities and another vehicle of modern desecularization, NRMs, materializes in practices such as yoga and meditation with the use of angel cards and a keen interest in astrology.

In recognizing finer qualities in the popular religions of the past, post-Catholic folk religiosity happily embraces belief in spirits with faith in god's omnipotence. While the concept of modernization may be criticized for its tautological reasoning (Peng 2009), a key ingredient of modernity still advocates for the supremacy of an individual as 'the measure of all things'. If Ireland is to embrace its de-rationalized, heterogeneous and less-institutionalized religious landscape, it is also expected to deconstruct its Irishness so that ethno-religious identification of 'Irish' and 'Catholic' becomes decoupled.

Chapter 9

MIGRANT RELIGIONS AND THE IRISH STATE

Abel Ugba

Taking African transnational Pentecostalism as the main example and focusing mostly on the decades since the Celtic Tiger economic boom (Sweeney 1998), this chapter provides a critical assessment of the development and dynamics of migrant religions within the Irish state. The Celtic Tiger period is germane to this analysis for two main reasons. One, although immigrants were present in Ireland long before the birth of the modern Irish state in 1922 (McKeon 1997; Rolston and Shannon 2002), their larger-scale presence and most visible religious and cultural activities have taken place since the Celtic Tiger period (Smith and Mutwarasibo 2000; Ugba 2009). Two, the sociocultural conditions and moral climate that resulted directly and indirectly from the economic prosperity of the Celtic Tiger years constituted an important context that has framed the history and activities of Pentecostal Africans and other immigrant religious formations such as Muslims. Although this analysis focuses primarily on African-led Pentecostalism, references will be made to Islam not least because the two faiths arguably constitute the most prominent interventions on Ireland's religious landscape in recent decades. Also, the two religions seemed to have received the most attention in public discourse in the period under review (Scharbrodt 2011; Montgomery 2013; Carr and Haynes 2015; Khan 2017). Moreover, there are similarities and dissimilarities in the experiences of the two groups which make for a richer and nuanced analysis.

This chapter reflects critically on the multidimensional experiences and encounters of Pentecostal Africans as they sought to establish a presence in Ireland's sociocultural and religious landscapes. It references the multiple levels of contacts and conflicts with the dominant Catholic church, the Irish Pentecostal 'other', the public and the Irish state. It highlights the aloofness of the Irish state and argues that this disposition translated into the absence of critical statutory frameworks for important and necessary dialogues and policies that could have made the presence and integration experiences of African Pentecostals less complicated. It suggests that the failure to put the framework and critical infrastructure in place has also limited – at least in the short term – the potential societal benefits from the presence of the 'religious other' in twenty-first-century Ireland. Following this introduction, the chapter will provide a brief overview of the multiple entanglements between religion and migration to situate the current developments in a meaningful historical context. This will be followed by a summary of the multiple features of the interfaces between religion and migration in postmodernism. Here, emphasis will be placed on the accelerated and diverse religion transnationalism, especially the increased migration of the religious 'other' from the Global South to the largely 'secular' Global North and the debates relating to how the nation states, mostly in the West, have attempted to manage this presence of religious and cultural minorities in their territory.

The chapter posits African transnational Pentecostalism as an unusual phenomenon that the Irish state and much of the public could not understand or engage with in the formative years of the religious movement. Similarly, media and public discourse of the activities of fledgling Muslim communities was largely coloured by anxieties and suspicions deriving mostly from the media discourse of 9/11 attacks in the United States (Scharbrodt 2011; Carr and Haynes 2015) and long-standing stereotypes about the oriental world (Said 1995). In concluding, the chapter states that the religious 'other' in postmodern Ireland arrived at a time when, due to a complex combination of factors, the state and much of the public lacked the motivation to understand or engage with it. Although the government actively discussed and proposed multiculturalism and integration initiatives at the time, none was directed specifically towards immigrant religious minorities, and there was certainly no recognition of the significance and role of religious ideologies in shaping both the self-perception of immigrants and their integration and acculturation aspirations.

Religion and migration in historical contexts

The relationship between religion and migration is hydra-headed and complex. For example, religion has been a major factor in voluntary and involuntary migrations within countries and internationally (Carling 2002; Gozdziak and Shandy 2002; Fiddian-Qasmiyeh et al. 2014). Religion is implicated in migration motives and decisions, for example, when believers relocate to escape religious persecution and biases, or when they embark on a voluntary mission to spread religious ideologies. The Jewish diaspora is often cited as one of the earliest examples of migration that is compelled by hostile circumstances or persecution, while the transmission of Buddhism along the Silk Road from the East to the West is often highlighted as a voluntary migration aimed at achieving religious-cum-economic purposes (Casanova 2001; Obadia 2012; Herrington 2013).

Transnational migrations that have been induced by religion, or in which religion has played a significant role, have included the presence of European Christian missionaries in various parts of Africa from the fifteenth century and the activities of Islam propagators in Africa (Levtzion and Pouwels 2000; Reese 2014). Since the second half of the twentieth century, this has also included the steady flows of variously motivated agents of religions from the Global South to the Global North to propagate religious ideologies and establish a presence in the sociopolitical and cultural landscapes of countries in the North (Obadia 2012; Herrington 2013). The flight of many Yazidis from Iraq (Hanish 2009; *The Economist* 2016) and Muslims from Myanmar (Ware and Laoutides 2019; Roy 2020) are recent examples of involuntary migrations that were provoked by religious persecution.

In addition to compelling and instigating migrations, religion is also a significant factor in how believers self-define and self-present in the immigration circumstances and in how they construct belongingness, social boundaries and commonalities (Haar 1998; Hunt and Lightly 2001; Hunt 2002; Ugba 2009; Adogame 2015). Often, religion is a familiar and dependable social, material and emotional resource that most immigrant believers are quick to deploy in new and challenging immigration circumstances. Immigrant religious activism is generally unhindered by precarious immigration statuses and the many other impediments that prevent immigrants from participating in politics, the labour market and workers' unionism. For this and other reasons, religious activism has become more dynamic and diverse in postmodernism, leading R. Stephen Warner (1998: 3) to conclude that religion means more to immigrants in the immigrant context than it did in their home countries because religious institutions become the places where new relationships are 'forged'. For Barbara Metcalf, 'the sense of contrast – contrast with a past or contrast with the rest of society – is at the heart of a self-consciousness that shapes religious style' (Metcalf 1996: 7). Penny Logan, who studied the Gujaratis in Britain, concluded that adult believers developed heightened religious awareness 'as a result of belonging to a minority group in a predominantly irreligious society' (Logan 1988: 124, cited in Vertovec 2000).

However, it must be acknowledged that the supposed multiplier and dynamic effects of the immigration experience on religious activism have been problematized by some analysts. Douglas Massey and Monica Higgins (2011: 1), for example, assert that 'immigration is a disruptive event that alienates immigrants from religious practice rather than "theologizing" them'. James Beckford (2019) has similarly acknowledged that immigration sometimes offers an escape from religion for some immigrants. These notions do not capture the experiences of Pentecostal African immigrants in Ireland. Not only have these groups grown from small and invisible communities in the 1990s to vibrant and dynamic community institutions, but they also are increasingly socially and culturally significant as bridges between African communities and mainstream Irish churches, interest groups and the larger society. Their dynamic growth and vast and near-ubiquitous presence within the African communities remain one of the most significant immigration-related interventions in the social and cultural landscapes in Ireland in recent decades. Their membership, socio-demographic profile and aspirations are being renewed and enriched by successive waves of migration from Africa and the increased number of Irish-born Africans in their ranks.

For a long time, much of the research on immigrant religions in the West (see Williams 1988; Kalilombe 1997; Mella 1994; Warner and Wittner 1998; Vásquez and Dewind 2014) adopted a functionalist analytical framework that focused mostly and disproportionately on the role of religious institutions in providing emotional, social and material support for believers as they strive to acclimatize and integrate. For example, Orlando Mella (1994: 114) concluded that Catholic Chilean refugees in Sweden utilized their faith to 'reconstruct a microcosm of the homeland in the host country' to offset the cultural marginalization and social isolation they experienced in the new environment. Gerrie ter Haar (1998: 159) similarly notes that Pentecostalism endowed African immigrant believers in the Netherlands with 'the spiritual strength and social contacts necessary to survive, and even to begin the long climb up the ladder of social responsibility in a country which, like most parts of Western Europe, has gradually become more hostile to foreigners, particularly when they are people of colour'. It must be noted that Haar's analyses, while largely functionalist, do examine the role of Pentecostal ideologies in constructing self and social identity. The functionalist approach to immigrant religion largely fails to prioritize the substance of beliefs and their transformative impact on believers, but it instead links religion's relevance primarily to its societal and social significance. Part of the reasons for this is the intentional and unintentional attachment to the secularization or 'death of god' thesis (Anidjar 2006; Leiter 2019) by some scholars in the West. Functionalist analysis of religion has often manifested in the penchant, also partly motivated by a secularist orientation, to subsume religion under the rubrics of culture (Krech 2000).

Religion, migration and the nation state in postmodernity

The increased presence of Pentecostal Africans and other immigrant religious formations in twenty-first-century Europe, including Ireland, has taken place against the backdrop of increased global migrations generally and of the migration of propagators of various religious ideologies from the Global South to the Global North (OECD 2020). Although this analysis focuses on post-Second World War, it must be acknowledged that the presence of the religious 'other' in Ireland has a long, rich and complex history (Gray 2016; Holmes 2017). This has led Tadhg Ó hAnnracháin (2019) to describe Ireland and the Netherlands as the two Western European countries that have been most impacted by confessional migration. This chapter references only one example – the migration of British Protestants to Ireland. Ó hAnnracháin paints a nuanced picture of the role that religion played in instigating migrations from Britain. The bulk of the immigrants who arrived from Britain to Ireland between 1580 and 1641 were Protestants. While religious motives, particularly the inclination towards evangelism, may have inspired the migration of some, for others religion acquired salience and a stronger identitarian purpose only as they negotiate self-identity and social belongingness in Ireland. Ó hAnnracháin states that the confessional identity of those Protestant migrants greatly impacted their self-ascribed as well as the externally imposed social identity and the staunch resistance and brutal repression or 'explosion of resentment in 1641–42' that they were subsequently subjected to (Ó hAnnracháin 2019: 11).

The absence of 'explosion of resentment' is not the only marker of the dissimilarities between the circumstances of the earlier Protestant immigrants in

Ireland and the more recent immigrant religious 'other' that this chapter focuses on. The most important marker of difference is perhaps the colonial context of that encounter and the related social and economic disparity that existed between the Protestant immigrants from Britain and the bulk of the native population. The post-Second World War presence of immigrant religions in Ireland, including African Pentecostalism and Islam, has only extended and enriched a complex history of disrupted and disruptive presences of the religious 'other' in Ireland.

Although the post-Second World War immigrant religious 'other' are not confronting the scale and type of repression encountered by the Protestant immigrants from Britain, their reception in Ireland and insertion into the mainstream society have, for various reasons and in different ways, been problematic. The challenge of incorporating religious minorities is replicated in various forms in other Western democracies. Religious ideologies nurtured in a different and mostly contrary sociocultural environment in the Global South increasingly seek a presence in the West in the era of globalization and mass migration. The contact and collision between nation states in the West and immigrant-led minority religions appear to have accelerated since the 9/11 attacks, and it has become a recurring theme in media and public discourses of multiculturalism, immigrant integration, secularism and the status and social location of cultural and religious minorities in Western democracies. As Beckford (2019: 15–35) notes, 'Arguments about religion and migration have become at least as contentious as those about "race", class, language, nationality and ethnicity in discussions of social cohesion, integration or assimilation.' Similarly, Peggy Levitt (1998: 75) describes religious globalization as 'the spread and thickening of transnational religious structures and movements that challenge the nation-state'. Academic researchers who have paid attention to this development have mainly focused on longer-established non-Christian religions with a large followership, such as Islam (Farrar 2012; Tottoli 2015). By focusing on African transnational Pentecostalism, this analysis aims to expand and enrich the discourse.

Although the new immigrant religions in Ireland have not encountered the challenges and brutal resistance experienced by the seventeenth-century Protestants from Britain, their presence has nonetheless been circumscribed by an uncongenial climate that has made their activities problematic. In the next section, I present a concise analysis of the history of African-led Pentecostal groups in Ireland and examine their connections to and interactions with various sectors of Irish society. I also discuss the religious and sociopolitical contexts that have framed their orientation and practice.

Migrant religions in Ireland: Contemporary contexts

African transnational Pentecostalism and Islam are among the religions that have perched on the wings of mass migrations to reach several countries in the West, including Ireland. Internal developments in Ireland, especially the economic boom of the 1990s known as the 'Celtic Tiger', resulted in new immigration policies that opened avenues for greater migrant inflows. Ireland's new-found economic wealth, and the higher international clout that came with it, made her more visible and attractive to migrants from various parts of the world. The other factors that contributed to the increase in immigration are the increase in global refugee flows that resulted from armed and civil conflicts in various countries (Collinson 1993; Faist 2000) and the general larger-scale movement of goods, services and people inspired by globalization. These flows moved mostly from the Global South to the Global North and East to West (Sassen 1998). Migrants from various African countries were among those who came into Ireland to meet the country's need for workers, transact business, study, join family members or seek political asylum (Cullen 2000).

Another contributor to the increased presence of African immigrants in Ireland from the 1990s is its geographical proximity to the UK. Apart from having a larger and more settled population of Africans, the UK has direct air links to many countries in Africa. Some African immigrants to Ireland from the 1990s had lived in the UK or travelled through it to reach Ireland. Others have friends or relatives there and they consume goods and services produced or mediated by their compatriots in the UK. These transnational involvements and activities have contributed to the evolution of the nascent African groups in Ireland into vibrant communities that have provided social and cultural reference points for new African immigrants. Another contributor is the linguistic affinity between Ireland and several countries in Africa. Immigrants from Anglophone African countries are generally more confident migrating to other English-speaking countries because they believe acculturation and social and economic mobility will be less problematic than in non-English-speaking countries.

Moreover, some Africans in Ireland came from countries with deep and strong religious connections to Ireland. Those connections were initiated and concretized through the activities of Irish Catholic priests and missionaries in several parts of the continent. As agents of the Catholic religious empire, Irish missionaries travelled to, and propagated religious ideologies in, countries such as Nigeria, Ghana and Sierra Leone. Some of the Africans who came to Ireland from the 1990s had interacted with Irish men and women who came to Africa as missionaries and educators (Ugba 2003). Much of that interaction, and the religious education that was imparted on them by the Irish missionaries, happened in their formative and impressionable years and likely shaped their impression of Ireland as a religious country with moral and spiritual values that were closely aligned with those from their African background and spirituality. Pentecostal Africans have struggled to reconcile their preconception of Ireland with the Celtic Tiger Ireland that confronted them after they arrived, as one church leader stated in an interview with me in the early days of the movement in Ireland:

> Right now, we believe God is leading us to pray for a spiritual revival in Ireland. Ireland is a Christian nation, but the bible says, 'by their fruits, you'll know them'. You don't measure Christianity by what they say; you measure it by the

fruits they show. And as I look around there seems to be so many fruits that do not look like Christian fruits.

Another affinity between Ireland and Africa relates to the role played by various Irish groups and the trade unions in the anti-apartheid struggles in Africa. As far back as the eighteenth century, Dublin, Limerick and other Irish cities hosted Black anti-slave trade activists like Olaudah Equiano and Frederick Douglass. However, Bill Rolston and Michael Shannon argue that the contexts of the various encounters between Ireland and Africa inevitably skewed the balance of power in favour of Ireland, a situation that has generally re-enforced a feeling of self-importance and superiority among the Irish. As they put it, 'the Irish had countless opportunities to be reminded of their relative superiority and while that lesson may have lain dormant at various times, it only needed the excuse of immigration to be awakened' (Rolston and Shannon 2002: 88).

By the end of the first decade of the twenty-first century, religious activism had become entrenched among Ireland's immigrant communities. For example, the Islamic Cultural Centre of Ireland in Clonskeagh in Dublin, which housed an ultra-modern Mosque and eatery and recreational facilities, had become a hub of cultural and religious activities for the fast-growing Muslim population and a magnet for visitors from various sectors of the Irish society. In November 2007, the Central Statistics Office (CSO) reported that the number of Muslims in the country had increased to 32,500, making Islam the third-largest religion in the State after the Catholics and the Church of Ireland. According to a press release by the CSO (2007: 1), 'just over 55 per cent of Muslims were either Asian or African nationals with 30.7 per cent having Irish nationality'. The majority of Muslims (94.2 per cent) lived in the cities or urban centres (CSO 2007: 1). In 2016, the population of Muslims had increased to 63,443, or 1.3 per cent of the population of Ireland. The average age of Muslims was twenty-six years whilst that of the general population was thirty-seven. Muslims were more likely than the general population to get married and less likely to be divorced. Significantly, a CSO report on the 2016 census showed that 'Irish nationals represented the largest nationality group among [the] Muslims in Ireland, accounting for 55.6 per cent of the total' (CSO 2016a). These factors pointed to bright and solid prospects for expanded and thriving Muslim communities in Ireland.

The growth prospects for Pentecostalism in Ireland were equally bright, according to the 2016 census. It noted that Pentecostal and Apostolic groups had increased from 3,152 in 2002 to 13,350 in 2016, an annual growth rate of almost 11 per cent. At an average age of 25.3 years, their membership is considerably younger than that of the general population and those of most religious groups in Ireland. Most Pentecostals live in Dublin. While over 55 per cent identified 'African' as their ethnicity, 66.4 per cent claimed Irish as their nationality (CSO 2016a). The comparatively younger population of Pentecostals and the high rate of naturalization suggest a bright prospect for the growth and expansion of these communities.

Migrant religion and the Irish state: Case study of Pentecostal Africans

Pentecostalism is an umbrella of related doctrines and practices that are based on the Holy Spirit experience of the disciples of Jesus during the Feast of Pentecost in the first century (see Acts 2.1-46). It is not uncommon for Pentecostals from different groups and even the same group to hold divergent interpretations of core biblical teachings. But they are unified, and differentiated from many non-Pentecostal Christian formations, by the overriding importance they place on the transformative and restorative power of the Holy Spirit, the literal appropriation of biblical texts and the claim to rebirth or being born again. Among Pentecostals, there is a near-unanimous acceptance of the role of the Holy Spirit as a super enabler that invests its harbourer with supernatural ability to overcome various material, emotional and spiritual challenges. Although the divergent appropriation of beliefs has frequently resulted in conflicts and schisms, this has invested Pentecostalism with flexibility and made it adaptable to various contexts. It is a feature that has aided the rapid global spread of Pentecostalism.

Pentecostal churches were among the first, and perhaps the most prominent, community institutions established by new African immigrants in Ireland. From the late 1990s, they provided visible evidence of religious activism among newer African immigrants, especially in major cities such as Dublin, Galway, Cork and Donegal. The groups vary by size, doctrines, transnational connections and history. The socio-demographic profile of the various groups generally comprises mostly young men and women who have migrated from various African countries for diverse reasons, including to propagate Pentecostalism and establish multiracial and multi-ethnic congregations. They also comprise African immigrants from other EU countries and, increasingly in the last decade, children of first- and second-generation African immigrants, the majority of whom are also Irish citizens.

By the late 1990s, the presence of these congregations was being acknowledged in media and public discourse, but they were primarily portrayed as exotic, racially exclusive and subaltern institutions that merely provided a semblance of home for their African members. Academic studies of African transnational Pentecostalism did not exist in the Irish context when I commenced my research in 2001. Therefore, the privilege and excitement to be the pioneering researcher of this significant and new phenomenon in Ireland were tempered with logistical and intellectual challenges. The logistical challenges mainly related to issues of access to research sites and participants and overcoming the suspicion and mistrust of church members who were relatively new in Ireland and were still entangled in the struggle to establish legal residence and social acceptance. The uncertainties and anxieties of the time sometimes translated into various degrees of suspicion of the 'outsider', including other Africans. My pre-existing links in the community, most of which I had established when I co-published and edited Metro Éireann (www.metroeireann.com), helped to break down access barriers and establish an 'insider' status relatively quickly. The absence of documented and reliable academic research on this group was one of the main intellectual challenges. The semi-scholarly information about immigrant religions that existed consisted mainly of publications by the churches themselves, a report by the Irish Council of Churches (ICC 2003) and a few reports in the mainstream media, mostly the *Irish Times* (Cullen 2000; McCann 2000; Haughey 2002).

To address the dearth of independent and scholarly material, I triangulated several data-gathering methods and theoretical frameworks in my investigation. The methods included ethnographic observation, a quantitative survey, semi-structured interviews, semiotic analysis of printed material and critical analysis of audio sermons. I also had several hours of informal interactions and conversation with research participants who had become my acquaintances and visited me and my family with their families. Those visits translated into unique avenues to study my informants in a natural environment as I conversed and interacted with them and observed their interactions with one another. Those informal meetings and our discussions provided deeper and robust insights into the beliefs, experiences and perspectives of my informants, and they enriched my accounts immeasurably. I also actively cultivated key informants or 'cultural interpreters' (Richardson 1990, 1995; Van Mannen 1995; Wolcott 1995) in the groups that I investigated. They consisted of influential men and women, mostly officials, who were regular participants in the affairs of the groups and had a rich knowledge of, and insight into, doctrines and praxis. They played a pivotal role in enlisting the support and trust of research participants. The other main intellectual challenge was how to define and delineate the research to invest it with the intellectual rigour, depth, comprehensiveness and insight befitting a pivotal intellectual investigation of this new development in Ireland. Here, the interventions and suggestions of mentors and colleagues in the Department of Sociology at Trinity College Dublin proved invaluable.

The relationship of African Pentecostals with the Irish (or white) Pentecostal 'other' has oscillated between competition and cooperation. Some African Pentecostals who had attended 'Irish' Pentecostal churches left because the way of worship in those churches did not cohere with the experience they had had in their home countries. An African Pentecostal who had attended an Irish Pentecostal church said he relocated to an African church because the 'way' they prayed in the Irish-led church differed from the way 'we pray in Africa'. Others left because the services were devoid of vibrant singing, music and dancing, and the themes that dominated the prayers and sermons did not connect with their daily experiences and struggles in Ireland.

The distinction that Pentecostal Africans create between themselves and white-dominated Irish Pentecostal groups is smaller and less significant than the one they create between themselves and the mainline churches, especially the dominant Catholic establishment. They generally believe that the Catholic church is spiritually dead or in 'spiritual darkness' because it has deviated from some biblical doctrines, embraced formalistic worship and ceased to demand moral accountability from its members. In the words of the leader of a leading African Pentecostal church,

> As a born-again Christian, my life should be based on the bible. When people see me, they should know that I live by the bible … this is not common in the Catholic Church. They just go through catechism and the Simple Prayer book. The Catholics have their Bible called Apocrypha.

Describing the 'cold' reception he was accorded the only time he visited a Catholic church, an African Pentecostal said he felt 'as if I wasn't a Christian'.

However, this opposition to the mainline churches has not hindered African Pentecostal groups from forming a relationship of convenience with these churches at times. For example, some African Pentecostal groups have rented, or freely avail of, church halls from Catholic parishes for their Sunday and midweek meetings. These arrangements have sometimes ended acrimoniously. For example, the leader of an African Pentecostal group stated that a priest from whom they had rented a hall became envious and terminated the cooperation because of the rapid increase in the number of those attending the services of the African group. The priest worried that the African group could in time draw the members of his church away. Other arrangements have broken down after the officials of the mainline church accused African Pentecostals of orchestrating loud worship meetings or engaging in services that lasted longer than the agreed time.

The ambivalent relationship that Pentecostal Africans maintain with the mainstream churches is replicated in their relationship with the larger society. Although they oppose and, in some cases, detest some of the social trends and habits of the majority society, they nonetheless rely on the institutions, infrastructure and services provided by the society. Most African Pentecostal groups oppose alcohol consumption in any quantity, sex before and outside of marriage, non-Christian music and music festivals, and a host of other activities that are common across the majority society. These markers of difference have not only created social boundaries between them and the larger society but also constitute formidable impediments to their evangelism and 'reverse mission' goals.

An unintended consequence of the rapid expansion and increased visibility of both Pentecostal African groups and Muslim communities is unwanted attention from racist and anti-immigrant groups, and secularist and atheistic interest groups. These groups are, for diverse and sometimes conflicting reasons, opposed to the presence and activities of minority immigrant religions in Ireland. For example, the Immigration Control Platform campaigned vigorously for more restrictive immigration policies. Additionally, the Irish government, while confirming its commitment to the Geneva Convention, has nonetheless failed to criticize government ministers who publicly made unsubstantiated distinctions between 'genuine' refugees and those they qualified as 'bogus', 'economic migrants' or 'welfare scroungers' (Cullen 2000; Guerin 2002). In the early twenty-first century, vitriolic anti-immigration discourse in a section of the Irish media quickly translated into a moral panic and racially motivated attacks directed mostly at Black Africans. They culminated in the defacing of the shops and homes of Africans in North Dublin, Parnell Street and Tallaght (Lentin 2001; Lentin and McVeigh 2002, 2006; Olusola 2002). The hostilities hindered the evangelism intentions and activities of

Pentecostal Africans. A pastor and the members of his group, for example, decided to abandon their street evangelism initiatives after officials at a Dublin train station threatened to call the Gardaí (Irish police) because they were distributing leaflets to visitors and commuters. As the terrified church leader puts it, 'I want to preach the gospel; I don't want to go to jail. So, we've been a bit wiser since then.'

A 2004 referendum that abolished *jus soli* citizenship was a culmination of sustained agitation mostly by anti-immigration activists and is recognized as a landmark moment. Comhall Fanning has argued that the redefinition of Irish citizenship through the referendum and the other measures by the Irish state created the 'non-citizen'. 'Non-citizens' were portrayed as 'transient and not belonging to the nation-state' (Fanning 2019: 11). Punitive employment laws and social welfare policies such as the Direct Provision (DP), the state-sponsored system of accommodation for asylum seekers, compounded the social and economic isolation of asylum seekers and made their survival precarious. As Fanning (2019: 10) puts it, 'When citizenship is combined with the provision of welfare and healthcare, it could be viewed as the right to survive.' While DP and other state policies segregated asylum seekers physically and socioculturally from the mainstream society, African-initiated churches provided a conducive environment where many could articulate their challenges and seek various solutions with input from co-worshippers and church leaders.

Another major development that has framed the presence and activities of new immigrant religions in Ireland is the steady ascent of secularism and atheism – a development that has stunned and challenged Ireland's Pentecostal African immigrants who have arrived in the country with a self-defined 'reverse mission' mandate. The fundamental premise of reverse mission is that Christian beliefs and moral values are disappearing rapidly in the West and the duty to halt the slide and make a sterile Christianity landscape vibrant again belongs to Africans who themselves have been impacted by, and benefited from, the seeds of Christianity that the European missionaries propagated in Africa many centuries ago. Pentecostals and evangelical Christians in Africa and the diaspora are among the most fervent agents of reverse mission. Many Pentecostal African immigrants arrived in Ireland with a preconceived notion of Ireland as a 'Christian' country – although Ireland has officially been a secular state since a 1973 amendment to the constitution. However, Pentecostal immigrants have been confronted with not only a dramatic upturn in the number of atheists and agnostics but also the critical and disdainful attitude of a growing segment of the population of Ireland towards religion generally, but especially towards institutional religion. For example, the number of those with no religion, including atheists and agnostics, had increased dramatically from 67,413 in 1991 to 277,237 in 2011 and 481,388 in 2016 (CSO 2016a). Worryingly for African Pentecostal agents of reverse mission, atheism and agnosticism are spreading fastest among the younger age groups, including students in secondary and tertiary institutions (CSO 2016b: 72–3).

The emotional and social disentanglement from religion by many in Ireland had been impacted by the incessant revelations in the 1990s and 2000s of sexual and physical abuse among Catholic clergy and the historical abuse in orphanages and homes for single mothers owned and managed by the Catholic church (Inglis 1998; Bethune 2012; Regan 2013). But for Pentecostal Africans, a significant marker of the repudiation of Christian values by Ireland was when it voted by close to 66 per cent in 2018 to repeal the Irish constitution's Eighth Amendment, which proscribed abortion and equated the right to life of an unborn foetus to that of a pregnant woman. The Taoiseach (Prime Minister) Leo Varadkar subsequently described the result of the referendum as 'a culmination of a quiet revolution that's been taking place in Ireland' ('Reaction: "The Country Has Listened"' 2018). It was a revolution that has no doubt heightened the uncongenial climate for Pentecostal Africans. It is one that is likely to further complicate the landscape for this religious movement and the other migrant religions because it widens the chasm between them and the larger Irish society, and complexifies the social and moral contexts in which they seek to train their younger generations to be religious. The 'culmination of a quiet revolution' seems to guarantee that the disinterest in, and lack of connection to, contemporary immigrant religions by the larger Irish society will continue for the foreseeable future.

Conclusion

In this chapter, African transnational Pentecostalism has been posited as one example of an immigrant religion that has taken roots in postmodern Ireland. The chapter has examined the circumstances in which African transnational Pentecostalism was introduced to Ireland and highlighted the challenges its adherents encountered as they sought to stamp their religious practices and ideologies on Ireland's sociocultural and religious landscape. It has not been the aim of this chapter to present in-depth historiography of Islam in Ireland or trace the dynamics of its growth and influence. However, the occasional references to Islam in Ireland have provided insights that confirm various degrees of commonalities between the experiences of its adherents and those of Pentecostal Africans.

This chapter has highlighted that African Pentecostal groups have confronted antipathy from sections of the public and the media and battled state-sanctioned impediments to acculturation and integration, mostly in the form of policies that denied their members and other immigrants groups access to gainful employment, civic and political citizenship, and the infrastructure and space to actualize their religious practices in ways that cohere with their expectations. The other obstacles have included various forms of indirect discrimination, unintended biases and racially motivated micro and open aggressions from sections of the Irish public. Racially motivated aggressions have included attacks on individuals and properties. The experiences of pioneering African Pentecostals in Ireland have included degrees of cooperation and resistance from individual parishes within the dominant Catholic establishment in Ireland, mostly in Dublin.

Although the government, through proxies such as the National Consultative Committee on Racism and Interculturalism (NCCRI) and the Equality Authority, initiated policies and public consultations about multiculturalism and integration in the late 1990s and the first decade of the twenty-first century, it failed to recognize the cultural, sociopolitical and identitarian significance of religion for immigrants. It instead subsumed religion into the rubrics of culture and, consequently, showcased neither the desire nor genuine political will to initiate systematic and constructive dialogues with Ireland's nascent immigrant religious communities of the 1990s. This omission simultaneously deprived the immigrant religious formations of valuable resources and support that would have enhanced their insertion into the Irish society and diminished the contributions and benefits they potentially could bring to their new home.

Chapter 10

IRISH CATHOLICISM: WHERE HAS IT BEEN AND WHERE IS IT GOING?

Brian Conway

The Knock Marriage Bureau (hereafter, 'the Bureau') – also known as Knock Marriage Introductions – was founded by Fr Michael Keane, a priest of the archdiocese of Tuam in Knock, County Mayo, in 1967 (Neary 2011). Run by its priest-founder in its early days, it offered a Catholic dating service to prospective partners. The larger social context was the lack of meeting opportunities for men and women as emigration took hold in Western rural areas in the 1960s, even as other cultural practices of the era – such as attending dance halls – proliferated in more urbanized locations (Neary 2011).

The Bureau's approach involved a fairly straightforward procedure: prospective partners completed a questionnaire about themselves, their interests and so forth, and returned this to the Bureau along with photographs. Based on the information provided, the Bureau offered a number of introductions, depending on the number of available matches in its files (in terms of location, age, or perhaps educational background, etc.) (Gately 2019; McGrath 2019). This meant sending details about the match to each prospective partner. Once each partner agreed to meet, the Bureau exchanged their contact details and then stepped back, letting the individuals concerned make their own meeting arrangements.[1] Some of these meetings resulted in long-term relationships, and some not.

Over the years, the Bureau claimed to have helped bring about nearly a thousand marriages in this way. In 2019, however, the Bureau closed, citing the growth and popularity of online dating agencies that displaced its half a century or so role as a more traditional offline dating service (McCrave 2019). This is a good example of how needs in advanced modern societies once performed by religious groups become increasingly fulfilled by direct secular equivalents. As changes in the wider society take place – in this case, the diffusion of modern technologies – religion seems to lose its place and the secular world steps in. A kind of reshuffling of the religious-secular relation occurs. How can this dynamic be understood in the Irish case more generally?

This chapter attempts to apply sociologist Jörg Stolz and colleagues' relatively new theory of religious-secular competition (Stolz et al. 2016) to the case of Irish

Catholicism. This theory has been usefully proposed as an alternative to traditional theories of secularization and religious economy to account for religious change and continuity in modern societies. Although Stolz and colleagues developed and tested this theory primarily with the Swiss case in mind and focused mainly on the individual level of analysis, it also has application – although (yet) largely untested – to other national contexts.

While prior research has applied other perspectives such as the secularization framework to the Irish case (e.g. Hornsby-Smith 1992; Andersen 2016; Conway, forthcoming), to the best of my knowledge, no previous study has analysed it through this more recent theoretical approach. Thus, I investigate how this theory applies to the Catholic case at the individual (micro), organizational (meso) and societal (macro) levels.[2] More specifically, I examine trends in religious behaviours and beliefs, associational culture and vocations as well as the church's public legitimacy following decades of scandal, focusing on challenges to each from secular alternatives. In so doing, I show the relative suddenness of sharp reductions in the Catholic church's influence in the society. This chapter proceeds in three steps. I begin by setting forth the theoretical framing and then look at dynamics of competition between the religious and the secular at each level in turn. For each level I examine 'where Catholicism has been' and then focus on 'where Catholicism is going' in the future. As such, this chapter engages with the important issue of pathways of religious change. In so doing, I rely mostly on prior social survey- and historical-based studies. The final section provides a summary and conclusion.

Theorizing religious-secular competition

The basic insight of religious-secular competition theory is that from the 1960s modern societies came to be characterized by a growing competition between religious answers and secular answers to basic human questions and needs. The wider context here is the strengthening of various aspects of the society, including education, consumer culture, science and technology, and individual rights. Together, these sociocultural changes result in the emergence of a 'me-society', in which individuals are more and more questioning of the power of their former religious superiors (Stolz et al. 2016).

One sees this in the displacement of the priest as family counsellor by professional lay therapists, the growth of secular clubs and societies (e.g. Simon Community, Rotary) as an alternative to a religious associational culture (e.g. confraternities, sodalities) and the emergence of the secular media as rival 'pulpit' (Conway and Kilcoyne 1997) to the Catholic Church. Thus, this theory recognizes that religious-secular competition takes place at different levels of the society, from the individual to the organizational and societal. The main territory over which the religious and the secular compete include fulfilling quests for meaning and tackling personal crises, meeting needs for belonging and providing life opportunities, and defining what is a good and moral world. And outside forces such as pandemics, demographic shifts and technology can all be consequential for this struggle for influence. Sometimes the displacement of the religious by the secular (as in the opening vignette) is the outcome of this tension, but sometimes not. In some cases, alternative outcomes such as de-differentiation[3] may result (Stolz et al. 2016).

This perspective has been proposed as an informative alternative to prominent secularization and religious economy perspectives and, in particular, their tendency to make overly generalized claims (in the case of the religious economy perspective) or lose sight of specific historical factors (in the case of secularization theory). By taking a more person-led approach and bringing in contextual detail, this theory attempts to overcome these shortcomings, though empirically substantiating it is more difficult than might be assumed. Methodologically, Stolz and colleagues' approach relies on a mixed-methods research design, involving insights from interviews and large-scale social surveys. For example, on the qualitative side, the study compares the impact of growing up in a religious family (or not) on present-day religious identities and, on the quantitative side, the beliefs and practices of different generations (Stolz et al. 2016). Combined, this makes it possible to contextualize population-level trends and patterns in relation to the dynamics of individuals' lives unfolding across time and space. Within this framework, how might individual-level dynamics be understood?

Individual-level dynamics of competition

As mentioned, religious-secular competition theory posits an ongoing tension between the religious and secular worlds, with the latter usually winning out. This is reflected at the level of individual behaviours regarding such things as problem-solving, leisure and even religious practice itself. In the past, people sought help with problems within the family – such as marital discord – by seeking the assistance of a priest or religious (Stolz et al. 2016). Priests themselves sometimes received specialist training in marriage counselling to equip them with the skills and knowledge for this role. By contrast, today's personal problems are more and more tackled by secular lay expertise. This is reflected in the growth of an infrastructure of counselling services – in clinics instead of presbyteries – where ordinary people can avail of secular help.

For example, earlier research on help-seeking behaviour found that ordinary people rely upon a wide range of secular sources of help in tackling mental health difficulties and that these predominate over religious ones. Of secular professionals relied upon, psychiatrists, nurses and counsellors are relied on slightly more than are clergy in dealing with mental health issues. In addition, respondents tend to rate religious help as the least effective (Doherty and Moran 2009). Past research also found that clergy are relied upon *more* than certain secular supports such as psychologists, social workers, psychotherapists and the internet in tacking mental health difficulties. Regarding relative levels of reliance on secular versus religious help, in some cases (e.g. social workers, internet) clergy were only slightly more likely to be relied on, while compared to others (e.g. psychotherapists) clergy were about twice as likely to be relied upon (Doherty and Moran 2009).

Another aspect at this analytical level – and one which has received more attention in the literature – is individual religious behaviours. In the past, a strong religious service attendance norm resulted in crowded churches but this norm is now much weaker (Hornsby-Smith 1992; Donnelly and Inglis 2010; Andersen 2016; Conway, forthcoming). For example, weekly religious service attendance dropped from 82 per cent in 1981 to 40 per cent in 2008 (Pollack and Rosta 2017). In contemporary times, near-empty pews in religious services are not uncommon and church buildings frequently outsize their congregations, trying to hold out the further erosion of attendance. Even so, church attendance levels are relatively high compared to other European countries (Pollack and Rosta 2017).

The emptying of the pews is one thing, but their 'greying' is another. A visit to most Masses shows the preponderance of older-age categories among adherents and the relative absence of the young, a symbol of the displacement over time of more religious older cohorts by less religious younger ones. And large-scale social surveys bear this out. For example, past studies show an increase in 'nones' (i.e. respondents who self-identify as having no religious affiliation) among younger-age cohorts (Greeley and Ward 2000) and reductions in church attendance across different cohorts, even as their religious beliefs remain largely unchanged (Hirschle 2010). This trend is likely to continue as parental religious socialization, a key factor in perpetuating the Catholic faith across generations (Smith et al. 2014), diminishes.

Although the Catholic-specific practice of confession is not usually included in large-scale international social surveys measuring religiosity, it too appears to have eroded very significantly, symbolized by the repurposing of former confessionals as storage spaces or their jettisoning altogether.[4] According to national survey-based research, monthly confession rates reduced from 47 per cent in 1974 to 18 per cent in 1988–9 (Fahey 1992), before falling further to 9 per cent in 2007–8 (Mac Gréil 2009).[5] When this, coupled with reductions in church attendance, is considered alongside less dramatic declines in belief of 5 per cent or greater in the 1991–2008 time period[6] (Wilkins-Laflamme 2021), it adds up to a picture of diminishing traditional Catholicism. A key future challenge, then, for Catholic identity in Ireland – as more generally (Conway 2021) – is institutional retention.

Past studies suggest that secular alternatives are at least partially driving the fall off in religious behaviours. For example, a national survey-based study of patterns of religious commitment found that 10 per cent of respondents cited work as a reason for not attending weekly religious services (Mac Gréil 2009), suggesting that religious practice increasingly competes with other secular world activities. Apart from work, sport also makes growing claims on ordinary people's religious time. For example, Gaelic Athletic Association (GAA) training and competitive matches take place on Sundays, when they compete with religious worship services – and parishes more generally – for devotees' time. This has prompted church elites to lobby against secular schedules clashing with religious ones (Cardinal Urges GAA to Move Matches 2011). There are other examples too: the crowding out of traditional religious practices (e.g. family prayer and street processions) by aspects of consumer culture such as shopping, television and cinema. Here secular alternatives provide a functional equivalent to religion, more at the level of sociability than belief (Hirschle 2010).

It is also the case that this secular competition occurs within the religious domain itself, something which the religious-secular competition theory recognizes. For example, in recent times the sacraments of first communion and confirmation have become more and more commodified. This is reflected in the use of consumer goods such as high-end cars in religious ceremonies as well as the more traditional financial giving of the 'communion money' associated with the sacrament. In 2017 a priest in the diocese of Derry, Fr Paddy O'Kane, took issue with this growing materialistic outlook associated with the sacrament. While acknowledging the belonging and traditionalistic aspect of first communions for many children, he criticized its secularization by 'an orgy of sentimentality and materialism with miniature brides and bouncy castles and bursting bank accounts' (Priest Criticises Parents 2017).

Of course, this individual level of analysis interacts with organizational dynamics. For example, the church has been institutionally innovative in responding to these 'vacant pews' challenges, sometimes by bringing in elements of secular culture to appeal to a broader audience. One key site where this innovation takes place – as in the church more generally – is the parish (Adler, Bruce and Starks 2019), though this phenomenon has received less attention in past literature in the Irish case than one might expect. One good example of this is Portlaoise parish.[7] A Midlands town with a large, 1960s-era church building and adjacent contemporary parish centre, this vibrant parish attracts relatively high attendance rates for its services, which in the past included adaptations to the traditional Mass format via popular culture hymns sung by a Gospel choir.[8]

Unexpected external shocks such as the Covid-19 global pandemic can, however, upend devotees' faith lives. This sudden event has meant that many religious services moved online, displacing the bodily co-presence of offline, face-to-face services (Baker et al. 2020). While significant imagination has been brought to bear by parishes in doing this (Ganiel 2020a; O'Brien 2020), it may be that religion in the post-pandemic era may become increasingly privatized or abandoned altogether, as more and more adherents become accustomed to not going to religious services on a regular basis (Baker et al. 2020). However, this scenario is not inevitable. Another is that devotees will return to traditional collective religious services but with the expectation of online religious offerings as well (Ganiel 2020a). The pandemic era may even prompt a rebound of religious service attendance as adherents (re)discover its meaning in their lives (Ganiel 2020a), though how long any uptick might last is an open question. What of religious-secular competition at the organizational level?

Organizational-level dynamics of competition

It is not just the case that this secular-over-religious pattern exists at the individual level. It also applies at the meso level, the middle space between the individual and society. Here I centre the role of associational life (e.g. participation in local groups) and callings to the priesthood and religious life, and how these bring out the tension between the religious and secular worlds. According to historical studies, the church in Ireland promoted a significant civic life among adherents in a broad range of associations and groups, especially confraternities and sodalities (Lennon 2012). Being frequently named after saints of the Catholic church and operating under clerical authority (Lennon 2012), they provided a model for their members' lives. As such, these small groups of co-religionists – which sometimes had cross-cutting ties – fulfilled not only an important spiritual function such as bolstering the practice of prayer but also a social one of meeting other similarly minded people and forging friendships (Lennon and Kavanagh 2012). Additionally, the leadership of sodalities and confraternities frequently took a stand on social issues of the day (e.g. the treatment of Travellers) (Lennon and Kavanagh 2012), playing an interesting prophetic ministry role. As elsewhere (see Bullivant 2019), they were also part of a broader wrap-around Catholic milieu including parishes and street processions, where devotees' faith was sustained in their everyday lives. These devotional-oriented groups were supplemented by other groups such as the Society of St Vincent de Paul, which provided social assistance to the poor and needy (Lennon and Kavanagh 2012).

In 2021 some of these groups (e.g. Legion of Mary) still exist, but there are more secular equivalents of former Catholic organizations to which ordinary people can be attracted. For example, when asked in the early 1970s about her reasons for opting for a secular version of activism such as the Simon Community over the Society of St Vincent de Paul, one respondent in a relatively recent study of sodalities and confraternities noted, 'I was beginning to question my old, traditional Catholicism in a way which made me unwilling to help them in the name of some saint. I just wanted to help them for their own sakes, as fellow human beings' (Ní Chearbhaill 2012: 183–4). Here, a secular 'schema' (Sewell 1992: 10; see also Czarnecki 2015) is appealed to over a religious one in motivating civic activism. Additionally, internal competition within the Catholic case – as noted in other Catholic-majority societies (Diotallevi 2002; see also Driessen 2014) – may also have mattered. More specifically, it may be that within-Catholic diversity partly contributed to the decline of confraternities and sodalities and the parallel vitality of other groups. For example, the Legion of Mary, Pioneer Total Abstinence Association and the Society of St Vincent de Paul also vied for members among devotees with the added attraction of being more lay-led – and thus in tune with the currents of Vatican II (1962–5) – than their more devotional-oriented counterparts (Lennon and Kavanagh 2012).

Another aspect of the organizational level of analysis is the decline of Catholic vocations, though by no means unique to Ireland (Kerkhofs 1995). In the past, the church attracted many young people from the Catholic laity to enter novitiates or seminaries of which there was also a plentiful supply, as would-be priests, brothers and nuns. In the case of the male workforce, the numbers were so numerous that newly ordained clergy could not always rely on an appointment in their native church, prompting some to go abroad for ministry (Tierney 2010). Writing about

Irish society in the 1930–50s span, sociologist Liam Ryan argued that the strong appeal of the church to potential recruits owed something to its external-facing vision, with little or no direct competitors, within a then largely navel-gazing society: 'During that period, the Catholic Church was one of the few institutions in Ireland offering an ideal. The Church was looking out at the world and calling on young men and women to do something about the paganism and the poverty in which most of humanity lived' (Ryan 2000: 59). And young lay women and men duly responded in very large numbers.

The 1957–8 St Patrick's College, Maynooth, Third-Year Divinity class piece presented the headshots of sixty-three soon-to-be-ordained callings in clerical collar, arranged in neat rows around slightly larger photographs of the then reverend professor of Church Chant and Organ Fr Charles O'Callaghan, auxiliary Bishop (later Cardinal) William Conway and Pope Pius XII. After ordination in Maynooth in 1959, the new callings – with about 230 other diocesan callings in the high tide of that year[9] – would go on to take up appointments in parishes and church institutions. To put this in context, the pages of Maynooth's Kalendarium, the college's compendium that provides information about its academic life, reported just two ordinations to the priesthood in the 2020–1 academic year. In addition, twenty-eight diocesan seminarians (excluding seminarians from international dioceses or religious congregations) were enrolled in Maynooth across all seven years of the formation process in the 2019–20 academic year (Saint Patrick's College Maynooth 2020–1). Given that not all of these seminarians will likely be ordained, it represents a very small replacement cohort and almost another world compared to the situation in the late 1950s. Beyond Maynooth, many former novitiates and seminaries have now closed or been repurposed,[10] reflecting the sharp downward trending of callings in general (Conway 2011).

What explains the trend lines in the church's male workforce? Ordinations to the priesthood peaked before 1960, suggesting they were already in decline by the 1960s regardless of any dampening effect of Vatican II, a frequently mentioned explanation in the literature (e.g. Stark and Finke 2000; Fishman and Jones 2007; Conway 2016).[11] Sociologists have advanced a number of other explanations apart from Vatican II, one of which is the secular opportunity perspective. Putting to one side criticisms of the data brought to bear to evaluate this perspective (e.g. Stark and Finke 2000), its basic insight is that the opening up of a secular opportunity structure from the 1960s onwards in human service-oriented fields such as social work, teaching and nursing provided especially women, but also men, with options for a career that were previously largely captured by the church. Because the church had to compete more with direct secular alternatives, its own ranks diminished (Ebaugh, Lorence and Saltzman Chafetz 1996; Conway 2016).

Elsewhere, I have shown (Conway, forthcoming) that the absolute and relative number of nuns reduced after 1960. For example, in 1960 there were 14,157 nuns (444.99 per 100,000 Catholics) compared to 11,077 (251.35 per 100,000 Catholics) in 1990, representing a reduction of 3,080 nuns (−193.64 per 100,000 Catholics) in this thirty-year period. By 2015, the number of nuns declined further to 6,197 (112.38 per 100,000 Catholics). Looking at the trends in the 1960 to

2015 timeframe, there was reduction of nearly 8,000 nuns (−332.61 per 100,000 Catholics) in this time period, representing a 56 per cent decline. In roughly the same period (1961 to 2016), the female labour force participation rate rose from 30.86 per cent to 53.47 per cent, representing a 22.61 per cent increase (Ortiz-Ospina, Tzvetkova and Roser 2018). Following previous studies (Stark and Finke 2000), this suggests that not all or even most of the decline in the Catholic female workforce was driven by secular opportunity, as relatively modest increases in female labour market participation co-occurred with quite sharp decreases in the female workforce, but further research is needed to investigate this relationship more systematically.

As with the individual level of analysis, it is difficult to see how the church might engineer a turnaround of these trends and patterns. Only an exaggerated optimism could envisage the prospect, for example, of novitiates and seminaries filling up to pre-1960s levels again. It is much more likely that the church will continue to struggle to meet its personnel replacement needs, even if foreign clerical labour is drawn upon from non-Western countries such as Nigeria, as is already the case in some (arch)dioceses, to partially offset the loss of Irish personnel. This reflects the decentring of European Catholicism in the global church and the parallel growth of African Catholicism. Similarly, it is difficult to envisage organizational entities emerging which could reach the level of activity of earlier associations. Finally, what can be said about religious-secular competition at the societal level, especially in terms of church–society interactions?

Societal-level dynamics of competition

Addressing the congregation at his consecration as coadjutor bishop of Clonfert in St Brendan's Cathedral, Loughrea, in 1979, Bishop Joseph Cassidy, then the country's youngest bishop, memorably spoke of Ireland's changing religious-secular relationship:

> I take on this responsibility at a time of tension in the Church. Some like to describe it as a tension between a new affluence and an old faith. I do not accept that analysis. I see it rather as a tension between an old materialism and a new faith. … Ours is a young faith, not an old inheritance struggling for survival. (Donohoe 1979:13)

Historically, the church's inheritance in post-independence Ireland included relatively cooperative church–state interactions, expressed in the high levels of influence of its moral activism in national politics, even in the context of formal church–state separation (Fahey 1992; Buckley 2016). It has also fulfilled a significant social service provision role – in areas such as education, health and social welfare – underpinned by the church's numerous workforce (Fahey 1992; Grzymała-Busse 2015). This service-oriented church (Fahey 1992) has not, however, been known for the expansiveness of its contributions to Catholic theology, unlike its counterparts in continental Europe or Latin America (McDonagh 2012; see also Fahey 1992; Hornsby-Smith 1992).

Even so, in the intervening years, the church's public presence has experienced a kind of churning perhaps like never before. Here, the church's chief competitor has been the secular media, which increasingly subjects its stances – and the actions of its personnel – to a critical gaze (Pollak 1997; Donnelly and Inglis 2010) but has also helped empower it to amplify a stronger prophetic voice (Ganiel 2020b). And the media's role in people's everyday lives – and their degree of contact with it – should not be underestimated, as past time-use studies show that on an average day respondents spend two hours watching television, with only sleep and work occupying more of their daily time. Respondents spend an additional half hour or so reading a newspaper or magazine and listening to the radio on an average day (McGinnity et al. 2005).

Perhaps the clearest example of this competition is the challenge to its legitimacy brought on by the proximal factor of scandal, which began in 1992 as a scandal of personal piety associated with Bishop Eamonn Casey[12] (Donnelly and Inglis 2010; Donnelly 2016) and then unfolded (from the early 1990s onwards) as an ongoing series of scandals of child sexual abuse and leadership failings (Keenan 2012). In both cases, clerical misconduct was publicized in the media (Donnelly and Inglis 2010; Keenan 2012; Donnelly 2016), now ready to run negative, reputational damaging stories about the church (Donnelly and Inglis 2010). A further aspect of scandal related to historic abuses in church institutions such as Magdalene laundries and Mother and Baby Homes. It is also the case, perhaps partially influenced by scandal, that there is less appetite among the general populace for church influence in political life, with support for the view that religious leaders should not seek to exert influence on governmental decision making increasing from 69 per cent in 1991 to 79 per cent in 1998 (Pollack and Rosta 2017), a time period marked by heightened public scrutiny of the church's child sexual abuse scandals.

The most recent example of church-related scandal was the publication in 2021 of the *Report of the Commission of Investigation into Mother and Baby Homes*, which documented the treatment 'unmarried mothers' (Department of Children, Equality, Disability, Integration and Youth 2021: 2), as they were then known, received in state-funded and church-run Mother and Baby Homes. Like other scandals before it from the early 1990s onwards, media coverage of this scandal – as well as popular culture representation – placed before the society the church's dominance of sexual morality in earlier times, which unfavourably judged mothers who had children outside marriage. Within this moral framing, which arguably went against other Christian values such as mercy, fathers were largely exonerated.[13] The report also revealed the playing out of local church–state interactions, as against the more common focus on national-level ones, in the origins and running of Mother and Baby Homes. To take just one example, its account of Árd Mhuire in Dunboyne, County Meath, showed the cooperation between the Good Shepherd Sisters and local authority officials around issues such as the home's upkeep, based on letters of correspondence (Department of

Children, Equality, Disability, Integration and Youth 2021: 8). As such, these institutions were not inflicted by the church on the society and instead reflected a certain agency on the part of political elites and, more broadly, individual communities and families. For the young mothers themselves, their constrained lives meant that most had little or no alternative to being placed in a Mother and Baby Home.

While the media operates in general as a competitor to the church's power and influence, it nonetheless exercises impactful prophetic ministry, especially regarding the poor and needy in society. Trócaire, the Irish Bishops' Conference development agency, is arguably one of the hierarchy's most successful projects (Conway, forthcoming; see also Hornsby-Smith 1992) and was established by the Irish bishops in 1973 with Bishop Casey as its chairman in its early history (Ferriter 2006). This Catholic agency provides relief such as water and food and public goods such as education to ordinary people in some of the most downtrodden parts of the world, and not all co-religionists. Many of these efforts are financially supported by the traditional 'Trócaire box', a simple cardboard collection box and staple presence in many Irish households during Lent (Maye 2010). As an expression of Catholic-influenced mobilization, Trócaire brings Irish Catholicism into contact with global Catholicism, which in turn acts back on the national church's outward-looking focus.

The church's 'successful' prophetic ministry is not limited, however, to the global development space and includes a local/national focus as well (Conway, forthcoming). For instance, two of the most prominent and respected organizations responding to homelessness in Dublin – Focus Ireland and the Peter McVerry Trust – have a religiously inflected background, being founded by a nun and priest, respectively. Another nun established Cuan Mhuire, a network of centres serving people with addiction problems, whatever their circumstances (Costello 1985; see also Byrne 2017). Similarly, socio-economic policy advocacy group Social Justice Ireland is led by a priest.

In some cases, the secular media may actually contribute to bolstering the church's moral leadership (Ganiel 2020b). Not all elements of the secular world necessarily compete with the religious one; the religious can also co-opt the secular.

Although in the past the global church tended to perceive the media as somewhat of a threat, from the 1930s it became increasingly empowered by it, seeing its potential for communicating its message more widely (Chamedes 2019). In Ireland, this view took somewhat longer to take hold but was reflected, among other initiatives, in the 1969 establishment of the Catholic Communications Institute of Ireland, which trained church personnel in media (Ganiel 2020b). Later, the church hierarchy began the practice of appointing a media spokesperson, usually a bishop, to communicate its stances to the public (Flynn 1997; O'Mahony 1981). Today, church elites have also embraced social media, with the episcopal conference employing digital media technologies such as Facebook, Instagram and Twitter[14] and a number of individual bishops or archbishops having their own Twitter accounts.[15] Added to this is the frequent use of social media by parishes (Byrne 2017) and (arch)dioceses across the country. Overall, Catholic leaders began to better understand and develop more open relations with the media (Conway and Kilcoyne 1997; Daly 2011; Ganiel 2020b).

Even so, the liberalization of views in the general population – and distancing from Catholic positions – on issues such as abortion and same-sex relationships (Greeley and Ward 2000) suggests that the church increasingly finds significant elements of its prophetic ministry lacking in resonance with the wider society and even many of its own adherents (Conway, forthcoming), especially among younger generations who have grown up through the scandals over the years and have little or no experience of a pre-scandal church. In light of this past, it is difficult to see how the church could be 'rescued' from growing cultural indifference, even hostility, toward it. This means that it is likely to struggle with the strategic issue of prolonging the Catholic faith in the society in the years ahead. This is acknowledged even by the Irish bishops, who, in their opening statement in 2021 regarding initiating a process toward a National Synodal Assembly, noted the 'huge challenges to the faith over the past fifty years from the rapid transformation and secularization of society in Ireland'.[16]

Conclusion

This chapter has sought to apply religious-secular competition theory to the Irish case. Looking at the individual, organizational and societal levels, I showed trends regarding religious-secular competition as well as the future prospects for Catholicism in light of them.

Individual religious practices compete now more than before with a range of secular options for spending one's available time. Attending Mass is just one option among many on a Saturday evening or Sunday morning, and one which fewer adherents are willing to choose than before. This means that Ireland does not really have a Mass-attending culture anymore, at least not in comparison to the past. Additionally, pious Catholics, especially among young people, are a social minority. Similarly, few daughters and sons today see being a vowed religious or priest as a fulfilling life option, especially when secular alternatives for the more socially minded exist. Some of the Catholic infrastructure of small groups that might have motivated some of these callings in the first place has thinned out and, in the case of confraternities and sodalities, has disappeared.

At the societal level, the church's role as an institutional promoter of faith and morals, especially regarding sexual ethics has eroded significantly (Ryan 1995; Greeley and Ward 2000; Dillon 2007). Although Catholic authorities have learned to use the media more effectively, in the recent past, negative stories about the church have tended to predominate in media reportage (Donnelly and Inglis 2010). This is part of a scandal-driven collective re-evaluation of the church's past that has been taking place since the 1990s, and is not yet complete.[17] At the same time, the church, through its diverse units, has 'good enough' legitimacy to exert moral influence in other domains such as addiction, global development and housing (Conway, forthcoming), notwithstanding its image being tainted by scandal. Of course, these different analytical levels interact with one another and together construct Catholic identity. For example, high religious practice levels tend to foster vocations and numerous callings provide church authorities with greater legitimacy to speak out on moral and social issues. Conversely, low practice levels likely dampen callings and, in turn, the church's symbolic weight.

I have argued that the religious-secular competition perspective provides a useful theoretical framing for interpreting these changes in the Irish case, highlighting the secular-over-religion dynamic at the different analytical levels. Religious-secular competition theory rightly spotlights how the religious and the secular struggle with one another over basically same territory to guide the direction of future identities. However, in focusing on how the secular crowds out the religious, this binary-led perspective has less to say about religious-secular interactions. Future work could test this competition-driven theory more directly at the individual level, relying on social surveys and interview research.

Taken together, present-day Ireland is less Catholic than before but still a Catholic-majority society in the sense that a majority self-identify as Catholic even if not practicing at past levels. Thus, the church's relationship to the society exists more at the level of a 'broad' cultural and historical presence than as a 'deep' ongoing religious commitment among a large majority of the general populace. Even so, vibrancy and growth within Catholicism are also present, but these tend to be in pockets here and there (a kind of 'concentrated Catholicism') – for example, pilgrimage sites such as Knock,[18] select parishes such as Portlaoise parish and lay movements such as Neocatechumenal Way[19] or Catholic-based global activism. Vibrancy is also sporadic – for instance, priests ministering to the sick during the current pandemic or to the bereaved during tragic events – rather than being a feature of the society in general.

All of this suggests that Catholicism in Ireland has reached a moment in its history. In the span of the last four or five decades, it has moved from a social influence that was largely unrivalled to an influence that is now one among many. Looking ahead to twenty years from now, it is likely that the indicators of religiosity examined here (e.g. church attendance, vocations, prophetic ministry, etc.) will have slowly eroded even more. In this context, it is instructive to return to the Maynooth example mentioned earlier. Here, the relationship of the church to its neighbouring campus may well be a metaphor for its future place in Irish society writ large; founded as a Catholic seminary, which became the largest in the world (Corish 1995), its 'offspring' in 2021 is a state-funded university that shares a co-located campus. Compared to this competitor secular entity, Maynooth College is smaller, has less symbolic weight and inhabits older, more traditional buildings bearing the memory of a quietly fading past.

Chapter 11

THINKING BEYOND THE ISLAND: BUDDHISM, IRELAND AND METHOD IN THE STUDY OF RELIGIONS

Laurence Cox and Brian Bocking

Introduction

Historically, 'Irish' and 'Buddhist' have seldom gone together. Most commonly the phrase appears as an oxymoron or, more interestingly, as a thought experiment to represent a position *outside* the 'Protestant-Catholic' binary within which not just Irish religion but 'Ireland' and 'Irishness' have been widely understood. Thus, in 1906, the president of what is today University College Cork (UCC) – arguing for Catholic control of the National University – wrote, 'if the Grand Lama and his followers could establish a large colony in Ireland tomorrow, it is not improbable that in the course of a year or so they would be conceded a University adapted to the religion of Buddhists' (Cox 2013: 166).

At the other end of Eurasia in India and Burma, an 'Irish Buddhist' stood for something rather different. Rudyard Kipling's best-selling novel *Kim* (1900) and Bithia Croker's *Road to Mandalay* (1917) present respectively the son of an Irish soldier following a Tibetan Buddhist guru, and a part-Irish deserter who has ordained as a Burmese monk. The uneasy attraction for readers in these cases came from the awareness that Buddhism connected many of the British Empire's colonies in Asia – and that the Irish constituted a large proportion of the military whose job was to hold those colonies down. What might happen, even in fantasy, if the two were to join hands?

Empire, of course, produced both these situations. The academic study of religions has long discussed the construction of 'world religions' as forms through which colonialism categorized its subjects and through which those subjects staked claims for recognition on a world scale. This process led – in Ireland as in much of Asia – to the construction of nation states defined around relationships between 'the nation' and 'religion'. At the same time as 'Buddhism' was being articulated at the end of the nineteenth century as a single thing on a world stage – including by Irish figures such as U Dhammaloka, Charles Pfoundes, Lafcadio Hearn or John Bowles Daly – religion had become central to Irish popular politics and in ways that made Irish engagement with Buddhism qualitatively different to what happened in, for example, North America or Britain. For example, in sharp contrast to the United States and UK, Irish Theosophy had little use for Buddhism (Cox 2013, ch. 4).

Buddhism and the study of religions in Ireland

The multiple meanings of 'Irish Buddhist' noted above are shaped by this wider religious history, and until very recently *actual* Irish engagement with Buddhism has responded to the same situation: for example, presenting Buddhism as tolerant where dominant Irish Christianities were anything but, or as peaceful in contrast to the long history of sectarian violence. More subtle versions include the assertions that Buddhism is not about adherence to religious dogma, or about blind obedience to a religious institution, or about bringing up children in a religion understood as a form of ethnic membership. These are, of course, assertions to be understood as countering the dominant (ethnic, confessional and political) meanings of religion on the island – or as asserting Buddhism as 'not religious'. Previously these were more 'philosophical' and today perhaps more 'spiritual', hand in hand with the shifting emphasis from Buddhist *ideas* to Buddhist *practices*. More interestingly perhaps, Buddhism has also meant an engagement with a wider world of thought and culture beyond that defined by the 'Abrahamic' religions generally. As Asian Buddhists have arrived in Ireland, with their own complex histories, this picture becomes further complicated. From the point of view of the study of religions, of course, this means that the intersection between Ireland and Buddhism is a particularly productive and creative one for thinking about the changing and contested meanings of 'religion' and 'religions'.

Because of the institutional power of the Irish churches, the terrain of religious studies here has long been occupied by theologians – until recently still mainly concerned with training priests and now seeking ways to reinvest their cultural capital. In many universities the old Catholic philosophical curriculum (from Aristotle to Aquinas) still dominates, with little understanding or interest in Asian philosophy.[1] Irish history and sociology, too, tend to take 'religion' for granted in terms of its dominant meanings on the island. The study of Buddhism necessarily asks broader questions, in many ways, among them questions about what it means to engage with or 'belong to' 'a religion' such as Buddhism in a context of religious innovation and diversity. As just one illustration, Irish healthcare has always been dominated by religious organizations, with fixed rules for how Catholics and Protestants should be treated. Cox remembers the challenges of contributing to an Irish Health Service Executive document whose editors clearly wanted to be able to tell nurses and doctors that 'Buddhists want X, and do Y' when receiving healthcare. The editors struggled with the proposition that it might be better to *ask* the patient rather than seek a religious professional who would say what the patient *ought* to want, based on a binary ethno-religious identity.

From 2008 onwards, Bocking and his colleagues developed the first non-confessional department for the study of religions on the island. This logically started with study of terrain which was not already over-contested by theologians and which represented and reflected a 'new Ireland' which is far more culturally diverse than in the twentieth century, more inclined to engage in religious innovation and increasingly confident in acknowledging the realities of Ireland's history when part of the British Empire – including deep but forgotten bonds with Asia and discarded alternative visions of a free Ireland's future. Specialists in areas including Buddhism, Islam, Orthodox and African Christianities, Indian and indigenous religions represented the new 'Religions and Global Diversity' programme and its postgraduate branches, while the founding of the Irish Society for the Academic Study of Religions (ISASR) and its annual conferences brought in many of the scholars of 'Ireland's New Religious Movements' (Cosgrove et al. 2011).

The Irish past has of course long been contested, with a centuries-long conflict between native historiographical traditions tied to the Irish Catholic church and the vanished Gaelic aristocracy, on the one hand, and a colonial/Whig history which saw the British Empire as civilizing Ireland, on the other. This gave way in the late nineteenth and early twentieth centuries to the new kind of nationalist historiography spreading across Europe – and, in turn, Asia – which linked claims to geographical, ethnic and cultural uniqueness with the right to sovereignty. Towards the end of the twentieth century, the violent conflicts over the status of Northern Ireland, as well as revived Left and women's movements, saw a diversification of narratives of Irish culture and history. These ranged from attempts to remember and celebrate – rather than deny or decry – Irish involvement in Empire to more interesting approaches such as thinking Ireland in postcolonial terms and critiquing its racist past and present. These debates continue, on an island where history, Empire and religion are never far away.

The Irish study of Buddhism takes its place in this context, offering a way to understand in a global perspective both Irish collusion in the imperial (and Christian missionary) enterprise of the colonial period and Irish religious solidarity with the pan-Asian 'Buddhist revival' of the late nineteenth and early twentieth centuries (Turner, Cox and Bocking 2020: 9–14). 'At home', it enables an exploration of religiously shaped dissent from the dominant meanings of 'religion' as well as insights into many of the different 'new Irish' communities (as well as some new religious movements) and into how Irish culture is engaging – or failing to engage – with a context which is, once again, global rather than insular.

Research on Buddhism and Ireland

Academic research on the encounter between Buddhism and Ireland began with Cox's research for *Buddhism and Ireland* (2013),[2] developing his previous work on Irish social movements and countercultures. In November 2009, Cox and others organized the first ever Irish conference on the topic of 'Alternative Spiritualities,

New Religious Movements and the New Age in Ireland' at Maynooth University, which saw a first presentation of his own research with Maria Griffin on Irish Buddhism as well as a paper by John L. Murphy (Westcliff University, California) on the invention of 'Celtic Buddhism' and eleven other papers which referred in some way to Buddhism, often in the context of the Irish 'New Age' (Cox 2010; Cosgrove et al. 2011).

At that conference, the two authors of this chapter met for the first time and discovered a shared interest in the then-obscure figure of U Dhammaloka, now the subject of our book co-authored with Burmese Buddhism specialist Alicia Turner and published in 2020 as *The Irish Buddhist* (discussed below). Cox had discovered Dhammaloka (alias 'Larry O' Rourke') in European and US radical and freethinking (atheist) journals of the early 1900s and had just published a research note on the topic (Cox 2009), while Bocking, keen to discover research topics that might combine his own academic background with issues relevant to Ireland, discovered a reference by Alexey Kirichenko to an Irish Buddhist in colonial Burma, with a footnote acknowledging Alicia Turner as the source (Kirichenko 2009: 34). Turner, it transpired, had noted Dhammaloka's presence as an Irish Buddhist called Colvin (another alias) in Burmese newspapers of the early 1900s but knew little of him beyond brief reports of his controversial activities in colonial Rangoon (present-day Yangon). Our collaborative research into the elusive Dhammaloka occupied the next ten years, during which time Cox published *Buddhism and Ireland* (2013). *Buddhism and Ireland* revealed an extraordinary and unexpected story of archaeological, literary and 'lived' Buddhist connections with Ireland and Irish people over a vast span of time, starting with a bronze Buddha statue from Sri Lanka found in 1886 in a peat bog in County Meath – the 'Baltrasna Buddha', probably a product of Roman-era trade links (Cox 2013: 45–6) – and continuing up to the present.

For the pre-1850 period, Cox's research focused primarily on reception history. Rather than the traditional cataloguing of 'what Europeans knew about Buddhism', it took the known *material facts* of transmission (e.g. translations of medieval texts, library holdings of early modern texts, scholarship on literacy and printing, etc.) to map out as far as possible *when* Irish people came in contact with the specific features of Asian Buddhism transmitted by the Alexandrian and Graeco-Bactrian contacts, Mongol-era missions and early modern travellers, *which* Irish people encountered these and *what can be known* about how they were perceived and used. To the best of our knowledge, and despite widespread interest in the question of 'how Buddhism came to the West', this remains the only published research on the European encounter with Buddhism to attempt such a study for the pre-modern period.

Other than the Baltrasna Buddha, the first demonstrable knowledge of Buddhism in Ireland came with the development of patristic scholarship in the sixth- and seventh-century Irish church and hence familiarity with the Church Fathers' descriptions of Indian ascetics. Parallel to this transmission were the 'legendary Alexander' texts, translated into Middle Irish by the tenth or eleventh century, and *Barlaam and Josaphat*, the life of the Buddha transformed into a

Christian saint, translated into Irish by 1600. Along with Marco Polo, a series of mostly religious missions to the East generated accounts of the Buddhist world at the time of the Mongol Empire and its successor khanates. *Leabhar Ser Marco Polo* (The Book of Sir Marco Polo) was translated into Irish, probably in County Waterford, in 1460. Even more popular, however, were the travels of Odoric of Pordenone from Venice via Sri Lanka to Beijing and back via Tibet (*c*.1317–30), plagiarized in the massively popular *Travels of Sir John Mandeville*. *Buddhism and Ireland* demonstrated continuous Irish familiarity with this story in every century from the fourteenth to the nineteenth. Odoric's assistant, 'brother James of Ireland', is the first attested Irish encounter with living Buddhism (Cox 2013: 45–77).

In the early modern period, the Wars of Religion, plantation (i.e. British settlement of Ireland) and emigration led to a divergence between Irish Protestant and Catholic circuits of knowledge of the Buddhist world, both now increasingly based on contemporary encounters. Religious repression meant that Irish Catholic awareness of the Jesuit encounter with Asian Buddhism was often more developed in the Continental diaspora than on the island, while Protestant circuits of trade and colonization paid particular attention to sailors' accounts. In a highly literate island, these narratives circulated not only in expensive editions but also in serialized form and probably in inexpensive chapbooks. *Buddhism and Ireland* details what is known of the many copies still surviving and the multilingual circuits involved. The remarkable level of popular Irish knowledge of Buddhism attained by this means is epitomized in the work of Ireland's first commercial woman writer, Sydney Owenson, who casually references 'the *dalai lama* of little Thibet' in her successful 1806 novel *The Wild Irish Girl*.

This knowledge only grew during the nineteenth century. When in 1911 a bestselling travel book by the globetrotting American author Harry Franck (Franck 1910) made the name of 'Damalaku' and his fabled journey to Lhasa headline news in America (*Atlanta Constitution*, 30 July 1911) and beyond, it took a Dublin newspaper (the *Sunday Independent* of 6 August 1911) to correct the name to 'Dhammaloka' for its discerning readers. The nineteenth century had seen increasing numbers of Irish people – mostly men – encountering Buddhism in Asia with the spread of the British Empire. The single-largest contingent among these were soldiers and sailors, but the Irish in Asia included also colonial officers of every grade, among them Max Arthur Macauliffe, the Limerick-born judge and still-renowned scholar of Sikhism (Shackle and Bocking 2017), and Daniel H. R. Twomey, the Cork-born judge (and grandfather of the anthropologist Mary Douglas) who presided at Dhammaloka's Rangoon appeal hearing in 1911 (Turner, Cox and Bocking 2020: 3–4). Numerous also were Irish missionaries and traders and a large number of 'poor whites' (particularly but not only ex-soldiers and ex-sailors) living from casual labour and varyingly integrated into the multi-ethnic working-class populations of busy port cities – the kind of world from which Dhammaloka, the Dubliner, came.

As a result, countless Irish families had relatives or acquaintances in Asia, employment prospects in the Empire beckoned and everyday Irish knowledge of Buddhism increased dramatically. For many years, the first thing visitors to the National Museum in Dublin encountered was a *parinibbana* Buddha from Mandalay, captioned 'A trophy [*sic*] of Britain's newest colony exhibited to the people of her oldest' and immortalized in Molly Bloom's soliloquy in *Ulysses*; but this was just one of thousands of looted, excavated or purchased Buddhist artefacts and texts in museums and exhibitions, private hands and libraries. With the help of the late Michael Holland, university curator at UCC, we discovered a five-metre Sri Lankan wooden statue of the Buddha in UCC's archive. This was one among many material indications of the university's interest in Asia – generations of students would pursue medical and other careers in the colonies. The Cork city fathers, however, revealed an orientalist disdain for the statue when in 1907 they discussed not so much where, but rather whether, it should be preserved – in a newspaper controversy they were embarrassed for the philistinism of their response (Cox 2013: 128–30). Irish museums are only now beginning to engage with the decolonizing debate on returning such items.

An orientalizing approach extended even to the collection (or borrowing) of people, as in the 1925 visit to Ireland of Tibetan 'dancing lamas' brought to Dublin to dance and play music before showings of the new *Epic of Everest* movie documenting the 1924 Mallory/Irvine expedition (Cox 2013: 169–71).[3] Public interest in Asia at a distance, however, contrasted with a pervasive religious intolerance within Ireland that meant that none of the handful of people who identified as Buddhist in the available census returns seems to have done so publicly, with the wonderful exception of Robert Gibson (d. 1914) of Dromcollogher – a spiritualist, cooperative activist, suffragette ally and nationalist. Even though Vivian Butler Burke (see below) organized Wesak (Buddhist New Year's) celebrations in Dublin in 1935, she does not seem to have put her name to them within Ireland.

Collaborative digital humanities research: Restoring forgotten Irish religious lives

Most known Irish Buddhists of the period were thus to be found in Asia. Of these, two are already the subject of extensive research for other reasons: Lafcadio Hearn (1850–1904), famous for his writing on Japanese culture (Cox 2013: 236–41), and the transgender pioneer Michael/Laura Dillon (1915–1962) who, as Lobsang Jivaka, died a Buddhist novice in Ladakh (Cox 2013: 271–8). Research on other Irish Buddhists of this period consequently had to be done from scratch, usually in collaborative approaches. Much of our understanding of the early Irish Buddhist vanguard thus takes the form of a set of parallel biographies, constituting a prosopography where multiplicity has to substitute for individual depth in some cases. Along with U Dhammaloka/Laurence Carroll (another alias), research on Charles James William Pfoundes, John Bowles Daly and Vivian Butler Burke illustrates this approach.

The discovery and investigation in collaboration with Shin'ichi Yoshinaga (Kyoto) of Charles Pfoundes (né Pounds, 1840–1907) revealed an extraordinary pioneering Irish emigrant and mariner whose enduring passion for the culture and religion of Japan (where he lived for nearly thirty years from 1863 to 1876 and again from 1893 until his death in 1907) led him to launch in London in 1889 the first – and for well over a century entirely forgotten – official Buddhist Mission to the West. Pfoundes's 'Buddhist Propagation Society', based in London where Pfoundes lived between 1878 and 1892, was sponsored by Pure Land (Jodo Shinshu) Buddhists in Kyoto. Among several publications on Pfoundes beyond the account in *Buddhism and Ireland*, our most comprehensive is 'The First Buddhist Mission to the West: Charles Pfoundes and the London Buddhist Mission of 1889–1892', co-authored with Professor Yoshinaga, a scholar with unrivalled knowledge of esoteric and 'alternative' East-West translocal religious connections and interactions in the decades around 1900 (Bocking 2013; Bocking, Cox and Yoshinaga 2016; Bocking 2021).

John Bowles Daly (*c*.1844–*c*.1916) was a disillusioned Anglican clergyman, studied by Cox and Mihirini Sirisena. After the disestablishment of the (Anglican) Church of Ireland in 1869, he worked in the poor East End of London, became a Theosophist and accompanied Colonel Olcott to Ceylon (Sri Lanka). Here he became involved in the Buddhist Theosophical Society (BTS) schools, lay Buddhist schools with a modernist English-language curriculum set up by Ceylonese Buddhist reformists to counter Christian missionary schools. Daly's 1890 *pansil* (lay conversion) ceremony was conducted by Ceylonese chief monk Hikkaduwe Sumangala. Daly became principal of Mahinda College in Galle, Ceylon, before falling out with the BTS, worked briefly for the colonial authorities as Commissioner for Buddhist Temporalities (i.e. properties and revenues) and eventually left for India and then Australia (Cox 2013: 229–36; Cox and Sirisena 2016).

Another remarkable figure is Vivian Butler Burke (*c*.1881–1937). Some research on her life has been carried out by Turner, Cox and Margery Reynolds but more remains to be done (Cox 2014). Butler Burke was the daughter of a mixed (Catholic–Protestant) marriage whose parents had emigrated to the United States. Following their death, she returned to Ireland around 1920 and became involved in anti-Treaty republicanism.[4] Butler Burke's life mixed politics, art and spirituality; she corresponded with Mohandas Gandhi, the German journalist and satirist Kurt Tucholsky and the French dramatist and mystic Romain Rolland, worked with Irish poet Ella Young and was a friend of American actor and director Orson Welles. Around 1927 she responded to a request by reformist Asian Buddhists to set up a centre in Dublin and did so in her own house on Harcourt Terrace, until 1935 or 1937. Here she hosted events including the Wesak celebration and talks by Sri Lankan reformer A. P. de Zoysa, then completing a PhD in London. She was also an Irish contact for the Maha Bodhi Society in Calcutta led by Anagarika Dharmapala.

Dhammaloka and his world

Our research on U Dhammaloka began in 2009 when digital resources that have proved crucial to our research such as full-text online newspaper archives and digitized books and journals from the turn of the twentieth century were only starting to become available – along with the internet bandwidth to accommodate them. Since then, the range of resources and their accessibility has of course increased substantially, though English-language sources overwhelmingly predominate. The three authors of *The Irish Buddhist* (Turner, Cox, Bocking), with the often substantial help of dozens of academic colleagues around the world, communicated mainly by email and occasionally Skype, and met together in person perhaps five times during ten years of research, at academic events in Canada, Ireland and Japan. The work could not, however, have been done in times of Covid-19 – our online research was underpinned by three fully funded research projects enabling archival searches and publications by research assistants (Choompolpaisal 2013; Sirisena 2017), funded conferences, and travel for research and academic presentations in a dozen countries.

Our findings on Dhammaloka are comprehensively presented in *The Irish Buddhist: The Forgotten Monk Who Faced Down the British Empire*. The book substantially rewrites the early history of 'global Buddhism', a story hitherto told 'from above' about genteel scholars interested in Buddhist philosophical ideas. Our research delved into more than a thousand mostly fragmentary records to uncover the down-to-earth words and actions of a radical working-class Irish freethinker who 'went native' to become a sincere and fully observant Burmese-style Buddhist monk. Dhammaloka campaigned vocally across Asia for Buddhist values and traditions threatened by colonialism in a way that clearly shook the British establishment. However, *The Irish Buddhist* does not by any means proffer a plebeian inversion of the 'great man' theory of history. In contrast, the research reveals that Dhammaloka – like most Irish Buddhists of this period – could not have filled the role he did without the active strategic backing of Asian sponsors and supporters who found Dhammaloka as a 'white' monk useful to the anti-colonial cause. Dhammaloka was not 'the first Western Buddhist monk' (a chimera we deal with in the book) but he was certainly the first European to ordain other European Buddhist monks.

Publication of the book has generated significant interest and useful feedback from readers, and since publication, we have discovered more about two of the European Buddhist ordinands most closely associated with Dhammaloka. The first, M. T. de la Courneuve, was ordained personally by Dhammaloka at his Buddhist mission in Singapore; the second, Richard Laffère, by the head priest of Dhammaloka's home (Tavoy) monastery in Rangoon, and we take the opportunity to offer some of these new findings here. When writing *The Irish Buddhist*, all we knew of Dhammaloka's Singapore ordinand were his initials and surname, 'M. T. de la Courneuve'; that he was an Englishman who immediately prior to ordination had been a British colonial policeman in Perak (today's Malaysia); that he was ordained as U Dharmatrata in October 1904 and that, according to the Singapore *Straits Times* which described the ceremony in some detail, he was the son of a Deputy Commissioner (a very high rank) in the Burmese branch of the Indian Civil Service. Following publication of *The Irish Buddhist*, 'M. T.' was identified as Montague Thomas de la Courneuve who was born in India in 1878, attended school in Bristol, UK, in the 1890s and died of wounds in France during the First World War in April 1917.[5] His father Frederick, a coal mining engineer in Raniganj (now West Bengal), died in 1896 when Montague was eighteen. His uncle, Frederick's brother Stewart Howard Thomas de la Courneuve,[6] who was indeed a top-grade Deputy Commissioner in Burma, soon afterwards married – contrary to marriage laws of the time in both the UK and British India – Montague's widowed mother Lisette (née Stewart). The marriage was legal because it took place in Ceylon which was not part of British India and whose more liberal rules on matrimony allowed a woman to marry her deceased husband's brother. Thus, by 1904, the year of Montague's ordination by Dhammaloka, Stewart was Montague's stepfather as well as his uncle.

A decade previously, and more obviously relevant to this chapter on Buddhism, Stewart H. T. de la Courneuve had contracted another marriage – of a kind decidedly unusual for prominent civil servants in Burma – when he wed a Spanish-Portuguese woman who had been left orphaned in infancy by her parents' death during a trade voyage to Rangoon. The girl had been brought up by a local Burmese couple and the adoptive parents agreed to the marriage only if it was conducted according to Buddhist rites. Hence it was that around 1886 Montague's future stepfather publicly underwent a Burmese Buddhist marriage in the British capital Rangoon (followed within a decade by a Buddhist divorce, which freed him to marry his brother's widow Lisette, and his ex-wife to marry 'a Shan gentleman').[7] Montague was not, therefore, the first member of his family to submit to Buddhist law, and he would have been familiar with Buddhism in Burma for years before he ordained. After his ordination by Dhammaloka, Montague remained a monk for a year or more. He eventually emigrated to Canada where he married in 1912. In 1915 he enlisted in the Canadian Expeditionary Force, his religion on the attestation form (and subsequently on his Army death record) shown as 'Buddist' [sic]. Whether there were other self-declared Buddhists, Irish-ordained European ex-monks or otherwise, in Toronto around 1915 remains so far as we know an open question.

The second of Dhammaloka's close followers about whom more details have emerged only since publication of *The Irish Buddhist* was a Dublin civil engineer called Richard Lawson Laffère who went to Asia for work around 1902 and was ordained as U Vara in February 1905 in Rangoon. The ceremony was conducted by U Vicitta, head of the Tavoy monastery, Dhammaloka's Burmese home. Laffère had worked in the Malay States and Siam (present-day Malaysia and Thailand) before his ordination. As U Vara, he was reported to be assisting Dhammaloka with various Buddhist propagation projects during 1905 and, at some point thereafter, returned to lay life. By November 1906, according to the *Madras Weekly Mail*, he was working professionally in Madras (Chennai) and by 1907 was Assistant Engineer in charge of government buildings in the port of Bunder Abbas in the Persian Gulf (Administration Report of the Persian Gulf 1905–1910).[8] He died there on 22 June 1909, the consular death certificate recording his age as unknown. He was thirty.

There is a pattern. As with Montague de la Courneuve, the radical step (for a European) of ordination as a monk was by no means Laffère's first engagement with

Buddhism. In Dublin, where he had lived with relatives following the early death of both parents, he subscribed to *Light of Asia*, the magazine of the Jodo Shinshu mission in San Francisco (which incidentally used, as part of its rituals adapted for American devotees, a Buddhist hymn, 'Rejoice', arranged by Dhammaloka to the tune of 'Ye Banks and Braes O' Bonnie Doon').[9] Laffère was sent two copies of each issue, one probably forwarded by his relatives to wherever he was working in Asia. Next door to his address at 7 Gilford Road – and presumably in some way connected – was one of a tiny number of households with members who returned their religion as 'Buddhist' in the 1911 census. Its five residents (all boarders) comprised Dublin medical students Ralph Mecredy and Francis Crosslee, English journalist Arthur Garbutt (all much younger than Laffère) and widowed mother and daughter Elizabeth and Isobel Warrington, both India-born and living in Dublin since about 1900. Laffère's own younger relative at no. 7, Atha Laffère, was herself a rare Irish freethinker. It seems clear that in heading for Asia, Laffère was looking for more than engineering work. Like Montague de la Courneuve, he spent a year or so as a monk, but while we have a record of Montague self-identifying as a Buddhist ten years after his disrobing, we have, so far, no documentary evidence that would tell us whether Laffere continued to regard himself as a Buddhist up to the time of his death in 1909.

Ireland and Buddhism after Empire

With the independence of what became the Free State (1922), most of Ireland left the British Empire. Together with general imperial decline and the increasing confessionalism of both states (the Free State; from 1949 the Republic, and Northern Ireland), this meant that all kinds of exchange with Buddhist Asia declined considerably, so that 1950s Ireland knew considerably less about Buddhism than did the 1850s. Matters began to change with the birth of an Irish counterculture from the late 1960s on and Ireland's increasing role as a rural retreat for romantics from other Western countries. The years 1971 and 1972 saw the first public affirmations of Buddhism in Ireland for a century and, as the decade progressed, the first Buddhist centres appeared, in rural West Cork and working-class Dublin. A few people travelled directly from Ireland to Asia in search of Buddhist teaching, while members of the vast Irish diaspora elsewhere became interested in Buddhism and some Irish people encountered Buddhism in different forms in the UK, the United States and other Western societies.

This period was also that of 'the Troubles' and rising sectarian tension in Northern Ireland, as well as right-wing Catholic activism in the Republic culminating in the 1983 constitutional ban on abortion. Buddhist pioneers in this period thus still had to overcome strong cultural-religious resistance to their interest. Characteristically, Maura Soshin O' Halloran was Irish-American, involved in political and cultural radicalism, who then travelled to Japan for Zen training, receiving Dharma transmission shortly before her accidental death. Her diaries, published as *Pure Heart, Enlightened Mind*, have become globally known.

For later generations, particularly in the Republic, matters have been less fraught as feminism, LGBTQ+ activism and other forms of cultural change have dismantled much of the apparatus of Catholic power. In the 2016 census there were 9,758 self-identified Buddhists, of whom 53.7 per cent held Irish nationality, a proportion in line with previous figures. Western converts (not only Irish) outnumber immigrant Buddhists, not massively in absolute terms but very substantially in terms of the organization of Buddhist centres and temples.[10] There are thus two faces to Buddhism in today's Ireland: a public face dominated by Western converts and a private/family space in which immigrant communities are more significant.

More recent research and publications on Buddhism

Parallels between our research on Buddhism and similarly fruitful and innovative research projects in other areas of the academic study of religions are discussed in the introduction to this book. Since the publication of *Buddhism and Ireland* in 2013, Buddhist groups and communities in Ireland have evolved but not transformed, with numbers rising but a similar relationship between converts and immigrants to that sketched above. Numbers had grown by the 2016 census, reflecting a recovery from the 2007–8 economic crash. The Covid-19 pandemic that began in 2019 will almost certainly have affected the numbers of Asian Buddhists in Ireland in various ways, but the scheduled 2021 census which might have revealed trends was postponed until April 2022. Conversely, the move online forced by the pandemic represents absolutely nothing new for Buddhism in Ireland, which has always been shaped by physical distance, both from the homelands of Asian Buddhist traditions and the Western European or North American centres of newer Buddhist groups. If anything, Irish-based Buddhists are likely to find that what had previously been their online lifeline, not always much needed by Buddhists in Asia – or for that matter in the UK or the United States – is now massively boosted, as larger and better-resourced populations now require the scale of connection that smaller and more peripheral Buddhists have always needed.

Since its inception in 2014, the *Journal of the Irish Society for the Academic Study of Religions* (*JISASR*) has sought to encourage work by Irish scholars and/or work on Irish topics, as well as attracting contributions in any area of the academic study of religions from scholars worldwide. The first *JISASR* article specifically on Buddhism was Turner's ISASR keynote on the study of religion in 2014 (Turner 2014). The 2016 issue, a *Festschrift* for Bocking on his retirement, contained several articles covering a wide range of Buddhist-related topics: Kate Crosby and Janaka Ashin on the impact of international Buddhist networks on the Burmese nationalist monk Shin Ukkaṭṭha (Crosby and Ashin 2016), Cox and Sirisena on Daly (above), Michael Pye on the steady development of a distinctive female-led 'new religion' (the White Light Association) in culturally Buddhist Japan (Pye 2016), Tim Barrett on rival interpretations of Tokugawa Japanese writings on Buddhism and Confucianism (Barrett 2016), Stefania Travagnin on the life, mission and mummification of the transnational (China, Tibet, Taiwan) Buddhist woman Elder Gongga (Travagnin 2016); and, in 2017, Brigitta Kalmar on Tibetan Buddhist pilgrimage culture in India (Kalmar 2017).

Beyond these, Dr Tatsuma Padoan, lecturer in East Asian Religions at UCC and a specialist in Japanese religions, is completing (2022) a British Academy Newton International Research Project entitled 'A Semiotics of Sacred Geography: Understanding Pilgrimage and Holy Sites in a Comparative Perspective' (see Padoan 2021), while John Ó Laoidh (Maynooth), whose PhD research focused on the gendered aspects of pedagogy in transnational Korean (Son) Buddhism, has co-authored with Cox a 2021 article on Japanese Buddhism in Ireland for the *Journal of Religion in Japan* (Cox and Ó Laoidh 2021). A recent book by Antony Goedhals (Pretoria) on Hearn's 'neo-Buddhist' writings (Goedhals 2020) adds to our understanding of colonial-era Irish-Buddhist links, while Peter Doran (Queens University Belfast) has published a critical exploration of the political economy of mindfulness (Doran 2017) and Eilís Ward (National University of Ireland Galway) a book on Buddhism and neoliberal therapy culture (Ward 2021). The Irish Network for Studies in Buddhism plays its role in connecting Study of Religions scholars, theologians and Buddhists with occasional seminars and email communications.

Future prospects

Irish universities had a significant involvement with the Orientalist project in the decades between the highly controversial opening up of the Indian Civil Service to competitive examination in 1855 and Irish independence (see Cox 2013, ch. 3). In the mid-twentieth century, Asian Studies in the Republic of Ireland would be reduced to Biblical Studies and theological polemic gradually replaced by interfaith dialogue, as the purposes of Empire were replaced by those of Christian churches. The opening decades of the twenty-first century have seen a revival of Asian studies in various contexts, tied to increasing business links especially with China and India as well as Irish universities' attempts to recruit Asian students and develop their own Asian expertise. At the same time, the study of race and ethnicity, immigration and multicultural societies creates openings for the study of religions including different kinds of Buddhism within Ireland. Finally, the increased engagement of Irish Buddhists with the state, reflected in the founding in 2018 of a broad-based 'Irish Buddhist Union', signals a growing tendency of Buddhist institutions to seek access to the various possibilities for 'religions' offered by the architecture of the Irish state (historically constructed with only Catholicism and Protestantism in mind). These include opportunities for fostering more diverse and relevant forms of religious education at school level.

If Irish universities become able to offer the sort of systematic and specialized language teaching that has historically been the backbone of Buddhist studies in Europe, it is only likely to be for East Asian languages, and perhaps without the study of classical Chinese that is key to the East Asian Buddhist textual tradition. Similarly, the approach more common in North America of a focus on local Buddhism with an ethnographic emphasis on religious experience may be limited by the small size of Irish Buddhism overall.

However, Ireland's own postcolonial, diasporic and multi-ethnic situation offers a particular vantage point for the study of *globalizing* and *translocative* Buddhism from the mid-nineteenth century to the present; the UCC department from the start recognized this fact and established its strengths in the area of 'contemporary religions' (embracing broadly the nineteenth century to the present). This approach faces fewer (not no) linguistic constraints and fits with the Irish situation where only a small minority of self-described Buddhists in Ireland are affiliated with a physical centre or temple, so that the large majority of Buddhist practice on the island is mediated by online relationships, international organizations, global intercultural discourses and the circulation of books, artefacts, recorded talks and practices – all of these relevant for physical centres as well. The combination of Ireland's extensive global diaspora (estimated at around twelve times the six million population of the island, after nearly two centuries of sustained emigration) and Ireland's own increasingly international and multicultural population can in fact be a significant strength in this respect. This is illustrated by the research history sketched out in this chapter – and throughout this book in respect of other Irish research in the history of religions.

The Covid-19 pandemic will, we hope, have faded into history somewhat by the time this book is published, but Brexit – to all appearances a regressive process hardly begun at the time of writing and with no predictable outcome in the short, medium or long term – rather remarkably leaves Ireland as the only EU country apart from Malta where English (now dominant as the language of international research) is a native language – a significant element of Irish-English bilingualism notwithstanding. We might therefore expect to see some kinds of EU-funded research shift from British to Irish universities as a part of this; but the contours remain blurred at present. In terms of open questions for the Irish academic study of Buddhism, by far the most important research lacuna relates to the study of Asian Buddhists in Ireland. Unlike most post-imperial countries, where large numbers of immigrants from a small number of ex-colonies made the founding of religious institutions to serve their own religious needs relatively straightforward, immigration to Ireland is both very diverse and small in absolute numbers, meaning that immigrant-led Buddhist temples or organizations are rare. At present, only Soka Gakkai International and a Thai temple in Mitchelstown seem to be primarily or partially oriented towards immigrant Buddhists, although, of course, many centres and groups with largely Irish or white convert organizations have Asian teachers at least occasionally present.

This means that most Asian Buddhist practice in Ireland takes place either within public contexts constructed by and for Western converts or in largely private settings. It is furthermore massively diverse, both linguistically and culturally, the census picture revealing many different small groups of Asian Buddhists. The obvious hope is that the coming generation of 'new Irish' postgraduates, equipped with relevant language and cultural skills, will be able to carry out ethnographic research in at least some of these contexts at what is now, in the 2020s, a moment of transition between immigrant populations dominated by first-generation adults and their second-generation children.

An 'Irish Buddhist' is no longer an oxymoron. Instead, today Irish Buddhists may represent two equally interesting phenomena, in roughly equal numbers. One comprises immigrant communities from around Asia. If these groups are mostly unlikely to control their own religious institutions, buildings and teachings in Ireland as they would have done in Asia, some at least have a clear interest in articulating their identity in religious terms. The other comprises Westerners, typically brought up within one of Ireland's dominant religious communities, engaging in some of the forms of internationally mediated religious exploration, including Buddhist forms that are often said to characterize late modernity. These two categories of 'Asian' and 'Western' are, of course, increasingly likely to overlap and blend, and in this respect too, the academic study of Buddhism offers a privileged vantage point into some key areas of 'religion' – which has always been one of the island's most widely recognized languages.

Postface

MAPPING THE RELIGIOUS FIELD IN IRELAND

Tom Inglis

Sometimes it seems to me that describing and analysing the history and development of the religious field in Ireland is like putting together a jigsaw the pieces of which are still being made. It can be argued that the religious field in Ireland is unique, because the Catholic church remained so powerful for so long and had major social, political, economic and psychological consequences. However, the field has changed dramatically in the last fifty years. Many pieces have been added to the jigsaw and Gladys Ganiel provides a good overview of these in her chapter. Other chapters in this volume provide new insights and understandings about the way the religious field has evolved, particularly in relation to minority religions and alternative ways of being religious.

However, given that the Catholic church still dominates the field, it is important to map the changes that are taking place within it and among Irish Catholics. Brian Conway describes and analyses these changes by focusing on how secular groups and organizations are taking over roles and functions that were previously the preserve of religious groups, particularly the Catholic church. We see this in education, health and, especially, in social welfare. But it is perhaps most evident in soul care. The media and the market have become the main sources as to how to live a good life, how to take care of ourselves, our minds and bodies, our families. They have also become, particularly through debate and discussion in the media, a major threat to the church's monopoly over the meaning of life.

But there are other changes. For years the church and its rituals were at the heart of parish life. People lived their lives in Catholic time and space. There is an argument that in terms of community integration the role of the church is increasingly being usurped by the Gaelic Athletic Association, not just in bringing young people and their parents together but also, as we saw at the height of the Covid-19 pandemic, in providing social services. At an institutional level, a major change has been in the way the church is no longer the moral guardian of the media and state. The roles have been reversed, and it is now the media and the state that have forced the church to confess to the sins and crimes that its members committed during the time it held a monopoly over morality. It has not helped that the hierarchy and religious orders have often come across as more concerned with protecting their own interests rather than those of the victims of abuse.

One of the reasons why the church became and remained so powerful was its ability to suppress opposition to its dominance. From the foundation of the Irish state, the church was able, for the next fifty years, to silence the expression of alternative voices. Amy Heath-Carpentier and Jenny Butler articulate that during the nationalist upheaval, the struggle to imagine a different political future for Ireland was linked to different ways of being religious. This experimentation was strongest among a Protestant, intellectual, literary set and, as Heath-Carpentier observes, was particularly strong amongst women. Once political independence was gained, the emergence of the Catholic church as the dominant force in the religious and many other social fields, and its determination to undermine the influence of Protestantism, meant that such experimentation was suppressed. Although she does not show it directly, Heath-Carpentier's chapter reminds us how little religious opposition there was during this period. There was no appetite to be religiously adventurous, to try to seize some control of the church by those, particularly women, who have suffered most from its teachings and regulations. The church made sure that there was nothing to bother the tranquil lives of the laity and the laity was happy to hold onto the religious beliefs, attitudes and values that the church provided.

Ganiel draws attention to the way being religious, particularly being Catholic or Protestant, was different in Northern Ireland. Again, this connects with the finding that religion tends to be more important to people in times of conflict and social upheaval. Identity with and attachment to the Catholic church and Protestant denominations has remained high. But, returning to Conway's analysis, the question is to what extent secular groups in the North are replacing the sense of identity, bonding and belonging that has been linked to religious denominations and groups.

Síle de Cléir reveals the rich variety of religious rituals and experiences there were in Ireland prior to the Catholic church developing its monopoly position. Being religious was less about organized rituals and ceremonies within churches and more about stories, songs, poems and prayers that involved local saints. There were, then, thousands of different religious flowers in the religious field. The demise of this syncretic form of religion that blended pagan, Celtic and Christian ways of being religious was directly related to the campaign to bring the church under Roman control.

The Ultramontane campaign led by Cardinal Paul Cullen during the latter half of the nineteenth century not only brought religion into churches but also cemented the idea that the Catholic church was the one true church. This, along with centuries of colonial oppression and Protestant ascendancy, made being Protestant in the new Republic difficult. Deirdre Nuttall and Tony Walsh capture the subtle but effective means by which Catholics symbolically dominated Protestants in the new era of Catholic hegemony. And yet, as they observe, while Protestant numbers declined significantly in the first seventy years of the new state, many prospered in various occupational fields. However, their religious difference led them to having different social and cultural lives. Protestants became the quintessential 'other'. They were marginalized, excluded and sometimes hounded out of social life by the Catholic church, particularly Archbishop John Charles McQuaid. This hounding was epitomized by the strict enforcement of the *Ne Temere* decree. The result was a cultural strategy whereby Protestants were careful to keep their heads down and live quiet lives among themselves.

The influx of immigrants from the beginning of the 1990s brought new energy to the field of Irish Protestantism. There were new vibrant communities of Pentecostalists, Baptists and Presbyterians who were proud to be Protestant. In focusing specifically on transnational African Pentecostals, Abel Ugba reveals how despite very difficult conditions there was a determination to create and maintain strong communities. In many respects, their otherness, their passion to be religious and to hold onto very conservative beliefs and values helped them become more religious than their Protestant and Catholic counterparts. In an increasingly secular and individualist culture, they have been a beacon of religious fervour.

One of the consequences of the Catholic church developing such a monopoly position in the religious field was that while Catholics became good at being Catholic, they became less interested in exploring, debating and discussing religion. This may help explain why Irish Catholics seem to go straight to embracing a secular life rather than seeking out new ways of relating to the supernatural and transcendental dimensions of their life. They threw out, so to speak, the religious baby with the Catholic bathwater. As Vesna Malešević documents, there has been a steady growth in new religious movements, but it would seem that in comparison to other Western societies the numbers are low. Approximately 2.5 per cent of the 2016 Census indicated that they belonged to 'other religions' (which included Islam, Hinduism and Buddhism, as well as new religious movements). A further 2.5 per cent reported that they did not belong to any religion. So, despite the arrival of new religious products, the majority of Irish people are still happy to live a secular life or continue to take what is on offer in the Catholic supermarket.

The reason for such strong religious inertia is undoubtedly linked the dominance of the Catholic church within primary and secondary education. Given the passing of the same-sex marriage and abortion referendums, which legalized both in Ireland for the first time in 2015 and 2018, respectively, one might expect that there would be greater resistance to church control of education. However, it would seem that the majority of Irish parents are not very disturbed by the lack of choice when it comes to schooling. This may be, as Patricia Kieran suggests, because the religious education curriculum is neither stridently orthodox Catholic nor, it would seem, taught by very committed Catholic teachers.

Laurence Cox and Brian Bocking have focused on the history of Buddhism in Ireland and the contribution of Irish people to its worldwide development. This is important work in filling in the missing pieces in the historical and contemporary mapping of this religious field. They note that approximately half of the ten thousand Buddhists in Ireland today are immigrants from Asia and the other half are Irish people brought up as Catholic or Protestant. What needs to be explored is the number of people who engage in yoga, meditation and mindfulness, which, while not necessarily directly linked to Buddhism, have an elective affinity with its teachings and practices. It is right to draw attention to the growing number of people who grew up as Catholics and who have become disenchanted with and alienated or completely detached from the church. It would seem that there is little or nothing that makes the church interesting or attractive to these people. There are many others, perhaps the majority, who have little interest in the church and religion but who, when it comes to being religious, like being Catholic and participating in church rituals.

The religious field in Ireland is changing rapidly. The monopoly the Catholic church held over the meaning of life, how to be spiritual, how to reach out to the transcendental and how to live a good life, has been broken. There are new answers, new providers, new religious movements. And yet when it comes to being religious, it would seem that most of those brought up as Catholics are still happy to identify themselves as such and, when needed, to make use of the church's services. This volume, then, arrives at a fortuitous time as Ireland's religious landscape continues to undergo significant transformations and adaptations. The volume reflects a new interest, energy and enthusiasm for studying religion. It shines important lights on aspects of Irish religion that have previously remained hidden from view. It raises questions that have not been asked before and suggests topics for future research.

NOTES

Preface

1 For more on the complexities of language in describing the island of Ireland, see M. Daly, 'The Irish Free State/Éire/Republic of Ireland/Ireland: "A Country by Any Other Name"?' *Journal of British Studies* 46, no. 1 (2007): 72–90. DOI: 10.1086/508399.

Chapter 1

1 By contrast, the co-authors of this introduction are both what are affectionately known in Ireland as 'blow-ins' – namely those who arrived on the wind. An alternative term would be 'academic migrants'. Our adventitious status provides a rather threadbare excuse for any misrepresentations and misunderstandings in this introduction and provides an opportunity to thank our 'cultural brokers'.
2 ASR is a broad term for approaches that aim to understand the nature and role of religions in a wider culture without making religious claims themselves or using religious premises as an analytical framework i.e. 'non-confessional' approaches.
3 ASR does occupy a prominent place in the EASR Constitution (3:i): 'The objective of the EASR shall be to promote the academic study of religions through the international collaboration of all scholars normally resident in Europe whose research has a bearing on the subject.' See https://www.easr.eu/constitution-and-byelaws/ (accessed 27 September 2021).
4 Here, the discussions about 'what's in a name' differ across the national histories of ASR; those languages that allow for the notion of *scientia* as a name for all academic knowledge production are in a better place to provide a distinct understanding of a *science des religions, scientia dei religioni, Religionswissenschaft, religiewetenschap* and so forth. A good summary of arguments is provided in the special issue of the journal *Religion*: *Religion at 50: Past and Futures* (Stausberg and Engler 2020). Another clarification helpful in the Irish context is the difference between the term 'religious studies' and ASR, since R/religious S/studies is closely identified with the school subject (also called R/religious E/education, etc.; see Kieran, this volume) that often presents knowledge about religions in close relationship with theology and constructs them as 'the other' of Christianity.
5 'Confessional' here denotes any religiously engaged position which views the study of religion(s) as part of its own faith formation. The Constitution of ISASR states (in line with the IAHR constitution), 'The Society is a forum for the critical, analytical and cross-cultural study of religions, past and present. It is not a forum for confessional, apologetical, interfaith or other similar concerns.' See https://isasr.wordpress.com/about/constitution/ (accessed 27 September 2021).
6 The organization 'Universities Ireland' that promotes collaboration between all universities on the island of Ireland lists ten members: UCC (University College

Cork), UCD (University College Dublin), DCU (Dublin City University), MIC (Mary Immaculate College, University of Limerick), MU (Maynooth University), NUIG (National University of Ireland Galway), QUB (Queen's University Belfast), TCD (Trinity College Dublin), WIT (Waterford Institute of Technology) and Open University in Ireland with TU (Technical University) Dublin.

7 Within TCD, Patrick Claffey notably introduced a course on 'World Christianities', teaching about African and Asian forms of Christianity and the variety of migrants' religions; Brad Anderson's project on digital sacred texts provides another such innovative approach.

8 Some former elements of which have expanded within the School of Languages, Literatures and Cultural Studies (see https://www.tcd.ie/nmes/staff/ (accessed 27 September 2021)).

9 Ireland's Jewish community has attracted the attention of historians (e.g. Hyman 1973; Keogh 1998; Rivlin 2011). Ulster University's interdisciplinary research project with NUIG 'Representations of Jews in Irish Literature' is described at https://www.ulster.ac.uk/research/topic/english/projects/representations-of-jews-in-irish-literature (accessed 27 September 2021).

10 See jisasr.org.

11 Themed 'Borders and Boundaries: "Religion" on the Periphery', the programme of this conference is still available and telling, not only in respect to its situation (during the Brexit negotiations) but also showing the breadth and scope of ASR in both countries. It was also the first time the British Association for the Study of Religions (BASR) had held its conference in Northern Ireland, made possible through collaboration with ISASR. https://basrblog.files.wordpress.com/2018/08/basr-isasr-information-booklet-1-september-2018.pdf (accessed 27 September 2021).

12 At least one pre-publication reviewer has chided us for not highlighting more scholars past and present in Ireland and abroad, but no one has yet attempted a comprehensive survey of ASR in Ireland and global ASR scholarship on Irish religions on which we could draw for this introduction. Perhaps the limitations of our survey will encourage more extensive work on this topic.

13 Further details including profiles of the nine-strong research team and research outputs are at http://hiddengalleries.eu/about/ (accessed 27 September 2021).

14 Records of the Centre's activities since 2013 are at https://mewsc.wordpress.com/about/ (accessed 27 September 2021).

15 https://www.bayreuth-academy.uni-bayreuth.de/en/people/Fellows-list/Dr_-Abel-Ugba/index.php (accessed 27 September 2021).

16 https://calvin.edu/centers-institutes/nagel-institute/projects/african-advance/awarded-grants/ (accessed 27 September 2021).

17 Dhammaloka: https://dhammalokaproject.wordpress.com/ (accessed 27 September 2021).

18 See https://www.youtube.com/watch?v=gj1VS04pZh4 (accessed 27 September 2021).

19 For 'the five best books on Northern Ireland', see Todd's essay headed 'It Would Have Been More Embarrassing to Mistake Someone's Religion Than Their Gender, and Equally Inconceivable …' at https://irishhistoriansinbritain.org/?p=766 (no date) (accessed 27 September 2021).

20 https://sites.google.com/site/coldwarkirby (accessed 27 September 2021).

21 For more on this project, funded by the Irish Research Council, 2012–13, and DCAL MAGUS, 2014–15, see https://radicalreligionblog.wordpress.com/about/ (accessed 27 September 2021).

22 The nature of today's Irish political parties, for example, may be something of a closed book to outside observers, not least because, apart from Labour and the Green Party, their names do not readily identify themselves with international political traditions. Sinn Féin ('Ourselves') is widely known for its role as the party of all-Ireland nationalism; the two parties that have previously governed the Republic and are currently (2021) together in government in coalition with the Greens are Fianna Fáil ('Soldiers of Destiny') and Fine Gael ('Tribe of the Irish'). These two parties are descended from opposing sides in the civil war of 1922–3 which accompanied the establishment of the Irish Free State (Fianna Fáil regarding the oath of allegiance to the British crown as a betrayal), rather than from any decisive differences in political ideology or economic policy.

23 The worldwide Irish diaspora is estimated at around seventy million, more than ten times the population of the island of Ireland. As just one indication of its scale and significance, exactly half of the forty-six presidents of the United States to date, including Roosevelt, Truman, Kennedy, Reagan, Clinton, Obama and Biden, have been of Irish descent.

24 The term *Vergangenheitsbewaeltigung* is intrinsically linked to the period of German history during 1933–45 under nationalist socialism and how to analyse, 'work through' and learn to live with responsibility for war crimes committed during the Second World War and responsibility for the Holocaust. It refers to the public debate that was initiated in large part by writers, artists and scholars and which found its way into the teaching curriculum of German schools but became part of revisionist and populist developments. The other model that has often figured in such conversations is the South African 'Truth and Reconciliation Commission' approach as a way of processing a complicated and traumatic past.

25 The remainder comprise 5.5 per cent Church of Ireland (Anglican) schools, one Jewish and two Islamic schools, and various forms of mixed-denomination schools.

26 Ganiel here takes an 'all-Ireland' approach, with the exception of Protestantism in the Republic which is addressed by Nuttall and Walsh (this volume).

27 See, for example, Klostergaard-Petersen et al. (2018) for the cognitive and evolutionary approach; the journal *Material Religion*, edited by S. Dees, A. Maldonado-Estrada, S. Brent Plate and K. Rakow; Grieser and Johnston (2017) for the *Aesthetics of Religion*; and Koch (2016) for the European tradition of an economics of religion.

Chapter 2

1 While in prison, Markievicz, a military and political leader in the Irish revolutionary period, wrote numerous letters to her sister, Eva Gore-Booth. Gore-Booth's life partner, Esther Roper, edited and published a collect of these letters (Markievicz [1934] 1986b: 208–9).

2 Advanced nationalists 'shared a worldview which can best be described as advanced nationalism and a tendency to be more separatist and idealistic than the more pragmatic Home Rule party' (Lynch 2015: 15). In this context, I expand this definition by including women who embraced multiple progressive movements, particularly feminism.

3 Examples include Sinn Féin politician, suffragist and education pioneer Mary MacSwiney (1872–1942) and Sinn Féin politician, founding member of Cumann na mBan and Fianna Fáil politician Kathleen Clarke (1878–1972).

4 Kimberlé Crenshaw (1993) devised intersectionality to name how single-identity analyses of discrimination fail to address oppression in instances that occur across multiple identity categories. Further, single-identity analyses also create a false sense of unity.
5 These are correspondences (micro–macro, cosmic relationships), living nature (animated landscape), imagination and meditations as vehicles for communication between the worlds and transmutation (often ritualized) (Faivre 1994: 10–13).
6 Neither concentrates on the Irish context exclusively, and while some may argue this distinction matters little, Maud Gonne and Ella Young did make a distinction due to nationalist qualms.
7 Though born in England, Besant embraced her mother's Irish heritage and was a lifelong nationalist. She promoted, not without controversy, Indian nationalism as well.
8 Russell adopted the name 'Æ' as an abbreviation of 'Æona', a 'Gnostic term for the spiritual offspring of the deity' (Goodrick-Clarke 2006: 555). Studies of Irish esotericism include Goodrick-Clarke (2006), Foster (1989) and Selina Guinness's response to Foster (Guinness 2003).
9 Despard was born in England, but she identified with her father's Anglo-Irish family (County Roscommon). She also married into the Despard family of County Laois. A progressive, Despard was involved in Irish politics from around 1906, and she embraced Irish republicanism. She relocated to Ireland permanently around 1921 (Clarke 2009).
10 Androcentric religions privilege men in leadership and theology and feature male gods exclusively, which includes the dominant forms of Christianity in Ireland.
11 Christ (1982) addressed more than five hundred participants at the Great Goddess Re-emerging conference at the University of California, Santa Cruz.
12 Women's or feminist spirituality is not a unified movement with delineated beliefs, canon or governing body. Rather, it is a diverse set of individuals, beliefs and practices grouped under this amorphous term.
13 Twenty-three years prior to the Easter Rising, Dr Douglas Hyde's (1892) lecture to the National Literary Society, 'The Necessity for De-Anglicising Ireland', argued for the revitalization of the Irish language.
14 Most of the women in this study were neither rural nor Catholic-born, and one could argue that they appropriated beliefs and practices from their counterparts in rural Ireland.
15 As assessed by historians Margaret Ward (1995b) and Senia Pašeta (2013).
16 Such as Jennie Wyse Power (1858–1941), Alice Furlong (1866–1946) and Ethna Carbery (1864–1902).
17 Including the aforementioned Gonne, Young and Markievicz.
18 A woman who was independent, progressive, syncretic in religion and who conceptualized gender in ways akin to the twenty-first rather than the turn of the twentieth century. Kraft (2013: 357).
19 Helen Laird Curran, nationalist and actress with the Irish National Theatre Society. She is also known by her stage name, Honor Lavelle.
20 Likely during the October 1889 lecture tour of Colonel Henry S. Olcott, president of the Theosophical Society (1889: 150).
21 These include Cesca Trench (2005: 250) and Padraic Colum (1931: 4).
22 See Goodrick-Clarke (1985).
23 Æ formed his own Hermetic Society twice, once in 1898 and again in 1909 after fissions emerged in Theosophy (Goodrick-Clarke 2006: 555).

24 Born in England, Móirín Nic Shionnaigh's given name was Olive Fox. She is alternatively listed as Maureen or Moireen Fox in primary sources.
25 When Blavatsky died, Besant was set to ascend to the Outer Head of the Esoteric Section, but the American, William Quan Judge, contested. Judge broke with Besant in 1895, splitting Theosophical Society between Besant's group, which was headquartered in India, and his, which was headquartered in Pasadena, California.
26 I derive the date of Young and Gonne's first meeting by comparing *Flowering Dusk* and Gonne's first mention of Young in her March 1902 letter to W. B. Yeats (Gonne 1993: 486).
27 Elsa Gidlow was a prominent lesbian poet and journalist based in California.
28 Historians of Wicca credit Ray and Rosemary Buckland with transporting British Wicca to the United States in 1963 (Clifton 2006).
29 Frances Georgiana Chenevix Trench's father was the Vicar of Orpington in Kent, and her grandfather was Richard Chevenix Trench, the Archbishop of Dublin (1864–84).
30 Included in 'Constance Markievicz to Eva Gore-Booth, 29 Dec. 1916' (Markievicz 1986a: 156–9).
31 This is discussed by Young (1945), Gonne (1995) and Trench (2005).
32 The fourth gospel being the Gospel of John, which is the most mystical gospel and thus a common source of contemplation within Western esotericism.
33 St Patrick's College is a pontifical university established in 1795 for the training of Roman Catholic priests.

Chapter 3

1 For instance, folklore studies comprise a significant part of the study of Irish language and literature in both the University of Limerick and the National University of Ireland Galway.
2 See, for instance, the notable difference in attitude to the (rural) St John's Eve bonfires and the May Eve bonfires in Limerick city in the 1970s on the part of one informant/collector in National Folklore Collection, vol. 1855, 98–100.
3 See, for example, Ó Duilearga (1981), Ó Cróinín and Ó Cróinín (1981) and Ó Ceannabháin (1983).
4 Ó Súilleabháin (1967), Danaher (1972); see also Evans (1957) and Gregory (1920).
5 See, for instance, ATU425 'The search for the lost husband' as told by Peig Sayers, 'The Woman Who Went to Hell', in Ó Súilleabháin (2012: 134–9).
6 Peig Sayers's oral narrative: Almqvist and Héalaí (2009, 2020) and Jackson (1939).
7 Sayers and Ní Chinnéide (1974), Ní Mhainnín and Ó Murchú (1998), Sayers (1962).
8 Jackson uses the spelling 'Cuán' in the text of the story but 'Cúán' in the notes. To avoid confusion, I have used 'Cúán' in this quote from Jackson's notes and in all other references to the saint.
9 The translations of this story are by the author.
10 Author's personal experience, July–August 2018.
11 Almqvist and Héalaí (2009: 51–2 (Irish version), 203–4 (English version)).
12 Almqvist and Ó Héalaí (2009: 55–6 (Irish version), 207–8 (English version)). For other examples of this belief, see Ó Duilearga (1981: 265–6) and Ó Cróinín and Ó Cróinín (1981: 213).

13 For an account of the involvement of members of the Jesuit order in Irish-language studies and Irish-language publishing, for example, see A. Titley et al. (2013); for an account of the involvement of members of the Christian Brothers' order, see M. Ó Cearúil (1996).

Chapter 5

1 For an exception, see Marianne Elliott's (2009) historical account.
2 There are, of course, notable north/south differences within the island's Christian denominations, see Elliott (2009).
3 This chapter neglects sociological studies of Protestantism in the Republic, a topic discussed elsewhere in this volume. But see Mennell et al. (2000), Crawford (2010) and, for an interdisciplinary study of the everyday religion of Protestant women, Jackson (2020).
4 Reports on public inquiries into abuse in Ireland, and the media coverage that accompanied them, have been the occasion for the exposure of the horror and extent of abuse, including inquiries into the Diocese of Ferns (Ferns Report 2005), the Archdiocese of Dublin (Murphy Report 2009), the Commission to Inquire into Child Abuse in reformatory and industrial schools (Ryan Report 2009), the Diocese of Cloyne (Cloyne Report 2011), the Magdalene Laundries (McAleese Report 2013), and the Mother and Baby Homes Commission of Investigation (2021).
5 For discussion of these and other attendance figures from the European Social Survey, see O'Mahony (2013). The 2016 figure is from the European Social Survey.
6 Ó Féich and O'Connell analyse European Values Survey data.
7 The 'highly religious' index combined self-assessment of religion's importance in one's life, attendance, frequency of prayer and belief in God; see https://www.pewresearch.org/fact-tank/2018/12/05/how-do-european-countries-differ-in-religious-commitment/ (accessed 7 April 2021).
8 Work in the cognitive science of religion has investigated the relationship between Catholic abuse scandals and 'credibility enhancing displays' (CREDs) – instances of practising what is preached – as well as 'credibility undermining displays' (CRUDs) – not practising what is preached, or religious hypocrisy. A small-scale empirical study conducted in the Republic hypothesized that exposure to scandal might reduce the potency of CREDs, especially in the absence or decline of other religious CREDs (in the family and wider culture), thus contributing to declines in belief and practice. It found one-off exposures to CREDs or CRUDs did not impact belief or practice, but consistent exposure to CREDs over time bolstered belief and practice. See Turpin, Andersen and Lanman (2018).
9 In these studies Conway found that the Irish Catholic bishops were more likely to use secular discourses to justify their position in the public sphere than bishops in these other countries. This reflected a perceived need to appeal to a more secularizing society. It also was partly a result of having more resources for accessing and commissioning social scientific research.
10 Higher attendance rates among Catholics are in line with international trends, where Catholics tend to out-attend Protestants because of the importance placed on receiving the Eucharist.
11 Monthly attendance figures from the Northern Ireland Life and Times Survey.

12 An updated book analysed the rise of the DUP in the early 2000s (Bruce 2007). Alternatively, Veronique Altglas (2022) suggests that sociologists of religion have over-emphasized the role of religious ideas and beliefs in Northern Ireland's conflict, while neglecting issues of class, inequalities, and sectarian discrimination.
13 For an alternative perspective, see Sandal (2017).
14 For an anthropological study that includes a discussion of African immigrant religion, see Murphy and Maguire (2012).
15 The Redeemed Christian Church of God is a denomination of Nigerian origins.
16 On new religious movements, see also Mulholland (2019). Peter Mulholland usefully situates the rise of new religious movements in a context that also produced a Catholic charismatic movement and Marian apparitions.
17 See, for example, an edited volume by Queen's University Belfast sociologists of religion Altglas and Wood (2018).

Chapter 6

1 Johnston Graf explores Yeats's interest in eugenics in later life and its connection to his concern with preserving the Protestant ascendancy; while this is an important factor to note in how it may have influenced his views on Irish nationhood, the examination of it is beyond the scope of this chapter.
2 Other notable contributors to Bean na hÉireann were Joseph Plunkett and Roger Casement, whose father had an interest in spiritualism.
3 The 1798 Rebellion that took place between 24 May and 23 September 1798 was a major uprising against British rule in Ireland, led by the revolutionary reform group the United Irishmen.

Chapter 7

1 In general, when this chapter refers to 'Ireland' we are referring to the entity that is independent Ireland, known as the Republic of Ireland since the foundation of the state.
2 There is an extensive but separate literature on Protestantism in Northern Ireland, an extraordinarily different phenomenon from that in the Republic. Readers interested in exploring this field should consult the work of such authors as Claire Mitchell, Gladys Ganiel, Ruth Dudley Edward or Glen Jordan.
3 The account emerged as part of an ongoing research inquiry focused on gathering and exploring narratives informing Protestant identity in Ireland. The project is sponsored by the Centre for the Study of Irish Protestantism at Maynooth University, County Kildare.
4 Corpus Christi, a specifically Catholic church holiday focused on Eucharistic adoration and emphasizing an explicitly Catholic understanding of Mass, Eucharist and church. It was observed throughout the country, frequently with great shows of pomp and triumphalism.
5 'Garda Síochána', Guardians of the Peace, the Irish police force.
6 This small group, usually Protestant (but not universally so), maintained their links with Britain following independence; their children continued to be educated in English public schools, and politically they looked to Westminster rather than to Dublin. It is a remarkable anomaly of Irish life that, despite significant evidence to the contrary, it was the assumptive world of this tiny grouping which was projected

onto the whole Protestant minority – the vast majority of whom had no associations whatsoever with the category.

7   The Irish War of Independence was largely a guerilla conflict fought between the Irish Republican Army (IRA) and forces of the British Crown between 1919 and 1921. It constituted the concluding episode in the long and often brutal process of Ireland achieving political independence from the UK.

8   About 25 per cent of all the country's Big Houses (of which there were two thousand) were destroyed and some more modest homes were also targeted.

9   It should be noted, however, that other minorities also experienced forms of 'othering', include groups who experienced much more severe forms: the Traveller community, for example, is overwhelmingly Catholic, but Travellers were also seen as outsiders and marginalized in other ways – as they are to this day. Travellers continue to suffer horrifying levels of discrimination and diverse attempts to justify this. Less recognized, perhaps, is the history of anti-Semitism in Ireland. Although the Irish Jewish community was very small even at its peak, anti-Jewish sentiment was widespread in early independent Ireland, supported by negative popular views of Jews by the media and conspiracy theories held, and sometimes propagated, by politicians. See, for example, Hanley (2020) and Kenny (2017).

10 The *Ne Temere* decree of 1910 ruled that all children of marriages between a Roman Catholic and a non-Catholic must be brought up as Catholics. Both parties had to sign an official document agreeing to this before the marriage could be performed. The Decree was enforced in Ireland with a ferocity unheard of even in other rigidly Catholic countries.

11 See, for example, the case of the Tilson marriage, when the Irish High Court ruled against the Protestant member of a marriage that had broken down. When Justice Gavin Duffy ruled on the Tilson case in the High Court, he said,

> We are a people of deep religious convictions. Accordingly, our fundamental law deliberately establishes a Christian constitution; the indifferentism of our decadent era is utterly rejected by us ... religion holds in the Constitution the place of honour which the community has always accorded to it in public opinion. The right of the Catholic Church to guard the faith of its children, the great majority, is registered in our fundamental document. (O'Connor 2008: 397)

12 A revisiting of this era of fear occurred in the 1970s, 1980s and early 1990s when 'the Troubles' in Northern Ireland were at their height. A significant number of Protestant churches (at least three in Dublin alone), halls and schools in the Republic were torched or their walls daubed with slogans proclaiming 'Prods Out'. The terror evinced by such actions was largely (but not wholly) ameliorated by the positive support proffered by many members of the majority community. For more on this, see Walsh (2013).

13 One example is the international Jacob's Biscuits, originating as a Quaker firm in Waterford, and Shaw's clothing stores with the slogan 'almost nationwide', initially a Methodist family concern.

14 This was the case until very recently, with Hubert Butler one of the few exceptions contributing to the exploration of Irish Protestant experience. Others, such as William Trevor, Alan Ford and Heather Crawford, are examples of Irish Protestant writers and academics domiciled largely abroad. Among other prominent writers and researchers in the area, Eugenio Biagini is Italian, and Miriam Moffitt and Denis Maguire, who are Irish, are not from Protestant backgrounds. This has begun to change in the last

two decades, however, as academics from within the minority community in Ireland begin to explore its experience. Ian d'Alton, Ida Milne and Tony Walsh, an author of this chapter, all constitute such examples.
15 Maguire and Murphy (2015), Nuttall (2020) and Ugba (2009) explore aspects of the influx of religious cosmopolitanism into Ireland. Some of the former represent international streams of theological Protestantism (e.g. sectors of Evangelicalism and Pentecostalism); the impact on Irish Protestantism has received little attention to date.

Chapter 10

1 I thank Hazel O'Brien and Brendan McNamara for inviting me to contribute to this edited volume and for their helpful comments on an earlier version of this chapter. This account is based on the Bureau's procedures outlined on its Facebook account. For more detail, see https://www.facebook.com/pg/Knock-Marriage-Introductions-416083628484851/about/?ref=page_internal (accessed 4 May 2021).
2 Although religious-secular competition theory distances itself from secularization theory, it is expressed in terms of a similar 'levels of analysis' framework found in the secularization literature (e.g. Dobbelaere 1999).
3 As an example, Charismatic Catholicism brings in elements of popular culture (e.g. music) to compete with secular alternatives (Stolz et al. 2016).
4 This confessional box-related trend is substantiated by the interviews of priests featured in the RTÉ documentary 'The Confessors' (12 October 2020).
5 See also Tierney (2010).
6 This is based on an International Social Survey Programme-derived aggregation of measures of belief in God, heaven, hell, religious miracles, God concerning himself with humans and God's existence giving meaning to life (Wilkins-Laflamme 2021).
7 For more detail see https://www.portlaoiseparish.ie/.
8 This account of Portlaoise parish is based on the author's personal knowledge of it. See also Byrne (2017). Similarly, other parishes (e.g. Newbridge parish) have been noted for their vibrancy (e.g. Martin 2020).
9 This figure for diocesan callings in 1959 is based on the author's calculation derived from the Vatican's statistical yearbook, *Annuario Pontificio* (Vatican Secretariat of State 1961), which reports ordinations (with a two-year lag) at the diocesan level.
10 Some former seminaries have been repurposed for secular uses, either closely related to their former use or not at all. For example, Carlow College today is a secular higher education institution. By contrast, the former Jesuit novitiate in Emo is now a public amenity. For more detail, see https://carlowcollege.ie/ and https://www.jesuit.ie/news/sentimental-journey-emo/ (accessed 24 May 2021).
11 See Clericus, an online research project which reports (among other things) enrolment and ordination trend lines for St Patrick's College, Maynooth. For more detail, see https://clericus.ie/ and https://www.maynoothuniversity.ie/arts-and-humanities-institute/news/clericus-project-student-testimonial (both accessed 24 May 2021).
12 The Bishop Casey scandal related to his relationship with a woman, Annie Murphy, and fathering of a child with her, which was publicized in the media in 1992. For more detail, see Ferriter (2006).

13 In his January 2021 statement following the publication of *the Report of the Commission of Investigation into Mother and Baby Homes*, Archbishop Michael Neary of Tuam noted that if the church at the time had held men as fathers more accountable, the fate of young mothers may have been more favourable. For more detail, see https://www.catholicbishops.ie/2021/01/13/statement-by-archbishop-michael-neary-on-the-publication-of-the-report-of-the-commission-of-investigation-into-mother-and-baby-homes/ (accessed 18 May 2021).
14 For more detail, see https://www.catholicbishops.ie/.
15 For example, the archbishop of Armagh, Eamon Martin, has his own Twitter account.
16 For more detail, see https://www.catholicbishops.ie/2021/03/10/statement-of-the-spring-2021-general-meeting-of-the-irish-catholic-bishops-conference/ (accessed 11 May 2021). In March 2021, the Irish Catholic Bishops' Conference announced its plans to convene a National Synodal Assembly within the next five years.
17 For an account of how Irish society is reckoning (or not) with its past connection to the church, see Scally (2021).
18 For example, in March 2021 Knock shrine was raised by Pope Francis from a national shrine to the level of an International Eucharistic and Marian Shrine. According to Mayo County Council Enterprise & Investment Unit, it is the most visited tourist site in Mayo, attracting 1.6 million visitors in 2015, versus 350,000 visiting nearby Croagh Patrick (Mayo County Council Enterprise & Investment Unit 2015). For more detail, see https://www.knockshrine.ie/.
19 This is reflected in the 2012 establishment of a Neocatechumenal Way-inspired archdiocesan seminary in Dundalk, County Louth. For more detail, see https://www.redmatarmagh.org/.

Chapter 11

1 University College Cork (UCC) is perhaps a significant exception, with Asian philosophy in the curriculum since the 2008 appointment of Graham Parkes and subsequently Adam Loughnane.
2 Australian theologian John D'Arcy May, who became director of the Irish School of Ecumenics at Trinity College Dublin in 1987, was already active in Buddhist-Christian theological dialogue circles.
3 Mathematician Mary Everest (the family name pronounced 'Eve-rest', not 'Ever-est') was the niece of Sir George Everest after whom the mountain was named. Her husband, George Boole, Professor of Mathematics at Queen's College Cork (now UCC) created Boolean algebra, basic to the design of computer circuits underpinning the kinds of digital humanities research discussed below.
4 I.e. opposition to the Treaty by which Ireland became a Free State (but a Dominion within the Commonwealth) while the United Kingdom retained the Protestant-dominated region now called Northern Ireland.
5 We are indebted to Dr Charles Booth (University of the West of England, Bristol) for the identification of Montague de la Courneuve arising from his research on Bristol colonial returnees in the First World War (Fedorowich and Booth 2021).
6 The surname 'Thomas de la Courneuve' reflects the family's French-Welsh antecedents.

7 The summary details here derive from numerous genealogical sources including Montague's war record, available at https://central.bac-lac.gc.ca/. item/?op=pdf&app=CEF&id=B2413-S021 (accessed 17 November 2021). We are grateful to descendants of the Stewart/Thomas de la Courneuve families for providing valuable items of information.
8 Also, Bandar Abbas and other spellings.
9 We are grateful to Professor Thomas A. Tweed (University of Notre Dame) who discovered and shared with us this remarkable musical link between Dhammaloka and Buddhists in San Francisco.
10 Not having been an imperial metropolis, immigration to Ireland lacks the large numbers from individual states which in other countries have led to substantial migrant Buddhist organizations.

REFERENCES

Chapter 1

Anderson, B., ed. (2020), *From Scrolls to Scrolling: Sacred Texts, Materiality and Dynamic Media Cultures*, Berlin: de Gruyter.

Anderson, B., and Kearney, J., eds (2018), *Ireland and the Reception of the Bible: Social and Cultural Perspectives*, London: Bloomsbury.

Beckerlegge, G. (2021), 'The Making of the Ideal Transnational Disciple: Unravelling Biographies of Margaret Noble/Sister Nivedita', in P. Bornet (ed.), *Translocal Lives and Religion*, 57–88, Sheffield: Equinox.

Berglund, J., Shanneik, Y., and Bocking, B., eds (2016), *Religious Education in a Global-Local World: Boundaries of Religious Freedom*, Regulating Religion in Diverse Societies series, vol. 4, Dordrecht: Springer.

Bocking, B., Cox, L., and Yoshinaga, S. (2014), 'The First Buddhist Mission to the West: Charles Pfoundes and the London Buddhist Mission of 1889–1892', *DISKUS*, 16 (3): 1–33. Available online: https://cora.ucc.ie/handle/10468/9812 or http://diskus.basr.ac.uk/index.php/DISKUS/article/view/51/44 (both accessed 25 July 2021).

Butler, J. (2020a), 'Contemporary Pagan Pilgrimage: Ritual and Re-storying in the Irish Landscape', *NUMEN: International Review for the History of Religions*, 67 (5–6): 613–36.

Butler, J. (2020b), 'Entering the Magic Mists: Irish Contemporary Paganism, Celticity and Indigeneity', in G. Harvey (ed.), *Indigenizing Movements in Europe*, 13–30, Sheffield: Equinox.

Carr, J. (2016), *Experiences of Islamophobia: Living with Racism in the Neoliberal Era*, London: Routledge.

Carr, J., and Fanning, B. (2019), 'Muslim Dilemmas in the Republic of Ireland: Anti-Extremism and Self-Regulation in the Context of Super-Diversity', *Islam and Christian-Muslim Relations*, 30 (2): 1–15.

Claffey, P. (2007), *Christian Churches in Dahomey-Benin: A Study of Their Socio-Political Role*, Studies of Religion in Africa Series, vol. 31, Leiden: Brill.

Claffey, P., Bereska, T., and Szustek, T. (2016), *Atlantic Tabor: The Pilgrims of Croagh Patrick*, Dublin: Liffey Press.

Conway, B. (2013), 'Social Correlates of Church Attendance in Three European Catholic Countries', *Review of Religious Research*, 55 (1): 61–80.

Conway, B. (2021), 'The Sociology of Catholicism: A Review of Research and Scholarship', *Sociology Compass* [online], 15 (4): e12863. Available online: https://doi-org.ucc.idm.oclc.org/10.1111/soc4.12863 (accessed 25 July 2021).

Cosgrove, O., Cox, L., Kuhling, C., and Mulholland, P., eds (2011), *Ireland's New Religious Movements*, Newcastle upon Tyne: Cambridge Scholars.

Cox, L. (2010), 'Current Debates: New Religion(s) in Ireland "Alternative Spiritualities, New Religious Movements and the New Age in Ireland" Conference Report, NUI Maynooth, 30–31 October 2009', *Irish Journal of Sociology*, 18 (10): 100–11.

Cox, L. (2013), *Buddhism and Ireland: From the Celts to the Counter-Culture and Beyond*, Sheffield: Equinox.
Crowley, V. (2017), 'Olivia Durdin-Robertson: Priestess of Isis', in I. Bårdsen Tøllefsen and C. Giudice (eds), *Female Religious Leaders in New Religious Movements*, Palgrave Studies in New Religions and Alternative Spiritualities series, 141–64, London: Palgrave Macmillan.
Crowley, V. (2019), 'Pagan Experiences of Counselling and Psychotherapy', in S. Harvey, S. Steidinger and J. Beckford (eds), *New Religious Movements and Counselling: Academic, Professional and Personal Perspectives*, 113–29, Abingdon: Routledge.
de Cléir, S. (2014), 'Gaisce, greann agus grá: "Conall Gulban" agus féidearthachtaí na scéalaíochta gaisciúla' [Heroism, Humour and Love: "Conall Gulban" and the Scope of Heroic Storytelling], *Béaloideas* 82: 1–23 (with English summary).
de Cléir, S. (2017), *Popular Catholicism in 20th-Century Ireland: Locality, Identity and Culture*, London: Bloomsbury.
De Sondy, A. (2013), *The Crisis of Islamic Masculinities*, New York: Bloomsbury Academic.
De Sondy, A., Gonzalez, M. A., and Green, W. S. (2020), *Judaism, Christianity and Islam: An Introduction to Monotheism*, New York: Bloomsbury.
Faas, D., Foster, N., and Smith, A. (2020), 'Accommodating Religious Diversity in Denominational and Multi-Belief Settings: A Cross-Sectoral Study of the Role of Religion in Irish Primary Schools', *Educational Review*, 72 (5): 601–16.
Foley, T. (2016), 'Monotheism and Modernity: W. E. Hearn, Ireland, Empire, and the Household Gods', *Journal of the Irish Society for the Academic Study of Religions*, 3: 84–107. Available online: https://jisasr.org/archive/volume-3-2016/ (accessed 24 July 2021).
Foley, T. (2017), 'Dining Alone in Rawalpindi? Max Arthur Macauliffe: Sikh Scholar, Reformer, and Evangelist', *Journal of the Irish Society for the Academic Study of Religions*, 4: 7–32. Available online: https://jisasr.org/archive/current-issue-volume-4-2017/ (accessed 24 July 2021).
Fujiwara, S., Thurfjell, D., and Engler, S., eds (2021), *Global Phenomenologies of Religion: An Oral History in Interviews*, Sheffield: Equinox.
Ganiel, G. (2016), *Transforming Post-Catholic Ireland: Religious Practice in Late Modernity*, Oxford: Oxford University Press.
Ganiel, G., and Yohanis, J. (2019), *Considering Grace: Presbyterians and the Troubles*, Dublin: Merrion Press.
Goodman, N. (1978), *Ways of World-Making*, Indianapolis: Hackett.
Gray, B. (2016), 'The Politics of Migration, Church, and State: A Case Study of the Catholic Church in Ireland', *International Migration Review*, 50 (2): 315–51.
Gribben, C. (2007), *God's Irishman: Theological Debates in Cromwellian Ireland*, Oxford: Oxford University Press.
Gribben, C. (2021), *The Rise and Fall of Christian Ireland*, Oxford: Oxford University Press.
Grieser, A. (2021), '"European History of Religion" Revisited: Modelling a Pluralist Approach', in C. Auffarth, A Grieser, and A. Koch (eds), *Religion in Culture – Culture in Religion: Burkhard Gladigow's Contribution to Shifting Paradigms in the Study of Religion*, 185–216, Tübingen: Tübingen University Press.
Grieser, A., and Johnston, J., eds (2017), *Aesthetics of Religion: A Connective Concept*, Berlin: de Gruyter.
Guzy, L. (2013), *Marginalised Music: Music, Religion and Politics from the Bora Sambar Region of Western Odisha*, Zürich: Lit.

Guzy, L., and Kapaló, J., eds (2017), *Marginalised and Endangered Worldviews: Comparative Studies on Contemporary Eurasia, India and South America*, Berlin: Lit.

Hadromi-Allouche, Z. (2018a), 'Images of the First Woman: Eve in Islamic Fāl-nāma Paintings', *Biblical Reception*, 5: 31–55.

Hadromi-Allouche, Z. (2018b), ' "My God? Your Lord!": A Qur'anic Response to a Biblical Question', *Journal of the International Qur'anic Studies Association*, 3: 79–110.

Heath-Carpentier, A. (2021), 'Revolution and Revelation: A Study of the Religiopolitical Lives and Legacies of Two Irish Republican Friends, Maud Gonne and Ella Young', *Journal of the Irish Society for the Academic Study of Religions* (online), 8: 1–32.

Hyman, L. (1973), *The Jews of Ireland: From the Earliest Times to the Year 1910*, Shannon: Irish University Press.

Ibrahim, V. (2011), 'The Mir of Ireland: Nationalism and Identity of an Early "Muslim" Migrant', *Temenos: Nordic Journal of Comparative Religion*, 46 (2). Available online: https://doi.org/10.33356/temenos.4513 (accessed 25 July 2021).

Inglis, T. (1987), *Moral Monopoly: The Catholic Church in Modern Irish Society*, Dublin: Gill and Macmillan.

Inglis, T. (1998), *Moral Monopoly: The Rise and Fall of the Catholic Church in Modern Ireland*, Dublin: UCD Press.

Kapaló, J. (2019), *Inochentism and Orthodox Christianity: Religious Dissent in the Russian and Romanian Borderlands*, Abingdon: Routledge.

Kapaló, J., and Povedák, K., eds (2021), *The Secret Police and the Religious Underground in Communist and Post-Communist Eastern Europe*, Abingdon: Routledge.

Keogh, D. (1998), *Jews in Twentieth-Century Ireland*, Cork: Cork University Press.

Khan, A. H. (2013), 'Creating the Image of European Islam: The European Council for Fatwa and Research and Ireland', in J. S. Nielsen (ed.), *Muslim Political Participation in Europe*, 215–38, Edinburgh: Edinburgh University Press.

Kippenberg, H. G. (2002), *Discovering the Religious History in the Modern Age*, Princeton, NJ: Princeton University Press.

Kieran, P. (2021), 'A Brief History of Catholic Education in Ireland from the Penal Laws to Founding of the Free State (1922) and Beyond', in S. Whittle (ed.), *Irish and British Reflections on Catholic Education*, 67–80, Singapore: Springer Nature.

Kieran, P., and McDonagh, J. (2021), 'The Centre Cannot Hold: Decolonising the RE Curriculum in the Republic of Ireland', *British Journal of Religious Education*, 43 (1): 123–35.

Kirby, D. (2017), 'The Cold War and American Religion', *Oxford Encyclopaedia of Religion in America*, 24 May. Available online: https://oxfordre.com/religion/religion/view/10.1093/acrefore/9780199340378.001.0001/acrefore-9780199340378-e-398 (accessed 25 July 2021).

Kirby, D. (2021), 'Religious Women and the Northern Ireland Troubles', *Journal of Religious History* (preview online). DOI: 10.1111/1467-9809.12767.

Klostergaard Petersen, A., Saelid, G. I., Martin, L. H., Jensen, J. S., and Sørensen, J., eds (2018), *Evolution, Cognition, and the History of Religion: A New Synthesis*, Leiden: Brill.

Koch, A. (2016), 'Economics of Religion', in M. Stausberg and S. Engler (eds), *Oxford Handbook of the Study of Religion*, 355–64, Oxford: Oxford University Press.

Loughlin, E. (2020), 'Just One School Divested in 2020', *Irish Examiner*, 23 December. Available online: https://www.irishexaminer.com/news/arid-40196136.html (accessed 6 July 2021).

Madden, G. (2014), 'Bishop Michael Browne of Galway and Anti-Communism, 1937–1976', *Saothar (Journal of the Irish Labour History Society)*, 39: 21–31.

Madden, G. (2018), 'The Connolly Association, the Catholic Church, and Anti-Communism in Britain and Ireland during the Early Cold War', *Contemporary British History*, 32 (4): 492–510. DOI: 10.1080/13619462.2018.1519418.

McNamara, B. (2019), 'Eliding the Esoteric: R. J. Campbell and Early Twentieth Century Protestant Discourse in Britain', *Journal of Religious History*, 43 (4): 511–30.

McNamara, B. (2021), *The Reception of 'Abdu'l-Bahá in Britain; East Comes West*, Leiden: Brill.

Neary, A., Gray, B., and O'Sullivan, M. (2018), 'Lesbian, Gay and Bisexual Teachers' Negotiations of Civil Partnership and Schools: Ambivalent Attachments to Religion and Secularism', *Discourse Studies in the Cultural Politics of Education*, 39 (3): 434–47.

Nuttall, D. (2019), '"Cahill's Blood": Mr Cahill Makes the Cure', in J., Carey, C. Ó Ghealbháin, I. Tuomi and B. Hillers (eds), *Charms, Charmers and Charming in Ireland: From the Medieval to the Modern*, New Approaches to Celtic Religion and Mythology series, 145–58, Cardiff: University of Wales Press.

Nuttall, D. (2020), *Different and the Same: A Folk History of the Protestants of Independent Ireland*, Dublin: Eastwood Books.

O'Brien, H. (2019), 'The Marginality of "Irish Mormonism": Confronting Irish Boundaries of Belonging', *Journal of the British Association for the Study of Religions*, 21: 52–75. Available online: https://www.jbasr.com/ojs/index.php/jbasr/article/view/40/43 (accessed 25 July 2021).

O'Brien, H. (2020), 'What Does the Rise of Digital Religion during Covid-19 Tell Us about Religion's Capacity to Adapt?', *Irish Journal of Sociology*, 28 (2): 242–6. Available online: https://journals.sagepub.com/doi/pdf/10.1177/0791603520939819 (accessed 25 July 2021).

O'Toole, E. (2019), 'Ireland's Attempts to Secularise Its Schools Have Turned to Farce', *The Guardian*, 10 April. Available online: https://www.theguardian.com/commentisfree/2019/apr/10/ireland-secularise-schools-catholic-dublin-divestment (accessed 6 July 2021).

Padoan, T. (2019), 'Reassembling the Lucky Gods: Pilgrim Economies, Tourists, and Local Communities in Global Tokyo', *Journeys: The International Journal of Travel and Travel Writing*, 20 (1): 75–97. Available online: https://www.berghahnjournals.com/view/journals/journeys/20/1/journeys.20.issue-1.xml (accessed 25 July 2021).

Padoan, T. (2021), 'On the Semiotics of Space in the Study of Religions: Theoretical Perspectives and Methodological Challenges', in T.-A. Poder and J. Van Boom (eds), *Sign, Method, and the Sacred: New Directions in Semiotic Methodologies for the Study of Religion*, 189–214, Berlin: de Gruyter.

Pevarello, D. (2017), 'Criticism of Verbosity in Ancient Philosophical and Early Christian Writings: Jesus' Critique of the "Polylogia" of Pagan Prayers (Matthew 6:7) in Its Graeco-Roman Context', in A. Klostergaard Petersenand and G. van Kooten (eds), *Religio-Philosophical Discourses in the Mediterranean World*, Ancient Philosophy and Religion, vol. 1, 244–75, Leiden: Brill.

Pevarello, D. (2018), 'Pythagorean Traditions in Early Christian Asceticism', in L. I. Larsen and S. Rubenson (eds), *Monastic Education in Late Antiquity: The Transformation of Classical Paideia*, 256–77, Cambridge: Cambridge University Press.

Rivlin, R. (2011), *Jewish Ireland: A Social History*, Dublin: History Press.

Ruane, J. (2021), 'Long Conflict and How It Ends: Protestants and Catholics in Europe and Ireland', *Irish Political Studies*, 36 (1): 109–31. Available online: https://doi.org/10.1080/07907184.2021.1877900 (accessed 27 September 2021).

Ruane, J., and Todd, J. (2010), 'Ethnicity and Religion: Redefining the Research Agenda', *Ethnopolitics*, 9 (1): 1–8. DOI: 10.1080/17449050903557377.
Sakaranaho, T., and Martikainen, T. (2015), 'The Governance of Islam in Finland and Ireland', *Journal of Religion in Europe*, 8 (1): 7–30.
Scharbrodt, O., Sakaranaho, T., Khan, A. H., Shanneik, Y., and Ibrahim, V., eds (2015), *Muslims in Ireland: Past and Present*, Edinburgh: Edinburgh University Press.
Shackle, C., and Bocking, B. (2017), 'Representing Sikhism: Essays in Memory of the Irish Scholar Max Arthur Macauliffe', *Journal of the Irish Society for the Academic Study of Religions*, 4 (1): 1–6. Available online: https://jisasr.org/archive/current-issue-volume-4-2017/ (accessed 25 July 2021).
Shanneik, Y. (2015), 'Remembering Karbala in the Diaspora: Religious Rituals among Iraqi Shii Women in Ireland', *Religion*, 45 (1): 89–102.
Shanneik, Y. (2016), '"They Aren't Holy": Dealing with Religious Differences in Irish Primary Schools', in J. Berglund, Y. Shanneik and B. Bocking (eds), *Religious Education in a Global-Local World*, 165–80, Dordrecht: Springer.
Stausberg, M. (2007), 'The Study of Religion(s) in Western Europe (I): Prehistory and History until World War II', *Religion*, 37 (4): 294–318. DOI: 10.1016/j.religion.2007.10.001.
Stausberg, M. (2009), 'The Study of Religion(s) in Western Europe III: Further Developments after World War II', *Religion*, 39 (3): 261–82. DOI: 10.1016/j.religion.2009.06.001.
Stausberg, M., and Engler, S., eds (2020), *Religion at 50: Past and Futures*, special issue of *Religion*, 50 (1).
Stringer, A. (2016), 'Addressing the Problem of Socio-Economic-Classification', in A. Day (ed.), *Contemporary Issues in the Worldwide Anglican Communion: Powers and Pieties*, 149–68, Farnham: Ashgate.
Stringer, A. (2019), 'The Congregation as a Station for Social Integration – an Analysis of Congregants' Personal Networks with an Interpretation Using Giddens' Theory of Structuration', *Journal of the Irish Society for the Academic Study of Religions*, 7: 35–58. Available online: https://jisasr.files.wordpress.com/2020/01/the-congregation-as-a-station-for-social-integration-an-analysis-of-congregantse28099-personal-networks-with-an-interpretation-using-giddense28099-theory-of-structuration-pdf.pdf (accessed 27 September 2021).
Todd, J. (2018), *Identity Change after Conflict: Ethnicity, Boundaries and Belonging in the Two Irelands*, New York: Palgrave Macmillan.
Todd, J., and Ruane, J. (2016), 'Ethnicity and Religion', in K. Cordell and S. Wolff (eds), *Routledge Handbook of Ethnic Conflict*, 67–78, Abingdon: Routledge.
Turner, A., Cox, L., and Bocking, B. (2020), *The Irish Buddhist: The Forgotten Monk Who Faced Down the British Empire*, New York: Oxford University Press.
Ugba, A. (2009), *Shades of Belonging: Pentecostal Africans in Twenty-First Century Ireland*, Trenton, NJ: Africa World Press.
Ugba, A. (2011), 'When "Home" Is Nowhere: Re-assessing African Diasporic Experience in 21st Century Ireland', in P. Duibhir, R. McDaid and A. O'Shea (eds), *All Changed? Culture and Identity in Contemporary Ireland*, 71–81, Dublin: Duras Press.
Walsh, T. (2021), 'Profound Encounters: The Love Feast and the Old German Baptist Brethren', *Journal of Plain Anabaptist Communities*, 2 (1): 1–27.
Woodlock, R. (2012), 'Muslim Wellbeing in Australia: An Analysis of Personal and National Wellbeing among a Sample of Muslims Living in New South Wales and Victoria', *Islam and Christian–Muslim Relations*, 23 (2): 181–200.

Woodlock, R. (2016), 'Identity and Islamophobia: An Australian Investigation', in D. Pratt and R. Woodlock (eds), *Fear of Muslims? International Perspectives on Islamophobia*, Boundaries of Religious Freedom: Regulating Religion in Diverse Societies series, vol. 3, 131–51, Switzerland: Springer.

Chapter 2

Annat, A. (2016), 'Ella Young's Vision', in A. Pilz and W. Standlee (eds), *Irish Women's Writing 1878–1922*, 191–208, Manchester: Manchester University Press.
Arthur, G. (1966), 'Gavin Arthur Talks about Ella Young Part 1, A', Dunes Center, James D. Cain recorded interview (audio file). Available online: http://dunescenter.org/dunes-collaborative/dunes-collaborative-products/conversations-about-ella-young/ (accessed 2 February 2019).
Beck, U. (2014), 'Individualization Is Eroding Traditions Worldwide', in U. Beck (ed.), *Ulrich Beck: Springerbriefs on Pioneers in Science and Practice*, vol. 2, 90–9, New York: Springer.
Christ, C. P. (1982), 'Why Women Need the Goddess: Phenomenological, Psychological, and Political Reflection', in C. Spretnak (ed.), *The Politics of Women's Spirituality: Essays on the Rise of Spiritual Power within the Feminist Movement*, 71–86, New York: Anchor Press/Doubleday.
Christ, C. P. (2012), 'Why Women, Men, and Other Living Things Still Need the Goddess: Remembering and Reflecting 35 Years Later', *Feminist Theology*, 20 (3): 242–55.
Christ, C. P., and Plaskow, J. (2016), *Goddess and God in the World: Conversations in Embodied Theology*, Minneapolis, MN: Fortress Press.
Clarke, F. (2009), 'Despard, Charlotte', Dictionary of Irish Biography. Available online: https://www.dib.ie/biography/despard-charlotte-a2542 (accessed 19 July 2021).
Clark Roof, W. (1993), 'Religion and Narrative', *Review of Religious Research*, 34 (4): 297–310. Available online: https://doi.org/10.2307/3511969.
Clifton, C. (2006), *Her Hidden Children: The Rise of Wicca and Paganism in America*, Lanham, MD: AltaMira Press.
Colum, P. (1931), *Ella Young: An Appreciation*, New York: Longmans, Green.
Crenshaw, K. (1993), 'Mapping the Margins: Intersectionality, Identity Politics, and Violence against Women of Color', *Stanford Law Review*, 43 (6): 1241–99. Available online: https://doi.org/10.2307/1229039.
Daly, M. (1973), *Beyond God the Father: Toward a Philosophy of Women's Liberation*, Boston: Beacon.
Dixon, J. (2001), *Divine Feminine: Theosophy and Feminism in England*, Johns Hopkins University Studies in Historical and Political Science, Baltimore, MD: Johns Hopkins University Press.
Eller, C. (1993), *Living in the Lap of the Goddess: The Feminist Spirituality Movement in America*, New York: Crossroads.
Faivre, A. (1994), *Access to Western Esotericism*, Albany: State University of New York Press.
Faivre, A., and Rhone, C., trans. (2010), *Western Esotericism: A Concise History*, Albany: State University of New York Press.

Flanagan, M. (1949), 'Witness Statement 246', Dublin: Bureau of Military History. Available online: https://www.militaryarchives.ie/collections/online-collections/bureau-of-military-history-1913-1921/reels/bmh/BMH.WS0246.pdf (accessed 1 July 2021).

Foster, R. F. (1989), 'Protestant Magic: W. B. Yeats and the Spell of Irish History', in *Proceedings of the British Academy*, 243–66, London: British Academy.

Ganiel, G. (2016), *Transforming Post-Catholic Ireland: Religious Practice in Late Modernity*, Oxford: Oxford University Press.

Geertz, C. ([1973] 2000), *The Interpretation of Cultures*, New York: Basic Books.

Gidlow, E. (1986), *Elsa, I Come with My Songs*, San Francisco: Booklegger Press.

Gonne, M. (1993), 'Gonne to Yeats, March 1902 letter 101n2', in A. Norman Jeffares and A. MacBride White (eds), *Always Your Friend: The Gonne-Yeats Letters, 1893–1938*, 486, New York.

Gonne, M. ([1938] 1995), *A Servant of the Queen*, ed. A. Norman Jeffares and A. MacBride White, Chicago: University of Chicago Press.

Gonne, M., and Yeats, W. B. (1993), *Always Your Friend: The Gonne-Yeats Letters, 1893–1938*, ed. A. Norman Jeffares and A. MacBride White, New York: Norton.

Goodrick-Clarke, N. (1985), 'The Occult Roots of Nazism, the Ariosophists of Austria and Germany', *WayBackMachine*. Available online: https://web.archive.org/web/20061003213650/http://lapismagazine.org/nazism.html (accessed 23 June 2019).

Goodrick-Clarke, N. (2006), 'The Dublin Hermetic Societies (1885–1939)', in W. J. Hanegraaff (ed.), *Dictionary of Gnosis & Western Esotericism* [ebook], 555–8, Leiden: Brill.

Gore-Booth, E. (1894), *Diary of Eva Gore-Booth* (1894), in the papers of Eva Gore-Booth (1870–1926), MIC 590 Reel 5, Belfast: Public Records Office of Northern Ireland (PRONI).

Gore-Booth, E. (1904), 'To Maeve', in G. Russell (ed.), *New Songs: A Lyric Selection Made by A.E.*, 49, Dublin: O'Donoghue.

Gore-Booth, E. (1905), *The Three Resurrections and the Triumph of Maeve*, London: Longmans, Green.

Gore-Booth, E. (1916), *The Death of Fionavar from the Triumph of Maeve*, London: Erskine MacDonald.

Gore-Booth, E. (1923), *A Psychological and Poetic Approach to the Study of Christ in the Fourth Gospel*, London: Longmans, Green. Available online: https://archive.org/details/MN41955ucmf_1 (accessed 25 October 2017).

Gore-Booth, E. (1926), *The Inner Kingdom*, London: Longmans, Green.

Gore-Booth, E. (1927), *The World's Pilgrim*, London: Longmans, Green.

Gore-Booth, E. (1929), 'The Inner Life of a Child', in E. Roper (ed.), *Poems of Eva Gore-Booth Complete Edition with the Inner Life of a Child and Letters and Biographical Introduction*, 51–60, New York: Longmans, Green.

Grand, S. (1894), 'The New Aspect of the Woman Question', *North American Review*, 158 (448): 270–6. Available online: https://www.jstor.org/stable/25103291 (accessed 25 July 2021).

Guinness, S. (2003), '"Protestant Magic" Reappraised: Evangelicalism, Dissent, and Theosophy', *Irish University Review*, 33 (1): 14–27.

Hanegraaff, W. J. (2006), 'Introduction', in W. J. Hanegraaff (ed.), *Dictionary of Gnosis & Western Esotericism* [ebook], vii–xiii, Leiden: Brill.

Hyde, D. ([1892] 2006), 'The Necessity for De-Anglicising Ireland', in M. Murphy and J. MacKillop (eds), *An Irish Literature Reader: Poetry, Prose, Drama*, 2nd edn, 139–49, New York: Syracuse University Press.

'Irish Suffrage Activities' (1913), *Irish Citizen*, 27 September: 154–5.

Ivakhiv, A. J. (2001), *Claiming Sacred Ground: Pilgrims and Politics at Glastonbury and Sedona*, Bloomington: Indiana University Press.

Joynt, M. (1912), 'Women and the State', *Irish Citizen*, 15 June: 27.

Kelly, A. (2012), 'Before the Gardnerians', Patheos, 12 October. Available online: https://www.patheos.com/blogs/aidankelly/2012/10/before-the-gardnerians-the-fellows hip-of-the-four-jewels-and-the-church-of-aphrodite/ (accessed 10 October 2016).

Kelly, A. (2016), *Hippie Commie Beatnik Witches: A Social History of the New Reformed Orthodox Order of the Golden Dawn*, 2nd rev. edn, Tacoma: Hierophant Wordsmith Press.

Kraft, S. E. (2013), 'Theosophy, Gender, and the "New Woman"', in M. Rothstein and O. Hammer (eds), *Handbook of the Theosophical Current*, 357–73, Leiden: Brill.

Levenson, L., and Natterstad, J. H. (1986), *Hanna Sheehy-Skeffington: Irish Feminist*, Syracuse, NY: Syracuse University Press.

Liebmann Jacobs, J. (1989), *Divine Disenchantment: Deconverting from New Religions*, Bloomington: University of Indiana Press.

Lynch, R. (2015), *Revolutionary Ireland, 1912–1925*, New York: Bloomsbury.

Macardle, D. (1956), 'A Poet of the Celtic Twilight – Transcript', Ireland: UCD Archives (RTÉ written archives radio talk scripts P260/671).

Macardle, D. (2020), 'The Return of Niav', in D. Macardle (ed.), *Earth-bound and Other Supernatural Tales*, 39–51, Dublin: Swan River Press.

MacCurtain, M. (1987), 'Moving Statues and Irishwomen', *Studies: An Irish Quarterly Review*, 76 (302): 139–47. Available online: https://www.jstor.org/stable/30090851 (accessed 25 July 2021).

Markievicz, C. (1909), 'To Miss Nora Cassidy and the Young Girls of Ireland', *Bean na h'Eireann*, 9: 14.

Markievicz, C. ([1915] 1995), 'Buy a Revolver', in M. Ward (ed.), *In Their Own Voice: Women and Irish Nationalism*, 45–7, Dublin: Attic Press.

Markievicz, C. (1923), 'Mr. Arthur Griffith and the Sinn Féin Organisation', *Éire*, 18 August: 25.

Markievicz, C. ([1934] 1986a), 'Constance Markievicz to Eva Gore-Booth, 29 Dec. 1916, Aylesbury Prison', in E. Roper (ed.), *Prison Letters of Countess Markievicz*, 156–9, London: Virago Press.

Markievicz, C. ([1934] 1986b), 'Constance Markievicz to Eva Gore-Booth, undated, 1918–1919, Holloway Jail', in E. Roper (ed.), *Prison Letters of Countess Markievicz*, 208–9, London: Virago Press.

Molony, H. (1934), Witness Statement 391, Dublin: Bureau of Military History. Available online: http://www.bureauofmilitaryhistory.ie/reels/bmh/BMH.WS0391.pdf (accessed 12 January 2018).

National Archives Ireland (1911a), '11 Grosvenor Place, Rathmines & Rathgar West, Dublin', 1911 Census. Available online: http://www.census.nationalarchives.ie/pages/1911/Dublin/Rathmines___Rathgar_West/Grosvenor_Place/65752/ (accessed 6 February 2019).

National Archives Ireland (1911b), '14 Kingston, Dundrum, Dublin', 1911 Census. Available online: http://www.census.nationalarchives.ie/pages/1911/Dublin/Dundrum/Kingston/94478/ (accessed 6 February 2019).

'National Literary Society' (1901), *The Freeman's Journal*, 18 December: 7.
O'Brolchain, M. (1949), BMH Witness Statement 321, Dublin: Bureau of Military History. Available online: https://www.militaryarchives.ie/collections/online-collections/bureau-of-military-history-1913-1921/reels/bmh/BMH.WS0321.pdf (accessed 12 March 2021).
Pašeta, S. (2013), *Irish Nationalist Women, 1900–1918*, New York: Cambridge University Press.
Rigby, K. (2001), 'The Goddess Returns: Ecofeminist Reconfigurations of Gender, Nature, and the Sacred', in F. Devlin-Glass and L. McCredden (eds), *Feminist Poetics of the Sacred*, 23–54, New York: Oxford University Press.
Russell, G., ed. (1904), *New Songs: A Lyric Selection Made by A.E.*, Dublin: O'Donoghue.
Sheehy Skeffington, A. (1991), *Skeff: The Life of Owen Sheehy Skeffington: 1909–1970*, Dublin: Lilliput Press.
Sheehy Skeffington, M. (2017), 'The Role of Hanna and Francis Sheehy Skeffington, Feminists, Nationalists, Pacifists, Socialists in Early Twentieth Century Ireland' (lecture), 28 September.
Theosophical Society (1889), 'Theosophical Activities', *Lucifer*, 5 (26): 146–51.
Tiernan, S. (2012), *Eva Gore-Booth: An Image of Such Politics*, New York: Manchester University Press.
Trench, F. (2005), *Cesca's Diary 1913–1916: Where Art and Nationalism Meet*, ed. Hilary Pyle, Dublin: Woodfield Press.
Ward, M. (1995a), *In Their Own Voice: Women and Irish Nationalism*, Dublin: Attic Press.
Ward, M. (1995b), *Unmanageable Revolutionaries: Women and Irish Nationalism*, London: Pluto Press.
Ward, M. (2019), *Fearless Woman: Hanna Sheehy Skeffington, Feminism, and the Irish Revolution*, Dublin: University College Dublin Press.
Young, E. (1906), *Poems*, Dublin: Maunsel.
Young, E. (1910), *Celtic Wonder-Tales*, Dublin: Maunsel.
Young, E. (1922), *The Weird of Fionavar*, Dublin: Talbot Press.
Young, E. (1938), *Marzilian and Other Poems*, Oceano: Harbison & Harbison.
Young, E. (1945), *Flowering Dusk: Things Remembered Accurately and Inaccurately*, London: Longmans, Green.
Young, E. (1950), 'Ella Young Talks with Alan Watts Part 1', Dunes Center (audio recording, 4.10). Available online: http://dunescenter.org/dunes-collaborative/dunes-collaborative-products/conversations-about-ella-young/ (accessed 10 January 2021).

Chapter 3

Almqvist, B., and Ó Héalaí, P., eds (2009), *Labharfad le Cách / I Will Speak to You All*, Dublin: New Island.
Almqvist, B., and Ó Héalaí, P., eds (2020), *Níl Deireadh Ráite / Not the Final Word*, Dublin: New Island.
Burke, P. (1978), *Popular Culture in Early Modern Europe*, London: Maurice Temple Smith.
Danaher, K. (1972), *The Year in Ireland*, Cork: Mercier.
de Cléir, S. (2010), 'Ritual and the City Context: Limerick 1925-1960', *Béascna: Journal of Folklore and Ethnology*, 6: 1–19.

de Cléir, S. (2017), *Popular Catholicism in 20th-Century Ireland: Locality, Identity and Culture*, London: Bloomsbury.
Dundes, A. (1980), 'Who Are the Folk?', in A. Dundes (ed.), *Interpreting Folklore*, 1–19, Bloomington: Indiana University Press.
Evans, E. E. (1957), *Irish Folk Ways*, London: Routledge and Kegan Paul.
Fuller, L. (2002), *Irish Catholicism since 1950: The Undoing of a Culture*, Dublin: Gill and Macmillan.
Gregory, A. (1920), *Visions and Beliefs in the West of Ireland*, London: G. P. Putnam's Sons.
Harris, A. (2013), *Faith in the Family: A Lived Religious History of English Catholicism, 1945–82*, Manchester: Manchester University Press.
Harrold, P. (1994), 'Park and Its People: Origin and Folklore', in K. Hannan and P. J. O'Donnell (eds), *Patrick's People: Historical Perspectives on an Ancient and Developing Community*, 67–70, Limerick: n.p.
Holbek, B. (1982), 'The Many Abodes of Fata Morgana or the Quest for Meaning in Fairy Tales', *Journal of Folklore Research*, 22 (1): 19–28.
Hughes, H. (1991), *Croagh Patrick (Cruach Phádraig – the Reek): An Ancient Mountain Pilgrimage*, Westport: Harry Hughes.
Hyde, D. (1906), *Abhráin Diadha Chúige Connacht, or, The Religious Songs of Connacht: A Collection of Poems, Stories, Prayers, Satires, Ranns, Charms Etc.*, Dublin: M. H. Gill.
Jackson, K., ed. (1939), *Scéalta ón mBlascaod*, Dublin: An Cumann le Béaloideas Éireann (also available as *Béaloideas*, 8 (1938): 3–96).
Larkin, E. (1976), *The Historical Dimensions of Irish Catholicism*, New York: Arno Press.
Lysaght, P. (1995), 'An Choróin Mhuire in Iar-thuaisceart Thír Chonaill sa Bhfichiú Haois: Suíomh do Dheabhóid Mheánaoiseach Eorpach i Gcráifeacht agus Saol Traidisiúnta na nDaoine', *Sinsear: The Folklore Journal*, 8: 13–54.
MacCurtain, M. (1989), 'Fullness of Life: Defining Female Spirituality in Twentieth-Century Ireland', in M. Luddy and C. Murphy (eds), *Women Surviving: Studies in Irish Women's History in the 19th and 20th Centuries*, 233–63, Dublin: Poolbeg.
MacNeill, M. (1962), *The Festival of Lughnasa: A Study of the Survival of the Celtic Festival of the Beginning of the Harvest*, Oxford: Oxford University Press.
MagFhloinn, B. (2016), *Blood Rite: The Feast of St Martin in Ireland*, Helsinki: Folklore Fellows' Communications.
Magliocco, S. (2014), 'Religious Practice', in R.F. Bendix and G. Hasan-Rokem (eds), *A Companion to Folklore*, 2nd edn, 136–53, Oxford: Wiley Blackwell.
McGrath, T. G. (1991), 'The Tridentine Evolution of Modern Irish Catholicism: A Re-Examination of the "Devotional Revolution" Thesis', *British Catholic History*, 20: 512–23.
Messenger, J. C. (1972), 'Folk Religion', in R.M. Dorson (ed.), *Folklore and Folklife: An Introduction*, 217–32, Chicago: University of Chicago Press.
National Folklore Collection (2017), 'UNESCO Memory of the World'. Available online: https://www.ucd.ie/irishfolklore/en/about/unescomemoryoftheworld/ (accessed 22 April 2021).
National Folklore Collection, vol. 1855, 98–100.
National Museum of Ireland (n.d.), 'National Museum of Ireland: Country Life'. Available online: https://www.museum.ie/en-IE/Museums/Country-Life (accessed 22 April 2021).
Ní Mhainnín, M., and Ó Murchú, L., eds (1998), *Peig: A Scéal Féin*, Dingle: An Sagart.
Nic Einrí, U. (2001), *An Cantaire Siúlach: Tadhg Gaelach*, Dingle: An Sagart.

Ó Ceannabháin, P., ed. (1983), *Éamon a Búrc: Scéalta*, Dublin: An Clóchomhar.
Ó Cearúil, M., ed. (1996), *Gníomhartha na mBráithre: Aistí Comórtha ar Ghaelachas na mBráithe Críostaí*, Dublin: Coiscéim.
O'Connor, A. (2012), 'The "Sacred Isle" of Saints and Scholars Revisited: Exploring Irish Spirituality, Religious Folklore and Cultural Identity', in R. Uí Ógáin, W. Nolan and E. Ó hÓgáin (eds), *Sean, Nua agus Síoraíocht: Féilscríbhinn in Ómós do Dháithí Ó hÓgáin*, 363–74, Dublin: Coiscéim.
Ó Cróinín, S., and Ó Cróinín, D., eds (1981), *Seanachas Amhlaoibh Í Luínse*, Dublin: Comhairle Bhéaloideas Éireann.
Ó Crualaoich, G. (2003), *The Book of the Cailleach: Stories of the Wise-Woman Healer*, Cork: Cork University Press.
Ó Duilearga, S., ed. (1981), *Seán Ó Conaill's Book: Stories and Traditions from Iveragh*, trans. Máire MacNeill, Dublin: Comhairle Bhéaloideas Éireann.
O'Flynn, C. (1998), *There Is an Isle: A Limerick Boyhood*, Cork: Mercier.
Ó Giolláin, D. (2005), *An Dúchas agus an Domhan*, Cork: Cork University Press.
Ó Héalaí, P. (2012), *An Slánaitheoir ag Siúl ar an Talamh: Innéacs Scéalta Faoi Phearsana an Tiomna Nua i mBéaloideas na hÉireann, Maille le Réamhrá agus Staidéar*, Dingle: An Sagart.
Ó hEochaidh, S., and Ó Catháin, S., eds (1977), *Fairy Legends from Donegal*, trans. M. Ní Néill, Dublin: Comhairle Bhéaloideas Éireann.
Ó hÓgáin, D. (1990), *Myth, Legend and Romance: An Encyclopaedia of the Irish Folk Tradition*, London: Ryan Publishing.
Ó Súilleabháin, S., ed. (1952), *Scéalta Cráibhtheacha*, Dublin: An Cumann le Béaloideas Éireann (also available as 'Scéalta Cráibhtheacha', *Béaloideas*, 21 (1951–2)).
Ó Súilleabháin, S. (1967), *Irish Folk Custom and Belief*, Cork: Mercier.
Ó Súilleabháin, S., ed. (2012), *Miraculous Plenty: Irish Religious Folktales and Legends*, trans. W. Caulfield, Dublin: Folklore of Ireland Council.
Primiano, L. (1995), 'Vernacular Religion and the Search for Method in Religious Folklife', *Western Folklore*, 54 (1): 37–56.
Sayers, P. (1962), *An Old Woman's Reflections*, trans. S. Ennis, Oxford: Oxford University Press.
Sayers, P., and Ní Chinnéide, M. (1974), *Peig: The Autobiography of Peig Sayers of the Great Blasket Island*, trans. B. Mac Mahon, Dublin: Talbot Press.
Sciorra, J. (1999), '"We Go Where the Italians Live": Religious Processions as Ethnic and Territorial Markers in a Multi-Ethnic Brooklyn Neighborhood', in R. A. Orsi (ed.), *Gods of the City: Religion and the American Urban Landscape*, 310–40, Bloomington: Indiana University Press.
Taylor, L. J. (1995), *Occasions of Faith: An Anthropology of Irish Catholics*, Dublin: Lilliput.
Thomas, K. (1971), *Religion and the Decline of Magic: Studies in Popular Religion in Sixteenth and Seventeenth-Century England*, New York: Scribner.
Titley, A., O'Riordan, M., Breathnach, D., and Ní Mhurchú, M., eds (2013), *An Chuallacht Léannta: Ceiliúradh ar Iosánaigh agus Léann na Gaeilge*, Dublin: Foilseacháin Ábhair Spioradálta.
Tyers, P., ed. (1982), *Leoithne Aniar, Baile an Fheirtéaraigh: Cló Dhuibhne*.
UCC Anthropology (n.d.), 'What Is the Cork Folklore Project?'. Available online: https://www.ucc.ie/en/anthropology/research/researchprojects/corkfolkloreproject/ (accessed 22 April 2021).

Uí Ógáin, R. (2012), 'Guí an Phobail – Amhráin Bheannaithe ó Iarthar Chontae na Gaillimhe', in S. Ó Cadhla and D. Ó Giolláin (eds), *Léann an Dúchais: Aistí in Ómós do Ghearóid Ó Crualaoich*, 36–49, Cork: Cork University Press,

Uther H. J. (2004a), *The Types of International Folktales: A Classification and Bibliography, Part I*, Helsinki: Folklore Fellows' Communications.

Uther, H. J. (2004b), *The Types of International Folktales: A Classification and Bibliography, Part II*, Helsinki: Folklore Fellows' Communications.

Wildman, C. (2011), 'Religious Selfhoods and the City in Inter-War Manchester', *Urban History*, 38: 103–23.

Chapter 4

Akenson, D. (2012), *A Mirror to Kathleen's Face: Education in Independent Ireland 1922–1960*, Abingdon: Routledge.

Bastide, D. (2006), *Teaching Religious Education 4–11*, London: Routledge.

Biesta, G., Aldridge, D., Hannam, P., and Whittle, S. (2019), *Religious Literacy: A Way Forward for Religious Education? A Report Submitted to the Culham St Gabriel's Trust*. Available online: https://www.reonline.org.uk/wp-content/uploads/2019/07/Religious-Literacy-Biesta-Aldridge-Hannam-Whittle-June-2019.pdf (accessed 10 July 2021).

Byrne, G., and Francis, L. J., eds (2019), *Religion and Education: The Voices of Young People in Ireland*, Dublin: Veritas.

Byrne, G., and Kieran, P., eds (2013), *Toward Mutual Ground: Pluralism, Religious Education and Diversity in Irish Schools*, Dublin: Columba Press.

Catholic School Partnership (2015), *Catholic Primary Schools in a Changing Ireland: Sharing Good Practice on Inclusion of All Pupils*, Dublin: Veritas.

Conboy, S. (2016), 'The Question of Religious/Belief Diversity in Irish Multidenominational Primary Schools', *ETBI*, Spring: 32–7.

Conboy, S. (2017), 'What Are Community National Schools?', *ETBI*, Spring: 3–4.

Conboy, S. (2019), 'Ten Years of State Multidenomnational Schools', in *Education Matters Ireland's Yearbook of Education: Primary 2018=2019*, 24–8, Castleisland: Education Matters.

Conway, E. (2012), 'The Future of Catholic Schools – the Forum on Patronage and Pluralism: Cultural Marker and Wake-Up Call', *The Furrow*, June: 369–77.

Conway, E. (2015), 'Vatican II on Christian Education: Can It Guide Us through Today's "Educational Emergency"?', in N. Coll (ed.), *Vatican II and Ireland: Its History and Its Prospects*, 253–73, Dublin: Columba Press.

Coolahan, J. (1981), *Irish Education History and Structure*, Dublin: Institute of Public Administration.

Coolahan, J., and O'Donovan, J. (2009), *A History of Ireland's School Inspectorate, 1831–2008*, Dublin: Four Courts Press 2009.

Coolahan, J., Hussey, C., and Kilfeather, F. (2012), *The Forum on Patronage and Pluralism in the Primary Sector: Report of the Forum's Advisory Group*, Dublin: Department of Education and Skills.

Cullen, S. (2013), 'Toward an Appropriate Religious Education for Future Teachers of Religious Education: Principles for a Theological Education Approach', PhD thesis, Dublin City University.

Cunnane, F. (2004), *New Directions in Religious Education*, Dublin: Veritas.

Darmody, M., and Smyth, E. (2013), *Governance and Funding of Voluntary Secondary Schools in Ireland*, Dublin: ESRI.

Department of Education (1926), *Report of the Department of Education for the School Year 1924–1925 and the Financial and Administrative Years 1924–25–26*, Dublin: The Stationery Office.

Department of Education (1965), *Rules for National Schools under the Department of Education*, Dublin: The Stationery Office.

Department of Education (1971), *Curaculum na Bunscoile*, Dublin: The Stationery Office.

Department of Education and Skills (1999), *Primary School Curriculum Introduction*, Dublin: The Stationery Office.

Department of Education (2019), 'Statistical Bulletin Enrolments'. Available online: https://www.education.ie/en/Publications/Statistics/Data-on-Individual-Schools/ (accessed 10 July 2021).

Dermody, A., Kelly, A., and Ward, F. (2010), *Signposts: Lessons for Living*, Dublin: Original Writing.

Dineen, F. (2021), 'Religious Education in Catholic Schools: Troubling Times or Routine Ructions?', in S. Whittle (ed.), *Irish and British Reflections on Catholic Education*, 187–98, Singapore: Springer.

Dineen, F., and Lundie, D. (2017), 'Does Religious Education Matter to Teachers in Catholic Primary Schools? Concerns and Challenges', in M. Shanahan (ed.), *Does Religious Education Matter?*, 101–13, London: Routledge.

Doherty, D. (2020), '"Why Do You Bother Writing Those Books?" Religious Book Publishing and Its Possible Significance for Lifelong Religious Education', doctoral thesis, DCU.

Donnelly, P. (2001), 'A Study of Higher-Order Thinking in the Early Years Classroom through Doing Philosophy', *Irish Educational Studies*, 20 (1): 278–95.

Donnelly, P. (2004), 'Wondering and the World and the Universe: Philosophy in the Early Years', *Irish Review*, 31: 51–65.

Durcan, T. J. (1972), *History of Irish Education from 1800*, Bala, North Wales: Dragon Books.

Educate Together (2004), *Learn Together Ethical Education Curriculum*, Dublin: Educate Together.

Educate Together (2018), *What Is an Educate Together National School?* Available online: https://www.educatetogether.ie/app/uploads/2018/09/What-is-an-Educate-Together-National-School_-Brochure.pdf (accessed 10 July 2021).

Educate Together and the Humanist Association of Ireland (2017), *Lessons on Humanism 1st/2nd Class*, Dublin: Educate Together and HAI.

Faas, D., Smith, A., and Darmody, M. (2018), 'Children's Agency in Multi-Belief Settings: The Case of Community National Schools in Ireland', *Journal of Research in Childhood Education*, 32 (4): 486–500.

Fischer, K. (2016), *Schools and the Politics of Religion and Diversity in the Republic of Ireland: Separate but Equal?*, Manchester: Manchester University Press.

Fitzgerald, G. (2010), 'How Religion Made Its Way into the Primary School System', *Irish Times*, 13 February.

Glendinning, D. (2012), 'The Irish Constitution: Education and Human Rights in Recognised Schools'. Available online: https://www.ihrec.ie/download/pdf/dr_glendenning_ihrc_law_society_10th_annual_human_rights_conference_13_october_2012.pdf (accessed 10 July 2021).

Government of Ireland (1937), *Constitution of Ireland*, Dublin: Government Publications.

Grimmitt, M. (1973), *What Can I Do in RE?*, Essex: Mayhew-McCrimmon.
Grimmitt, M. (1987), *Religious Education and Human Development: The Relationship Between Studying Religions and Personal, Social and Moral Education*, Essex: McCrimmons.
Groome, T. (2011), *Will There Be Faith:? A New Vision for Educating and Growing Disciples*, San Francisco: HarperOne.
Harmon, M. (2018), '"I Am a Catholic Buddhist": The Voice of Children on Religion and Religious Education in an Irish Catholic Primary School', Doctor of Education thesis, Dublin City University.
Henry, S. (2021), 'The Queerness of Education: Rethinking Catholic Schooling beyond Identity', in S. Whittle (ed.), *Irish and British Reflections on Catholic Education*, 121–31, Singapore: Springer.
Heinz, M., Davison, K., and Keane, E. (2018), '"I Will Do It but Religion Is a Very Personal Thing": Teacher Education Applicants' Attitudes towards Teaching Religion in Ireland', *European Journal of Teacher Education*, 41 (2): 232–45.
Hession, A. (2015), *Catholic Primary Religious Education in a Pluralist Environment*, Dublin: Veritas.
Hull, J. (1984), *Studies in Religious Education*, Lewes: Falmer Press.
Hyland, A. (1989), 'The Multidenominational Experience in the National School System in Ireland', *Irish Educational Studies*, 8: 89–114.
Hyland, A., and Bocking, B. (2015), 'Religion, Education, and Religious Education in Irish Schools', *Teaching Theology and Religion*, 18 (3): 252–61.
Irish Episcopal Conference (1977), *Children of God Series*, Dublin: Veritas.
Irish Episcopal Conference (2010), *Share the Good News*, Dublin: Veritas.
Irish Episcopal Conference (2015), *Catholic Preschool and Primary Religious Education Curriculum for Ireland*, Dublin: Veritas.
Irish Episcopal Conference (2019), *Grow in Love Sixth Class Teacher's Manual*, Dublin: Veritas.
Irish National Teachers' Association (2003), *Teaching Religion in the Primary School: Issues and Challenges*, Dublin: INTO.
Irwin, J. (2013), 'Towards Change: Exploring Tensions in Ethical-Religious Pedagogy in Irish Primary Education', in G. Byrne and P. Kieran (eds), *Toward Mutual Ground: Pluralism, Religious Education and Diversity in Irish Schools*, 177–86, Dublin: Columba Press.
Keast, J. (2007), *Religious Diversity and Intercultural Education: A Reference Book for Schools*, Strasbourg: Council of Europe Publishing.
Kennedy, D. (2021), 'Encounters with Truth: The Hermeneutical Task of Religious Education in the Republic of Ireland', PhD thesis, Dublin City University.
Kieran, P., and Hession, A., eds (2005), *Children, Catholicism and Religious Education*, Dublin: Veritas.
Kieran, P., ed. (2019), *Connecting Lives: Interbelief Dialogue in Contemporary Ireland*, Dublin: Veritas.
Kieran, P., and McDonagh, J. (2021), 'The Centre Cannot Hold: Decolonising the RE Curriculum in the Republic of Ireland', *British Journal of Religious Education*, 43 (1): 123–35.
King, J. (1970), *Religious Education in Ireland*, Dublin: Fallons.
Kuusisto, A., and Gearon, L., eds (2017), *Value Learning Trajectories: Theory, Method, Context*, Münster: Waxmann.

Lane, D. (2007), *Challenges Facing Religious Education in Contemporary Ireland*, Dublin: Veritas.
Lane, D. (2013), *Religion and Education: Re-imagining the Relationship*, Dublin: Veritas.
Lane, D. (2021), *Theology and Ecology in Dialogue: The Wisdom of Laudate Si'*, Mahwah, NJ: Paulist Press International.
Larkin, E. (1972), 'The Devotional Revolution in Ireland 1850-75', *American Historical Review*, 77 (3): 625–52.
Lodge, A. (2021), 'Moving beyond "Let's Have Another Mass": Post-Secular Approaches to Exploring Had Expressing a Faith-Based Ethos in the Pluralist Public Square of an Irish University', paper presented to the Annual Conference of the ESAI, 25–26 March 2021. Available online: https://www.dcu.ie/sites/default/files/inline-files/anne-lodge-moving-beyond-lets-have-another-mass-esai-paper-march-2021_2.pdf (accessed 13 July 2021).
Lodge, A., and Jackson, M. (2014), *Come & C: Report of the Diocesan Parish Survey*, Diocesan Office of the United Dioceses of Dublin and Glendalough.
Lodge, A., and Lynch, K., eds (2005), *Diversity at School*, Dublin: Institute of Public Administration.
Lodge, A., Tuohy, D., and Fennelly, K. (2011), *Our Schools, Our Community*, General Synod Board of Education.
McConville, P. (1965), 'Catechetics: Reviews for Religion Teachers', *The Furrow*, 16 (9): 559–62.
McGrady, A., Francis, L., and McKenna, U. L. (2019), 'Catholic Identities, Religious Faith and Moral Values: An Empirical Enquiry among 16 to 19 Year-Old Male Students in the Republic of Ireland', in G. Byrne and L. Francis (eds), *Religion and Education: The Voices of Young People in Ireland*, 125–44, Dublin: Veritas.
McKenna, U., Ipgrave, J., and Jackson, R. (2008), *Inter Faith Dialogue by Email in Primary Schools: An Evaluation of the Building E-bridges Project*, Münster: Waxmann.
Mahon, E., and O'Connell, D. (2015), *Grow in Love Junior Infants Teacher's Manual*, Dublin: Veritas.
Mawhinney A. (2012), 'A Discriminating Education System: Religious Admission Policies in Irish Schools and International Human Rights Law', *International Journal of Children's Rights*, 20 (4): 603–23.
Meehan, A., and O'Connell, D. (2021), 'Religious Education in Irish Catholic Primary Schools: Recent Developments, Challenges and Opportunities', in S. Whittle (ed.), *Irish and British Reflections on Catholic Education: Foundations, Identity, Leadership Issues and Religious Education in Catholic Schools*, 199–210, Singapore: Springer.
Mitchel, J. (1913), *Jail Journal*, Dublin: M. H. Gill.
Mullally, A. (2018), 'We Are Inclusive but Are We Being Equal?', in *Challenges to Community National Schools Regarding Religious Diversity*, Doctor of Education thesis, Dublin City University.
NCCA (2018), *Goodness Me, Goodness You: Third to Sixth Class*, Dublin: National Council for Curriculum and Assessment.
NCCA (2020), *Draft Primary Curriculum Framework for Consultation*, Dublin: National Council for Curriculum and Assessment.
Neary, A. (2013), 'Lesbian and Gay Teachers' Experiences of "Coming Out" in Irish Schools', *British Journal of Sociology of Education*, 34 (4): 583–602.
Neary, A., Gray, B., and O'Sullivan, M. (2018), 'Lesbian, Gay and Bisexual Teachers' Negotiations of Civil Partnership and Schools: Ambivalent Attachments to

Religion and Secularism', *Discourse Studies in the Cultural Politics of Educa*tion, 39: 434–47.

Nugent, M., and Donnelly, J. (2013), 'Only Secular Schools Respect Every Person's Human Rights Equally', in G. Byrne and P. Kieran (eds), *Toward Mutual Ground: Pluralism, Religious Education and Diversity in Irish Schools*, 187–94, Dublin: Columba.

O'Brien, C. (2019), 'More than 100 Catholic Primary Schools Have Closed over Past Decade', *Irish Times*, 20 March.

O'Buachalla, S. (1988), *Educational Policy in Twentieth Century Ireland*, Dublin: Wolfhound Press.

O'Connell, D. (2018), 'Catholic Primary Schools – on Rapidly Thinning Ice', *The Furrow*, December: 660–70.

O'Connell, D, Ryan, D. C., and Harmon, M. (2018), 'Will We Have Teachers for Catholic Primary Schools in Ireland?', in S. Whittle (ed.), *Religious Education in Catholic Schools*, Frankfurt: Peter Lang.

O'Donoghue, T. A. (1999), *The Catholic Church and the Secondary School Curriculum in Ireland 1922-62*, New York: Peter Lang.

O'Donoghue, T., and Harford, J. (2011), 'A Comparative History of Church–State Relations in Irish Education', *Comparative Education Review*, 55 (3): 315–41.

O'Donoghue, T., and Harford, J. (2012), 'Contesting the Limond Thesis on British Influence in Irish Education since 1922: A Comparative Perspective', *Comparative Education Review*, 48 (3): 337–46.

Organisation for Security and Co-operation in Europe (2007), *Toledo Guiding Principles on Teaching about Religions and Beliefs in Public Schools*, Warsaw: Sungraf.

Parker-Jenkins, M., and Masterson, M. (2013), 'No Longer "Catholic, White and Gaelic": Schools in Ireland Coming to Terms with Cultural Diversity', *Irish Educational Studies*, 32 (4): 477–92.

Park, N. (2019), 'Why Secular Education Is Good for Children, Good for Religion and Good for Society', in P. Kieran (ed.), *Connecting Lives: Interbelief Dialogue in Contemporary Ireland*, 171–82, Dublin: Veritas.

Renehan, C. (2014), *Openness with Roots: Education in Religion in Irish Primary Schools*, Cambridge: Cambridge Scholars.

Rogan, E. (1987), *Irish Catechesis: A Juridico-Historical Study of the Five Plenary Synods, 1850-1956*, Roma: Pontificia Gregoriana.

Scally, D. (2021), *The Best Catholics in the World: The Irish, the Church and the End of a Special Relationship*, London: Penguin Books.

Selim, A. (2014), *Islam and Education in Ireland*, Dublin: Veritas.

Shanahan, M., ed. (2017), *Does Religious Education Matter?*, London: Routledge.

Smart, N. (1968), *Secular Education and the Logic of Religion*, New York: Humanities Press.

Smyth, E., Lyons, M., and Darmody, M., eds (2013), *Religious Education in a Multicultural Europe: Children Parents and Schools*, London: Palgrave Macmillan.

Stapleton, C. (2021), 'Catholic Education at the Coalface of a Kaleidoscope of Identities', *Pastoral Care in Education*. Available online: https://doi.org/10.1080/02643 944.2021.1898664 (accessed 28 May 2021).

Stratford Jewish NS (2019), *School Handbook*. Available online: http://www.stratfordns.ie/content/files/STRATFORD_NS_HANDBOOK_2019_-_2020_final_HH_20th_june_2019.pdf (accessed 30 March 2021).

Sullivan, John (2017), 'A Space Like no Other', in M. Shanahan (ed.), *Does Religious Education Matter?*, 1–18, London: Routledge.

Teach Don't Preach (2007), ' Minister Hanafin Announces New Community National Schools for Two Dublin Locations'. Available online: https://www.teachdontpreach.ie/2012/01/13-december-2007-minister-hana fin-announces-new-community-national-scho ols-for-two-dub lin-locations-responding-to-dive rse-needs-of-chang ing-society/ (accessed 10 July 2021).

Titley, E. B. (1983), *Church, State, and the Control of Schooling in Ireland, 1900–1944*, Dublin: Gill and Macmillan.

Tuohy, D. (2013), *Denominational Education and Politics: Ireland in a European Context*, Dublin: Veritas.

Van Nieuwenhove, R. (2012), 'The End of Catholic Education in Ireland: Further Reflections on the Forum on Patronage and Pluralism', *The Furrow*, June: 278–85.

Walsh, B., ed. (2016), *Essays in the History of Irish Education*, London: Palgrave Macmillan.

Whittle, S., ed. (2021), *Irish and British Reflections on Catholic Education*, Singapore: Springer.

Wilkinson, J., ed. (2001–10), *Follow Me Series*, Dublin: Board of Education of the General Synod of the Church of Ireland.

Wilkinson, J. (2021), 'The Church of Ireland Primary School in an Expanding Educational Marketplace: The Use of School Websites to Promote School Identity and Ethos', *Irish Educational Studies*, 40 (1): 71–85.

Ziebertz, H. G., and Riegel, U., eds (2009), *How Teachers in Europe Teach Religion*, Münster: Lit.

Chapter 5

Altglas, V. (2022), *Religion and Conflict in Northern Ireland: What Does Religion Do?* London: Palgrave Pivot.

Altglas, V., and Wood, M., eds (2018), *Bringing the Social Back into the Sociology of Religion: Critical Approaches*, Leiden: Brill.

Andersen, K. (2010), 'Irish Secularization and Religious Identities: Evidence of an Emerging New Catholic Habitus', *Social Compass*, 57 (1): 15–39.

Baillie, S. (2002), *Evangelical Women in Belfast: Imprisoned or Empowered?*, New York: Palgrave.

Breen, M., ed. (2017), *Values and Identities in Europe: Evidence from the European Social Survey*, London: Routledge.

Breen, S., and Healy, A. E. (2014), 'Secularization in Ireland: Analysing the Relationship between Religiosity and Demographic Variables in Ireland from the European Social Survey 2002–2012', *International Journal of Religion in Spirituality in Society*, 3 (4): 113–25.

Breen, S., and Reynolds, C. (2011), 'The Rise of Secularism and the Decline of Religiosity in Ireland: The Pattern of Religious Change in Europe', *International Journal of Religion and Spirituality in Society*, 1 (2): 195–212.

Brewer, J. (2010), *Peace Processes: A Sociological Approach*, Cambridge: Polity.

Brewer, J., with Higgins, G. (1998), *The Mote and the Beam: Anti-Catholicism in Northern Ireland, 1600–1998*, Basingstoke: Macmillan Press.

Brewer, J., with Higgins, G., and Teeney, F. (2011), *Religion, Civil Society and Peace in Northern Ireland*, Oxford: Oxford University Press.

Bruce, S. (1986), *God Save Ulster: The Religion and Politics of Paisleyism*, Oxford: Clarendon Press.

Bruce, S. (2007), *Paisley: Religion and Politics in Northern Ireland*, Oxford: Oxford University Press.
Casanova, J. (2006), 'Rethinking Secularization: A Global Comparative Perspective', *Hedgehog Review*, 8 (1–2): 7–22.
Cloyne Report (2011), *Report on the Commission of Investigation into the Catholic Diocese of Cloyne*, Dublin: Government Publications.
Conway, B. (2013), 'Social Correlates of Church Attendance in Three European Catholic Countries', *Review of Religious Research*, 55 (1): 61–80.
Conway, B. (2014a), 'Religious Public Discourses and Institutional Structures: A Cross-National Analysis of Catholicism in Chile, Ireland, and Nigeria', *Sociological Perspectives*, 57 (2): 149–66.
Conway, B. (2014b), 'Religious Institutions and Sexual Scandals: A Comparative Study of Catholicism in Ireland, South Africa, and the United States', *International Journal of Comparative Sociology*, 55 (4): 318–41.
Conway, B., and Spruyt, B. (2018), 'Catholic Commitment around the Globe: A 52-Country Analysis', *Journal for the Scientific Study of Religion*, 57 (2): 276–99.
Cooke, D. (1996), *Persecuting Zeal: A Portrait of Ian Paisley*, Dingle: Brandon Books.
Cox, L. (2012), 'Current Debates: New Religion(s) in Ireland', *Irish Journal of Sociology*, 18 (1): 100–11.
Crawford, H. (2010), *Outside the Glow: Protestants and Irishness in Independent Ireland*, Dublin: UCD Press.
Donnelly, S. (2016), 'Sins of the Father: Unravelling Moral Authority in the Irish Catholic Church', *Irish Journal of Sociology*, 24 (3): 315–39.
Donnelly, S., and Inglis, T. (2010), 'The Media and the Catholic Church in Ireland: Reporting Clerical Child Sex Abuse', *Journal of Contemporary Religion*, 25 (1): 1–19.
Elliott, M. (2009), *When God Took Sides: Religion and Identity in Ireland – Unfinished History*, Oxford: Oxford University Press.
Ferns Report (2005), *Report on the Catholic Diocese of Ferns*, Dublin: Government Publications.
Ganiel, G. (2006), 'Ulster Says Maybe: The Restructuring of Evangelical Politics in Northern Ireland', *Irish Political Studies*, 21 (2): 137–55.
Ganiel, G. (2008), *Evangelicalism and Conflict in Northern Ireland*, New York: Palgrave.
Ganiel, G. (2016a), *Transforming Post-Catholic Ireland: Religious Practice in Late Modernity*, Oxford: Oxford University Press.
Ganiel, G. (2016b), 'Secularism, Ecumenism, and Identity on the Island of Ireland', in J. C. Wood (ed.), *Christianity and National Identity in Twentieth-Century Europe*, 73–90, Gottingen: Vandenhoeck & Ruprecht.
Ganiel, G. (2019), 'Religious Practice in a Post-Catholic Ireland: Towards a Concept of "Extra-Institutional Religion"', *Social Compass*, 66 (4): 471–87.
Ganiel, G. (2020), *People Still Need Us*, Belfast: Irish Council of Churches.
Ganiel, G. (2021a), 'Praying for Paisley: Fr Gerry Reynolds and the Role of Prayer in Faith-Based Peacebuilding – a Preliminary Theoretical Framework', *Irish Political Studies*, 36 (1): 72–91.
Ganiel, G. (2021b), *Something Other than a Building*, Belfast: Irish Council of Churches.
Ganiel, G. (2021c), 'Online Opportunities in Secularizing Societies? Clergy and the COVID-19 Pandemic in Ireland', *Religions*, 12 (6): 437. Available online: https://doi.org/10.3390/rel12060437 (accessed 29 July 2021).

Ganiel, G., and Dixon, P. (2008), 'Religion, Pragmatic Fundamentalism and the Transformation of the Northern Ireland Conflict', *Journal of Peace Research*, 45 (3): 419–36.
Ganiel, G., and Marti, G. (2014), 'Northern Ireland, America and the Emerging Church Movement: Exploring the Significance of Peter Rollins and the Ikon Collective', *Journal of the Irish Society for the Academic Study of Religions*, 22: 26–47.
Gray, B., and O'Sullivan Lago, R. (2011), 'Migrant Chaplains: Mediators of Catholic Church Transnationalism or Guests in Nationally Shaped Religious Fields?', *Irish Journal of Sociology*, 19 (2): 94–110.
Green, B. (2012), 'Book Review', *Sociology*, 46 (6): 1235–6.
Hayes, B., and Dowds, L. (2010), *Vacant Seats and Empty Pews*, Belfast: Ark Research Update 65.
Hayes, B., and Dowds, L. (2015), 'Religion and Attitudes towards Gay Rights in Northern Ireland: The God Gap Revisited', in S. Brunn (ed.), *The Changing World Religion Map*, 3321–40, Dordrecht: Springer.
Healy, A. E., and Breen, M. (2014), 'Religiosity in Times of Insecurity: An Analysis of Irish, Spanish and Portuguese European Social Survey Data, 2002–2012', *Irish Journal of Sociology*, 22 (2): 4–29.
Hilliard, B. (2003), 'The Catholic Church and Married Women's Sexuality: Habitus Change in Late 20th Century Ireland', *Irish Journal of Sociology*, 12 (2): 28–49.
Inglis, T. (1987), *Moral Monopoly: The Catholic Church in Modern Irish Society*, Dublin: Gill and Macmillan.
Inglis, T. (1998), *Moral Monopoly: The Rise and Fall of the Catholic Church in Modern Ireland*, Dublin: UCD Press.
Inglis, T. (2000), 'Irish Civil Society: From Church to Media Domination', in T. Inglis, Z. Mach and R. Mazanek (eds), *Religion and Politics: East-West Contrasts from Contemporary Europe*, 49–67, Dublin: UCD Press.
Inglis, T. (2007), 'Catholic Identity in Contemporary Ireland: Belief and Belonging to Tradition', *Journal of Contemporary Religion*, 22 (2): 205–20.
Inglis, T. (2014), *Meanings of Life in Contemporary Ireland: Webs of Significance*, New York: Palgrave Macmillan.
Jackson, D. (2020), *Spirituality at the School Gate: The Importance of Encounter*, Eugene: Wipf and Stock.
Kitching, K. (2013), 'Governing "Authentic" Religiosity? The Responsibilisation of Parents beyond Religion and State in Matters of School Ethos in Ireland', *Irish Journal of Sociology*, 21 (1): 17–34.
Kmec, V., and Ganiel, G. (2019), 'The Strengths and Limitations of the Inclusion of Religious Actors in Peace Processes in Northern Ireland and Bosnia and Herzegovina', *International Negotiation*, 24 (1): 136–63.
Malešević, V. (2010), 'Ireland and Neo-Secularisation Theory', *Irish Journal of Sociology*, 18 (1): 22–42.
McAleese Report (2013), *Report of the Inter-Departmental Committee to Establish the Facts of State Involvement with the Magdalen Laundries*, Dublin: Government Publications.
McGarry, J., and O'Leary, B. (1995), *Explaining Northern Ireland: Broken Images*, London: Wiley & Sons.
Mennell, S., Elliott, M., Stokes, P., Rickard, A., and O'Malley-Dunlop, E. (2000), 'Protestants in a Catholic State – a Silent Minority in Ireland', in T. Inglis, Z. Mach and R. Mazanek (eds), *Religion and Politics: East-West Contrasts from Contemporary Europe*, 68–92, Dublin, UCD Press.

Mitchel, P. (2003), *Evangelicalism and National Identity in Ulster, 1921–1998*, Oxford: Oxford University Press.
Mitchell, C. (2004), 'Is Northern Ireland Abnormal? An Extension of the Sociological Debate on Religion in Modern Britain', *Sociology*, 38 (2): 237–54.
Mitchell, C. (2005), *Religion, Identity and Politics in Northern Ireland: Boundaries of Belonging and Belief*, Aldershot: Ashgate.
Mitchell, C., and Ganiel, G. (2011), *Evangelical Journeys: Choice and Change in a Northern Irish Religious Subculture*, Dublin: UCD Press.
Mother and Baby Homes Report (2021), *Report of the Commission of Investigation into Mother and Baby Homes*, Dublin: Government Publications.
Mulholland, P. (2019), *Love's Betrayal: The Decline of Catholicism and the Rise of New Religions in Ireland*, Oxford: Peter Lang.
Murphy, F., and Maguire, M. (2012), *Integration in Ireland: The Everyday Lives of African Migrants*, Manchester: Manchester University Press.
Murphy, L. (2010), *Believing in Belfast: Charismatic Christianity after the Troubles*, Chapel Hill: Carolina Academic Press.
Murphy Report (2009), *Report on the Commission of Investigation into the Catholic Archdiocese of Dublin*, Dublin: Government Publications.
Nic Ghiolla Phádraig, M. (1995), 'The Power of the Catholic Church in the Republic of Ireland', in P. Clancy, S. Drudy and K. Lynch (eds), *Irish Society: Sociological Perspectives*, 593–619, Dublin: Institute for Public Administration.
Nic Ghiolla Phádraig, M. (2009), *Religion in Ireland: No Longer an Exception?*, Belfast: Ark Research Update 64.
Norris, P., and Inglehart, R. (2011), *Sacred and Secular: Religion and Politics Worldwide*, Cambridge: Cambridge University Press.
O'Brien, H. (2019), 'The Marginality of "Irish Mormonism": Confronting Irish Boundaries of Belonging', *Journal of the British Association for the Study of Religions*, 21: 52–75.
O'Brien, H. (2020a), 'Institutional Gender Negotiations in Irish Mormon Congregations', in A. Hoyt and T. G. Petrey (eds), *The Routledge Handbook of Mormonism and Gender*, 405–18, London: Routledge.
O'Brien, H. (2020b), 'What Does the Rise of Digital Religion during Covid-19 Tell Us about Religion's Capacity to Adapt?', *Irish Journal of Sociology*, 28 (2): 242–6.
O'Connell, P., Collins, M., Creighton, M., and de Silva Pedroso, M. (2019), *Irish Social Attitudes in 2018–19: Topline Results from Round 9 of the European Social Survey*, Dublin: Geary Institute.
Ó Féich, P., and O'Connell, M. (2015), 'Changes in Roman Catholic Beliefs and Practices in Ireland between 1981 and 2008 and the Emergence of the Liberal Catholic', *Journal of Contemporary Religion*, 30 (2): 231–47.
O'Mahony, E. (2013), *Religion and Beliefs among Catholics in Ireland: A Short Review of Recent ESS Data*, Dublin: Irish Bishops Conference.
Pembroke, S. (2013), 'The Role of Industrial Schools and Control over Child Welfare in Ireland in the Twentieth Century', *Irish Journal of Sociology*, 21 (1): 52–67.
Pew Research Center (2018), *Being Christian in Western Europe*. Available online: https://www.pewforum.org/2018/05/29/being-christian-in-western-europe/ (accessed 16 July 2021).
Ribberink, E., Achterberg, P., and Houtman, D. (2013), 'Deprivatization of Disbelief? Non-Religiosity and Anti-Religiosity in 14 Western European Countries', *Politics and Religion*, 6 (1): 101–20.

Ritter C., and Kmec, V. (2017), 'Religious Practices and Networks of Belonging in an Immigrant Congregation: The German-speaking Lutheran Congregation in Dublin', *Journal of Contemporary Religion*, 32 (2): 269–81.
Robinson, L. (2014), *Embodied Peacebuilding: Reconciliation as Practical Theology*, Oxford: Peter Lang.
Röder, A. (2017), 'Old and New Religious Minorities: Examining the Changing Religious Profile of the Republic of Ireland', *Irish Journal of Sociology*, 25 (3): 324–33.
Ryan Report (2009), *Report on the Commission to Inquire into Child Abuse in Reformatory and Industrial Schools*, Dublin: Government Publications.
Sandal, N. (2017), *Religious Leaders and Conflict Transformation: Northern Ireland and Beyond*, Cambridge: Cambridge University Press.
Scharbrodt, O., Sakaranaho, T., Khan, A. H., Shanneik, Y., and Ibrahim, V., eds (2015), *Muslims in Ireland: Past and Present*, Edinburgh: Edinburgh University Press.
Scull, M. (2019), *The Catholic Church and the Northern Ireland Troubles*, Oxford: Oxford University Press.
Stringer, A. (2013), 'Congregation and Social Structure: An Investigation into Four Northern Irish Memberships', *Social Compass*, 60 (1): 22–40.
Todd, J. (2014), 'Social Structure and Religious Division: Comparing the Form of Religious Distinction in the Two Irish States', in J. Wolffe (ed.), *Catholics, Protestants and Muslims: Irish 'Religious' Conflict in Comparative Perspective*, 42–58, Basingstoke: Palgrave.
Todd, J. (2018), *Identity Change after Conflict: Boundaries and Belonging in the Two Irelands*, London: Palgrave.
Turpin, T. (2019), 'Leaving Roman Catholicism', in D. Enstedt, G. Larsson and T. T. Mantsinen (eds), *Handbook of Leaving Religion*, 186–99, Leiden: Brill.
Turpin, H., Andersen, M., and Lanman, J. (2018), 'CREDs, CRUDs, and Catholic Scandals: Experimentally Examining the Effects of Religious Paragon Behaviour on Co-Religionist Belief', *Religion, Brain and Behaviour*, 9 (2): 43–55.
Ugba, A. (2009), *Shades of Belonging: African Pentecostals in Twenty-First Century Ireland*, Trenton, NJ: Africa World Press.
Weatherred, J. L. (2014), 'Child Sexual Abuse and the Media: A Literature Review', *Journal of Child Sexual Abuse*, 24 (1): 16–34.
Wells, R. (2010), *Hope and Reconciliation in Northern Ireland*, Dublin: Liffey.
Yeates, N. (2011), 'The Irish Catholic Female Religious and the Transnationalisation of Care: An Historical Perspective', *Irish Journal of Sociology*, 19 (2): 77–93.

Chapter 6

Bevir, M. (2003), 'Theosophy and the Origins of the Indian National Congress', *International Journal of Hindu Studies*, 7 (1/3): 99–115.
Bradley, A. (2000) '"Fumbling in a Greasy Till": Nation and Class in Yeats's "Responsibilities"', *Irish University Review*, 30 (2): 289–314.
Bramsbäck, B. (1971), 'William Butler Yeats and Folklore Material', *Béaloideas* 39 (41): 56–68.
Bryson, M. E. (1977), 'Metaphors for Freedom: Theosophy and the Irish Literary Revival', *Canadian Journal of Irish Studies*, 3 (1): 32–40.

Costigan, G. (1973), 'Romantic Nationalism: Ireland and Europe', *Irish University Review*, 3 (2): 141–52.
Duggan, C. (2018), 'The Theosophical Society and Politics: Esoteric Discourse, Esoteric Monism, and Theosophical Identity in Late 19th and Early 20th Century Britain and Ireland', PhD diss., University College Cork, Ireland.
Githens-Mazer, J. (2006), *Myths and Memories of the Easter Rising: Cultural and Political Nationalism in Ireland*, Dublin: Irish Academic Press.
Guinness, S. (2003), '"Protestant Magic" Reappraised: Evangelicalism, Dissent, and Theosophy', *Irish University Review*, 33 (1): 14–27.
Hewitt, S. (2015), '"An Initiated Mystic": Modernization and Occultism in Synge's "The Aran Islands"', *New Hibernia Review/Iris Éireannach Nua*, 19 (4): 58–76.
Johnston Graf, S. (2005), 'An Infant Avatar: The Mature Occultism of W. B. Yeats', *New Hibernia Review/Iris Éireannach Nua*, 9 (4): 99–112.
Kehoe, E. (2016), 'Daughters of Ireland: Maud Gonne MacBride, Dr Kathleen Lynn and Dorothy Macardle', in E. Biagini and D. Mulhall (eds), *The Shaping of Modern Ireland: A Centenary Assessment*, 139–57, County Kildare: Irish Academic Press.
Kelleher, M. (2019), 'Literary Revival', in J. Crowley, D. Ó Drisceoil and M. Murphy (eds), *Atlas of the Irish Revolution*, 85–93, Cork: Cork University Press.
Lane, L. (2003), '"It Is in the Cottages and Farmers' Houses That the Nation Is Born": AE's "Irish Homestead" and the Cultural Revival', *Irish University Review*, 33 (1): 165–81.
Mills Harper, M., and Paul, C. E., eds (2008), 'Editors' Introduction', in *The Collected Works of W.B. Yeats Volume XIII: A Vision: The Original 1925 Version*, xi–xiii, New York: Scribner.
Morris, C. (2003), 'Becoming Irish? Alice Milligan and the Revival', *Irish University Review*, 33 (1): 79–98.
Morris, C. (2012), *Alice Milligan and the Irish Cultural Revival*, Dublin: Four Courts Press.
Murphy, R. (2008), *Ella Young: Irish Mystic and Rebel*, Dublin: Liffey Press.
Nally, C. (2010), *Envisioning Ireland: W. B. Yeats's Occult Nationalism*, Bern: Peter Lang.
Nuttall, D. (2020), *Different and the Same: A Folk History of the Protestants of Independent Ireland*, Dublin: Eastwood Books.
Regan, S. (2006), 'W.B. Yeats: Irish Nationalism and Post-Colonial Theory', *Nordic Irish Studies*, 5: 87–99.
Reynolds, L. (1982), 'The Irish Literary Revival: Preparation and Personalities', in R. O'Driscoll (ed.), *The Celtic Consciousness*, 383–99, Portlaoise: Dolmen Press.
Ryan, L. (2020), 'Nationalism and Feminism: The Complex Relationship between the Suffragist and Independence Movements in Ireland', in L. Connolly (ed.), *Women and the Irish Revolution: Feminism, Activism, Violence*, 17–32, County Kildare: Irish Academic Press.
Sinnett, A. P. (1883), *Esoteric Buddhism*, 1st edn, London: Trübner.
Steele, K., ed. (2004), 'Introduction: Maud Gonne and the Irish Nationalist Press, 1895-1946', in *Maud Gonne's Irish Nationalist Writings 1895-1946*, xix–xxxviii, Dublin: Irish Academic Press.
Steele, K. (2019), 'Constance Markievicz and the Politics of Memory', in L. Ryan and M. Ward (eds), *Irish Women and Nationalism: Soldiers, New Women and Wicked Hags*, 62–79, County Kildare: Irish Academic Press.
Welch, R. (2000), *The Concise Oxford Companion to Irish Literature*, Oxford: Oxford University Press.
Williams, M. (2016), *Ireland's Immortals: A History of the Gods of Irish Myth*, Princeton, NJ: Princeton University Press.

Young, E. (1909), *The Coming of Lugh: A Celtic Wonder-Tale*, 1st edn, Dublin: Maunsel.
Young, E. (1910), *Celtic Wonder-Tales*, illustrated by Maud Gonne, 1st edn, Dublin: Maunsel.

Chapter 7

Abbott, R. (2002), 'Robert Abbott', in C. Murphy and L. Adair (eds), *Untold Stories: Protestants in the Republic of Ireland*, 17–20, Dublin: Liffey Press.
Akenson, D. H. (1975), *A Mirror to Kathleen's Face: Education in Independent Ireland 1922–1960*, Montreal: Magill and Queen's.
Bielenberg, A. (2013), 'Exodus: The Emigration of Southern Irish Protestants during the Irish War of Independence and the Civil War', *Past and Present*, 218 (1): 199–233.
Burman, E. (1994), *Deconstructing Developmental Psychology*, London: Routledge.
Bury, R. (2017), *Buried Lives: The Protestants of Southern Ireland*, Dublin: History Press.
Butler, H. (1985), *Escape from the Anthill*, Mullingar: Lilliput Press.
Caird, D. A. (1984), 'Protestantism and National Identity', in J. McLoon (ed.), *Being Protestant in Ireland: Co-operation North, in Association with the Social Study Conference*, Summer School St Kieran's College Kilkenny, 4–8 August 1984, Co-operation North.
Coulter, C. (2002), 'Carol Coulter', in C. Murphy and L. Adair (eds), *Untold Stories: Protestants in the Republic of Ireland*, 63–6, Dublin: Liffey Press.
Crawford, H. (2010), *Outside the Glow: Protestants and Irishness in Independent Ireland*, Dublin: University College Dublin Press.
CSO (2016), 'Census of Population 2016 – Profile 8 Irish Travellers, Ethnicity and Religion'. Available online: https://www.cso.ie/en/releasesandpublications/ep/p-cp8iter/p8iter/p8rnc/ (accessed 10 March 2021).
Davies, B., and Gannon, S. (2006), *Doing Collective Biography*, Maidenhead: McGraw Hill Education (UK).
d'Alton, I. (2009), 'A Vestigial Population? Perspectives on Southern Irish Protestants in the Twentieth Century', *Eire-Ireland*, 44 (3): 9–42.
de Souza Santos, B. (1999), 'On Oppositional Postmodernism', in R. Munck and D. O'Hearn (eds), *Critical Theory: Contributions to a New Paradigm*, 29–43, London: Zed Books.
de Sousa Santos, B. (2018), *Another Knowledge Is Possible*, New York: Verso.
Foucault, M. (1982), 'The Subject and Power', *Critical Inquiry*, 8 (4): 777–95.
Foucault, M. (1988), *Politics, Philosophy, Culture: Interviews and Other Writings, 1977–84*, New York: Routledge.
Foucault, M. (1998), *The History of Sexuality 1: The Will to Knowledge*, London: Penguin.
Foucault, M. (2019), *Power: The Essential Works of Michel Foucault 1954–1984*, London: Penguin UK.
Foucault, M., and Faubion, J. D. (1994), *Power: Essential Works of Foucault 1954–1984*, London: Penguin.
Freire, P. (1977), *Cultural Action for Freedom*, London: Penguin.
Hanley, B. (2020), '"The Irish and the Jews Have a Good Deal in Common": Irish Republicanism, Anti-Semitism and the Post-War World', *Irish Historical Studies*, 44 (165): 57–74.

Hart, P. (1996), 'The Protestant Experience of Revolution in Southern Ireland', in R. English and G. Walker (eds), *Unionism in Modern Ireland*, 81–98, London: Palgrave Macmillan.

Guinnane, T. W. (1997), *The Vanishing Irish: Households, Migration and the Rural Economy in Ireland, 1850–1914*, Princeton, NJ: Princeton University Press.

Kenny, C. (2017), 'Sinn Féin, Socialists d "McSheeneys": Representations of Jews in Early Twentieth-Century Ireland', *Journal of Modern Jewish Studies*, 16 (2): 198–218.

Lennon, C. (2005), *Sixteenth-Century Ireland: The Incomplete Conquest*, Dublin: Gill and Macmillan.

Macourt, M. (2008), *Counting the People of God; the Census of Population and the Church of Ireland*, Dublin: Church of Ireland Publishing.

Maguire, M., and Murphy, F. (2015), 'Ontological (in)Security and African Pentecostalism in Ireland', *Ethnos*, 8 (5): 1–23.

McGarry, P. (2013), 'A Pluralist Protestant', *Irish Times*, 14 December.

Megahey, A. (2000), *The Irish Protestant Churches in the Twentieth Century*, Basingstoke: Springer.

Munck, R., and O'Hearn, D., eds (1999), *Critical Theory: Contributions to a New Paradigm*, London: Zed Books.

Murphy, C., and Adair, L., eds (2002), *Untold Stories: Protestants in the Republic of Ireland 1922-2002*, Dublin: Liffey Press.

Nuttall, D. (2020), *Different and the Same, a Folk History of the Protestants of Independent Ireland*, Dublin: Eastwood Books.

O'Connor, C. (2008), 'Marriage, "a Grave Injury to our Church" an Account of the 1957 Fethard-on-Sea Boycott', *History of the Family*, 12 (4): 395–401.

Ó Giolláin, D. (2000), *Locating Irish Folklore: Tradition, Modernity, Identity*, Cork: Cork University Press.

O'Leary, R. (2000), 'Religious Intermarriage in Dublin: The Importance of Status Boundaries between Religious Groups', *Review of Religious Research*, 41 (2): 471–87.

Ryan, A. B. (2001), *Feminist Ways of Knowing*, Leicester: National Institute of Adult Continuing Education.

Ryan, A. B. (2005), 'Methodology: Collecting Data', in M. Antonesa, H. Fallon, A. B Ryan, A. Ryan and T. Walsh (eds), *Researching and Writing Your Thesis*, 70–89, Maynooth: NUI Maynooth.

Semple, P. (2008), *The Rector Who Wouldn't Pray for Rain*, Dublin: Gill and Macmillan.

Tanner, M. (2003), *Ireland's Holy Wars: The Struggle for a Nation's Soul*, New Haven, CT: Yale University Press.

Tobin, R. (2012), *The Minority Voice: Hubert Butler and Southern Irish Protestantism, 1900–1991*, Oxford: Oxford University Press.

Todd, J., Rougier, N., O'Keefe, T., and Cañás Bottos, L. (2009), 'Does Being Protestant Matter? Protestants, Minorities and the Re-making of Ethnoreligious Identity after the Good Friday Agreement', *National Identities*, 11 (1): 87–99.

Trahar, S. (2010), *Developing Cultural Capability in International Higher Education: A Narrative Inquiry*, London: Routledge.

Turner, V. (1990), 'Are There Universals of Performance in Myth, Ritual and Drama?' in R. Schneider and W. Appel (eds), *By Means of Performance*, 18–19, Cambridge: Cambridge University Press.

Ugba, A. (2009), *Shades of Belonging: African Pentecostals in Twenty-First Century Ireland*, Trenton, NJ: Africa World Press.

Walsh, T. (2006), 'Experiencing Transculturalism', in B. Treacy, A. Martin and T. Walsh (eds), *No Longer Strangers*, 85–102, Dublin: Dominican Publications.

Walsh, T. (2013), 'Narratives of Irish Protestant Identity', PhD thesis, University of Bristol, Bristol.

Chapter 8

Allen, M. (2000), 'From Ecstasy to Power: Marian Apparitions in Contemporary Irish Catholicism', *Anthropological Journal on European Cultures*, 9 (1): 11–35.

Barker, E. (2015), 'New Religious Movements', in G. Ritzer (ed.), *The Blackwell Encyclopaedia of Sociology*. Available online: https://doi.org/10.1002/9781405165518.wbeosn020.

Beaman, L. (2013), 'The Will to Religion: Obligatory Religious Citizenship', *Critical Research on Religion*, 1 (2): 141–57.

Beckford, J. A. (1986), *NRMs and Rapid Social Change*, London: Sage.

Bellah, R. (1976), 'New Religious Consciousness and the Crisis in Modernity', in C. Y. Glock (ed.), *The New Religious Consciousness*, 333–52, Berkeley: University of California Press.

Berger, P. L. (1967), *The Sacred Canopy: Elements of a Sociology of Religion*, New York: Doubleday.

Bird, F., and Reimer, B. (1982), 'Participation Rates in New Religious and Para-Religious Movements', *Journal for the Scientific Study of Religion*, 21 (1): 1–14.

Bromley, D. (1983), 'Conservatorships and Deprogramming', in D. Bromley and J. T. Richardson (eds), *The Brainwashing/Deprogramming Controversy*, 267–24, New York: Edwin Mellen.

Bromley, D. (2016), 'Categorizing Religious Organizations', in J. R. Lewis and I. B. Tollefsen (eds), *The Oxford Handbook of NRMs, Vol 2*, 17–24, Oxford: Oxford University Press.

Bromley, D., and Melton, J. G. (2012), 'Reconceptualizing the Types of Religious Organization: Dominant, Sectarian, Alternative, and Emergent Tradition Groups', *Nova Religio: The Journal of Alternative and Emergent Religions*, 15 (3): 4–28.

Bruce, S. (2002), *God Is Dead: Secularization in the West*, Oxford: Blackwell.

Butler, D. J. (2015), '"A Most Difficult Assignment": Mapping the Emergence of Jehovah's Witnesses in Ireland', in S. Brunn (ed.), *The Changing World Religion Map*, 1615–34, Dordrecht: Springer. Available online: https://doi.org/10.1007/978-94-017-9376-6_85 (accessed 25 July 2021).

Casanova, J. (1994), *Public Religions in the Modern World*, Chicago: University of Chicago Press.

Castaño, Á., Bélanger, J. J., and Moyano, M. (2021), 'Cult Conversion from the Perspective of Families: Implications for Prevention and Psychological Intervention', *Psychology of Religion and Spirituality*, advance online publication. Available online: https://psycnet.apa.org/doi/10.1037/rel0000410 (accessed 29 July 2021).

Central Statistics Office (2011), 'Profile 7 Religion, Ethnicity and Irish Travellers – Ethnic and Cultural Background in Ireland'. Available online: https://www.cso.ie/en/census/census2011reports/census2011profile7religionethnicityandirishtravellers-ethnicandculturalbackgroundinireland/ (accessed 22 November 2021).

Central Statistics Office (2016), 'Census of Population 2016 – Profile 8 Irish Travellers, Ethnicity and Religion'. Available online: https://www.cso.ie/en/releasesandpublicati ons/ep/p-cp8iter/p8iter/p8rrc/ (accessed 14 July 2021).
Christopher, S., Fearon, J., McCoy, J., and Nobbe, C. (1971), 'Social Deprivation and Religiosity', *Journal for the Scientific Study of Religion*, 10 (4): 385–92.
Chryssides, G. (2011), *Historical Dictionary of New Religious Movements*, Lanham, MD: Scarecrow Press.
Clark, J. (2012), 'Secularization and Modernization: The Failure of a "Grand Narrative"', *Historical Journal*, 55 (1): 161–94.
Corish, M. (1996). 'Aspects of the Secularization of Irish Society', in E. G. Cassidy (ed.), *Faith and Culture in the Irish Context*, 115–32, Dublin: Veritas.
Cosgrove, O., Cox, L., Kuhling, C., and Mulholland, P. (2011), 'Editors' Introduction: Understanding New Religious Movements in Ireland', in O. Cosgrove, L. Cox, C. Kuhling and P. Mulholland (eds), *Ireland's New Religious Movements*, 1–27, Newcastle upon Tyne: Cambridge Scholars.
Cox, L. (2014), 'Buddhism in Ireland: The Inner Life of World-Systems', *Études Irlandaises*, 39 (2): 161–72.
Davie, G. (2013), 'Religion in 21st-Century Europe: Framing the Debate', *Irish Theological Quarterly*, 78 (3) 279–93.
Dawson, L. L. (1998), 'The Cultural Significance of NRMs and Globalization: A Theoretical Prolegomenon', *Journal for the Scientific Study of Religion*, 37 (4): 580–95.
Dawson, L. L., ed. (2003), *Cults and NRMs: A Reader*, London: Wiley Blackwell.
de Cléir, S. (2017), *Historical Background in Popular Catholicism in 20th-Century Ireland: Locality, Identity and Culture*, 1–16, London: Bloomsbury Academic. Available online: http://dx.doi.org/10.5040/9781350020610.ch-001 (accessed 14 July 2021).
Diani, M. (1993), 'Themes of Modernity in New Religious Movements and New Social Movements', *Social Science Information*, 32 (1): 111–31.
Donnelly, S., and Inglis, T. (2010), 'The Media and the Catholic Church in Ireland: Reporting Clerical Child Sex Abuse', *Journal of Contemporary Religion*, 25 (1): 1–19.
Draper, S., and Baker, J. (2011), 'Angelic Belief as American Folk Religion', *Sociological Forum*, 26 (3): 623–43.
Durkheim, E. ([1915] 2012), *The Elementary Forms of the Religious Life*, trans. J. Ward Swain, The Project Gutenberg. Available online: https://www.gutenberg.org/ files/41360/41360-h/41360-h.htm (accessed 14 July 2021).
Eggleton, M. (1999), 'Belonging to a Cult or New Religious Movement: Act of Free Will or Form of Mind Control?', in C. Lamb and M. D. Bryant (eds), *Religious Conversion: Contemporary Practices and Controversies*, 263–77, London: Cassell.
Flynn, C., and Kunkel, S. (1987), 'Deprivation, Compensation, and Conceptions of an Afterlife', *Sociological Analysis*, 48 (1): 58–72.
Fuller, L. (2004), *Irish Catholicism since 1950: The Undoing of Culture*, Dublin: Gill and Macmillan.
Gallagher, E. V. (2007), 'Compared to "What"? "Cults" and "New Religious Movements"', *History of Religions*, 47 (2–3): 205–20.
Ganiel, G. (2016), *Transforming Post-Catholic Ireland: Religious Practice in Late Modernity*, Oxford: Oxford University Press.
Giddens, A. (1991), *Modernity and Self-Identity: Self and Society in the Modern Age*, Cambridge: Polity Press.
Glock, C. Y., and Stark, R. (1965), *Religion and Society in Tension*, Chicago: Rand McNally.

Greeley, A. (2003), *Religion in Europe in the End of the Second Millennium*, New Brunswick: Transaction Publishers.
Healy, J. P. (2011), 'Involvement in a New Religious Movement: From Discovery to Disenchantment', *Journal of Spirituality in Mental Health*, 13 (1): 2–21.
Heelas, P., Woodhead, L., Seel, B., Szerszynski, B., and Tusting, K. (2005), *The Spirituality Revolution – Why Religion Is Giving Way to Spirituality*, Oxford: Blackwell.
Hjelm, T. (2018), 'Peter L. Berger and the Sociology of Religion', *Journal of Classical Sociology*, 18 (3): 231–48.
Inglis, T. (2002), 'Sexual Transgression and Scapegoats: A Case Study from Modern Ireland', *Sexualities*, 5 (1): 5–24.
Jameson, F. (1984), 'Periodizing the 60s', *Social Text*, 9 (10): 178–209.
Johnson, B. (1957), 'A Critical Appraisal of the Church-Sect Typology', *American Sociological Review*, 22 (1): 88–92.
Johnson, B. (1963), 'On Church and Sect', *American Sociological Review*, 28: 539–49.
Johnson, B. (1971), 'Church and Sect Revisited', *Journal for the Scientific Study of Religion*, 10: 124–37.
Kaelble, H. (2003), 'Social History in Europe', *Journal of Social History*, 37 (1): 29–35.
Karpov, V. (2010), 'Desecularization: A Conceptual Framework', *Journal of Church and State*, 52 (2): 232–70.
Kızılgeçit, M., and Ören, A. (2019), 'Psychological Reasons of Participation to NRMs: Quest of the Individual or Success of the Movement? Yeni Dini Hareketlere Katılımının Psikolojik Nedenleri: Bireyin Arayışı mı Hareketin Başarısı mı?', *ilted: ilahiyat tetkikleri dergisi / Journal of Ilahiyat Researches*, 51 (1): 445–56.
Kmec, V. (2014), 'Religion as a Response to the Crisis of Modernity: Perspectives of Immigrants in Ireland', in G. Ganiel, H. Winkel and C. Monnot (eds), *Religion in Times of Crisis*, 33–53, London: Brill.
Kuhling, C. (2014), 'The New Age Movement in the Post-Celtic Tiger Context: Secularization, Enchantment and Crisis', *Études Irlandaises*, 39 (2): 101–13.
Larkin, E. (1972), 'The Devotional Revolution in Ireland, 1850–75', *American Historical Review*, 77 (3): 625–52.
Lehmann, C. (2016), *The Money Cult: Capitalism, Christianity, and the Unmaking of the American Dream*, New York: Melville House.
Malešević, V. (2010), 'Ireland and Neo-Secularization', *Irish Journal of Sociology*, 18 (1): 1–34.
Malešević, V. (2019), 'Religious Regulation in Ireland', in *Oxford Research Encyclopaedia of Politics*, Oxford: Oxford University Press. Available online: https://doi.org/10.1093/acrefore/9780190228637.013.805.
Martin, D. (2005), *On Secularization: Towards a Revised General Theory*, Aldershot: Ashgate.
Melton, J. G. (2000), 'Emerging Religious Movements in North America: Some Missiological Reflections', *Missiology*, 28 (1): 85–98.
Molteni, F., and Biolcati, F. (2018), 'Shifts in Religiosity across Cohorts in Europe: A Multilevel and Multidimensional Analysis Based on the European Values Survey', *Social Compass*, 65 (3): 413–32.
Mouzelis, N. (2012), 'Modernity and the Secularization Debate', *Sociology*, 46 (2): 207–23.
Mulholland, P. (2011), 'Marian Apparitions, the New Age and the FÁS Prophet', in O. Cosgrove, L. Cox, C. Kuhling and P. Mulholland (eds), *Ireland's New Religious Movements*, 176–200, Newcastle upon Tyne: Cambridge Scholars.
Niebuhr, R. (1957), *The Social Sources of Denominationalism*, New York: Henry Holt.

O'Brien, H. R. (2018), 'Being Mormon in Ireland: An Exploration of Religion in Modernity through a Lens of Tradition and Change', PhD thesis, University of Exeter, UK.

O'Connor, P. (2001), *Emerging Voices: Women in Contemporary Irish Society*, Dublin: Institute of Public Administration.

Olson, P. (2006), 'The Public Perception of "Cults" and "New Religious Movements"', *Journal for the Scientific Study of Religion*, 45 (1): 97–106.

Pabst, A. (2012), 'The Western Paradox: Why the United States Is More Religious but Less Christian than Europe', in L. N. Leustean (ed.), *Representing Religion in the European Union: Does God Matter*, 169–84, London: Routledge.

Penet, J. C. (2008), 'From Idealised Moral Community to Real Tiger Society: The Catholic Church in Secular Ireland', *Journal of Irish Studies*, 3: 143–53.

Peng, Y. (2009), 'Modernization Theory', *Chinese Studies in History*, 43 (1): 37–45.

Pew Research Center (2021), 'More Americans Than People in Other Advanced Economies Say COVID-19 Has Strengthened Religious Faith'. Available online: https://www.pewforum.org/2021/01/27/more-americans-than-people-in-other-advancedeconomies-say-covid-19-has-strengthened-religious-faith/ (accessed 12 May 2021).

Possamai, A. M. (2015), 'Popular and Lived Religions', *Current Sociology*, 63 (6): 781–99.

Praising in Tongues (1977), [TV programme] RTÉ. Available online: https://www.rte.ie/archives/2017/0131/848993-charismatic-renewal-in-ireland/ (accessed 14 July 2021).

Richardson, J. (2007), 'A Critique of "Brainwashing" Claims about New Religious Movements', in L. L. Dawson (ed.), *Cults and NRMs: A Reader*, 160–6, Oxford: Blackwell.

Richardson, J. (2017), 'Definitions of Cult: From Sociological-Technical to Popular-Negative', in L. L Dawson (ed.), *Cults in Context*, 36–44, London: Routledge.

Roberts, C. (2009), 'Astrology in Ireland in the Post-War Era', paper presented at *Alternative Spiritualities, the New Age and New Religious Movements in Ireland Conference*, 30–31 October 2009, Maynooth: NUI Maynooth.

Robbins, T., and Bromley, D. (1999), 'Social Experimentation and the Significance of American New Religions: A Focused Review Essay', *Research in the Social Scientific Study of Religion*, 4: 1–28.

Royle, E. (1974), *Victorian Infidels: The Origins of the British Secularist Movement 1791–1866*, Manchester: Manchester University Press.

Rubinstein, M. (2019), 'New Religious Movements', in *Encyclopaedia Britannica*. Available online: https://www.britannica.com/topic/new-religious-movement (accessed 15 July 2021).

Saliba, J. A., and Melton, J. G. (2003), *Understanding New Religious Movements*, Oxford: AltaMira.

Scientology Blog (2021), 'Scientology Prayer for Total Freedom Shared in Online Interreligious Prayer Meeting in Response to the COVID-19 Pandemic'. Available online: https://www.scientologyreligion.org/blog/scientology-prayer-for-total-freedom-shared-in-online-interreligious-prayer.html (accessed 12 May 2021).

Seward, R. R., Stivers, R. A., Igoe, D. G., Amin, I., and Cosimo, D. (2005), 'Irish Families in the Twentieth Century: Exceptional or Converging?', *Journal of Family History*, 30 (4): 410–30.

Spickard, J. V. (2006), 'Narrative versus Theory in the Sociology of Religion: Five Stories of Religion's Place in the Late Modern World', in J. A. Beckford and J. Wallis (eds), *Theorising Religion: Classical and Contemporary Debates*, 176–7, Hampshire: Ashgate.

Stark, R., and Bainbridge, W. S. (1985), *The Future of Religion: Secularization, Revival and Cult Formation*, Berkeley: University of California Press.
Taylor, C. (1991), *The Ethics of Authenticity*, Cambridge, MA: Harvard University Press.
Troeltsch, E. (1931), *The Social Teachings of the Christian Churches*, trans. O. Wyon, London: Allen and Unwin.
Wallis, R. (1984), *The Elementary Forms of the New Religious Life*, London: Routledge.
Wallis, R. (2017), 'Three Types of New Religious Movements', in L. L. Dawson (ed.), *Cults in Context*, 46–64, London: Routledge.
We the Irish: The Pastor (1971), [TV Documentary] RTÉ. Available online: https://www.rte.ie/archives/2016/1011/823190-ireland-a-land-of-many-faiths/ (accessed 14 July 2021).
Weber, M. (1958), *The Protestant Ethic and the Spirit of Capitalism*, New York: Charles Scribner's Sons.
Weber, M. (1963), *The Sociology of Religion*, Boston: Beacon Press.
White, J. H. (1984), *Church and State in Modern Ireland, 1923–79*, 2nd edn, London: Gill and Macmillan.
Wilson, B. (1970), *Religious Sects: A Sociological Study*, London: Weidenfeld and Nicolson.
Wilson, B. (2003), 'Secularization: Religion in the Modern World', in P. Clarke and S. Sutherland (eds), *The Study of Religion, Traditional and New Religions*, 195–208, London: Routledge.
Young, E. A. (2012), 'The Use of the "Brainwashing" Theory by the Anti-Cult Movement in the United States of America, Pre-1996', *Zeitschrift für junge Religionswissenschaft*, 7: 5–19.

Chapter 9

Adogame, A. (2015), *The African Christian Diaspora: New Currents and Emerging Trends in World Christianity*, London: Bloomsbury.
Anidjar, G. (2006), 'Secularism', *Critical Inquiry*, 33 (1): 52–77. Available online: https://doi.org/10.1086/509746.
Beckford, J. A. (2019), 'Religions and Migrations – Old and New', *Quaderni Di Sociologia*, 80 (80): 15–32. Available online: https://doi.org/10.4000/qds.2599.
Bethune, B. (2012), 'Losing Their Religion: The Catholic Church Is Falling Apart in Ireland, and Not Just Due to Scandal', *Maclean's (Toronto)*, 125 (22): 32–4.
Carling, J. (2002), 'Migration in the Age of Involuntary Immobility: Theoretical Reflections and Cape Verdean Experiences', *Journal of Ethnic and Migration Studies*, 28 (1): 5–42.
Carr, J., and Haynes, A. (2015), 'A Clash of Racializations: The Policing of "Race" and of Anti-Muslim Racism in Ireland', *Critical Sociology*, 41 (1): 21–40. Available online: https://doi.org/10.1177/0896920513492805.
Casanova, J. (2001), 'Religion, the New Millennium, and Globalization (2000 Presidential Address)', *Sociology of Religion*, 62 (4): 415–41. Available online: https://doi.org/10.2307/3712434.
Collinson, S. (1993), *Europe and International Migration*, London: Pinter for Royal Institute of International Affairs.
CSO (2007), *2006 Census of Population – Volume 13*, Dublin: Central Statistics Office.

CSO (2016a), *Census of Population 2016 – Profile 8 Irish Travellers, Ethnicity and Religion*. Available online: www.cso.ie/en/releasesandpublications/ep/p-cp8iter/p8iter/p8rnc/ (accessed 15 June 2021).

CSO (2016b), *Census 2016 Summary Results - Part 1*, Dublin: Central Statistics Office.

Cullen, P. (2000), *Refugees and Asylum Seekers in Ireland*, Cork: Cork University Press.

Faist, T. (2000), *The Volume and Dynamics of International Migration and Transnational Social Spaces*, Oxford: Oxford University Press.

Fanning, C. (2019), 'The Creation of "the Citizen" Requires at the Same Time the Active Creation of "the Non-Citizen". Ireland as a Case Study', *Trinity Social & Political Review*, 29 (1): 9–21.

Farrar, M. (2012), *Islam in the West: Key Issues in Multiculturalism*, Houndsmills: Palgrave Macmillan.

Fiddian-Qasmiyeh, E., Loescher, G., Long, K., and Sigona, N. (2014), *The Oxford Handbook of Refugee and Forced Migration Studies*, Oxford: Oxford University Press.

Gozdziak, E. M., and Shandy, D. J. (2002), 'Editorial Introduction: Religion and Spirituality in Forced Migration', *Journal of Refugee Studies*, 15 (2): 129–35. Available online: https://doi.org/10.1093/jrs/15.2.129.

Gray, B. (2016), 'The Politics of Migration, Church, and State: A Case Study of the Catholic Church in Ireland', *International Migration Review*, 50 (2): 315–51. Available online: https://doi.org/10.1111/imre.12165.

Guerin, P. (2002), 'Racism and the Media in Ireland: Setting the Antiimmigration Agenda', in R. Lentin and R. McVeigh (eds), *Racism and Anti-racism in Ireland*, 91–101, Belfast: Beyond the Pale.

Hanish, S. (2009), 'Christians, Yazidis, and Mandaeans in Iraq: A Survival Issue', *Domes (Milwaukee, Wis.)*, 18 (1): 1–16. Available online: https://doi.org/10.1111/j.1949-3606.2009.tb00104.x.

Haughey, N. (2002), 'Nigerians Are Flocking to Their Own Churches', *Irish Times*, 28 October. Available online: https://www.irishtimes.com/news/nigerians-are-flocking-to-their-own-churches-1.1102431 (accessed 12 July 2021).

Herrington, L. M. (2013), 'Globalization and Religion in Historical Perspective: A Paradoxical Relationship', *Religions*, 4 (1): 145–65. Available online: https://doi.org/10.3390/rel4010145.

Holmes, A. (2017), 'Protestants and "Greater Ireland": Mission, Migration, and Identity in the Nineteenth Century', *Irish Historical Studies*, 41 (160): 275–85. Available online: https://doi.org/10.1017/ihs.2017.39.

Hunt, S. (2002), '"Neither Here nor There": The Construction of Identities and Boundary Maintenance of West African Pentecostals', *Sociology*, 36 (1): 147–69.

Hunt, S., and Lightly, N. (2001), 'The British Black Pentecostal "Revival": Identity and Belief in the New Nigerian Churches', *Ethnic and Racial Studies*, 24 (1): 104–24.

ICC (2003), *Research Project into Aspects of the Religious Life of Refugees, Asylum Seekers and Immigrants in the Republic of Ireland*, Belfast: Irish Council of Churches.

Inglis, T. (1998), *Moral Monopoly: The Rise and Fall of the Catholic Church in Modern Ireland*, Dublin: University College Dublin Press.

Kalilombe, P. (1997), 'Black Christianity in Britain', *Ethnic and Racial Studies*, 20 (2): 308–15.

Khan, A. (2017), 'Narratives of Muslim Migration to Ireland', *Muslim World*, 107 (3): 401–31. Available online: https://doi.org/10.1111/muwo.12200.

Krech, V. (2000), 'From Historicism to Functionalism: The Rise of Scientific Approaches to Religions around 1900 and Their Socio-Cultural Context', *Numen*, 47 (3): 244–65. Available online: https://doi.org/10.1163/156852700511540.
Leiter, B. (2019), 'The Death of God and the Death of Morality', *The Monist*, 102 (3): 386–402. Available online: https://doi.org/10.1093/monist/onz016.
Lentin, R. (2001), 'Responding to the Racialisation of Irishness: Disavowed Multiculturalism and Its Discontents', *Sociological Research Online*, 5 (4). Available online: http://www.socresonline.org.Uk/5/4/lentin.html (accessed 15 June 2021).
Lentin, R., and McVeigh, R. (2002), *Racism and Anti-Racism in Ireland*, Belfast: BTP.
Lentin, R., and McVeigh, R. (2006), *After Optimism? Ireland, Racism and Globalisation*, Dublin: Metro Eireann.
Levitt, P. (1998), 'Local-Level Global Religion: The Case of U.S.-Dominican Migration', *Journal for the Scientific Study of Religion*, 37 (1): 74–89.
Levtzion, N., and Pouwels, R., eds (2000), *The History of Islam in Africa*, Athens: Ohio University Press.
Logan, P. (1988), 'Practising Hinduism: The Experience of Gujarati Adults and Children in Britain', Unpublished report, Thomas Coram Research Unit, University of London Institute of Education.
Massey, D. S., and Higgins, M. E. (2011), 'The Effect of Immigration on Religious Belief and Practice: A Theologizing or Alienating Experience?', *Social Science Research*, 40 (5): 1371–89. Available online: https://doi.org/10.1016/j.ssresearch.2010.04.012.
McCann, T. (2000), 'Using Faith to Feel at Home', *Irish Times*, 14 October.
McKeon, B. (1997), 'Africans in Ireland in the 18th Century', *African Expression*, 4 (Autumn).
Mella, O. (1994), *Religion in the Life of Refugees and Immigrants*, Stockholm: Centre for Research in International Migration and Ethnicity (CEIFO).
Metcalf, B. (1996), 'Introduction: Sacred Words, Sanctioned Practice, New Communities', in B. Metcalf (ed.), *Making Muslim Space in North America and Europe*, 1–27, Berkeley: University of California Press.
Montgomery, V. (2013), 'Multicultural Ireland? Muslim Women and Integration in Ireland', *Irish Political Studies*, 28 (3): 434–49. Available online: https://doi.org/10.1080/07907184.2013.823087.
Obadia, L. (2012), 'Globalisation and New Geographies of Religion: New Regimes in the Movement, Circulation, and Territoriality of Cults and Beliefs', *International Social Science Journal*, 63 (209–10): 147–57. Available online: https://doi.org/10.1111/issj.12034.
Ó hAnnracháin, T. (2019), 'Religious Refugees or Confessional Migrants? Perspectives from Early Modern Ireland', *Journal of Early Modern Christianity*, 6 (1): 3–18. Available online: https://doi.org/10.1515/jemc-2019-2005.
OECD (2020), *International Migration Outlook 2020*, Paris: OECD. Available online: https://doi.org/10.1787/ec98f531-en.
Olusola, J. (2002), 'Stop Telling Me to Go Back Home – This Is My Home', *Irish Times*, 30 July. Available online: https://www.irishtimes.com/news/stop-telling-me-to-go-back-home-this-is-my-home-1.1090178 (accessed 12 July 2021).
'Reaction: "The Country Has Listened. Women Have Spoken"' (2018), *Irish Times*, 26 May. Available online: https://www.irishtimes.com/news/polit ics/reaction-the-country-has-listened-women-have-spoken-1.3509 819 (accessed 15 June 2021).
Reese, S. (2014), 'Islam in Africa/Africans and Islam', *Journal of African History*, 55 (1): 17–26. Available online: https://doi.org/10.1017/S0021853713000807.

Regan, E. (2013), 'Church, Culture and Credibility: A Perspective from Ireland', *New Blackfriars*, 94 (1050): 160–76. Available online: https://doi.org/10.1111/nbfr.12012.
Richardson, L. (1990), *Writing Strategies: Reaching Diverse Audiences*. Thousand Oaks, CA: Sage.
Richardson, L. (1995), 'Narrative and Sociology', in J. Van Mannen (ed.), *Representation in Ethnography*, 198–221, Thousand Oaks, CA: Sage.
Rolston, B., and Shannon, M. (2002), *Encounters: How Racism Came to Ireland*, Belfast: Beyond the Pale.
Roy, C. A. (2020), 'An "Un-Imagined Community": The Entangled Genealogy of an Exclusivist Nationalism in Myanmar and the Rohingya Refugee Crisis', *Social Identities*, 26 (5): 590–607. Available online: https://doi.org/10.1080/13504 630.2020.1782731.
Said, E. (1995), *Orientalism*, London: Penguin.
Sassen, S. (1998), *Globalisation and Its Discontents: Essays on the New Mobility of People and Money*, New York: New Press.
Scharbrodt, O. (2011), 'Shaping the Public Image of Islam: The Shiis of Ireland as "Moderate" Muslims', *Journal of Muslim Minority Affairs*, 31 (4): 518–33.
Smith, S., and Mutwarasibo, F. (2000), *Africans in Ireland: Developing Communities*, Dublin: African Cultural Project.
Sweeney, P. (1998), *The Celtic Tiger: Ireland's Economic Miracle Explained*, Dublin: Oak Tree Press.
The Economist (2016), 'Iraq's Yazidis: Freedom on Hold', 13 August. Available online: https://www.economist.com/middle-east-and-africa/2016/08/13/free dom-on-hold (accessed 24 November 2021).
ter Haar, G. (1998), *Halfway to Paradise: African Christians in Europe*, Cardiff: Cardiff Academic Press.
Tottoli, R., ed. (2015), *Routledge Handbook of Islam in the West*, London: Routledge.
Ugba, A. (2003), 'African Churches in Ireland', *Asyland Magazine of the Irish Refugee Council*, Autumn: 10–11.
Ugba, A. (2009), *Shades of Belonging: Pentecostal Africans in Twenty-First Century Ireland*, Trenton, NJ: Africa World Press.
Van Mannen, J. (1995), 'An End to Innocence: The Ethnography of Ethnography', in J. Van Mannen (ed.), *Representation in Ethnography*, 1–35, Thousand Oaks, CA: Sage.
Vásquez, M., and Dewind, J. (2014), 'Introduction to the Religious Lives of Migrant Minorities: A Transnational and Multi-Sited Perspective', *Global Networks (Oxford)*, 14 (3): 251–72. Available online: https://doi.org/10.1111/glob.12058.
Vertovec, S. (2000), 'Religion and Diaspora', paper presented at the Conference on 'New Landscapes of Religion in the West', School of Geography and the Environment, University of Oxford, 27–29 September 2000.
Ware, A., and Laoutides, C. (2019), *Myanmar's 'Rohingya' Conflict*, Oxford: Oxford University Press.
Warner, R. S. (1998), 'Immigration and Religious Communities in the United States', in S. R. Warner and J. G. Wittner (eds), *Gatherings in Diaspora: Religious Communities and the New Immigration*, 3–34, Philadelphia: Temple University Press.
Warner, R. S., and Wittner, J. G., eds (1998), *Gatherings in Diaspora: Religious Communities and the New Immigration*, Philadelphia: Temple University Press.
Williams, R. B. (1988), *Religion and Immigrants from India and Pakistan*, Cambridge: Cambridge University Press.

Wolcott, H. F. (1995), 'Making a Study "More Ethnographic"', in J. Van Mannen (ed.), *Representation in Ethnography*, 79–111, Thousand Oaks, CA: Sage.

Chapter 10

Adler, G. J., Jr, Bruce, T. C., and Starks, B., eds (2019), *American Parishes: Remaking Local Catholicism*, New York: Fordham University Press.

Andersen, K. 2016. 'Ireland in the Twenty-First Century: Secularization or Religious Vitality?', in D. Pollack, O. Müller and G. Pickel (eds), *The Social Significance of Religion in the Enlarged Europe: Secularization, Individualization and Pluralization*, 51–76, Abingdon: Routledge.

Baker, J. O., Martí, G., Braunstein, R., Whitehead, A. L., and Yukich, G. (2020), 'Religion in the Age of Social Distancing: How Covid-19 Presents New Directions for Research', *Sociology of Religion*, 81 (4): 357–70.

Buckley, D. T. (2016), *Faithful to Secularism: The Religious Politics of Democracy in Ireland, Senegal, and the Philippines*, New York: Columbia University Press.

Bullivant, S. (2019), *Mass Exodus: Catholic Disaffiliation in Britain and America since Vatican II*, Oxford: Oxford University Press.

Byrne, P. (2017), *All Will Be Well: Digital Dispatches from the Parish*, Dublin: Columba Press.

'Cardinal Urges GAA to Move Matches Clashing with Mass' (2011), *Irish Times*, 3 August. Available online: https://www.irishtimes.com/news/cardinal-urges-gaa-to-move-matches-clashing-with-mass-1.588090 (accessed 2 March 2021).

Chamedes, G. (2019), *A Twentieth-Century Crusade: The Vatican's Battle to Remake Christian Europe*, Cambridge, MA: Harvard University Press.

Conway, B. (2011), 'The Vanishing Catholic Priest', *Contexts*, 10 (2): 64–5.

Conway, B. (2016), 'Contexts of Trends in the Catholic Church's Male Workforce: Chile, Ireland and Poland Compared', *Social Science History*, 40 (3): 405–32.

Conway, B. (2021), 'The Sociology of Catholicism: A Review of Research and Scholarship', *Sociology Compass*, 15 (4): e12863. Available online: https://doi.org/10.1111/soc4.12863.

Conway, B. (forthcoming), 'Except Ireland? Secularization and the Irish Case', in E. M Meunier and P. Portier (eds), *Catholicisms within the Context of New Forms of Public Space Regulation: Comparative Overview*, Ottawa: University of Ottawa Press.

Conway, E., and Kilcoyne, C., eds (1997), *Twin Pulpits: Church & Media in Modern Ireland All Hallows College July 1997*, Dublin: Veritas.

Corish, P. J. (1995), *Maynooth College 1795–1995*, Dublin: Gill & Macmillan.

Costello, A. G. (1985), *In God's Hands: The Story of Sister Mary Consilio and Cuan Mhuire*, Dublin: Veritas.

Czarnecki, D. (2015), 'Moral Women, Immoral Technologies: How Devout Women Negotiate Gender, Religion, and Assisted Reproductive Technologies', *Gender & Society*, 29 (5): 716–42.

Daly, E. (2011), *A Troubled See: Memoirs of a Derry Bishop*, Dublin: Four Courts Press.

Department of Children, Equality, Disability, Integration and Youth (2021), Final Report of the Commission of Investigation into Mother and Baby Homes. Available online: https://www.gov.ie/en/publication/d4b3d-final-report-of-the-commission-of-investigation-into-mother-and-baby-homes/ (accessed 2 March 2021).

Dillon, M. (2007), 'Decline and Continuity: Catholicism since 1950 in the United States, Ireland, and Quebec', in L. W. Tentler (ed.), *The Church Confronts Modernity: Catholicism since 1950 in the United States, Ireland, & Quebec*, 239–67, Washington, DC: Catholic University of America Press.

Diotallevi, L. (2002), 'Internal Competition in a National Religious Monopoly: The Catholic Effect and the Italian Case', *Sociology of Religion*, 63 (2): 137–55.

Dobbelaere, K. (1999), 'Towards an Integrated Perspective of the Processes Related to the Descriptive Concept of Secularization', *Sociology of Religion*, 60 (3): 229–47.

Doherty, D. T., and Moran, R. (2009), *Mental Health and Associated Health Service Use on the Island of Ireland*, Health Research Board Research Series 7. Available online: https://www.ucd.ie/issda/t4media/NPWDS%20Report%202008.pdf (accessed 9 April 2021).

Donnelly, S. (2016), 'Sins of the Father: Unravelling Moral Authority in the Irish Catholic Church', *Irish Journal of Sociology*, 24 (3): 315–39.

Donnelly, S., and Inglis, T. (2010), 'The Media and the Catholic Church in Ireland: Reporting Clerical Child Sex Abuse', *Journal of Contemporary Religion*, 25 (1): 1–19.

Donohoe, J. B. (1979), 'New Bishop Receives Big Welcome', *Connacht Tribune*, 28 September: 13.

Driessen. M. D. (2014), *Religion and Democratization: Framing Religious and Political Identities in Muslim and Catholic Societies*, Oxford: Oxford University Press.

Ebaugh, H. R., Lorence, J., and Saltzman Chafetz, J. (1996), 'The Growth and Decline of the Population of Catholic Nuns Cross-Nationally, 1960–1990: A Case of Secularization as Social Structural Change', *Journal for the Scientific Study of Religion*, 35 (2): 171–83.

Fahey, T. (1992), 'Catholicism and Industrial Society in Ireland', in J. H. Goldthorpe and C. T. Whelan (eds), *The Development of Industrial Society in Ireland*, 241–63, Oxford: Oxford University Press.

Ferriter, D. (2006), *What If? Alternative Views of Twentieth-Century Ireland*, Dublin: Gill & Macmillan.

Fishman, R. M., and Jones, K. (2007), 'Civic Engagement and Church Policy in the Making of Religious Vocations: Cross-National Variation in the Evolution of Priestly Ordinations', in G. Giordan (ed.), *Vocation and Social Context*, 127–51, Leiden: Brill.

Flynn, T. (1997), 'Speaking for the Churches: The Church and the Media', in E. Conway and C. Kilcoyne (eds), *Twin Pulpits: Church & Media in Modern Ireland All Hallows College July 1997*, 23–8, Dublin: Veritas.

Ganiel, G. (2020a), 'People Still Need Us': A Report on a Survey of Faith Leaders on the Island of Ireland during the Covid-19 Pandemic, Irish Council of Churches/Irish Inter-Church Meeting. Available online: https://pure.qub.ac.uk/en/publicati ons/people-still-need-us-a-report-on-a-survey-of-faith-leaders-on-the (accessed 3 March 2021).

Ganiel, G. (2020b), 'Clerical Modernisers and the Media in Ireland: The Journalism of Fr Gerry Reynolds', *Contemporary British History*, 34 (4): 629–51.

Gately, S. (2019), 'Knock Marriage Introductions Maintains its Attraction', *CatholicIreland. Net*. Available online: https://www.catholicireland.net/knock-marriage-introductions-maintains-attraction/ (accessed 23 February 2021).

Greeley, A., and Ward, C. (2000), 'How "Secularised" Is the Ireland We Live In?', *Doctrine & Life*, 50: 581–17.

Grzymała-Busse, A. (2015), *Nations under God: How Churches Use Moral Authority to Influence Policy*, Princeton, NJ: Princeton University Press.

Hirschle, J. (2010), 'From Religious to Consumption-Related Routine Activities? Analyzing Ireland's Economic Boom and the Decline in Church Attendance', *Journal for the Scientific Study of Religion*, 49 (4): 673–87.

Hornsby-Smith, M. P. (1992), 'Social and Religious Transformation in Ireland: A Case of Secularization?', in J. H. Goldthorpe and C. T. Whelan (eds), *The Development of Industrial Society in Ireland*, 265–90, Oxford: Oxford University Press.

Keenan, M. (2012), *Child Sexual Abuse & the Catholic Church Gender, Power, and Organizational Culture*, Oxford: Oxford University Press.

Kerkhofs, J., ed. (1995), *Europe without Priests*, London: SCM Press.

Lennon, C., ed. (2012), *Confraternities and Sodalities in Ireland: Charity, Devotion and Sociability*, Dublin: Columba Press.

Lennon, C., and Kavanagh, R. (2012), 'The Flowering of the Confraternities and Sodalities in Ireland, c.1860–c.1960', in C. Lennon (ed.), *Confraternities and Sodalities in Ireland: Charity, Devotion and Sociability*, 76–96, Dublin: Columba Press.

Mac Gréil, M. (2009), *The Challenge of Indifference: A Need for Religious Revival in Ireland*, Maynooth: Survey and Research Unit, Department of Sociology, National University of Ireland Maynooth.

Martin, E. (2020), 'Archbishop Eamon Martin Congratulates Father Paul Dempsey on His Appointment as Bishop of the Diocese of Achonry', Irish Catholic Bishops' Conference. Available online: https://www.catholicbishops.ie/2020/01/27/archbishop-eamon-martin-congratulates-father-paul-dempsey-on-his-appointment-as-bishop-of-the-diocese-of-achonry/ (accessed 2 April 2021).

Maye, B. (2010), *The Search for Justice: Trócaire: A History*, Dublin: Veritas.

Mayo County Council Enterprise & Investment Unit (2015), Destination Mayo: A Strategy for the Future Development of Tourism in County Mayo 2015–2020. Available online: https://eagenda.mayo.ie//FilesUpLoaded/2015341524Item%20no%202%20Destination%20Mayo%20Tourism%20Strategy%202015-2020.pdf (accessed 24 March 2021).

McCrave, C. (2019), 'Match-Making Service "Knock Marriage Bureau" to Close after More than 50 Years', *The Journal*. Available online: https://www.thejournal.ie/knock-marriage-bureau-to-close-after-50-years-4639898-May2019/ (accessed 23 February 2021).

McDonagh, E., ed. (2012), *Faith and the Hungry Grass: A Mayo Book of Theology*, Dublin: Columba Press.

McGinnity, F., Russell, H., Williams, J., and Blackwell, S. (2005), *Time-Use in Ireland 2005: Survey Report*, Dublin: Economic and Social Research Institute. Available online: https://www.esri.ie/system/files/media/file-uploads/2016-03/BKMNINT183.pdf (accessed 7 May 2021).

McGrath, P. (2019), 'Knock Marriage Introductions Closes after 50 years in Operation', *RTÉ*. Available online: https://www.rte.ie/news/connacht/2019/0517/1050072-knock-marriage-introductions-closure/ (accessed 3 March 2021).

Neary, M. (2011), 'Homily of Archbishop Neary for Funeral Mass of Fr Michael Keane, RIP', *Irish Catholic Bishops' Conference*. Available online: https://www.catholicbishops.ie/2011/08/31/homily-archbishop-neary-funeral-mass-fr-michael-keane-rip/ (accessed 3 March 2021).

Ní Chearbhaill, M. (2012), 'Charity, Church and the Society of St Vincent de Paul', in C. Lennon (ed.), *Confraternities and Sodalities in Ireland: Charity, Devotion and Sociability*, 169–85, Dublin: Columba Press.

O'Brien, H. (2020), 'What Does the Rise of Digital Religion during Covid-19 Tell Us about Religion's Capacity to Adapt?', *Irish Journal of Sociology*, 28 (2): 242–6.

O'Mahony, T. P. (1981), 'A Link Man for the Church', *Irish Press*, 28 July: 9.

Ortiz-Ospina, E., Tzvetkova, S., and Roser, M. (2018), 'Women's Employment', *OurWorldInData.org*. Available online: https://ourworldindata.org/female-labor-supply (accessed 22 April 2021).

Pollak, A. (1997), 'The Religious Journalist', in E. Conway and C. Kilcoyne (eds), *Twin Pulpits: Church & Media in Modern Ireland All Hallows College July 1997*, 121–32, Dublin: Veritas.

Pollack, D., and Rosta, G. (2017), *Religion and Modernity: An International Comparison*, Oxford: Oxford University Press.

'Priest Criticises Parents Who Reduce First Communion to "Orgy of Materialism with Miniature Brides"' (2017), *Catholic Herald*, 29 May. Available online: https://catholicherald.co.uk/priest-criticises-parents-who-reduce-first-communion-to-orgy-of-materialism-with-miniature-brides/ (accessed 2 March 2021).

Ryan, L. (1995), 'The Family as a System', in J. M. Feheney (ed.), *Education and the Family: Papers to Mark the 150th Anniversary of Edmund Rice*, 64–80, Dublin: Veritas.

Ryan, L. (2000), 'Strengthening Irish Identity through Openness', in R. O'Donnell (ed.), *Europe: The Irish Experience*, 55–68, Dublin: Institute of European Affairs.

Saint Patrick's College Maynooth (2020–1), *Kalendarium 2020–21*. Available online: https://maynoothcollege.ie/files/images/Final-Kalendarium-2020-2021.pdf (accessed 20 April 2021).

Scally, D. (2021), *The Best Catholics in the World: The Irish, the Church and the End of a Special Relationship*, Dublin: Penguin/Sandycove.

Smith, C., Longest, K., Hill, J., and Christoffersen, K. (2014), *Young Catholic America: Emerging Adults in, Out of, and Gone from the Church*, Oxford: Oxford University Press.

Sewell, W. H., Jr. (1992), 'A Theory of Structure: Duality, Agency, and Transformation', *American Journal of Sociology*, 98 (1): 1–29.

Stark, R., and Finke, R. (2000), 'Catholic Religious Vocations: Decline and Revival', *Review of Religious Research*, 42 (2): 125–45.

Stolz, J., Könemann, J., Schneuwly Purdie, M., Englberger, T., and Krüggeler, M. (2016), *(Un)Believing in Modern Society: Religion, Spirituality, and Religious-Secular Competition*, Abingdon: Routledge.

Tierney, M. (2010), *No Second Chance: Reflections of a Dublin Priest*, Dublin: Columba Press.

Vatican Secretariat of State, Central Office of Church Statistics (1961), *Annuario Pontificio*, Vatican City: Vatican Publishing House.

Wilkins-Laflamme, S. (2021), 'A Tale of Decline or Change? Working toward a Complementary Understanding of Secular Transition and Individual Spiritualization Theories', *Journal for the Scientific Study of Religion*. Available online: https://doi.org/10.1111/jssr.12721 (accessed 29 July 2021).

Chapter 11

'Administration Report of the Persian Gulf (1905–1910)', in Qatar Digital Library, 'Administration Reports 1905–1910 [62v] (129/616)', 15, London: British Library India Office Records. Available online: https://www.qdl.qa/en/archive/81055/vdc_100023487519.0x000082 (accessed 19 July 2021).

Barrett, T. (2016), 'Michael Pye, Translating Drunk – and Stark Naked: Problems in Presenting Eighteenth Century Japanese Thought', *Journal of the Irish Society for the Academic Study of Religions*, 3: 236–49.

Bocking, B. (2013), 'Flagging Up Buddhism: Charles Pfoundes (*Omoie Tetzunostzuke*) among the International Congresses and Expositions, 1893–1905', *Contemporary Buddhism*, 14 (1): 17–37.

Bocking, B. (2021), 'Charles Pfoundes and the Forgotten First Buddhist Mission to the West: Some Research Questions', in P. Bornet (ed.), *Translocal Lives and Religion: Connections between Asia and Europe in the Late Modern World*, 171–92, Sheffield: Equinox.

Bocking, B., Cox, L., and Yoshinaga, S. (2016), 'The First Buddhist Mission to the West: Charles Pfoundes and the London Buddhist Mission of 1889-1892', *DISKUS: The Journal of the British Association for the Study of Religions*, 16 (3): 1–33.

Choompolpaisal, P. (2013), 'Tai-Burmese-Lao Buddhisms in "Modernising" Ban Thawai (Bangkok): The Dynamic Interaction Between Ethnic Minority Religion and British–Siamese Centralization in the Late Nineteenth/Early Twentieth Centuries', *Contemporary Buddhism*, 14 (1): 94–115.

Cosgrove, O., Cox, L., Kuhling, C., and Mulholland, P., eds (2011), *Ireland's New Religious Movements*, Cambridge: Cambridge Scholars.

Cox, L. (2009), 'Laurence O' Rourke / U Dhammaloka: Working-Class Irish Freethinker, and the First European Bhikkhu?', *Journal of Global Buddhism*, 10: 135–44.

Cox, L. (2010), 'Current Debates: New Religion(s) in Ireland "Alternative Spiritualities, New Religious Movements and the New Age in Ireland" Conference Report', NUI Maynooth, 30–31 October 2009', *Irish Journal of Sociology*, 18 (1): 100–11.

Cox, L. (2013), *Buddhism and Ireland*, Sheffield: Equinox.

Cox, L. (2014), 'Buddhism in Ireland: The Inner Life of World-Systems', *Études Irlandaises*, 39 (2): 161–72.

Cox, L., and Ó Laoidh, J. (2021), 'Japanese Buddhism in Ireland', *Journal of Religion in Japan*, 11 (1): 1–29.

Cox, L., and Sirisena, M. (2016), 'Early Western Lay Buddhists in Colonial Asia – John Bowles Daly and the Buddhist Theosophical Society of Ceylon', *Journal of the Irish Society for the Academic Study of Religions* (published online ahead of print 2021). Available online: https://doi.org/10.1163/22118349-01002008 (accessed 30 November 2021).

Crosby, K., and Ashin, J. (2016), 'All Too Human: The Impact of International Buddhist Networks on the Life and Posthumous Conviction of the Burmese Nationalist Monk, Shin Ukkaṭṭha (1897–1978)', *Journal of the Irish Society for the Academic Study of Religions*, 3: 219–35.

Doran, P. (2017), *A Political Economy of Attention, Mindfulness and Consumerism: Reclaiming the Mindful Commons*, London: Routledge.

Fedorowich, K., and Booth, C. (2021), '"Returning Home to Fight": Bristolians in the Dominion Armies, 1914–1918', in D. E. Delaney, M. Frost and A. L. Brown (eds),

Manpower and the Armies of the British Empire in the Two World Wars, 72–85, Ithaca: Cornell.

Franck, H. A. (1910), *A Vagabond Journey around the World: A Narrative of Personal Experience*, New York: Century.

Goedhals, A. (2020), *The Neo-Buddhist Writings of Lafcadio Hearn: Light from the East*, Leiden: Brill.

Kalmar, B. (2017), 'Re-imagining Tibetan Buddhist Pilgrimage Culture in India', *Journal of the Irish Society for the Academic Study of Religion*, 5: 40–68.

Kirichenko, A. (2009), 'From *Thathanadaw* to Theravāda Buddhism: Constructions of Religion and Religious Identity in Nineteenth- and Early Twentieth-century Myanmar', in T. D. DuBois (ed.), *Casting Faiths: Imperialism and the Transformation of Religion in East and Southeast Asia*, 23–45, Basingstoke: Palgrave Macmillan.

Padoan, T. (2021), 'On the Semiotics of Space in the Study of Religions: Theoretical Perspectives and Methodological Challenges', in T. A. Poder and J. Van Boom (eds), *Sign, Method, and the Sacred:New Directions in Semiotic Methodologies for the Study of Religion*, 189–214, Berlin: de Gruyter.

Pye, M. (2016), 'Recent Trends in the White Light Association (*Byakkō Shinkōkai*)', *Journal of the Irish Society for the Academic Study of Religions*, 3: 186–97.

Shackle, C., and Bocking, B. (2017), 'Representing Sikhism: Essays in Memory of the Irish Scholar Max Arthur Macauliffe', *Journal of the Irish Society for the Academic Study of Religions*, 4: 1–6.

Sirisena, M. (2017), 'The Dissident Orientalist: An Interpretation of U Dhammaloka's 1909 Tour of Ceylon', *Interventions*, 19 (1): 126–43.

Travagnin, S. (2016), 'Elder Gongga (1903–1997) between China, Tibet and Taiwan: Assessing Life, Mission and Mummification of a Buddhist Woman', *Journal of the Irish Society for the Academic Study of Religions*, 3 (1): 250–72.

Turner, A. (2014), 'Religion, the Study of Religion and Other Products of Transnational and Colonial Imaginings', *Journal of the Irish Society for the Academic Study of Religions*, 1: 12–25.

Turner, A., Cox, L., and Bocking, B. (2020), *The Irish Buddhist: The Forgotten Monk Who Faced Down the British Empire*, New York: Oxford University Press.

Ward, E. (2021), *Self*, Cork: Cork University Press.

INDEX

abortion
  Catholic Church and 63, 65, 142
  constitutional ban on 153
  Eighth Amendment, repeal of 12, 64, 130, 160
  Northern Ireland, attitudes in 68
Abrahamic faiths 8, 145
Abundant Life 72
abuse
  in industrial schools 66, 72, 117
  in Magdalene laundries 117, 140
  in Mother and Baby Homes 100, 140
  reports on public inquiries 66, 168 n.4
  see also Catholic Church abuse scandals
academic study of religions (ASR) 163 nn.2–4
  ASR, term 4, 163 n.2
  in BA and MA programmes 6
  development of 3, 5, 6, 19, 146
  dissertation topics 12–13
  EU-funded project 7
  multidisciplinary context 18
  in the post-secular university 19
  'Religions and Global Diversity' programme 146
  research, approach to 4–5
  research projects in Ireland 7–8
  research scholars in Ireland 9, 164 n.12
  role for 5
  School of Religion, TCD 6
  sub-disclipinary fields, development of 18
  in universities 5–6, 18
  world religions, colonialism and 144
Æ *see* Russell, George William
aesthetics of religion 8, 18
Africa
  affinity with Ireland 125
  anti-apartheid struggles 125
  Christianity in 10
  Islam propagators in 120
  migration from 121, 124
  religious connections to Ireland 124
African Catholicism, growth of 139
African immigrants
  English-speaking 124
  from EU countries 126
  in Ireland 124, 126
  Irish citizenship and 126
  Pentecostal churches established by 126
  racist attacks on 128, 130
  UK and 124
African Pentecostalism 17, 119, 120, 123, 130, 160
  academic research 126–7
  in Ireland 119, 121–2, 123
  Irish state, aloofness of 119, 120
African Pentecostals 16, 72, 115, 160
  antipathy experienced by 130
  bible and 127–8
  Catholic Church, perception of 127–8
  Catholic parishes, relationship with 128
  Celtic Tiger Ireland and 124–5
  diaspora 9
  in Europe 122
  in Germany 9
  indirect discrimination 130
  in Ireland 9, 72, 115, 121, 122
  Ireland, preconception of 124, 129
  Irish (or white) Pentecostal 'other' and 127
  the Irish state and 126–30
  in the Netherlands 122
  re-evangelization of the Irish 128, 129
  religion in Ireland, views on 129–30
  repeal of Eighth Amendment, views on 130
  reverse mission mandate 129
agnostics 115, 117, 129
alienation 108, 109–10
  of Irish Protestants 91, 92, 102
  see also marginalization

Alive O (1996–2004) programme 53
All Hallows Seminary, Dublin 113
Almqvist, B., and Ó Héalaí, P. 40, 41
alternative spiritualities 107, 109, 113–15
'Alternative Spiritualities, New Religious Movements and the New Age in Ireland' (2009) 6, 146–7
alternative therapies 115, 116
American 'Plain' churches 10–11
American Psychiatric Association 111
Andersen, Karen 65
Anderson, Brad 10, 164 n.7
androcentric religion 22, 24, 30, 166 n.10
angel card reading 115, 118
Anglican Church 10, 48, 71, 150
  see also Church of Ireland
Anglo-Irish, the 79
  ascendancy, loss of 79
  cultural nationalism, contributions to 85
  esotericism and 79
  perception of 85
  Romanticism and 85
  see also Protestant Ascendancy
Anglo-Norman invasion of Ireland 85
Anglo-Saxon world 118
anomie 109–10
anthropological studies 5, 7–8, 32, 53, 66–7, 71
anti-clerical movement 114
anti-communism 10
anti-religious sentiment 14, 67
anti-Semitism 170 n.9
anti-slave trade activists 125
Apostolic churches 94, 125
Archdiocese of Dublin, Murphy Report (2009) 66, 168 n.4
Árd Mhuire, Dunboyne, County Meath 140–1
Arthur, Gavin 26, 27
Ascendancy *see* Protestant Ascendancy
asceticism 9, 147
Asia
  Buddhist revival 146
  Ireland and 146, 149
  Irish people working in 148, 149
  missions to 148
Asian Buddhism
  British Empire and 144, 148
  Catholic knowledge of 148
  Irish knowledge of 148
  Jesuit encounter with 148
  knowledge of 147
  Protestant knowledge of 148
Asian Buddhists
  Covid-19 pandemic, effects of 154
  in Ireland 145, 150, 154, 156, 160
ASR *see* academic study of religions
astrology 27, 81, 114, 118
asylum seekers 124, 129
  see also refugees
atheism 16, 115, 117, 129
Atheist Ireland 60
ATU international tale-type index 37, 38
Aunya (goddess) 27
automatic writing 79, 80–1, 89

Baháʼí, studies of 9, 71
Baillie, Sandra 71
Baptists 48, 105, 160
Barrett, Tim 154
Barrett, William Fletcher 83
BASR *see* British Association for the Study of Religions
Bastide, Derek 52
Bean na hÉireann (journal) 88, 169 n.2
Beck, Ulrich 30
Becker, Howard 112
Beckerlegge, Gwilym 8
Beckford, James 110, 121, 123
belief, declines in 135
belief fluidity 61
belief (term) 33
  Caitliceach, as qualifying adjective 33
  creideamh, Irish term for 33
  Protastúnach, as qualifying adjective 33
belief-specific teaching (BST) 59
Bellah, Robert 110
Berkley Center for Religion, Peace and World Affairs 108
Besant, Annie (1847–1933) 22, 25, 83, 166 n.7, 167 n.25
Bible
  African Pentecostals and 127–8
  Hebrew Bible 8
  Protestant schools and 48
  use and impact of 10
Bible-related folklore 38

Blavatsky, Helena 80, 83, 167 n.25
Bocking, Brian 7, 9, 17, 146, 147
    Festschrift for 154
Boole, George 172 n.3
Boyne River, pilgrimage to 26–7
Bramsbäck, Birgit 84
Breen, Michael J. 67
    and Healy, Amy Erbe 66
    and Reynolds, Caillin 65
Brendan, St (d. *c*.575) 40–1
    Navigatio Sancti Brendani 41
Brewer, John 70
    Mote and the Beam, The: Anti-Catholicism in Northern Ireland 69
    Religion, Civil Society and Peace in Northern Ireland 71
Brexit 11, 12, 73, 156
Brigid (goddess) 25
Brigid, St 25, 38
British Academy 9, 155
British Association for the Study of Religions (BASR) 7, 164 n.11
British Empire
    Asian Buddhism and 144, 148, 149
    Dhammaloka and 151
    Ireland and 146
    Irish independence from 153–4
    military, Irishmen in 144
    spread of 148, 149
Bromley, David G., and Melton, J. Gordon 112–13
Bruce, Steve, *God Save Ulster* 69
Bryson, Mary 80
BST *see* belief-specific teaching
Buckland, Ray and Rosemary 27, 167 n.28
Buddha, *Barlaam and Josaphat* and 147–8
Buddha statues
    Baltrasna Buddha 147
    parinibbana Buddha 149
    Sri Lankan wooden statue in UCC 149
Buddhism 17–18, 26, 106, 109
    Asian Buddhists, arrival in Ireland 145
    assertions about 145
    colonialism and 144
    European Buddhists 151–3
    Europeans knowledge of (pre-1850) 147
    historic concerns about 144
    immigrants and 154
    interfaith dialogues 108
    in Ireland 114, 115, 153–4, 155, 156–7, 160
    Ireland and 146–9
    Irish diaspora and 153
    Irish engagement with 145
    Irish study of 146
    Japanese 155
    Jodo Shinshu 150, 153
    Korean (Son) Buddhism 155
    online services 154
    publications on 154–5
    Pure Land 150
    revival in Asia 146
    in San Francisco 173 n.9
    study of religions in Ireland and 145–6
    transmission from East to West 120
    Wesak (Buddhist New Year) 149, 150
    Western converts 154
    see also Irish Buddhists
Buddhist Mission to the West 150
Buddhist Propagation Society 150
Buddhist Theosophical Society (BTS) 150
Bureau of Military History 21
Burke, Peter 33
Burma 147, 151, 152, 154
Butler Burke, Vivian (*c*.1881–1937) 149, 150
Butler, Hubert 170n14
Butler, Jenny 9, 15, 77–89, 159

C of I *see* Church of Ireland
Calvinist literary cultures 10
Canada 151, 152
Carlow College 171 n.10
Carr, James 8
    Experiences of Islamophobia: Living with Racism in the Neoliberal Era 8
Casement, Roger (1864–1916) 27, 169 n.2
Casey, Eamonn, Bishop 140, 141, 171 n.12
Cassidy, Joseph, coadjutor bishop of Clonfert 139
catechetics/catechesis 47, 48, 51, 53
catechisms 42, 48, 53, 114, 128
Catholic charismatic movement 114, 169 n.16
Catholic Church 106
    attendance at services, decline in 17, 135, 142
    charitable and developmental work 17

216 Index

confession, practice of 135
congregation, 'greying'of 135
Corpus Christi, celebration of 90–1, 96, 102
critical attitudes towards 66
decline of 62, 66, 117, 133, 143, 161
dominance in Ireland 114, 160
education, control of 160
Free State and 20, 63, 93, 95
image, tainted by scandals 142–3
institutional church 65, 66
interdenominational system, views on 48–9
in Ireland 73, 132–43, 158, 159, 160
Irish Catholics, typology of 65, 66
Irish Constitution, special position in 64, 114, 116
Mass attendance 64, 67
media communications 142
media (secular) and 64, 133, 140, 141, 158
Ne Temere decree 93, 96, 97, 98, 100, 160
non-attendance, reasons for 135
in Northern Ireland 73
Parnell, rejection of 88
Pentecostals, relationship with 17
perception of 29, 127–8
post-Famine period 42
power in Ireland 106, 160
primary schools, patronage of 14, 45
religious associational culture 133
religious-secular competition and 133–4
Romantic nationalism, perception of 84
secular culture, elements of 136
service-oriented 139–40
social media, use of 141
social policies influenced by 63
social teaching 63
state, separation from 116
Ultramontane campaign 159
vacant pews, challenges of 135, 136
vocations, decline of 17, 137, 142
women and 21, 23, 64, 107
see also Catholic Church abuse scandals; Penal Laws
Catholic Church abuse scandals
child sexual abuse 107, 117, 129–30, 140
clerical abuse 4, 17, 64, 67–8, 129–30, 140
'credibility enhancing displays' (CREDs) 168 n.8
'credibility undermining displays' (CRUDs) 168 n.8
impact of abuse scandals 64, 72–3, 94, 133
media (secular) coverage of 17, 64, 66
in Mother and Baby homes 130
victims, treatment of 159
Catholic clergy
abuse scandals 4, 17, 64, 67–8, 129–30, 140
organizations established by 141
reliance on 134–5
vocations, decline of 17, 137
Catholic Communications Institute of Ireland 141
Catholic culture 113, 117
Catholic *habitus* 14, 15, 63, 64, 65, 66
Catholic hierarchy
civil rights, lobbying for 49
faith, challenges to 142
interdenominational schools, children banned from 49
media communications 141, 142
medical services in Protestant hospitals 99
perception of 159
scandal of personal piety 140
secular discourses 168 n.9
social media, use of 141–2, 172 n.15
state education resisted by 49
Trócaire established by 141
Catholic religiosity 67–8
Catholic religious education (RE) 53–5
Alive O (1996–2004) programme 53
anthropology, influence of 53
challenges facing 55
Children of God series (1973–2005) 53
confessional approach 50, 51, 53, 54, 56, 58, 60, 61
curriculum framework (IEC) 54
Grow in Love (2015–20) programme 54–5
heteronormativity of 55
kerygmatic and experiential approach 54

On Our Way series 53
pluralism and 53
pre-service teachers and 55
shared Christian praxis 54–5
sociology, influence of 53
teacher in-service support, need for 55
Catholic revival 113, 114
Catholic schools 51
  catechetical RE programmes 51
  catechism 48, 53
  challenges facing 55
  kaleidoscope of identities in 55
  LGBTQI families, inclusion of 55
  religious education (RE) in 53–5
Catholic seminaries 113, 138, 139, 143
  repurposing of 171 n.10
Catholic theology 139–40
Catholicism
  African 139
  alternative religions substituted for 109
  anti-Catholicism in Northern Ireland 69
  associations and groups 137
  changes in 10, 104
  Confirmation, commodification of 136
  confraternities/soldalities 137
  conservative, erosion of 94
  cultural Catholicism 66, 67
  devotional-oriented groups 137
  European Catholicism 139
  ex-Catholicism 67
  feminism and 23
  First Communion, commodification of 136
  folk Catholicism, coexistence with 113
  fundamentalist 90, 93, 95–6, 104
  global 141
  golden age of 85
  in Ireland 15, 113, 114, 116, 132–43
  Irish identity and 78, 89, 93, 106
  Jansenism and 114
  modernization, late nineteenth century 44
  national identity and 63
  nationalism and 20, 21, 31, 77
  in Northern Ireland 15
  older traditions and 42
  perception of 116
  persistence in Ireland 15
  post-Catholic Ireland and 66
  post-Famine growth in Ireland 42
  religious-secular competition, Stolz's theory of 17
  sacraments, commodification of 136, 161
  street processions 90–1, 96, 137
  traditional religion and 43
  Tridentine 114
  see also folk Catholicism; Penal Laws
Catholics
  church attendance in Northern Ireland 68–9
  church attendance in the Republic 63
  compartmentalization of practice 66
  creative type 65
  cultural type 65
  decline in numbers 94
  disaffected 94
  discrimination 92, 93, 97
  disenchanted 14, 66, 68, 161
  disillusioned ex-Catholics 16, 66–7
  dispossession in the seventeenth century 92
  ex-Catholics 16, 66–7
  individualist type 14, 65, 66
  institutional church, distancing from 65, 66
  liberal Catholics 65
  orthodox type 65
  population in Ireland 64, 115, 125
  Protestants, association discouraged 93
  self-identification as 143, 161
  typology of Irish Catholics 65
  see also Penal Laws
Celtic culture 85–6, 88
  legend of St Cuán and the serpent 38–40, 41
Celtic Festivals
  Beltaine (*Bealtaine*) 26, 39
  Lughnasa 43
  Samhain 36, 114
Celtic influence 36
Celtic Literary Society 25
Celtic mythology 86, 88
Celtic religious culture 36
Celtic Revival 15, 16, 82
  Anglo-Irish and 85
  development of 83

instigators of 78
O'Grady's role in 83
playwright, Alice Milligan 78, 88
Ulster people's contribution to 88
Yeats and 78, 79, 84
Celtic Tiger 12, 16, 64, 117, 119, 123–4
African immigrants' views on 124–5
immigration policies 123–4
Celts, the 84, 85–6
censorship 63, 116
Central Statistics Office (CSO)
Census (1911) 153
Census (2016) 62, 72, 94, 115, 117, 125, 154, 160
Ceylon (Sri Lanka) 150, 152
Ceylonese Buddhist reformers 150
Christian missionary schools 150
Mahinda College in Galle 150
charismatic Catholics 72, 171 n.3
charismatic Christians 71
charismatic renewal movement 114, 169 n.16
charitable schools 48
Chíl Chuáin (Kilquane) 38, 39
child abuse
Catholic Church and 107, 117, 129–30, 140
Ryan Report (2009) 66, 168 n.4
Children of God series (1973–2005) 53
Children of God (the Family) 106, 112, 114
China 155
Chinese language 156
Christ, Carol (theologian) 25, 29, 166 n.11
'Why Women Need the Goddess' 24
Christian missionaries 120, 146, 150
Christian theology 28
women, Aristotelian concepts of 24
Christianity 10, 62, 109
African forms of 16, 129
in Celtic Tiger Ireland 124–5
early Irish Christianity 36
Eastern European 7
formation of 8
Graeco-Roman literature and 8
Hellenistic philosophy and 8
pre-Christian, use of term 36
supernatural forces and 39
Christians, charismatic 71, 72, 171 n.3

Church of Aphrodite 27
church attendance 168 n.10
Covid-19 pandemic, effects of 17, 72, 136
reductions in 17, 135, 142
Church Education Society 49
Church Fathers 147
Church of the Flying Spaghetti Monster 115
Church of Ireland 30, 55, 91
Census (2016) 64
Church Education Society created by 49
disestablishment of 55, 150
General Synod Board of Education 55–6
patron to co-educational primary schools 55
population decline 94, 104
population in Ireland 125
schools 165 n.25
self-identified Catholics and 105
see also Anglican Church
Church of Ireland religious education 55–6
aims of RE programme 56
diversity of perspectives 56
Follow Me (FM) programme 56
learn about approach 56
learn from approach 56
Reformed tradition 56
themes of RE programme 56
Church of Ireland schools
approach to RE 52
post-primary 46
primary 45
RE programme 55–6
RE in schools 51, 52
Church of Scientology 108, 115
church-state interactions 106, 107, 116
in Mother and Baby Homes 140–1
in post-independence Ireland 139
church-state separation 116, 139
Cill Chuáin (Kilquane) 39–40
civil rights movement 109
Claffey, Patrick 7, 10, 164 n.7
clairvoyance 82
Clarke, Kathleen (1878–1972) 165 n.3
climate change 18
Cloyne Report (2011) 168 n.4

CNS *see* Community National Schools
co-educational primary schools 55
cognitive science of religion 18, 168 n.8
Cold War 10
Collins, Michael 83
colonial history of Ireland 91–4
  British Protestants, plantation of 92
  Catholics, dispossession of 92
colonialism 67, 95, 97
  British colonialism, legacy of 95, 97
  Buddhism and 144
  world religions and 144
Commission to Inquire into Child Abuse (Ryan Report 2009) 66, 168 n.4
Community National Schools (CNS) 47, 49, 50, 51, 57, 58–60
  belief nurturing 59
  belief-specific teaching (BST) 59
  Catholics, sacramental preparation 59
  establishment 58
  Ethical Education and Goodness Me Goodness You! 47
  GMGY, difficulties with 59
  GMGY new curriculum, NCCA and 59–60
  Goodness Me Goodness You! (GMGY) 58–60
  learning into/learning about/learning from approaches 58
  multi-belief and values curricula 47
  RE, belief strand of GMGY 60
Conboy, Seamus 58–9
conflict
  role of religion in 5, 10
  see also Troubles, the
confraternities 17, 42, 133, 137, 142
Confucianism 154
Connolly, James 27
Constitution of Ireland (1937)
  Catholic Church, special position of 64, 114, 116
  Eight Amendment, addition of 153
  Eighth Amendment, repeal of 12, 64, 130
  primary education 49–50
consumer culture 133, 136
consumerism 106, 117, 118
contraception 63, 93, 99
Conway, Brian 10, 17, 158, 159

Conway, Brian, and Spruyt, Bram 67–8
Conway, William, auxiliary Bishop (*later* Cardinal) 138
Corpus Christi 90–1, 96, 102, 169 n.4
Corrymeela Community 71
Cosgrave, O. et al., *Ireland's New Religious Movements* 146
Costigan, Giovanni 85
Counter-Reformation 43
Cousins, James Henry 78, 83
Cousins, Margaret (1878–1954) 22, 30
Covid-19 pandemic 18, 108, 156
  Asian Buddhists in Ireland, effects on 154
  church attendance, effects on 17, 72, 136
  faith, effects on 108
  GAA, social services provided by 158
  interfaith dialogues and 108
  lockdowns 72
  online services and 17, 72, 136
Cox, Laurence 6, 9, 17, 145, 146–7, 150
  and Bocking, Brian 144–57, 160
  Buddhism and Ireland 9, 147, 148, 154
Cox, Laurence, and Ó Laoidh, John 155
Cox, Laurence, and Sirisena, Mihirini 150, 154
Crenshaw, Kimberlé 166 n.4
Croagh Patrick, County Mayo 43, 113
Croker, Bithia, *Road to Mandalay* 144
Crosby, Kate, and Ashin, Janaka 154
Crowley, Vivianne 11
CSO *see* Central Statistics Office
Cuan Mhuire 141
Cuán, St 38–40, 41
Cullen, Paul, Cardinal 159
Cult Awareness Centre, Dublin 115
Cult Awareness Network 115
cult (term) 110, 111
cults 110–11, 112, 113
  anti-cult sentiment 115
  in Ireland 113
  visionary cults 115
  see also new religious movements (NRMs); sects
cultural nationalism 13, 24, 43
  ideology of 33
  importance in Ireland 85

Protestants and 15, 25, 77, 78, 82, 85
utilization of 85
Cumann Gaelach na hEaglaise 30
Cumann na mBan 21, 30, 86, 88, 165 n.3
Cunnane, Finola 47
Curran, Helen Laird (Honor Lavelle) 166 n.19
customs
    bonfires 167 n.2
    calendar custom 36, 37
    hierarchies of value 34
    types of 34

Dalkey School Project 49
Daly, John Bowles (*c*.1844–*c*.1916) 144, 149, 150
    Buddhist Temporalities 150
    Buddhist Theosophical Society (BTS) 150
Daly, Mary 24
Danaher, Kevin, *Year in Ireland, The* 32
Davies, Bronwyn, and Gannon, Suzanne 103
DCU *see* Dublin City University
de Cléir, Síle 11, 13, 32–44, 159
de la Courneuve, Frederick 152
de la Courneuve, Lisette (*née* Stewart) 152
de la Courneuve, Montague Thomas 151–2, 153
de la Courneuve, Stewart Howard Thomas 152
De Sondy, Amanullah 8
de Souza Santos, Boaventura 102, 103
de Zoysa, A. P. 150
Democratic Unionist Party (DUP) 68, 69
Department of Education 50
deprivation 110, 111
Dermody, A. et al., *Signposts: Lessons for Living* 57
desecularization 16, 107, 115, 117, 118
    see also secularization
Despard, Charlotte (1844–1939) 22, 166 n.9
devotions
    church-centred forms of 42, 43
    Counter-Reformation movements 43
    cult of the Sacred Heart 43
    Tridentine nature of 43
Dhammaloka, U 7, 9, 18, 144, 150–3
    alias Carroll, Laurence 149
    alias Colvin 147
    alias O'Rourke, Larry 147
    European Buddhist monks ordained by 151–3
    Rangoon appeal hearing 148
    'Rejoice' Buddhist hymn arranged by 153
    Singapore, mission to 151
Dharmapala, Anagarika 150
Dharmatrata, U 151, 152
Diani, Mario 110
digital humanities 18, 149–50
digital religion 10
Dillon, Michael/Laura (1915–62) 149
Direct Provision (DP) 129
discourses 95–6
    basic functions of 95
    dominant grouping, members of 96
    Foucault's concept of discourse 95, 96
    power, maintenance of 96
discrimination 166 n.4
    African Pentecostals and 130
    anti-Catholic 93, 97
    anti-immigrant 17, 128, 129
    Protestants and 93, 97, 100
Divine Light Mission 114
divorce 20, 99
    Buddhists and 152
    Catholic Church and 63, 65, 116
    Irish referenda on 12, 64
    Muslims and 125
Dixon, Joan 22
Doherty, Donna 47
Dominican Order 43
Donnelly, Philomena 60
Donnelly, Susie 64
Doran, Peter 155
Douglas, Mary 148
Douglass, Frederick 125
Dublin City University (DCU)
    religious education (RE) 6
    School of Theology, Philosophy and Music 5
Dudeism 112
Dudley Edwards, Owen 114
Duggan, Colin 83
Durdin-Robertson, Olivia (1917–2013) 11

e-forum (2016) 72
early Christianty 8, 41
early Irish Christianity 36, 41
EASR *see* European Association for the Study of Religions
Easter Rising (1916) 27, 30, 31, 80, 86, 88
'Easter 1916' (Yeats) 81
ecofeminist movement 24
ECONI *see* Evangelical Contribution on Northern Ireland
economics of religion 18, 165 n.27
Economist, The 121
ecumenical dialogue 61
ecumenics 5, 10, 71
ecumenism 93
Educate Together (ET) 45, 47, 51, 56
   Charter 57
   equality-based education 57
   establishment, reasons for 57
   Ethical Education and Goodness Me Goodness You! 47
   Learn Together Ethical Education Curriculum (2004) 57–8
   learning from approach 58
   Lessons on Humanism 57
   multi-belief and values curricula 47
education
   Catholic Church and 139
   Irish Constitution (Article 42.4) and 49–59
   religious bodies, involvement 46
   third-level, expansion of 117
   see also national system of education; religious education (RE); schools; universities
education about religion and beliefs and ethics (ERBE) 47, 51, 60, 61
Education Act (1998) 50
Education and Training Boards Ireland (ETBI) 45, 59
Elim Pentecostalist Church 114
emigration
   from Ireland 16, 93, 96, 132
   of Protestants 92, 93, 96, 97, 103
   see also immigrants; immigration; migration
English Catholicism 34
English language 156
Epic of Everest (film, 1924) 149

Equality Authority 130–1
equality-based education 52, 56–8
   see also Educate Together
Equiano, Olaudah 125
ERBE *see* education about religion and beliefs and ethics
esotericism 22, 78
   influence of 77, 81–2, 84, 88–9
   Irish revolutionaries and 77
   Protestant Ascendancy and 89
   Western 13, 15, 21
ET *see* Educate Together
ETBI *see* Education and Training Boards Ireland
ethics, faith communities and 108
ethnographic studies 9, 36, 72
ethnological research 32, 33
Europe
   Buddhism, knowledge of (pre-1850) 147
   Buddhist Studies in 155–6
European Association for the Study of Religions (EASR) xiii, 3–4, 6
European Buddhists 151–3
European Catholicism, decentring of 139
European Economic Community (EEC) 116
European missionaries 120
European pluralism 8
European Social Survey 66, 67
European Union (EU) 11
   African immigrants from 126
   EU funded projects 7, 156
European Values Surveys 65, 67
euthanasia 12, 65
Evangelical Contribution on Northern Ireland (ECONI) 70, 71
evangelical Protestants
   in America 108
   in Ireland 104
   in Northern Ireland 68, 69–70
   types of 70
evangelical women 71
evangelicalism
   empirical types of 70
   in Northern Ireland 9–10, 68, 69–70, 71
   political aspects of 68, 69, 71
   Protestant identity and 69

Evangelicals 112
Everest, Sir George 172 n.3
Everest, Mary 172 n.3
ex-Catholics 16, 66–7
extra-institutional religion 21, 30
   concept of 10, 66
   Irish nationalism as 31

Faas, Daniel et al. 12, 57, 60
fairies
   belief in 113
   see also *sidhe*
fairy legends 36, 86
fairytales 37
faith, Covid-19 pandemic and 108
faith schools 46, 52–3, 60
Faivre, Antoine 22
Faivre, Antoine, and Rhone,
   Christine 21–2
Family, the (Children of God) 106, 112, 114
Fanning, Comhall 129
fantasy 38, 104
Feiseanna Ceoil, An 99
Fellowship of the Four Jewels 26, 27
Fellowship of Mount Shasta 27
feminism 21, 23, 88, 154
feminist spirituality 24, 166 n.12
feminist theology 28–9
Ferns Report (2005) 168n4
Fethard Boycott 100
fiction-based religions 112, 115, 116
Fine, the (organization) 26
Fiorenza, Elisabeth Schüssler 21
Flanagan, Marie (*née* Perolz) 31
Focus Ireland 141
Foley, Tadhg 8
folk, concept of 33
folk Catholicism
   coexistence with Catholicism 113
   healing, religious 114
   holy well traditions 42, 43, 113
   Mass rocks, open-air Masses at 113
   revival of 106, 114
   see also Penal Laws
folk culture, idealization of 85
folk religion 13, 16, 33, 106, 118, 159
   organized religion and 113
   patterns 113
   revival of practices 114, 116

folk tradition
   Christianity as a term of reference 36
   May Eve bonfires 167 n.2
   'otherworld', use of the term 36
   St John's Eve bonfires 167 n.2
   understanding religion in 35–7
   see also Celtic Festivals; rituals
folklore
   collectors of 88
   oral traditions 32
   religious elements in 35–7
   religious elements, meaning/
      interpretation of 37–42
   in rural communities 33
   Russell's (Æ) interest in 82
   in urban communities 33
   Yeats's interest in 79, 81
   Young's interest in 24
folklore collection
   hierarchies of value 34
   in Ireland 33, 34, 35–7
   Irish language, importance of 33
   National Folklore Collection 32
Folklore of Ireland Council 35–6
folklore scholarship 34–5, 167 n.1
Follow Me (FM) programme 56
Foras Pátrúnachta, An 45, 49
   Irish-medium schools 49, 56
   multi-denominational schools 56–7
Forum and Patronage and Pluralism
   Report (2012) 51
Foster, Robert Fitzroy 79
Foucault, Michel 16, 91, 94, 102
   discourse, concept of 95, 96
   domination 97–8
   history 97
   power, concept of 94–5, 104
   subject, use of term 102
Fournier, E. E. 25
Fox, Charlotte Milligan 88
Francis, Pope 172 n.18
Franck, Harry 148
fraternities, decline of 17
Free Presbyterian Church 69
Free State xiii, 11, 153
   Catholic Church's role 20, 63, 93
   Catholic religion and 63
   Catholic self-image of 15, 31, 63, 77, 93

censorship 63
economic policies 63
national schools, management of 45, 49
protectionism 63
Protestant schools 49
Protestants, integration of 92-3
Protestants, sidelining of 15, 93
religious instruction (RI) 47
social policies, Catholic Church's influence on 63
Freire, Paolo 102, 103

Gaelic Athletic Association (GAA) 135, 158
Gaelic culture, Protestants and 16, 92
Gaelic League 30, 84, 88
Gaeltacht areas 33-4, 43
Ganiel, Gladys
  evangelicalism 9-10
  extra-institutional religion, concept of 10, 21, 30
  sociology of religion 5, 14, 16, 62-73, 158, 159
Gay Liberation movement 109
Geertz, Clifford 24, 31
gendered ideologies 22
gendered structural oppression 22
General Synod Board of Education 55-6
Geneva Convention 128
Germany 5, 9
Gibson, Robert 149
Giddens, Anthony 117
Gidlow, Elsa (1898-1986) 27, 167 n.27
Gifford sisters 30
Githens-Mazar, Jonathan 84-5
Glendenning, Dympna 49
global Catholicism 141
Global North
  migration to 120, 122, 124
  transnational migrations 120-1
global religious movements 114
Global South
  migration from 120, 122, 123, 124
  religious ideologies in 123
  transnational migrations 120-1
globalization 93, 108, 117, 123, 124
  religious globalization 123
  tradition, effects on 109

Glock, Charles, and Stark, Rodney 111
God
  belief in 171n6
  symbolization as male 24
Goddess, symbol of 24, 25
Goedhals, Antony 155
Golden Dawn *see* Hermetic Order of the Golden Dawn
Gongga, Elder 155
Gonne, Iseult 30, 87
Gonne, Maud (1866-1953) 13, 22
  Catholicism, conversion to 30
  Celtic Revival 78
  daughter, Iseult 30, 87
  death of son 87
  illustrations by 25, 86
  Inghinidhe na hÉireann founded by 25, 88
  Irish nationalism and 87-8
  L'Irelande Libre, contribution to 87
  Millevoye, relationship with 87
  occult, interest in 87
  perception of 87
  reincarnation, vision of 30
  renegotiation of religion 26, 30
  Romantic nationalism 87
  theatrical performances 87-8
  Western esotericism, interest in 30
  Yeats and 80, 87, 167n26
Good Friday Agreement (1998) 11, 68
Good Shepherd Sisters 140-1
Goodman, N., ways of world-making 18
Goodness Me Goodness You! (GMGY) 58-60
  new curriculum, NCCA and 59
  pluralist approach 59-60
  Toledo Guiding Principles, influence of 60
Gore-Booth, Eva (1870-1926) 13, 20, 22, 23-4
  Christianity, renegotiation of 29
  Death of Fionavar from the Triumph of Maeve, The 25
  'Inner Life of a Child, The' 28
  labour activism 28
  letters from Constance (sister) 165 n.1
  Mary Magdalene, depiction of 28-9
  the 'New Woman' 28-9

poetry 23–4, 28, 86–7
Psychological and Poetic Approach to the Study of Christ in the Fourth Gospel, A 28, 29
suffrage and 28
theological works 28, 29
theosophy, interest in 86
Three Resurrections and Triumph of Maeve, The 25
Gospel choir 136
Gospels, the 54, 167 n.32
Graham, Billy, missions to Ireland 16, 114
Grand, Sarah (1854–1943) 28
Gray, B. 12
Gregory, Augusta, Lady 79
Gribben, Crawford
  God's Irishmen: Theological Debates in Cromwellian Ireland 10
  'Radical Religion in the Trans-Atlantic World, 1500–1800' project 10
  Rise and Fall of Christian Ireland, The 10
Grieser, Alexandra 8, 12
Griffin, Victor, Dean of St Patrick's Cathedral, Dublin 100
Grimmitt, Michael 52
Groome, Tom 54
Grow in Love (2015–20) programme 54–5
Guinness, Selina 79
Gujaratis, in Britain 121
Guzy, Lidia 7–8

Hadromi-Allouche, Zohar 8
Hanafin, Mary 58
Hanegraaff, Wouter 21
Hare Krishna (ISKCON) 112, 115, 118
Harris, Alana 34
healing practices 115
  among Pentecostal Africans 9
  healing powers, belief in 114
  holy wells, belief in 113
Health Service Executive (HSE) 145
Healy, A. E., and Breen, M. 67
Healy, John, Archbishop of Tuam 43
Healy, John Paul 110
Hearn, Lafcadio (1850–1904) 8, 144, 149, 155
Hearn, William Edward (1826–88) 8
Heath-Carpentier, Amy 11, 13, 20–31, 159

Heavenly Culture, World Peace and the Restoration of Light (HWPL) 108
Hebrew Bible 8
Henry, Seán 55
Hermetic Order of the Golden Dawn 15, 22, 80
Hermetic Society 26, 80, 86
Hewitt, Seán 81–2
Hikkaduwe Sumangala (Buddhist monk) 150
Hill of Tara, pilgrimages to 30
Hilliard, Betty 64
Hinduism 26, 108, 109, 160
  interfaith dialogues 108
  in Ireland 113, 115
  Vedas, the 30, 83
Holbek, Bengt 37
Holy Catholic Ireland 77
holy wells 37, 40–1, 42, 43, 113
'homeless mind' 110
homelessness in Dublin 141
homosexuality 65, 68
Horan, Revd Richard 114
Houghton, Cherrie (*née* Matheson) 81
Humanist Association of Ireland 57
Hurley, Michael, SJ 5
HWPL *see* Heavenly Culture, World Peace and the Restoration of Light
Hyde, Douglas (1860–1949) 24, 35, 37, 79
  Irish language, views on 166 n.13
  Religious Songs of Connacht 32
Hydes-Lee, Georgina (Georgie) (*later* Yeats) 80, 81
Hyland, Áine, and Bocking, Brian 47–8

IAHR *see* International Association for the History of Religions
ICC *see* Irish Council of Churches
identity 94–105
  change, evangelical contributions to 10
  ethnic and religious identity in Ireland 67, 159
  Irish identity 78, 89, 93, 106
  islands of identity 42
  of minority groups 94
  power and 94–7
  religion and 12, 16, 31, 37, 42, 68
  see also Irish identity; Protestant identity

ideology of separate spheres 23
  private/domestic sphere, women and 22, 23
  public sphere, men and 22
  religion and 22
IEC *see* Irish Episcopal Conference
immigrants
  anti-immigrant activism 128, 129
  Buddhist 154, 156, 157, 160
  marginalization of 104
  Protestant 104, 160
  re-evangelization of the Irish 72, 128
  religion and 71–2, 94, 119–31
  religion, importance of 121
  religious activism 121, 125
  self-consciousness of 121
immigration
  anti-immigration rhetoric 17
  to Ireland 18, 71–2, 94, 104, 106, 156, 160
Immigration Control Platform 128
India 7, 144, 150
  British India 152
  culture 84
  Irish universities and 155
  partition of 11
  religions 146
  sacred music of 8
  Tibetan Buddhist pilgrimage culture 155
Indian ascetics 147
Indian Civil Service 151, 155
Indian Home Rule movement 83
Indian nationalism 83–4, 166 n.7
individualism 109, 112, 118
industrial schools 66, 72, 117
Inghinidhe na hÉireann 20, 25, 27
  Bean na hÉireann journal 88
  membership 25
  perception of 25
  repository of empowering symbols created 25
Inglis, Tom xiv, 14–15, 158–61
  Irish Catholics, typology of 65, 66
  Moral Monopoly: The Catholic Church in Modern Irish Society 14, 63
  Rise and Fall of the Catholic Church in Modern Ireland, The 63–4
inter-religious literacy 54, 55

interdenominational schools 49, 51
interdenominational (term) 47
interfaith dialogue 108, 155
International Association for the History of Religions (IAHR) 4, 6
international folk narrative repertoire 37
International Society for Krishna Consciousness *see* ISKCON
involuntary migration 120, 121
Ipgrave, Julia 60
Iraq, flight of Yazidis from 121
Ireland
  colonial history of 91–4
  ethnic categories in 92
  migrations from Britain 122
  Protestant migrants 122
Ireland, Republic of
  African immigrants' preconception of 124–5, 129
  anti-religious sentiment 67
  Buddhism in 153–4
  Catholic Church and 20
  Catholicism, persistence of 15
  changes in the new millennium 93–4
  church-state hegemony 106
  counterculture 153
  cultural diversity of 146
  economic growth 63, 64, 116
  ethno-religious environment 16
  Holy Catholic Ireland, image of 77
  immigration 18, 71–2, 94, 106, 156, 160
  immigration policies 123–4, 128, 130
  multiculturalism 16, 57, 94
  partition of 11, 12
  political parties 165 n.22
  post-Catholic Ireland 66
  post-primary schools 45–6
  primary schools 45
  protectionism, end of 63
  Protestant minority in 90, 96, 101
  Protestants' experience of 15, 16
  religious education at primary level 45–61
  religious persistence in 14, 15, 65, 66
  revolutionary period (1912–23) 11, 13
  secularization 14–15
  social changes (1960s, 1970s) 106
  woman, conceptions of Ireland as 25, 87
  see also Celtic Tiger

Ireland's Eye 26
Irenaeus, St 53
Irish Agricultural Organisation Society 82
Irish Bishops' Conference 141
Irish Buddhism 147
Irish Buddhist Union 155
Irish Buddhists 9, 17, 18, 113, 144, 156, 157
  in Asia 149–50
  census returns 149, 153, 154
  multiple meanings of 144, 145
  see also Buddhism; Burke, Vivian Butler; Daly, John Bowles; Dhammaloka, U; Hearn, Lafcadio; Pfoundes, Charles James
Irish Citizen 22–3, 88
Irish Citizen Army (ICA) 21
Irish citizenship
  African immigrants and 126
  redefinition of 129
Irish Civil War (1922–3) 20
Irish Council of Churches (ICC) 127
Irish Council of Imams 115
Irish Countrywomen's Association (ICA) 99
Irish diaspora 12, 156
  Buddhism and 153
  estimated size of 165 n.23
Irish Episcopal Conference (IEC) 51, 53, 54
  RE curriculum framework (2015) 54
Irish Folk Song Society 88
Irish Folklore Commission 35
Irish healthcare, religion and 145
Irish history
  British ignorance of 12
  protagonists, stereotyping of 12
Irish Homestead 82
Irish identity, Catholicism and 78, 89, 93, 106
Irish independence 153–4
  Protestants' role in 77–8
Irish Ireland, concept of 77–8
Irish Journal of Sociology 72
Irish language 30
  decline of 42
  importance in folklore collection 33
  Irish-medium schools 49, 56–7
  Jesuit order and 168 n.13

Leabhar Ser Marco Polo 148
literary tradition, hybridity of 32
Middle Irish, Alexander texts translated into 147
oral religious tradition in 35
promotion of 24
religious tradition and 43
traditional prayers 42
'vernacular' traditions preserved in 13, 33
Irish missionaries 17, 124
Irish Mormons 10, 72
Irish national identity, Catholicism and 63
Irish nationalism/nationalists
  Anglo-Irish and 86
  Asian anti-imperial group, links with 114
  Catholicism and 20, 21, 31, 77
  as extra-institutional religion 31
  feminism and 88
  mythic themes as emblem of 87–8
  nationalists, advanced 165 n.2
  Protestants and 78
  women at the heart of 20, 21
Irish Network for Studies in Buddhism 155
Irish Religious Beliefs (RTÉ series) 114
Irish School of Ecumenics (ISE) 5
Irish Society for the Academic Study of Religions (ISASR) 3–4, 6, 146, 154
  annual conferences 7
  Constitution 163 n.5
  journal *JISASR* 7
Irish Society of Diviners 114
Irish Statesman 81
Irish Times 127
Irish Women's Franchise League (IWFL) 31
Irish-medium schools 49, 56–7
Irishness
  Celtic culture and 79
  concept of 77–8, 97, 104
  deconstruction of 118
  definition of true Irishness 95
  exclusion of Protestants 78
ISASR see Irish Society for the Academic Study of Religions
ISE see Irish School of Ecumenics
Isis, Irish High Priestess of 11

ISKCON (Hare Krishna) 112, 115, 118
Islam 16, 17, 109, 117
   in Ireland 9, 113, 115, 119, 123, 125, 130, 160
   propagators in Africa 120
   in Western countries 123
Islamic Cultural Centre of Ireland 61, 125
Islamic schools 165 n.25
Islamic studies 8, 61
Islamophobia 8
islands of identity 42
Ivakhiv, Adrian J. 25
IWFL *see* Irish Women's Franchise League

Jackson, Kenneth 38, 39
Jackson, Robert, interpretative approach 60
Jacob's Biscuits 170 n.13
James of Ireland 148
Jansenism 114
Japan 9, 150, 154
   Buddhism 155
   Pure Land (Jodo Shinshu) Buddhists 150
   Tokugawa writings 154
   Zen training 153
Japanese mountain asceticism 9
Jediism/Jediists 112, 115
Jehovah's Witnesses 114, 115
Jesuits, Irish-language publications 168 n.13
Jesus, story-based pedagogy and 54
Jesus Centre in Dublin City 72
Jewish community in Ireland 114, 164 n.9
Jewish schools 49, 51, 52, 165 n.25
JISASR see Journal of the Irish Society for the Academic Study of Religions
Jivaka, Lobsang 149
Jodo Shinshu 150, 153
Johnson, Benton 112
Johnston Graf, Susan 81, 169 n.1
Jonestown massacre 110
Journal of the Irish Society for the Academic Study of Religions (*JISASR*) 7, 8–9, 154–5
Journal of Religion in Japan 155
Joyce, James
   Dubliners 83
   Ulysses 83, 149

Joynt, Maud (1868–1940) 13, 22
   article in the *Irish Citizen* 22–3
Judaism 109, 114
Judge, William Quan 26, 167 n.25
Jung, Carl Gustav 11

Kalmar, Birgitta 155
Kapaló, James, 'Creative Agency and Religious Minorities' 7
Keane, Revd Michael 132
Kearney, Jonathan 10
Kelleher, Margaret 81
Kelly, Aidan 26
Kieran, Patricia 10, 12, 14, 45–61, 160
King, J. D. 53
Kipling, Rudyard, *Kim* 144
Kirby, Dianne 10
   'Religion and the Cold War' 10
   'Religious Women and the Troubles' 10
Kirichenko, Alexey 147
Kmec, Vladimír 70
Knock Marriage Bureau 132
Knock shrine, County Mayo 143, 172 n.18
Korean (Son) Buddhism 155
Kraft, Siv Ellen 22
Kuusisto, Arniika, and Gearon, Liam 46
kyriarchy 13, 21, 22, 29, 31

Laffère, Atha 153
Laffère, Richard Lawson 151, 152–3
Laird, Helen (1874–1957) 25, 26
land, the, figurations as divine 25–6
Lane, Dermot 51, 52
Larkin, Emmet 42, 43
Late, Late, The (chat show) 64
Learn Together Ethical Education Curriculum (Educate Together 2004) 57, 58
legends
   fairy legends 36, 86
   St Brendan, Easter Sunday mass 40–1
   St Cuán and the Serpent 38–40, 41
Legion of Mary 91, 137
Lemass, Seán 116
Levitt, Peggy 123
LGBTQI families 55, 154
Liebmann, Janet 29
Light of Asia 153

Limerick City
    anti-slave trade activists 125
    Catholic religion in 41–2
    St Patrick, sayings and anecdotes about 43
L'Irlande Libre 87
literacy
    expansion across society 114
    inter-religious 54, 55
    religious 50, 51, 54
Literary Revival 77, 78, 83, 84
    Celtic mythology and 86, 88–9
'lived experience' 13–14
Lodge, Anne 49
Logan, Penny 121
Loyola Institute 5
Lughnasa (Celtic festival) 43
Lutheran congregation 72
Lysaght, Patricia 43

McAleese Report (2013) 168n4
Macardle, Dorothy (1889–1958) 23, 27–8
Macauliffe, Max Arthur 7, 8–9, 148
McDonald, Revd Michael 43
McNamara, Brendan, *Reception of 'Abdu'l-Bahá in Britain, The: East Comes West* 9
MacNeill, Máire 43
McQuaid, John Charles, Archbishop (1895–1973) 16, 93, 160
Macra na Feirme (farming organization) 99
MacSwiney, Mary (1872–1942) 165 n.3
MacSwiney, Muriel (*née* Murphy) (1892–1982) 23
McVerry, Peter, SJ 141
Madden, Gerard 10
Magdalene laundries 117, 140, 168 n.4
Magic Circle 16, 114
magic as part of fantasy 37–8
magical groups 15
magical practices 79, 80, 84
Magliocco, Sabina 34
Maha Bodhi Society, Calcutta 150
Mahinda College, Galle, Ceylon 150
Malešević, Vesna 16, 65, 106–18, 160
Mallory/Irvine expedition 149
Mandeville, Sir John, *Travels of Sir John Mandeville* 148

Manson Family 110
Marginalised and Endangered Worldviews Study Centre (MEWSC) 7
marginalization
    effects of 103
    of immigrants 104
    of minority-belief children 57
    of Protestants 93, 96, 97, 98, 102, 103, 104
    of women 21
    see also alienation
Marian apparitions 115, 169 n.16
Markievicz, Constance (*née* Gore-Booth) (1868–1927) 13, 20, 21, 22, 24, 86
    address to the Irish Women's Franchise League 20, 31
    Bean na hÉireann, contributions to 88
    Churches, perception of 29
    illustrations 25
    imprisonment 25, 165 n.1
    letters to Eva (sister) 165 n.1
    pen names 88
    pilgrimage to the River Boyne 26–7
    Protestant Ascendancy background 22
    Young, Ella and 27
marriage
    Buddhist rites 152
    Ceylonese rules 152
    Fethard Boycott and 100
    'mixed' marriages 93, 98, 100
    same-sex 12, 64, 160
    see also Knock Marriage Bureau; *Ne Temere* decree
marriage bar 116
marriage counselling 134
Martin, Eamon, Archbishhop of Armagh 172 n.15
Martin, St, feast of 36
Massey, Douglas, and Higgins, Monica 121
Mater Dei Institute 5
materialism 106, 117, 118, 136
Mathers, Samuel Liddell MacGregor 80
May Day, legend associated with 39
May Eve 167 n.2
Maynooth University (MU) 6, 30–1
    Centre for the Study of Irish Protestantism 169 n.3
    female Dean of Faculty appointed 30–1

international conference, Maynooth (2009) 6, 146–7
me-society, emergence of 133
media (secular)
　abuse, coverage of 64, 66
　Catholic Church and 64, 133, 140, 141, 142
　as moral guardian 158–9
　as rival 'pulpit' 133
　role in everyday lives 140
　Vatican II, coverage of 64
meditation 115, 118, 161
Mella, Orlando 122
Melton, J. Gordon 109
mental health issues 134
Messenger, John 33
Metcalf, Barbara 121
Methodist religious education (RE), *Follow Me* (FM) programme 56
Methodist schools 46, 51
Methodists 48, 72
methodological agnosticism 5
Metro Éireann 126
MEWSC *see* Marginalised and Endangered Worldviews Study Centre
migrant chaplains 72
migrant religions 16, 115, 117
　contemporary contexts 123–5
　in Ireland 119–31
migration
　involuntary 120, 121
　new religious movements (NRMs) and 109
　religion and 120–2
　to Ireland 16
　voluntary 120
　see also emigration; immigrants; immigration
Millevoye, Lucien 87
Milligan, Alice 88–9
　'At Maynooth' (poem) 88
　'Bonnie Charlie' (poem) 88
　Celtic Revival and 78, 88
　Glimpses of Erin (tourist guide) 88
　pen name, Iris Olkyrn (I.O.) 88
　Shan Van Vocht, editorship of 88
mindfulness 155, 161
missionaries
　in Ceylon 150

Christian 120, 146, 150
European 120, 129
Irish 17, 124, 148
Mitchell, Claire 69, 71
Model schools 50
modernization 106, 107, 109, 116, 118
Molony, Helena 27, 30, 88
'Money Cult' 117
monotheism 8
Moonies 106, 114, 115
morality 29
　the church and 158
　media and 158–9
　religious 116
Moran, Gabriel 53
Mormons 10, 72, 106, 114, 115
Morris, Kenneth Vennor (Cenydd Morus) 86
Mother and Baby Homes
　Catholic-run 140–1
　Protestant-run 100
　report into (2021) 140
　state funding of 140
Mother and Baby Homes Commission of Investigation (2021) 168 n.4
motherland, weaponization of 25–6
Mouzelis, Nicos 117
MU *see* Maynooth University
Mulholland, Peter 169n16
multi-denominational religious education 56–8, 61
multi-denominational schools 45, 46, 51
　Dalkey School Project 49
　Educate Together (ET) 56
　learning about approach to RE 52
　learning from approach to RE 52
　learning into approach to RE 52
　new state model, CNS 58
　patron bodies 45, 56
　types in Ireland 56–7
　see also Community National Schools
multi-denominational (term) 47, 59
multiculturalism 16, 57, 94, 131
Murphy, John L. 147
Murphy, Liam 71
Murphy Report (2009) 66, 168 n.4
Murphy, Rose 86
museums 8, 32, 149

Muslim schools 46, 49, 51
Muslims 108
  African 125
  Asian 125
  in Australia 8
  flight from Myanmar 121
  integration in Ireland 8, 72
  interfaith dialogues 108
  in Ireland 113, 114, 115, 119, 125
  Irish nationality 125
  population in Ireland 125
  in Western societies 8
Myanmar, Muslims' flight from 121
mysticism 26
mythology 24
  Celtic 82, 86, 88
  Irish mythology 82–3
  Russell's (Æ) use of 82–3
  Tuatha Dé Danann 88
  Yeats's use of 82–3

Nally, Claire 79, 85
National Catechetical Programme 53
National Consultative Committee on Racism and Interculturalism (NCCRI) 130–1
National Council for Curriculum and Assessment (NCCA) 50, 51
  Draft Primary Curriculum Framework (2020) 48, 61
  GMGY, new curriculum 59–60
  Wellbeing, focus on 60
National Directory for Catechesis in Ireland 53
  Share the Good News 53
National Folklore Collection 32
National Synodal Assembly 142, 172 n.16
national system of education
  Catholic authorities' views on 48
  establishment in Ireland 47, 49, 113–14
  interdenominational system 48
  literacy, expansion of 114
  RE partitioned from secular subjects 48
  religious education, use of term 47
  Stanley Letter and 47, 48
  see also primary schools
nationalist organizations, prohibition of women 25
nationalist women 13, 20, 21, 29–30, 31

NCCA *see* National Council for Curriculum and Assessment
NCCRI *see* National Consultative Committee on Racism and Interculturalism
Ne Temere decree (1910) 170 n.10
  Catholic Church's enforcement of 93, 96, 97, 160
  effects of 100
  enforcement in Ireland 93, 96, 97, 98, 160, 170 nn.10–11
  existential threat to the minority 98
  Irish state's support of 93
  Protestant silence about 100, 102
Neary, A. et al. 12
Neary, Michael, Archbishop of Tuam 172 n.13
neo-paganism 24, 25–6, 27
  earth gendered as female 25
  Irish sources to construct 26
  see also paganism
Neo-Pentacostalism 112
neo-secularization 65–6
Neocatechumenal Way 143, 172 n.18
neoliberal therapy culture 155
Netherlands 5, 108, 122
neuro-humanities *see* digital humanities
New Age movement 115, 118
New Age spiritualities 106, 116, 118
new religious movements (NRMs) 106, 107, 109–13, 110, 161
  alternative spiritualities in Ireland 113–15
  charismatic leaders and 109
  common characteristics 109
  counterculture, part of 110
  deprivation and 110, 111
  fundamentalist NRMs 109
  main (ideal) types of 112
  modernity and 110
  proliferation in the 1960s/1970s 109, 160
  proliferation in Ireland 116, 160
  proselytization and 114
  re-emergence of 116
  reasons for joining 111
  social change, response to 110
  typologies of 111–13
  in the United States 110, 114

world-accommodating movements 112
world-affirming movements 112
world-rejecting movements 112, 118
New Testament, index of stories about 38
Newfoundland 9, 11
Newton International Research Project 155
Ní Shéaghdha, Nóra 39–40
Nic Einrí, Úna 43
Nic Shionnaigh, Móirín (Olive Fox) 26, 27, 167 n.24
Niebuhr, H. Richard 111–12
Nigeria 124, 139
9/11 attacks in the United States 120, 123
Nivedita, Sister (Margaret Noble) 8
'no religion'
  in Census returns 64–5, 115, 117, 129
  North-South comparisons 73
  younger-age cohorts and 135
Noble, Margaret (Sister Nivedita) 8
Nolan, Finbar (faith healer) 114
non-Christian religions 71, 72
non-Christian religious phenomena 36
nonconformist minister 90–1, 94, 95–6, 97, 102–3
nonconformists 15, 90–1, 97
Norris, Pippa, and Inglehart, Ronald 67
Northern Ireland
  Anglican Church 10
  anti-Catholicism 69
  Calvinistic theology, Protestant identity and 69
  Catholic community 68
  Catholicism 15
  church attendance 68–9
  evangelical movement, Calvinistic 68
  evangelicalism 9–10, 68, 69–70, 71
  Good Friday Agreement (1998) 11, 68
  migration of Southern Protestants 93
  partition and 11, 63, 68
  peacebuilding organizations 70, 71
  politics, religion and 69
  power-sharing assembly 68, 70
  Protestant community 68, 90, 159
  Protestantism 15
  religion as an ethnic-marker 15, 69
  religious differences 63, 68, 159
  secularization 68, 69
  sociology of religion in 68–71
  Troubles, the 10, 20, 62, 68, 69, 146, 153
  unionist privilege in 68, 70
NRMs *see* new religious movements
numerology 81
nuns
  Mother and Baby Homes and 140–1
  organizations established by 141
  reduction in number of 138–9
  see also religious orders
Nuttall, Deirdre 11, 78
Nuttall, Deirdre, and Walsh, Tony 5, 15, 90–105, 159

O'Brien, Hazel 10, 72
O'Brolchain, Máire (*née* Ní Cillín) 25
O'Callaghan, Revd Charles 138
occult/occultism 15, 77, 78, 83, 87, 89
  Æ's interest in 82–3
  Georgie Yeats's interest in 80, 81
  Gonne and 87
  sex-magic, practice of 81
  Synge's interest in 81
  vision of ancient Ireland 84
  Yeats's interest in 79, 80, 82–3
O'Connor, Anne 38
Ó Crualaoich, Gearóid 35, 41
O'Donoghue, Thomas 53
Odoric of Pordenone 148
O'Driscoll, Teig 30
Ó Giolláin, Diarmuid 32
O'Grady, Standish 83
O'Halloran, Maura Soshin 153
  Pure Heart, Enlightened Mind 153
Ó hAnnracháin, Tadhg 122
Ó Héalaí, Pádraig 38
Ó hEochaidh, S., and Ó Catháin, S. 37
Ó hÓgáin, Dáithí 41
O'Kane, Revd Paddy 136
Ó Laoidh, John 155
Olcott, Colonel Henry S. 150, 166 n.20
'Ollthaigh' (Ulsterwomen), special powers of 41
On Our Way (RI series) 53
online dating agencies 132
online religious services
  Buddhist 154, 156
  interfaith programme 108
  in Ireland 72, 136
oral history 10, 32

Oral History Online 10
oral tradition 38
Organization for Security and
  Co-operation in Europe (OSCE) 60
oriental world, stereotypes about 120
Orthodox Christians 115, 117
OSCE *see* Organization for Security and
  Co-operation in Europe
Ó Súilleabháin, Seán
  Miraculous Plenty 34, 38
  Scéalta Cráibhtheacha 34, 38
'othering' 170 n.9
  of Protestants 93, 96, 99–101, 160
otherworld
  in Irish folk tradition 36, 79
  legend of St Cuán and the Serpent
    38–40, 41
  piseoga 36
  themes and beliefs 36–7
  see also fairies; fairy legends; *sidhe*
Owenson, Sydney, *Wild Irish Girl, The* 148

Pabst, Adrian 117
Padoan, Tatsuma, 'Semiotics of Sacred
  Geography, A' 9, 155
pagan beliefs, in Ireland 113
pagan festivals, in Ireland 114
pagan symbols 84
pagan (term) 36
paganism 114, 115
  contemporary 9, 11
  see also neo-paganism
paideia (educational cultures) 8
Paisley, Revd Ian 10, 69, 70
Palatines 48
Para-Religious movements 109
paranormal 83
Parnell, Charles Stewart 87, 88
partition of India 11
partition of Ireland 11, 12, 68
  churches post-partition 62
  Northern Ireland and 11, 63, 68
  religious differences solidified by 63
Pastafarians 115
patriarchy 22, 29
Patrick, St 38, 39, 43
peace processes
  (1) intellectual spaces 70
  (2) institutional spaces 70

(3) market spaces 70
(4) political spaces 70
role of religion in 5, 70
sociology of 70
peacebuilding
  church leaders, role of 71
  Corrymeela Community 71
  ECONI 70, 71
  evangelical contributions to 10
  faith-based 71
  institutional religions and 70, 71
  marginal actors (mavericks) 70, 71
  minority religious groups and 70–1
  in Northern Ireland 71
  prayer, role of 71
Pearse, Pádraig 86
Penal Laws (1695–1829) 11, 48, 85, 113
Pentecostal Africans *see* African
  Pentcostals
Pentecostal churches 17, 94, 104, 126,
  127
Pentecostal ideologies 122
Pentecostalism 126
  growth in Ireland 125
  Holy Spirit, the role of 126
  multi-ethnic congregations 126
  multiracial communities 126
Peter McVerry Trust 141
Peter, St 29
Pevarello, Daniele 8
Pew Research Center 64–5, 108
Pfoundes, Charles James (*né* Pounds)
  (1840–1907) 144, 149–50
  Buddhist Mission to the West 150
  Buddhist Propagation Society 150
  Japan, culture and religion of 9, 150
phenomenological tradition 5
philosophy
  Asian 145, 172 n.1
  children and 59, 60
  Hellenistic 8
pilgrimage(s)
  older practices 43
  places of 42
  'Semiotics of Sacred Geography,
    A' 9, 155
  Tibetan Buddhist 155
  to holy wells 113
  to Knock, County Mayo 143

Pioneer Total Abstinence Association 137
piseoga 36
Pius XII, Pope 138
Plaskow, Judith (1947–present) 29
pluralism 8, 51, 53, 57, 116
political parties in Ireland 165 n.22
Polo, Marco 148
   Leabhar Ser Marco Polo 148
popular culture 33
popular religion 33
Portlaoise parish, County Laois 136, 143
Portugal 6, 65, 67
post-Catholic folk religion 116, 118
post-Catholic Ireland 10, 66, 72
post-primary schools 45–6
   Catholic 45–6
   Church of Ireland 46
   Methodist 46
   multi-denominational 46
   Presbyterian 46
   Protestant ethos 46
   Society of Friends 46
post-secular university 19
postmodernism 120
   immigrant religious activism in 121
power
   discourses and 95–6
   Foucault's concept of 94–5, 97–8, 104
   fundamentalist Catholic
     nationalism and 95
   institutionalization of 95
   making power visible 96–7
   resistance to 97–8
prayer
   decline of Irish language and 42
   increase in 72
   peacebuilding, role in 71
   rosary prayer 43, 113
   sociology of prayer 71
   sociopolitical effect of 71
pre-Christian times 36, 113
pre-modern societies 32
Presbyterian Church 10
Presbyterian religious education 56
Presbyterian schools 46, 51
Presbyterians 22, 48, 105, 115
primary schools
   Catholic Church and 14, 45
   central place and potency of RE 46–7

Church of Ireland 45
   ERBE curriculum recommendation 51
   faith school sector 46, 52
   Forum and Patronage and Pluralism
     Report (2012) 51
   Irish-medium 49
   Jewish 46, 49, 52
   multi-denominational 14, 45, 49
   Muslim 46, 49
   religious education (RE) 14, 45–61
Primiano, Leonard 33
proselytization 54
   Catholic concerns 48
   in Ireland 114
   new religious movements and 114
Protestant Ascendancy 15, 22, 78, 85, 159
   esotericism, interest in 89
   exploitation of urban and rural
     workers 22
   perception of 91, 169 n.6
   Romantic nationalism and 84, 89
Protestant businesses 99, 101, 170 n.13
Protestant denominations 159
   growth in 72, 94
   immigrants and 94
   in Ireland 114
Protestant dissenters 48
Protestant identity 94
   British colonialism, legacy of 95
   change and liminality 103–5
   community 98–9, 101, 102
   complexity 101–2
   existential unsustainability,
     implications of 103
   facets of 98–105
   fundamentalist Catholicism and 95–6
   'identity in opposition' 101, 104
   in Northern Ireland 69
   in the Republic 5, 90, 97
   silence 99–101, 102
   subjected forms of feeling 102–3
Protestant schools
   Bible reading 48
   Free State and 49
   RE, approach to 52
   Reformed Christian tradition 52
   religious instruction 48
Protestant society, characterization
   of 98–9

Protestant women 159
  Hermetic Order of the Golden
    Dawn and 22
  Theosophical Society and 22
Protestant writers 170 n.14
Protestantism
  as an acceptable alternative 94
  colonial history and 91–4, 97
  demonization of 97
  disaffected Catholics and 94
  ethno-national identity in NI 15
  growth in numbers 94, 104
  in the Irish Republic 10, 101
  in Northern Ireland 15, 169 n.2
  perception of 15, 29, 97
  privilege, association with 92
  resilience of 105
  Synge's rejection of 78, 81–2
  traditional communities, decline in 105
  women's mission 23
Protestants
  alienation, sense of 91, 92, 102
  Catholic Church holidays and 90–1, 96
  Catholics discouraged from association
    with 93
  church attendance in Northern
    Ireland 68–9
  co-religionists in Northern Ireland,
    abandonment by 97
  colonial history of Ireland 91–4, 97
  cross-community organizations and 99
  cultural legacy 99
  discrimination 93, 97, 100
  diverse experiences of 101
  diversity within 92
  educational system 98–9
  emigration 92, 93, 96, 97, 103
  evangelicalism and 69–70
  Fethard Boycott 100
  in the Free State 92
  Gaelic culture and 16, 92
  growth in numbers 94, 104
  immigrants from Britain 122–3
  immigration, effects of 104, 160
  in Ireland 90, 92–3, 159–60
  Irish independence, role in 77–8
  Irishness, exclusion from concept
    of 77–8
  marginalization 93, 96, 97, 98, 102, 104

  medical system 98–9, 101
  migration to Ireland (1580–1641) 122–3
  in Northern Ireland 68–9, 90
  'othering' of 93, 96, 99–101, 160
  pejorative terms for 92
  population decline 93
  sidelining of 15, 90–1
  social marginalization of 93, 98
  social and religious stigma 93
  targeting of in the revolutionary period
    15, 92, 97
  'under siege', sense of being 96, 97
  see also evangelical Protestants;
    Ne Temere decree; Protestant
    denominations
psychography see automatic writing
Puck Fair, County Kerry 114
Pure Land (Jodo Shinshu) Buddhists 150
Pye, Michael 154

Quakers 46, 48, 51
  see also Society of Friends
Queen's University Belfast (QUB) 7, 155
queering of RE 61
Qur'an 8, 49
Quranic Studies 61

racism 16, 128, 130
Rastafarians 115
recession (2008) 12
reconciliation, Christian approaches to 10
reconstruction of religion 21, 28–9, 30
Redeemed Christian Church of God 72,
  169 n.15
Redemptorists' Archconfraternity of the
  Holy Family 42
referenda
  abortion 12, 64, 160
  blasphemy 12
  Catholic mores, abandonment of 64
  divorce 12, 64
  Eight Amendment of the
    Constitution 12, 64
  jus soli citizenship 129
  same-sex marriage 12, 64, 160
Reformation 92
  Counter-Reformation and 43
reformatory schools 66
  see also industrial schools

Reformed faiths 52, 56, 92
refugees 124
    Catholic Chilean 122
    in Ireland 128
    Muslims from Myanmar 121
    Yazidis from Iraq 121
    see also asylum seekers
Regan, Stephen 79
reiki healing 115
reincarnation 13, 30, 79
religion
    African forms of 16
    as an ethnic-marker 15, 69
    belief/commitment, rewards of 111
    communal rituals and 107
    in contemporary Ireland 107
    criteria for designation 115
    as a cultural identifier 11
    disillusionment with 16, 66–7, 118
    dominant meanings in Ireland 145
    feminism and 23
    functionalist analysis of 122
    Geertz's definition of 31
    identity and 12, 16, 31, 37, 42
    immigrants and 71–2, 94, 119–31
    interpretation of the word 47
    involuntary migration and 120, 121
    in Irish folk tradition 35–7
    in Limerick city 41–2
    localized aspect of 37, 42
    migration and 120–2
    migrations from Britain and 122–3
    nationalist women and 21, 30, 31
    non-confessional approach to 5
    'official' and 'unofficial' 33
    peace processes and 70
    popular 33
    reconstruction of 28–9
    rejection of 21, 22–3
    renegotiation of 21, 29–31
    replacement of 21, 23–8
    role in conflict 5
    role in peacebuilding 5
    science and 108
    social significance of 69
    study of, two-tiered model 33
    subjectivization of 109
    transnational migrations and 120–1
    vernacular 33
    voluntary migration and 120
    see also folk religion; traditional religion
religion and media studies 18
religion (term) 32–3
reiligiún (Irish term) 33
religiosity
    Catholic 67–8
    degrees of 116
    indicators of 143
    individual 116, 117
    social surveys measuring 135
    subjectivized 118
religious, interpretation of the word 47
religious activism, immigrants and 121, 125
religious authority, decline of 65
religious book publishing 47, 114
religious change, secularization and 107–9
religious decline
    measurement of 63
    in Northern Ireland 68–9
    in the Republic of Ireland 64, 65–6, 68, 94, 135
    in traditional and orthodox faiths 117, 135
religious education (RE)
    academic study, historical backdrop to 48–9
    aims of 50
    approaches to (learning about/learning from) 52
    Catholic RE, conceptualization of 51
    Catholic schools, RE in 53–5
    confessional approach 50, 51, 53, 54, 56, 58, 60, 61
    doctoral programmes, establishment of 61
    foundational principles of 61
    hermeneutical task in Ireland 61
    legal context 49–50
    main types in Ireland 50–3
    nation-wide state system, absence of 46
    patronage system 46, 50
    phenomenological approach 52, 58, 59
    at primary level in Ireland 14, 45–61
    in schools, debate about 46
    terms, proliferation of 46–8, 60–1
    transition, process of 47–8, 60–1
    types in Ireland 50–3

UCC conference 'RE21: Religious Education in a Global-Local World' 9
vocabulary, lack of consistency and vision 47
see also Catholic religious education; Church of Ireland religious education; multi-denominational religious education; National Council for Curriculum and Assessment; religious instruction (RI)
religious folklore
  international folk narrative and 37
  local legends 38–41
  St Brendan, Easter legend 40–1
  St Cuán and the Serpent 38–40
religious globalization 123
religious instruction (RI)
  Catholic *On Our Way* series 53
  in Free State policy documents 47
  kerygmatic approaches 53
  in Protestant schools 48
  Rules for National Schools 47, 50
  term, use of 47
  see also religious education (RE)
religious literacy
  development of key skills 54
  fostering 50, 51
  inter-religious literacy 54, 55
  spiritual literacy 54
religious minorities
  in Western democracies 16, 123
  see also African Pentecostalism; African Pentecostals; Buddhism; Islam; migrant religions; Mormons; Muslims; nonconformist minister; Protestantism; Protestants; Quakers
religious orders
  establishment in Ireland 113
  schools founded by 48
  vocations, decline of 137
  see also nuns
religious 'other'
  in post-modern Ireland 119, 120, 123
  post-Second World War 123
religious persecution, migrations provoked by 120, 121
religious persistence, in the Republic of Ireland 14, 15, 65, 66
religious revival 115–16

religious sense-experience 37
religious songs 35, 37
religious tradition
  in Cill Chuáin (Kilquane) 39
  cult of the Sacred Heart 43
  in Gaeltacht areas 43
  in Ireland 42–3
  rosary prayer 43, 113
  survival of 44, 113
  see also pilgrimage(s)
religious vitality 16, 107, 109
religious-secular competition
  areas of competition 133
  counselling services 134–5
  individual-level dynamics of competition 134–6
  organizational-level dynamics of competition 136–9
  outside forces and 133–4
  societal-level dynamics of competition 139–42
  theory of 17, 132–4, 136, 142, 143
Report of the Commission of Investigation into Mother and Baby Homes (2021) 140, 172 n.13
Reynolds, Revd Gerry 10, 71
Reynolds, Lorna 82
Reynolds, Margery 150
Rigby, Kate 13, 21, 24, 28, 29, 30
rituals 24, 26–7, 84, 159
  church rituals 107, 161
  Samhain-influenced 36
  see also Celtic Festivals; folk tradition
Robbins, Thomas, and Bromley, David 109–10
Röder, Antje 72
Rodgers, W. R. 40
Rogers, Jessie (theologian) 30–1
Rolston, Bill, and Shannon, Michael 125
Roman Catholic Church *see* Catholic Church
Romantic nationalism 84, 89
  agrarian culture, sentimentalization of 84
  Catholic Church's perception of 84
  in Europe 85
  folk culture, idealization of 85
  Gonne and 87
  influence of 77

Protestants and 84, 89
  rurality, perception of 84
  Yeats and 78–9
Romanticism 84, 85
Roof, Wade Clark 21
Roper, Esther 28, 165 n.1
rosary prayer 43, 113
Rosicrucian Society of England 80
Rotary International 133
RTÉ (Raidió Teilifís Éireann)
  'Confessors, The' (documentary) 171 n.4
  Irish Religious Beliefs (series) 114
  Late, Late, The (chat show) 64
Ruane, Joseph 10
Rubinstein, Murray 109
Russell, George William (Æ) (1867–1935) 22, 25, 26, 82–3
  adoption of 'Æ' 166 n.8
  agricultural cooperative movement 82
  Candle of Vision, The: Inner Worlds of the Imagination 82
  Celtic Revival and 78, 82
  Hermetic Society 166 n.23
  Homeward: Songs by the Way 82
  Irish Homestead, editorship of 82
  mythology, use of 82–3
  'Prince of Tir-na-nÓg, The' (painting) 82
  sidhe, paintings inspired by 82
  'Spirit of the Pool, The' (painting) 82
  'Stolen Child, The' (painting) 82
  theosophy, interest in 80, 82
  Ulysses (Joyce), appearance in 83
  'Warrior of the Sídhe, A' (painting) 82
Ryan, Anne 95
Ryan, Louise 88
Ryan Report (2009) 66, 168 n.4

sacraments
  Catholics and 65, 67, 136
  commodification of 136
  preparation for 14, 52, 54, 58, 59
sacred places 113
  see also Croagh Patrick; holy wells
St Brendan's Cathedral, Loughrea 139
St John's Eve 167 n.2
St Patrick's College, Maynooth 138, 143, 167 n.33

saintlore 38
saints, *Barlaam and Josaphat* 147–8
same-sex marriage 12, 64
same-sex relationships 142
Samhain (Celtic Festival) 36, 114
Satanists 115
Sayers, Peig 38
  identity, sense of 42
  Naomh Cuán agus an Phiast 38–40
  narrative technique 40, 41
  'Ollthaigh', special powers of 41
  oral narrative repertoire 38–41
  St Brendan legend 40–1
  use of the term 'Catholic' 42
Scharbrodt, Oliver, et al., *Muslims in Ireland* 9
schools
  charitable schools 48
  see also Catholic schools; Church of Ireland schools; Community National Schools; Educate Together; education; Jewish schools; Muslim schools; post-primary schools; Presbyterian schools; primary schools; Protestant schools
science, religion and 108
Scientology 112, 118
Seanad Éireann, Protestant members of 78, 92
second sight 80
Second Vatican Council *see* Vatican II
sects 111, 112, 113
  sectarian tendencies 112
  typologies 111, 112
  see also cults; new religious movements (NRMs)
secular clubs/societies 133, 158, 159
secularism 11, 16, 129, 160
secularization 10, 14, 116
  'death of god' thesis 122
  of faith schools 60
  individualism and 109
  in Ireland 62, 63, 64, 67, 107, 133
  modernization and 116
  North-South comparisons 72–3
  in Northern Ireland 68, 69
  portrayal of 118
  religious change and 107–9, 115–18

religious-secular competition as alternative to 134
theories of 133
in Western societies 63, 107–8
see also desecularization
Semple, Patrick 101
SEN see special educational needs
1798 Rebellion 169 n.3
sexual morality, Catholic Church and 140, 142
sexuality 63, 64
Shan Van Vocht (newspaper) 88
Shanahan, Mary 47
Sheehy Skeffington, Francis (1878–1916) 23, 30
Sheehy Skeffington, Hanna (1877–1946) 13, 22, 23, 30
'Life's Choosing' 23
Sheehy Skeffington, Owen (1909–70) 23
sídhe (other-worldly people) 82
ceol sídhe (faery music) 27, 30
Sikhism 8, 9, 55, 148
Simon Community 133, 137
Singapore 151–2
Sinnett, Alfred Percy, *Esoteric Buddhism* 80
Slieve Gullion, County Armagh 26
social changes
in the 1960s and 1970s 106
in Ireland 106
new religious movements (NRMs) and 110, 111
in Western countries 106
Social Justice Ireland 141
social media, Catholic hierarchy and 141–2, 172 n.15
Societas Rosicruciana in Anglia 80
Society of Friends (Quakers) 46, 56
Follow Me (FM) RE programme 56
Society for Psychical Research 83
Society of St Vincent de Paul 91, 137
sociologists of religion 14, 21, 73
all-island studies 62
ex-Catholics 16, 66–7
religion's decline, measurement of 63
'Sociology of Catholicism, The' (Conway) 10
sociology of peace processes 71
sociology of prayer 71

sociology of religion 5, 62–73
(1) the separation of religion from politics 63
(2) religion's decline in public influence and the privatization of religious belief 63
(3) declines in religious practice, belief and identification 63
explanatory frameworks 67
future directions 71–3
in Northern Ireland 68–71
in the Republic of Ireland 63–8
understanding 5, 62–73
universities and 73
sodalities 17, 133, 137, 142
Soka Gakkai International 112, 156
special educational needs (SEN) 54
spiritualism 30, 79, 106, 114, 115
automatic writing and 80–1
Sri Lanka 150
see also Ceylon
Stanley, Edward G. (1799–1869) 47, 48, 53
Stapleton, Catherine 55
Stark, Rodney, and Bainbridge, William 110, 111
Stausberg, Nucgaek 6
Steele, Karen 78, 88
Stella Matutina (Morning Star) 80
Stolz, Jörg 17, 132–3, 134
Straits Times 151
Stringer, Adrian 10, 71
suffrage
Gore-Booth and 28
Irish Citizen newspaper 22–3, 88
suffragists, Celtic myth and 88
Sullivan, John 50
supernatural belief 36, 37, 38, 113
supernatural forces 38–9
Sweden 5, 9, 108, 122
Synge, John Millington 78, 79, 81–2

Taylor, Lawrence J., *Occasions of Faith: An Anthropology of Irish Catholics* 32
TCD see Trinity College Dublin
Teach Don't Preach campaign 60
teachers
RE, teaching of 55
religious studies 5
training colleges 49, 51

telepathy 81
ter Haar, Gerrie 122
terminology of religious education 46–8, 60–1
Thai temple, Mitchelstown 156
theologians 145, 146
theology
   education and scholarship 30–1
   feminist theology 28–9
Theosophical Society 15, 26, 30, 80, 83, 112
   Protestant women and 22
   Russell (Æ) and 82
   split in 26, 167 n.25
theosophy 26, 79, 84, 106, 114
   Anglo-Irish and 86
   Cousins's interest in 83
   meaning of 82
   Russell's (Æ) interest in 80, 82, 83
   Yeats's interest in 80
   Young's interest in 86
therapists, professional 133
Thomas, Keith 33
Tibetan Buddhist pilgrimage 155
Tibetan 'dancing lamas' 149
Todd, Jennifer 10
Toledo Guiding Principles (OSCE) 60
traditional communities, saintlore in 38
traditional medicine 34
traditional religion 18, 107, 108, 110
   communal rituals 107
   modern Catholicism and 43
   see also religious decline
Trahar, Sheila 95
Transcendental Meditation 112, 114
transnational migrations, religion and 120–1
Travagnin, Stefania 154–5
Travellers, treatment of 137, 170 n.9
Trench, Cesca (1891–1918) 27, 30, 167 n.29
Tridentine Catholicism 114
Trinity College Dublin (TCD)
   Department of Sociology 127
   Irish School of Ecumenics 172 n.2
   School of Religion 5–6
   World Christianities course 164 n.7
Trócaire 141
Troeltsch, Ernst 111

Troubles, the (c.1968–98) 10, 20, 62, 68, 69, 153
   Protestants in the Republic, targeting of 170 n.12
Tuatha Dé Danann 88
Turner, Alicia 9, 147, 150
   Irish Buddhist, The (Turner et al.) 147, 151
   ISASR study of religion 154
Turner, Victor 104
Turpin, Hugh 66–7
Twomey, Daniel H.R. 148

UCC *see* University College Cork
Ugba, Abel 9, 16–17, 119–31, 160
Uí Ógáin, Ríonach 35
Ukkattha, Shin 154
Ulster, Celtic Revival in 88
Ulster Anti-Partition Council 88
Ultramontane campaign 159
UNESCO Memory of the World Register 32
Unification Church 112, 114, 115
United Irishmen 169 n.3
United Kingdom (UK), African immigrants and 124
United States of America (USA)
   Anglican Church 10
   anti-cult sentiment in 115
   cult, use of term 111
   new religious movements (NRMs) in 110, 114
   9/11 attacks in 120, 123
   sects and cults in 113
universities
   academic study of religions (ASR) 5–6, 146
   Asian studies 155–6
   EU-funded research 7, 156
   folklore studies 167 n.1
Universities of Ireland 163 n.6
University of California, Berkeley, Chair of Celtic Studies 27
University College Cork (UCC) 144
   Asian philosophy, study of 172 n.1
   Buddha statue in the archive 149
   conference (2013) centennial of Macauliffe's death 8–9
   East Asian religions 155

European Association for the Study of
  Religions (EASR) conference 3–4
 'RE21: Religious Education in a Global-
  Local World' 9
 'Religions and Global Diversity'
  programme 6–7, 8, 146
 Study of Religions department 3–4,
  6–7, 9, 156
University College Dublin (UCD) 10
 National Folklore Collection 32
unmarried mothers 140–1
urban religious activity 42

Vara, U 152
Varadkar, Leo 130
Vatican II (1962–5) 53, 93, 137, 138
 media/journalists' coverage of 64
 RE in Ireland, effects on 53
Vergangenheitsbewaeltigung 12, 165 n.24
vernacular religion 13, 33, 34
vernacular traditions 13
Vicitta, U 152
visionary cults 115
Vivekananda, Swami 8
vocations 137–8
 decline of 17, 137, 142
 decline, reasons for 138
 ordinations in Maynooth 138

Wallis, Roy 112, 113
Walsh, Tony 10, 15, 103
War of Independence (1919–21) 20, 92,
  170 n.7
 Protestants, targeting of 92, 97, 170 n.8
Ward, Eilís 155
Ward, Margaret 25
Warner, R. Stephen 121
Waterford Institute of Technology
 (WIT) 6
Watts, Alan (1915–73) 27
Weber, Max 111
Weekend Islamic School 49
Welch, Robert 85–6
Well of the Holy Women 113
Wellbeing, focus on, NCCA and 60
Westcott, William Wynn 80
Western esotericism 13, 15, 21–2, 24
 Irish nationalists and 78
 Protestant women and 22, 25

revolutionary politics and 22
 women and 22, 25, 30
Western Europe
 hostility towards foreigners 122
 religious revival in 115–16
Western societies
 Muslims in 8
 new religious movements
  (NRMs) in 160
 religious minorities in 123
 sects and cults in 113
 secularization in 63, 107–8
 traditional religion, decline in 107–8
 see also Western esotericism
White, J. H. 106
White Light Association 154
Wicca/Wiccans 112, 114, 167 n.28
Williams, Mark 82–3
Wilson, Brian 112
WIT *see* Waterford Institute of Technology
women
 Aristotelian concepts of 24
 Catholic Church and 21, 23, 64, 107
 Catholic women, changing role of 64
 evangelical women 71
 in Ireland's revolutionary period 13
 Irish nationalism and 20, 21
 kyriarchy 13
 nationalist women 13, 20, 21, 29–30, 31
 prohibition in nationalist
  organizations 25
 twentieth-century feminists 21
 unmarried mothers 140–1
 in the workforce 106, 139
Women's Movement 20
wonder tales 37–8
Woodlock, Rachel 8
world-accommodating movements 112
world-affirming movements 112
world-rejecting movements 112, 118

Yazidis 121
Yeats, Georgina (Georgie) (*née* Hydes-
  Lee) 80–1
Yeats, William Butler (1836–1939) 22,
  25, 26, 30
 Anglo-Irish background 78, 79
 automatic writing and 80–1
 Celtic culture, Irishness and 79

Celtic Revival and 78, 79, 84
Celtic Twilight, The 86
cultural nationalism and 78, 79
'Easter 1916' 81
esoteric interests 79, 80
eugenics, interest in 169 n.1
'folk', perception of 84
folklore, fascination with 79, 84
Gonne, Maud and 80, 87
Hermetic Order of the Golden Dawn, member of 80
Last Poems and Two Plays 79
magical practices 80
marriage 80
mythology, use of 82–3
numerology, study of 81
occultism, interest in 79, 80, 82
poetry 79
Romantic nationalism and 78–9
senator in the Free State 78
spiritualism practices 80
Stella Matutina and 80
theosophy, interest in 80
Vision, A 79
Wanderings of Oisin, The 79
yoga 16, 115, 118, 161
Yoshinaga, Shin'ichi 9, 149, 150
Young, Ella (1867–1956) 13, 22, 25, 83, 150
  Æ's rhyme 26

Celtic mythological themes 86
Celtic Revival and 78
Celtic Wonder-Tales 25, 86
Chair in Irish Myth and Lore, Berkeley 27, 86
Coming of Lugh 86
cultural nationalism 25
Earth, perception of 27
fairy legends, interest in 86
Flowering Dusk 22, 26, 167 n.26
folklore, interest in 79, 86
heather from Slieve Gullion 26
influence on women 27–8
Marzilian and other Poems 25
neo-paganism and 25, 26, 27
obituary 28
pilgrimage to the River Boyne 26–7
Poems 25
Presbyterianism, deconversion from 22
religion in rural Ireland, perception of 25
religious organizations established by 26
theosophy, interest in 86
United States, relocation to 27
Weird of Fionavar, The 25
Western esotericism and 25

Zen Buddhism 153
Zion National School 49

www.ingramcontent.com/pod-product-compliance
Lightning Source LLC
Chambersburg PA
CBHW062136300426
44115CB00012BA/1941